T0325754

Big Data and Knowledge Sharing in Virtual Organizations

Albert Gyamfi
Aalborg University, Denmark

Idongesit Williams
Aalborg University, Denmark

A volume in the Advances in
Knowledge Acquisition, Transfer,
and Management (AKATM) Book
Series

Published in the United States of America by
    IGI Global
    Engineering Science Reference (an imprint of IGI Global)
    701 E. Chocolate Avenue
    Hershey PA, USA 17033
    Tel: 717-533-8845
    Fax: 717-533-8661
    E-mail: cust@igi-global.com
    Web site: http://www.igi-global.com

Library of Congress Cataloging-in-Publication Data

Names: Gyamfi, Albert, 1974- editor. | Williams, Idongesit, editor.
Title: Big data and knowledge sharing in virtual organizations / Albert
  Gyamfi and Idongesit Williams, editors.
Description: Hershey, PA : Engineering Science Reference, [2019]
Identifiers: LCCN 2018029254| ISBN 9781522575191 (hardcover) | ISBN
  9781522575207 (ebook)
Subjects: LCSH: Knowledge management. | Telematics--Management. | Information
  technology--Management. | Big data.
Classification: LCC HD30.2 .B5443 2019 | DDC 658.4/038028557--dc23 LC record available at
https://lccn.loc.gov/2018029254

This book is published in the IGI Global book series Advances in Knowledge Acquisition, Transfer, and Management (AKATM) (ISSN: 2326-7607; eISSN: 2326-7615)

British Cataloguing in Publication Data
A Cataloguing in Publication record for this book is available from the British Library.

All work contributed to this book is new, previously-unpublished material.
The views expressed in this book are those of the authors, but not necessarily of the publisher.

For electronic access to this publication, please contact: eresources@igi-global.com.

Advances in Knowledge Acquisition, Transfer, and Management (AKATM) Book Series

ISSN:2326-7607
EISSN:2326-7615

Editor-in-Chief: Murray E. Jennex, San Diego State University, USA

MISSION

Organizations and businesses continue to utilize knowledge management practices in order to streamline processes and procedures. The emergence of web technologies has provided new methods of information usage and knowledge sharing.

The **Advances in Knowledge Acquisition, Transfer, and Management (AKATM) Book Series** brings together research on emerging technologies and their effect on information systems as well as the knowledge society. **AKATM** will provide researchers, students, practitioners, and industry leaders with research highlights surrounding the knowledge management discipline, including technology support issues and knowledge representation.

COVERAGE

- Cognitive Theories
- Cultural Impacts
- Information and Communication Systems
- Knowledge acquisition and transfer processes
- Knowledge management strategy
- Knowledge Sharing
- Organizational Learning
- Organizational Memory
- Small and Medium Enterprises
- Virtual communities

IGI Global is currently accepting manuscripts for publication within this series. To submit a proposal for a volume in this series, please contact our Acquisition Editors at Acquisitions@igi-global.com or visit: http://www.igi-global.com/publish/.

Titles in this Series

For a list of additional titles in this series, please visit:
https://www.igi-global.com/book-series/advances-knowledge-acquisition-transfer-management/37159

Knowledge-Intensive Economies and Opportunities for Social, Organizational, and ...
Miltiadis D. Lytras (Effat University, Saudi Arabia) Linda Daniela (University of Latvia, Latvia) and Anna Visvizi (Effat University, Saud Arabia)
Information Science Reference • ©2019 • 372pp • H/C (ISBN: 9781522573470) • US $185.00

The Role of Knowledge Transfer in Open Innovation
Helena Almeida (University of Algarve, Portugal) and Bernardete Sequeira (University of Algarve, Portugal)
Information Science Reference • ©2019 • 397pp • H/C (ISBN: 9781522558491) • US $195.00

Scholarly Content and Its Evolution by Scientometric Indicators Emerging Research ...
Zahid Ashraf Wani (University of Kashmir, India) and Tazeem Zainab (University of Kashmir, India)
Information Science Reference • ©2019 • 201pp • H/C (ISBN: 9781522559450) • US $135.00

Technological Innovations in Knowledge Management and Decision Support
Nilanjan Dey (Techno India College of Technology, India)
Information Science Reference • ©2019 • 322pp • H/C (ISBN: 9781522561644) • US $195.00

Effective Knowledge Management Systems in Modern Society
Murray E. Jennex (San Diego State University, USA)
Information Science Reference • ©2019 • 391pp • H/C (ISBN: 9781522554271) • US $195.00

Global Information Diffusion and Management in Contemporary Society
Zuopeng (Justin) Zhang (State University of New York at Plattsburgh, USA)
Information Science Reference • ©2019 • 331pp • H/C (ISBN: 9781522553939) • US $195.00

Contemporary Knowledge and Systems Science
W. B. Lee (Hong Kong Polytechnic University, China) and Farzad Sabetzadeh (Hong Kong Polytechnic University, China)
Information Science Reference • ©2018 • 340pp • H/C (ISBN: 9781522556558) • US $185.00

For an entire list of titles in this series, please visit:
https://www.igi-global.com/book-series/advances-knowledge-acquisition-transfer-management/37159

701 East Chocolate Avenue, Hershey, PA 17033, USA
Tel: 717-533-8845 x100 • Fax: 717-533-8661
E-Mail: cust@igi-global.com • www.igi-global.com

This book is dedicated to Rev. Francis and Esther Amuah.

Table of Contents

Detailed Table of Contents

Chapter 1

Nirali Nikhilkumar Honest, Charotar University of Science and Technology, India
Atul Patel, Charotar University of Science and Technology, India

Knowledge management (KM) is a systematic way of managing the organization's assets for creating valuable knowledge that can be used across the organization to achieve the organization's success. A broad category of technologies that allows for gathering, storing, accessing, and analyzing data to help business users make better decisions, business intelligence (BI) allows analyzing business performance through data-driven insight. Business analytics applies different methods to gain insight about the business operations and make better fact-based decisions. Big data is data with a huge size. In the chapter, the authors have tried to emphasize the significance of knowledge management, business intelligence, business analytics, and big data to justify the role of them in the existence and development of an organization and handling big data for a virtual organization.

Chapter 2

Serkan Polat, Istanbul Medeniyet University, Turkey
Fevzi Esen, Istanbul Medeniyet University, Turkey
Emrah Bilgic, Mus Alparslan University, Turkey

Virtual travel organizations, one of the most effective actors of tourism marketing, use information technology-based systems in parallel with the increasing use of information technologies. The competition in the tourism industries pushes virtual travel organizations to remain dynamic. Thus, customers can demand affordable and qualified tourism products. For this reason, it is inevitable for virtual travel organizations to use information technologies, in order to meet customers' demands efficiently and cost-effectively. Due to its nature, tourism products cannot be experienced before the sale. In order to analyze the expectations of the tourism customers, big-data-related technologies are valuable assets to the virtual travel organizations. From this point of view, managing massive data generated by tourism consumers is vital for the tourism supply chain. To the best of the authors' knowledge, there is no study relating big data and virtual travel organizations. In this chapter, the importance of five key concepts of big data have been discussed in terms of virtual travel organizations.

Chapter 3

Many industries prefer worldwide business operations due to the economic advantage of globalization on product design and development. These industries increasingly operate globalized multi-tier supply chains and deliver products and services all over the world. This global approach produces huge amounts of heterogeneous data residing at various business operations, and the integration of these data plays an important role. Integrating data from multiple heterogeneous sources need to deal with different data models, database schema, and query languages. This chapter presents a semantic web technology-based data integration framework that uses relational databases and XML data with the help of ontology. To model different source schemas, this chapter proposes a method based on the resource description framework (RDF) graph patterns and query rewriting techniques. The semantic translation between the source schema and RDF ontology is described using query and transformational language SPARQL.

Chapter 4

The authors in this chapter show the essence, dignity, current state, and development prospects of avatar-based management using blockchain technology for improving implementation of economic solutions in the digital economy of Russia. The purpose of this chapter is not to review the existing published work on avatar-based models for policy advice but to try an assessment of the merits and problems of avatar-based models as a solid basis for economic policy advice that is mainly based on the work and experience within the recently finished projects Triple H Avatar, an avatar-based software platform for HHH University, Sydney, Australia. The agenda of this project was to develop an avatar-based closed model with strong empirical grounding and micro-foundations that provides a uniform platform to address issues in different areas of digital economic and creating new tools to improve blockchain technology using the intelligent visualization techniques for big data analytics.

Chapter 5

Qaisar Iqbal, Universiti Sains Malaysia, Malaysia
Rashid Nawaz, University of Education, Pakistan

Information pollution, which usually refers to the overabundance of irrelevant, unsolicited, unwanted messages, is a major cause of concern for practitioners and academic researchers. Advances in the information and communication technologies has proliferated the production of information. Consequently, people are suffering from information pollution. Information pollution has made it difficult for employees and individuals to find the quality information quickly and conveniently from diverse information sources including print and electronic sources. This chapter sheds light on the relevant literature of information pollution and analyzes its causes in the Industry 4.0 era and puts forward suggestions for tackling this problem. This chapter emphasizes the significance of concrete efforts from computer scientists, academic professionals, and information professionals to devise strategies and techniques for refuting the effects of information pollution.

Chapter 6

Ezer Osei Yeboah-Boateng, Ghana Technology University College,
Ghana

Big data is characterized as huge datasets generated at a fast rate, in unstructured, semi-structured, and structured data formats, with inconsistencies and disparate data types and sources. The challenge is having the right tools to process large datasets in an acceptable timeframe and within reasonable cost range. So, how can social media big datasets be harnessed for best value decision making? The approach adopted was site scraping to collect online data from social media and other websites. The datasets have been harnessed to provide better understanding of customers' needs and preferences. It's applied to design targeted campaigns, to optimize business processes, and to improve performance. Using the social media facts and rules, a multivariate value creation decision model was built to assist executives to create value based on improved "knowledge" in a hindsight-foresight-insight continuum about their operations and initiatives and to make informed decisions. The authors also demonstrated use cases of insights computed as equations that could be leveraged to create sustainable value.

Chapter 7

In the era of big data, large amounts of data are generated from different areas like education, business, stock market, healthcare, etc. Most of the available data from these areas are unstructured, which is large and complex. As healthcare industries become value-based from volume-based, there is a need to have specialized tools and methods to handle it. The traditional methods for data storage and retrieval can be used when data is structured in nature. Big data analytics provide technologies to store large amounts of complex healthcare data. It is believed that there is an enormous opportunity to improve lives by applying big data in the healthcare industry. No industry counts more than healthcare as it is a matter of life and death. Due to rapid development of big data tools and technologies, it is possible to improve disease diagnosis more efficiently than ever before, but security and privacy are two major issues when dealing with big data in the healthcare industry.

Chapter 8

Social media receives growing interest from sports executives. Yet, very little is known about how to make use of such user-generated, unstructured data. By exploring tweets generated during Turkish Airlines Euroleague's Final Four event, which broadcasted the four tournaments of championship among four finalist teams, the authors studied how fans respond to gains and losses and how engaged they were during games through the course of the event. The authors found that favorable reactions were received when teams won, but the magnitude of unfavorable reaction was larger when teams lost. When it came to the organizer rather than the teams, the organizer of the event received most of the positive feedback. The authors also found that main source of tweets was smartphones while tablets were not among real-time feedback devices.

Chapter 9

Mahesh Pawar, Rajiv Gandhi Proudyogiki Vishwavidyalaya, India
Anjana Panday, Rajiv Gandhi Proudyogiki Vishwavidyalaya, India
Ratish Agrawal, Rajiv Gandhi Proudyogiki Vishwavidyalaya, India
Sachin Goyal, Rajiv Gandhi Proudyogiki Vishwavidyalaya, India

Network is a connection of devices in either a wired or wireless manner. Networking has become a part and parcel of computing in the present world. They form the backbone of the modern-day computing business. Hence, it is important for networks to remain alive, up, and reliable all the time. A way to ensure that is network traffic analysis. Network traffic analysis mainly deals with a study of bandwidth utilization, transmission and reception rates, error rates, etc., which is important to keep the network smooth and improve economic efficiency. The proposed model approaches network traffic analysis in a way to collect network information and then deal with it using technologies available for big data analysis. The model aims to analyze the collected information to calculate a factor called reliability factor, which can guide in effective network management. The model also aims to assist the network administrator by informing him whether network traffic is high or low, and the administrator can then take targeted steps to prevent network failure.

Chapter 10

Cihan Savaş, Kocaeli University, Turkey
Mehmet Samet Yıldız, Kocaeli University, Turkey
Süleyman Eken, Kocaeli University, Turkey
Cevat İkibaş, American University of Malta, Malta
Ahmet Sayar, Kocaeli University, Turkey

Seismology, which is a sub-branch of geophysics, is one of the fields in which data mining methods can be effectively applied. In this chapter, employing data mining techniques on multivariate seismic data, decomposition of non-spatial variable is done. Then k-means clustering, density-based spatial clustering of applications with noise (DBSCAN), and hierarchical tree clustering algorithms are applied on decomposed data, and then pattern analysis is conducted using spatial data on the resulted clusters. The conducted analysis suggests that the clustering results with spatial data is compatible with the reality and characteristic features of regions related to earthquakes can be determined as a result of modeling seismic data using clustering algorithms. The baseline metric reported is clustering times for varying size of inputs.

Chapter 11

Mehmet S. Aktaş, Yildiz Technical University, Turkey
Sinan Kaplan, Lappeenranta University of Technology, Finland
Hasan Abacı, Yildiz Technical University, Turkey
Oya Kalipsiz, Yildiz Technical University, Turkey
Utku Ketenci, Cybersoft, USA
Umut O. Turgut, Cybersoft, USA

Missing data is a common problem for data clustering quality. Most real-life datasets have missing data, which in turn has some effect on clustering tasks. This chapter investigates the appropriate data treatment methods for varying missing data scarcity distributions including gamma, Gaussian, and beta distributions. The analyzed data imputation methods include mean, hot-deck, regression, k-nearest neighbor, expectation maximization, and multiple imputation. To reveal the proper methods to deal with missing data, data mining tasks such as clustering is utilized for evaluation. With the experimental studies, this chapter identifies the correlation between missing data imputation methods and missing data distributions for clustering tasks. The results of the experiments indicated that expectation maximization and k-nearest neighbor methods provide best results for varying missing data scarcity distributions.

Preface

Globalization and the advancement in ICT has led to the emergence of more virtual organizations. Just as any other organizations, virtual organizations deal with big-data across their network, at the location of their teams and from external sources. What are the implications of the growing volume, variety, velocity and veracity of Big-data on their knowledge sharing endeavors? What are the problems associated with managing this Big-data? In addition, how best can these organizations manage big data to gain competitive advantage?

In order to address these questions, distinguished academics from United Kingdom, Spain, Australia, Russia, Finland, Malta, Ghana, India, Turkey, Malaysia and Pakistan, have contributed enriching and insightful chapters. The chapters in this book are contextualized within virtual organizations from different industries, ranging from tourism, education, and media to name a few. The Editorial advisory Board are from Spain, Denmark, India, and Ghana.

Readers of this book will gain deeper knowledge about the concepts and techniques for analyzing Big-data in virtual organizations. The models and techniques presented throughout the chapters would be outstanding in their applicability in virtual organizations. They cater for providing inspirations to the technically minded and non-technically minded persons alike.

The Editorial Team at IGI who, in the last 30 years, have published highly rated books made the production of this book possible. And we sincerely thank everyone, who contributed in making this book possible.

Albert Gyamfi
Aalborg University, Denmark

Idongesit Williams
Aalborg University, Denmark

Acknowledgment

We the editors want to specially thank the contributors to this book: Burçin Güçlü, Kamalendu Pal, Ezer Osei Yeboah-Boateng, Nirav Bhatt, Amit Thakkar, Serkan Polat, Fevzi Esen, Emrah Bilgic, Marcela Garza, Christopher Kennett, Qaisar Iqbal, Cihan Savaş, Mehmet Samet Yıldız, Süleyman Eken, Cevat İkibas, Ahmet Sayar, Mehmet S. Aktaş, Sinan Kaplan, Hasan Abacı, Oya Kalipsiz, Utku Ketenci, Umut O. Turgut, Mahesh Pawar, Vardan Mkrttchian, Ivan Palatkin, Leyla Gamidullaeva, Svetlana Panasenko, Nirali Nikhilkumar Honest, and Atul Patel for their immeasurable contribution to make this book a success. We were privileged to have worked with you on the dissemination of knowledge in this area of research.

We are also grateful to the Editorial Advisory Board, the team of peer reviewers and the Editorial Team from IGI for their assistance in making this book a reality. We are grateful to the assistant development editor from IGI and the project managers for the book, Ms. Marianne Caesar and Ms. Josephine Dadeboe for their immense contribution, guidance, and supervision in the course of this project.

Introduction

OVERVIEW OF THE BOOK

In the past few decades, Information and Communication Technologies (ICT) has played an important role in how organizations learn and share knowledge through knowledge management practices. As enterprise ICT applications and services evolve, so has the process of creating, sharing and managing knowledge in organizations evolved? Data from which knowledge is derived keeps increasing in Volume, frequency of production, and exists in different variety, some of which could be verified or otherwise. Just as non-virtual organizations, virtual organizations also engage in knowledge management practices, as a way of fostering organizational learning. As ICTs evolve, the amount of data available for the virtual organization also increases. What makes it challenging is the divergent nature of the sources of the data they have to deal with. As a matter of fact, the sources of data are becoming divergent by the day and they are often marketed in the form of analytics. These include the emerging market of data sellers who brand their product as "information needed by a group of organizations". Such information could be about potential customers, competitor habits, product consumption trend etc.

Moreover, there is also information from market research groups, consultants, blogs and even social media platforms such as LinkedIn. Meanwhile, there is information harnessed by the virtual organization internally, which could be documented or undocumented, as well as, structured or otherwise. The external and internally sourced information are often captured, stored, analyzed and shared to facilitate learning in the organizations. This is a trend that is bound to increase as the enabling ICTs such as 5G and the next generation mobile networks are currently being tested. We, thus, perceive that the linkages between technology, big data, and knowledge sharing will be on the increase, especially in virtual organizations. Hence, a book that seeks to clarify the interconnections between Big Data, and Knowledge sharing in Virtual organizations is timely if not strategic.

However, having followed the trend for nearly 4 years, we have realized the existence of more nagging questions that need to be addressed, so that solutions can be found to mitigate these existing challenges. In attempt to dealing with these issues, the idea of developing this book came into existence. In realty, each of these questions addressed in the book are not constants but dynamic and divergent in nature:

1. What challenges are virtual organizations facing?
2. What challenges could they be facing in future as ICTS evolve?
3. How are virtual organizations coping with big data?
4. What are the possibilities for using big data in virtual organizations?

The aim was not to answer all the questions in the book. Rather, to identify academics researching into big data, knowledge sharing and virtual organizations who can address one or more of these questions. This is because virtual organizations differ from one another in scope, nature and dynamics. Therefore no one answer fits all virtual organizations. As a result, different perspectives and approaches are provided in this book towards these questions. But that does not rob the reader of the insights to some of the answers to these questions and how they affect some virtual organizations.

As a result of the possibility provided by ICT and the cost advantages associated with virtual organizations, organizations either emerge as virtual organization or metamorphose into virtual organizations to save cost (Nami, 2008), attract remote talents (Cushard, 2018), maximize their financial and human resources (Kuruppuarachchi, 2006) and basically to attain some form of competitive advantage (Syler & Schwager, 2000). Reuters, Google, Facebook, Apple avensis etc. are examples of virtual organizations. However, virtual organization should not be confused with the establishment of branches. While companies aim at establishing branches to expand their market, their aim of establishing virtual organizations is to create flexibility in their operations to prevent them from being constrained to one location. It is important to note however, that the evolution of ICT is not the reason virtual organizations exist. Rather, the evolution of ICT can be seen as a catalyst for the evolution and the decisions by companies to metamorphose into virtual organizations. The fact is that virtual organizations are here to stay and in the future, there are likely to be more virtual organizations that are Small and Medium Sized Enterprises (SMEs). Therefore, there will be a lot of research in this direction and possible public interventions. Hence, the findings in this book will be useful for many decades to come.

WRITING STYLE AND CONTENT OF THE BOOK

The writing style of the book is a mixture of academic writing, report writing based on relevant research projects and experience based reporting. The chapters are enriching, enlightening and provocative. It is a book that will be of value to virtual organizations and non-virtual organizations dealing with big data. Such organizations will benefit from the technical inspirations provided in the book that can be adopted in the management of big data in virtual organizations; the privacy concerns in the management of big data in virtual organizations; and a sample based on an experiment on big data analysis conducted as an inspiration for small virtual organizations.

It is also a book that will be of value to academics, researcher and consultants researching in the field of knowledge management, organizational learning, computer science, information science, Information technology and information systems etc. These academics will benefit from with subjects, which include, Knowledge management, data mining, web semantics, cloud computing, avatar modelling, Industry 4.0, value creation and business analytics.

Furthermore, it is a book that will be of value to policy makers. Issues bordering on the ethical use and down sides of big data in virtual organizations are discussed in this book. These are some challenges that policy makers will have to deal with, if not now then in the future. In recent times, policy makers have been dealing with privacy issues when it comes to the processing of personal data. An example is the General Data Protection Regulation (GDPR) in the EU. As indicated in this book, virtual companies stand the risk of losing money due to information pollution. Policy initiatives are needed to regulate the data market to mitigate the effects of information pollution to companies. This is one of the provocative aspects arising from discussions in this book.

Although the book is of value to a wide range of stakeholders, it will benefit only those who have an interest in how organizations handle big data as well as those who need inspiration on how to handle big data. The overview of the chapters are presented in the next section.

OVERVIEW OF THE CHAPTERS

There are 11 chapters in this book.

- Chapter 1 provides an introduction to the fundamentals for the book. It explains the concept of knowledge management, Business analytics and virtual organizations and how these concepts relate.

- Chapter 2 describes the need for replacing existing traditional data management systems with systems that can manage big data. The chapter is very descriptive and informative on how the tourism industry consist of organizations that exist as virtual organization. An important fact of the chapter is the fact that data generated in the travel industry is actually becoming big data, insights of why this is so is explained in the chapter.

- Chapter 3 discusses the integration of heterogeneous enterprise data using ontology in supply chain management in virtual organizations. Due to globalization, industries are increasingly operating globalized multi-tier supply chains. Heterogeneous big data resides at various points of the supply chain. The chapter proposed for the need to unify the heterogeneous data to be able to cater for user needs. The chapter presents a heterogeneous data integration framework, which uses relational databases and XML data.

- Chapter 4 is inspires by the triple H avatar project. It explains the reflexive adaptation of block chain software that facilitate that facilitates e-learning and ubiquitous learning. The software presented is a self-modifying and self-learning software. The chapter also provides an insight on how the software is self-scalable as the volume of big data increases and how it adapts to the learning objectives of the users.

- Chapter 5 is an interesting chapter. It is not a chapter talking about the benefits of big data, but challenge of veracity with big data. The chapter argues that information credibility is an issue that plagued industries, pre industry 4.0. And with the advent of industry 4.0, virtual organizations will experience different degrees of information pollution in their big data, which might not make the big data useful at the end of the day.

- Chapter 6 discusses how big data sets generated from social media can be analyzed to derive value for media companies. The chapter introduces a model called the Multivariate Value Creation decision model to aid media executives in this endeavor.

- Chapter 7 is focused on the management of privacy when analyzing big data in the healthcare industry. This chapter does not focus on virtual organizations, however it provides tutorials on the technical issues surrounding the management of big data in the healthcare sector. What makes this chapter of significance is that it is focused on privacy related issues and provides steps to protect big data containing patient information.

- Chapter 8 is an empirically based chapter on the harvesting of big data. It provides a sample approach that could be useful for small virtual organizations on how to harvest big data from social media. The context of the chapter is the Evidence from Euroleague Basketball's Final Four Event: This chapter is written as a case study on how to manage big data from different sources. The experiment involved the authors exploring tweets generated during the Euroleague basketball Turkish airlines, final four. The authors studied how fans reacted to winning or losing of the games on twitter. Their methodology is well explained.

- Chapter 9 stresses the importance of networks in the transmission of big-data. One of the factors that will enable the efficient management of big data in virtual organizations, is if the networks handling the big –data are alive. The chapter presents a network model that is able to study and analyse network traffic based on a reliability factor. If the reliability factor is low, the network administrator is prompted to check the network. This serves as a proactive means of preventing network downtime for organizations.

- Chapter 10 is another chapter that provides a practical example on how to utilize big data for virtual organization in a particular industry. The context of the chapter are virtual organizations who operate Geographical Information Systems for the purpose of determining earthquake prone regions. The chapter provides an insight into how spatial patterns can be identified from big data with non-spatial attributes. The chapter reveals that clustering results with spatial data is compatible with the reality and characteristic features of regions related to earthquakes can be determined as a result of modeling seismic data using clustering algorithms.

- Chapter 11 deals with the challenges with missing data during data clustering. The missing data in the big data affects the quality of the data. This chapter provides an insight into how this problem can be solved.

CONCLUSION

It is common to say that the future is here or the future is yet to come. No one has ever said that the future was yesterday. Yesterday is never seen as the future. But the truth is that we are living in the future and oddly enough it began long before yesterday. Virtual organizations are growing by the day and in the years to come, we may end up with a world of virtual organizations. Each of these virtual organizations, just like the ones we have today will handle big data. It will be the backbone of their operations, just as it is today. This is why we say, the future was yesterday.

Therefore this book is timely and it is the hope of the editors that it will serve as a guiding light for existing virtual organizations and the ones to come.

Albert Gyamfi
Aalborg University, Denmark

Idongesit Williams
Aalborg University, Denmark

REFERENCES

Cushard, B. (2018). *Build a Virtual Workforce to Attract Talent and Reduce Costs*. Retrieved from Automatic Data Processing: https://www.adp.com/spark/articles/2018/06/build-a-virtual-workforce-to-attract-talent-and-reduce-costs.aspx

Kuruppuarachchi, P. (2006). Managing virtual project teams: how to maximize performance. Handbook of Business Strategy, 7(1), 71-78.

Nami, N. R. (2008). Virtual Organizations: An Overview. In *Intelligent Information Processing IV. IIP 2008. IFIP – The International Federation for Information Processing*. Boston, MA: Springer. doi:10.1007/978-0-387-87685-6_26

Syler, R., & Schwager, P. H. (2000). Virtual Organization as a Source of Competitive: A Framework from the Resource-Based. *AMCIS 2000 Proceedings, 390*.

Chapter 1

Knowledge Management and Business Analytics

Nirali Nikhilkumar Honest
Charotar University of Science and Technology, India

Atul Patel
Charotar University of Science and Technology, India

ABSTRACT

Knowledge management (KM) is a systematic way of managing the organization's assets for creating valuable knowledge that can be used across the organization to achieve the organization's success. A broad category of technologies that allows for gathering, storing, accessing, and analyzing data to help business users make better decisions, business intelligence (BI) allows analyzing business performance through data-driven insight. Business analytics applies different methods to gain insight about the business operations and make better fact-based decisions. Big data is data with a huge size. In the chapter, the authors have tried to emphasize the significance of knowledge management, business intelligence, business analytics, and big data to justify the role of them in the existence and development of an organization and handling big data for a virtual organization.

INTRODUCTION

Knowledge Management (KM) is a systematic way of managing the organization's assets for creating valuable knowledge that can be used across the organization to achieve the organization's success. KM consists of the processes, methods and systems that can help the organization to store, share, refine and transform the knowledge.

DOI: 10.4018/978-1-5225-7519-1.ch001

The organization can outline KM as the business objectives they want to achieve and apply the knowledge in new, old, or specific circumstances. KM is a continuous cycle which includes knowledge creation and improvement, knowledge distribution, knowledge addition and application. KM is a thoughtful and organized association of organization's people, process and technology to form a structured way of adding value and reuse the knowledge in innovative ways to expand, extend and exist in the competitive market. KM has main aspects of applying knowledge in all business activities among all the levels of the organization, and managing explicit and tacit knowledge. KM is an important aspect of any business organization as it offers the benefits to survive and stand in the global market, understand customers, establish and focus on key processes with continuous evolution and innovation, and adopt new technologies to enhance and expand the business.

Data, information and knowledge have important and noticeable meanings within KM. Data are facts or content which can be turned into information by analysis of data and adding value to it. Knowledge is a combination of related information, experiences and values with richer, and deeper perspective. Knowledge can be tacit or explicit. Tacit knowledge is personal, specific to particular context, and it is hard to formalize, capture and communicate. It is difficult to form a structure of how an individual has formed a view over a long period of time and transform it in to meaningful value. On the other hand, explicit knowledge can be easily collected, organized and transferred through digital means.

Business Intelligence (BI) is defined as "knowledge gained about a business through the use of various technologies which enable organizations to turn data into information". BI is also defined as "The processes, technologies and tools needed to turn data into information and information into knowledge and knowledge into plans that drive profitable business action". BI encompasses data warehousing, business analytics and knowledge management. BI allows us to use data strategically in responses to challenges and drive profitable business actions. BI can help in increasing efficiency in terms of minimizing the cost of servicing the customer, increasing effectiveness by allowing to access the information across every possible way, managing every opportunity and risk. BI can be thought of as a data refinery that turns data into actions and adds value. Effective decision making requires information that crosses organizational and functional boundaries, the new technology for understanding the past and predicting the future. A broad category of technologies that allows for gathering, storing, accessing and analyzing data to help business users make better decisions, BI allows analyzing business performance through data-driven insight. Business analytics applies different methods to gain insight about the business operations and make better fact based decisions. The application of BA allows to increase profitability, enhances data for future use, allows the business to to stand the competitive market and generate informative reports.

Big data is data with a huge size. It is used to describe collection of data that is huge in size and still it is growing exponentially with time. In other words, we can say that it is difficult to manage big data due to its three characteristics namely volume, velocity and variety. Volume means the data to handle is quiet large in amount, it can be in terabytes to zettabytes. Velocity means the data arrival rate is quiet high, so data arrives in great speed. Variety means data come in from different sources so they may be in different format like text, images, videos, etc. This data is so large and complex that traditional data management tools are not able to store or process it efficiently. The data found here is structured, semi-structured or unstructured. Structured data means the data that has a fixed format for example, data stored in relational database management system, Semi-structured data means data is not strictly in fixed form but it has some structure, for example data stored in an XML file, Unstructured data means data with unknown form or the structure, for example heterogeneous data containing a combination of simple text files, images, videos, etc. Any business organization will have to handle all the three types of data which can be huge in size and volume. The ability to process the Big data brings in multiple benefits such as, Business can use the social media data to form their business strategies, they can improve the customer service, identify risk for any product or service, provide better operational efficiency by making space for new data and identifying and moving the infrequently used data. The data products that result from developing a big data product include machine learning for classification algorithm, regression model or a segmentation model, recommender system that recommends choices based on user behavior, dashboard that helps to visualize aggregated data, and answering hypothesis or myths based on business objectives.

In the above content, the authors have tried to emphasize the significance of Knowledge Management, Business Intelligence, Business Analytics and Big Data, to justify the role of them in the existence and development of an organization. In the proposed chapters the authors mention the use and application of Knowledge management, Business Intelligence, Business Analytics and handling big data for a virtual organization. The objective is to cover the new approaches to handle and share the data in the virtual organization and focus on the new challenges raised to handle the data in such organization.

The Concept of Knowledge Management

According to Blackman (2008) phrase, 'Everything in nature and in the universe is an infinity of uniqueness', knowledge means taking the meaning and make sense to this infinity. To organize and store the data in a structured way information systems and databases are created as mentioned by Firestone & McElroy (2003).Knowledge Management (KM) is a systematic way of managing the organization's assets for creating valuable knowledge that can be used across the organization to achieve the organization's success. KM consists of the processes, methods and systems that can help the organization to store, share, refine and transform the knowledge. The organization can outline KM as the business objectives they want to achieve and apply the knowledge in new, old, or specific circumstances. KM is a continuous cycle which includes knowledge creation and improvement, knowledge distribution, knowledge addition and application. KM is a thoughtful and organized association of organization's people, process and technology as shown in figure 1, to form a structured way of adding value and reuse the knowledge in innovative ways to expand, extend and exist in the competitive market. KM has main aspects of applying knowledge in all business activities among all the levels of the organization, and managing explicit and tacit knowledge. KM is an important aspect of any business organization as it offers the benefits to survive and stand in the global market, understand customers, establish and focus on key processes with continuous evolution and innovation, and adopt new technologies to enhance and expand the business.

Each organization has its own key practices to apply and follow KM, so it is difficult to create generic models of KM. But in most cases the KM depends on the knowledge the way the organization serves its customers, employees, and other

Figure 1. People, process and technology the sources of knowledge management

stakeholders. It becomes very important the way the organization uses and reuses the information that is generated with the interactions among the customers, employees and other stake holders.KM mainly focuses on one of the many possible type of knowledge that resides in an organization, that is the knowledge the employees learn from doing the organization's work, here the knowledge is not the book knowledge it is learnt from the routine work that an employee performs. Examples of knowledge include: what an organization has learned about introducing new product or service, effective processes to capture and store the data, change in processes, etc. The role of KM comes here, how the employees using the earlier organization knowledge reduce their learning curve and as a result improve subsequent work process, or the organization carries out research and learn from the implementation related to the process, team and technology used can be overcome according to Shanmugam (2002).

Significance of Knowledge Management

The organizations to be successful and competitive today, need to continuously follow below activities,

1. Find an innovative way to translate the organization's experience into knowledge. This can be done by structured way of inter staff communication through a proper channel.
2. Transfer and control the knowledge across time and space. This can be done through the use of right technology to transfer the knowledge to an individual or a group, the content should be understood and used in a particular context, after understanding of the content the team can form new tasks and actions, which again goes as input to make it a better iterative process as depicted in Figure 2.

Figure 2. Iterative process of building, sharing and capturing experience to generate new knowledge

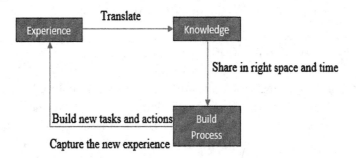

Knowledge management is very importantas it transforms the knowledge in the form of insights, understandings, and practical know-how that we all possess in other manifestations like books, technology, practices, and traditions within organizations of all kinds and in society in general. It helps to change the information into actionable knowledge and made available effortlessly in a usable form to the people who can leverage it according to their needs.

The key benefits that can be earned by applying KM are listed as below,

1. Organizations today are more universal; they are operating in multiple regions with varied culture. KM helps the organization to stand in the global market.
2. Organizations have to survive and adopt changes in the business and surrounding environment. KM helps the organization to derive self-learning ability to adopt the changing environment.
3. Employees of the organizations may change their work place, so with them their experience and work culture should not leave, KM helps the organization to capture the continuous knowledge and help the new employees to work with same skills and experience learnt from the past employees.
4. With the advances in the technology, the world is more connected and the customer expectations are increased for the availability of service by 24 X 7. KM helps the organization to handle the large pool of information in structured way, so the service can be rendered easily.

KM offers these benefits which are very significant for any organization to successfully compete in the global market.

Models of Knowledge Management

Knowledge management cycle is a process of transforming information into knowledge within an organization. It explains how knowledge is captured, processed, and distributed in an organization. There are different prominent models of knowledge management cycle, which includes the Meyer and Zack model, the Bukowitz and Williams's model, the McElroy model, and the Wiigmodel.

1. The Meyer and Zack Model

In the model the major stages of knowledge repository are analyzed and connected to the stages of a KM cycle. The stages include acquisition, refinement, storage/retrieval, distribution, and use. This cycle is also known as the "refinery." Acquisition deals with problems regarding the origin of main input, its cost, timeliness, control and accuracy. Refinement can be physical or logical, it deals with cleaning up, standardizing and structuring the content and adds value by creating readily usable knowledge and storing them. Storage or Retrieval forms a bridge between the upstream addition and refinement stages that feed the repository and downstream stages of product generation. Storage can be physical (file folders, printed information) as well as digital (database, knowledge management software). Distribution defines how the product is to be delivered to the end-user like fax, print, email and encloses not only the medium of delivery but also its timing, frequency, form, language, and so on.

The knowledge generated in the above phases is used and the performance is checked, to know the right content is used by the individual or a team. The repository provides management with the valuable knowledge of the organization. The cycles continuously renews the repository and refine the content. The Meyer and Zack model is one of the most complete picture of the key elements engaged in the knowledge management model. To be specific the notion of refinement is a crucial stage in the KM cycle and one that is often neglected as mentioned by Mohapatra, et al (2016).

2. Bukowitz and Williams Model

Bukowitz and Williams define a knowledge management process that outlines the way the organizations create, maintain and grow knowledge with greater value. In this model knowledge includes repositories, relationships, use of information technologies, deriving skill sets, means of communication, process to know how the things are done, response capturing, deriving organizational intelligence and handling external sources. The model has various stages like to get, use, learn and contribute. The first stage is to get information required in order to make decisions, solve problems, or innovate. The next stage is to use the gathered information in new and interesting ways in order to build the organizational innovation. Then the stage is to focus on learning form the experiences, to motivate generation of new ideas from the applied ideas. The last stage deals with encouraging employees to add what they have learnt to the common repository, so the individual knowledge can be made visible and available to the entire organization as mentioned by Mohapatra, et al (2016).

3. McElroy Model

This model describes different processes of knowledge life cycle that consists of the processes of knowledge creation and knowledge combination, with a series of response loops to organizational claims and the business-processing environment. It handles different claims like, problem claim, knowledge claim, new knowledge claim, evaluation of knowledge claim. The problem claim is an approach to learn and find the detected knowledge gap. The knowledge claim gives the response to the problem claims with the help of information gained as an individual or group. New knowledge claims are generated, tested and examined by the knowledge claim evaluation process, which result in new knowledge or unaccepted knowledge. Experience gained from the application of knowledge in the organizational knowledge base leads to new claims and resulting beliefs, triggering the cycle to begin all over again. The knowledge production process can include individual and group learning, codification of individual and group innovations, information addition process and knowledge integration. This model describes how knowledge is examined and a decision is made whether to include the knowledge in the organization's repository. The Km cycle focus on the processes to identify knowledge content that is of value to the organization and its stakeholders as mentioned by Mohapatra et al (2016).

4. WIIG Model

This model focus on different aspects like, business must provide service to the customers, the resources should be used properly, the business should be able to take wise decisions. KM process includes the creation, collection, distribution and use of quality knowledge. The KM cycle shows how the knowledge is built and used as individuals or as an organization. The knowledge building can be from external to internal sources, the information gathered is hold in a proper format. The knowledge can be accessed through the use of technology. It becomes embedded process to collect and disseminate the knowledge as mentioned by Mohapatra, et al (2016).

5. von Krogh and Roos Model

This model is the first model that precisely differentiates between individual knowledge and social knowledge. This model, analyzes how the knowledge gets to the workers of a company, how the knowledge comes in the organization, what does the knowledge mean to the employees and the organization, what can be the barriers of the organizational knowledge management. In this model, knowledge is to be found both in the mind of the people and in the links between them. The knowledge management is examined from the staff members, organization hierarchy, relations and network between the employees according to Virkus (2014).

6. Nonaka and Takeuchi Model

This model of KM has its base in a universal model of knowledge creation and the management of coincidence. There are four different modes of knowledge conversion, Socialization, Externalization, Combination and Internalization. Socialization is a technique of sharing tacit knowledge through observation, practice, and participation in formal or informal groups. Externalization is a technique of sharing tacit knowledge; it is a way to create explicit knowledge. Combination is the technique of integrating concepts into a knowledge system for example creating brief summary, generating review report, create database to organize the content. Internalization is the technique of converting explicit knowledge into tacit knowledge as mentioned by Mohapatra, et al (2016).

7. Choo Sense-Making KM Model

This model mainly focuses on Sense making, knowledge creation, decision making skills. This process plays a major role in the organization's knowledge creation, and its utilization. Sense making is a process to understand the changes, trends and governing rules that occur in the organization. After understanding the changes, it can help the organization to capture suitable information to exist in dynamic and changing environment. Knowledge creation is a process that allows an organization to create and organize information and generate new knowledge through organization learning, like improve the existing process, offer new services, improve product design, etc. Decision making process provides the options while taking decision and helps to select the best option. This model focuses on how informational elements are selected and given as input into organizational actions according to Virkus (2014).

8. Boisot I-Space Model

This model helps in differentiating the information that is important for the organization from the one that is less or not at all important. It emphasizes that information is extracted from data by means of observation. A Social Learning Cycle is proposed that adopts the I-Space to model the changing flow of knowledge. It has main phases as Scanning, Problem-Solving, Abstraction, Diffusion, Absorption, and Impacting. Scanning is a process of generating information from available data. Problem solving is a process which offers a structure to the insights of knowledge. Abstraction is generalization of knowledge to wide range of situations. Diffusion is sharing the new knowledge to particular scope of population. Absorption is applying new knowledge to variety of situations to generate new learning experiences and behavior which is tacit. Impacting is a process to apply fix practices in terms of artifacts, rules, policy, behavior patterns so knowledge becomes concrete. The model emphasizes that the organization need to adopt a dynamic KM approach to accommodate the dynamic nature of learning cycle according to Virkus (2014).

    As an abstract of all the models discussed above the KM process includes the knowledge acquisition, codification of knowledge and creations of tools. Under knowledge acquisition process the knowledge is captured and structured into readable form, some techniques like interviewing, observations, brainstorming, etc. can be applied to capture the knowledge. Under codification the tacit knowledge is converted into explicit knowledge by codifying it. This makes it easy to organize, store, locate, share and use the knowledge. Most common codified content is in terms of manuals, spreadsheets, databases, walkthrough, etc. After this process the last process is creation of knowledge tools, it allows to continuously transfer, combine and convert the different types of knowledge as users practice, interact and learn in the organization. Tools with various purpose can be created, like tools for document management, data warehouse, decision support system, project management, handling workflow, etc. Content creation and management tools are essential to structure and organize knowledge content for each retrieval and maintenance. It consists of the tools like Authoring Tools, Annotation Tools, Data Mining and Knowledge Discovery, Templates, Blogs, etc. Apart from knowledge creation knowledge sharing tools are also available, like File distribution, Electronic newsletter, Email, Group Calendars, Collaborative writing system, Video Communication System, Chat Systems, etc. These tools acts as enablers of knowledge flow and knowledge-sharing activities among personnel. Groupware invokes class of software that allows to work together while located remotely from each other.

Organization Maturity Models

The environment of an organization includes the set of norms, routines, unspoken rules of doing the work in the organization. The ways the organization works can be at different stages of maturity, to measure and assess this maturity different KM maturity models have been derived. The maturity model defines the stages through which an organization passes and improve their processes. This model acts as a guide for selecting process, improvement strategies by assisting the determination of the current process capabilities and the identification of issues most critical to quality and process improvement within a particular domain, like software engineering or systems engineering.

1. Capability Maturity Model

There are a number of organizational and KM maturity models, mostly derived from the Capability Maturity Model (CMM). The CMM was developed to describe the phases of software development processes, and the model was subsequently updated to the Capability Maturity Model Integration in 2000.The Capability Maturity Model describes five evolutionary levels in which an organization manages its processes. The five stages of the CMM are Initial, Repeatable, Defined, Manages and Optimized. In Initial phase the process is roughly defined, in repeatable phase the basic processes are set and they are enforced to execute, in Defined phase all the processes are precisely defined, standardized and connected to each other, in Managed phase all the processes are managed by collecting the details of data and quality requirements and in the Optimizing phase improvements required are planned based on the feedback and new ideas as mentioned by Sivasubramanian (2016).

2. Infosys KM Maturity Model

This model defines the areas of Knowledge Acquisition, Knowledge Dissemination and Knowledge Reuse. The organizational knowledge can be created through formal training. Once the knowledge is acquired it needs to be shared among the different level of organization. The knowledge earned is reused and updated based on the organizational changes and needs as mentioned by Sivasubramanian (2016).

3. CoP Maturity Models

The Wenger CoP life-cycle model provides a good characteristic to check whether informal networks exist within an organization and whether they are recognized and supported by the organization. The key features of the maturity model includes Paulk organizational maturity, Fujitsu organizational maturity, Paulzen and Percorganizational maturity, Forrester Group KM organizational maturity. Paulk organizational maturity approves the new technology or process within an organization to introduce new KM functions. Fujitsu organizational maturity provides a way to check how united or universal a culture is within the organization. Paulzen and Perc maturity is similar to Infosys KM model and gives an incremental introduction of KM initiatives into the organization. Forrester Group KM maturity describes how employees acquire content which can be used for incremental introduction of knowledge support services in the organization according to Agrifoglio (2015).

Applications of Knowledge Management

Knowledge Application Systems support the process through which some individuals utilize knowledge possessed by other individuals without actually acquiring, or learning, that knowledge. For a large enterprise or a government agency, the knowledge management applications are core building blocks for taking advantage of most essential information. Knowledge application technologies, which support direction and routines includes intranet search engine, document classification based on customized taxonomy, entity extraction, customer feedback analysis, expert systems, decision support systems, etc. The applications provide an easy was to access the data for informative decisions as mentioned by Laudon & Laudon (2002).

1. Intranet Search Engine

Being able to find what you need inside a company isn't always easy. Company intranets are an excellent starting point for making information available, but not every search box is equal. Accessing information often depends on users knowing where something is located. One of the most important knowledge management applications, therefore, is a strong, semantic search engine that can reach all enterprise content, and retrieve the precise items that you're looking for like marketing reports, product data sheets, customer information, patent records, etc. with the same speed and effectiveness that you would expect from a typical internet search.

2. Document Classification Based on Customized Taxonomy

Simply storing the company knowledge is useless, Effective enterprise search, therefore, starts with deploying classification and taxonomy development tools rooted in an understanding of language. The taxonomy must reflect your organization's unique vocabulary like the acronyms, products and project code names that your internal users know by heart, in order to be truly useful; a full understanding of meaning can help distinguish between different contextual uses of information. Both are essential for delivering precise information for search and other applications. For example, an energy company has its own language, which requires a specific and customized taxonomy that is able to associate content to the classes and nodes with great precision.

3. Entity Extraction

Identifying entities contained in people, places, locations, organizations, as well as customized organizational entities, can provide a useful view of unknown data sets by immediately revealing the who, what and where contained in your information. Entity extraction is an essential knowledge management application that helps transform unstructured data to data that is structured, and therefore machine readable and available for standard processing that can be applied for a number of business activities.

4. Customer Feedback Analysis

The opinions expressed online by your customers and users contain valuable insight about your companies, brands, competitors, products and services. Being able to analyze the signals and feedback left by consumers on social media, forums, reviews or classic survey mechanisms requires truly understanding what is being expressed and how. Semantic-powered knowledge management applications can cut through the slang, jargon and use of different languages to provide strategic value from customer feedback.

5. Expert System

An expert system is used to provide an answer to a problem, or clarify uncertainties where normally one or more human experts need to be consulted.

It can be used to create knowledge base which uses some knowledge representation to capture the main matter expert's knowledge. It is also used to collect that knowledge from the main matter expert's and codifying it according to the formalism. Expert systems may or may not have learning components but a third common element is that once the system is developed it is proven by being placed in the same real world problem solving situation as the human subject matter expert, typically as an aid to human workers or a supplement to some information system.

6. Decision Support System

A Decision Support System is a class of information systems that support business and organizational decision making activities. A properly designed DSS is an interactive software-based system intended to help decision makers compile useful information from a combination of raw data, documents, personal knowledge, or business models to identify and solve problems and make decisions. The DSS can be used to search, retrieve, generate solution, and solve new problems.

BUSINESS ANALYTICS

In any organization the use of Information Technology as mentioned by Scott Morton (1991) and Sharma, Yetton, & Zmud (2008) can increase the efficiency of work as mentioned by Wixom, B. and Watson, H. J. (2001). Business Analytics (BA) is the study of data by applying statistics on it. BA is a methodology to make a sound commercial decision as mentioned by Inmon, (2005), Bergeron (2000) and Hwang, Ku, Yen, and Cheng. (2004). This section provides an insight into the importance of analytics, the application of Business analytic and the advantages of applying business analytics.

Importance of Business Analytics

BA has an impact on the functioning of the whole organization. Therefore, BA can help improve profitability of the business, increase market share and revenue and provide better return to a shareholder. It facilitates the better understanding of data which can gain in operational efficiency at various levels of management in the organization. In the organization it is very important that how the information is utilized in a productive way so it makes the organization more competitive. BA combines available data with various well thought models to improve business decisions as mentioned by Cui, Damiani, & Leida, (2007). It converts available data into valuable information. This information can be presented in any required format, comfortable to the decision maker.BA applies the predictive models, optimization techniques for the better results which helps the management of business and customers to communicate in a productive way. BA requires the use of quantitative methods and evidence based data for modeling and decision making. BA can be possible only on large volume of data according to Stackowiak, Rayman, & Greenwald, (2007), so it uses the big data concept.

1. Benefits of Applying Business Analytics in Decision Making

The organizations use BA to take data driven decisions. The understanding gained by BA enables the organizations to automate and optimize their business processes as mentioned by Howson, (2006). The organizations are able to compete the global market by taking smart decisions based on the insight gained due to BA as mentioned by Kohavi, Rothleder, & Simoudis, (2002), the major insights include,

- Use and understand data to find new patterns and analyze the relationships among the data, by applying data mining.
- Most of the measurements are indirect, so it is necessary to apply quantitative and statistical analysis to obtain and analyze the results.
- Check the previous decisions using multivariate testing.
- Use predictive modeling as suggested by Negash (2004), and analytics to forecast the future results.

Business Analytics also provides support for companies in the process of making proactive tactical decisions, and BA makes it possible for those companies to automate decision making in order to support real-time responses.

2. Business Intelligence and Business Analytics

Business Intelligence (BI) and BA are similar, though they are not exactly the same. Business Intelligence involves the process of collecting data as mentioned by Tvrdikova (2007), from all sources and preparing it for Business Analytics as mentioned by Levy & Powell (1998). Business Intelligence is more of a first step for organizations to take when they need the ability to make data-driven decisions. BA, on the other hand, is the analysis of the answers provided by BI. While BI answers what happened, BA answers why it happened and whether it will happen again. BI includes reporting, automated monitoring and alerting, dashboards, scorecards, and ad hoc query; BA, in contrast, includes statistical and quantitative analysis, data mining, predictive modeling, and multivariate testing.

3. Considerations While Applying Business Analytics

Applying BA in any organization requires spending of time, money, violating privacy and taking risk to understand the problems and opportunities that can occur in business processes. The major challenges that can be faced while developing and implementing BA include,

- Support of senior management for allowing integrating the predictive models for the business processes.
- Support of infrastructure and tools to handle the data and processes.
- Avail data for modeling historical data and real time data for comparison in decision making.
- Support of agile approach to implement the right predictive models with the correct project management structure.
- Support of stakeholders to adopt the BA and predictive models.
- Support for change management for changing business rules and environment, and BA should be able to figure out the change in operations.
- Support for documentation of reports generated as results of BA, and explain how the results are generated.

4. Forming Best Practices for Business Analytics

Developing and implementing BA is a long process which requires the sound background of Organization in which the BA is to be applied. The organization can form some best practices for BA, so they can apply BA at all the levels of the organization to become more competitive and successful. The organization have to individually form the best practices for BA, here we list some of the most fitting best practices,

- Define the objective for using BA.
- Describe the business use case.
- Define your criteria for success and failure.
- Define how the data will be available and what internal and external factors are responsible for the generation of data.
- Select the right methodology.
- Check the models using the predefined success and failure criteria.

For any organization BA is important to gain competitive market and achieve success. When the BA best practices are formed and correctly implemented the organization will benefit from data-driven decision making.

Applying Business Analytics

In any organization, especially virtual organization, the role of IT is to provide applications for business transactions, business intelligence and collaborative applications. The business transaction applications are responsible for day to day operations and store data in the data repository, using a database system. The applications retrieve, store and manipulate the data using the database system.

Business intelligence applications analyze the business operations and generate information to help the business users understand, improve and optimize business operations. This information can be generated by analyzing and reporting the data produced by business transaction applications, and by processing the data stored in the data warehouse. A data warehouse provides the ability to gather data from various business transaction applications and integrate them into a single data repository. The data warehouse is data repository managed by a database system, and it uses languages as SQL to access and manipulate the data.

The diagram in Figure 3 demonstrates how knowledge management can help business users improve business processes. Initially Business intelligence applications were used to analyze data warehouse data and produced high level summarized data, measurements about business performance, but now it is used towards the business performance management applications that put these measurements into a business context, so they relate the data measurements to business goals and objectives. Applying the performance measurements into a business context improves the business decision making and action taking processing because the results become actionable. Putting the measurement into a business context creates business information. This information can be places in documents, spreadsheets,

Figure 3. Role of knowledge management in business

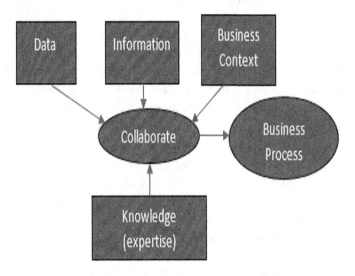

presentations, email, etc. in text, audio or video format. This data can be stored in the content repository which supports business metadata like author of the work, date produced, date updated, etc. apart from the data stored in the data repository. The content repository can manage the versioning, workflow, templates and search tools. Like a data repository a content repository is managed by a database system. After the business intelligence system give information, the business user's uses their expertise and knowledge to make decisions and take actions.

The decision making and action taking process may involve other user's participation and interaction. The interaction is supported by collaborative application and processing. This is a manual process of decision making. The knowledge of the business users can be captured as a set of business practices in the form of business rules, then decision making and action taking process can be automated. When business users make decisions and take actions they use their business knowledge to tie the actionable information to the business processes and activities they are responsible for their role in the organization. The ability to relate information to business processes is very important. Unfortunately, this aspect of the decision-making process is poorly supported by BI applications and BI vendors because the developers of these applications and software have a data-centric viewpoint of business operations, rather than a process-centric perspective. The ability to relate actionable information to business processes also provides the foundation for other ways of automating decision making and action taking. Less experienced business users could be given a guided-analysis workflow that helps them interpret actionable information, discover additional information, and make the right decision to fix business problems, optimize business processes and satisfy customer needs.

Advantages of Applying Business Analytics

Using business intelligence and analytics effectively is the crucial difference between companies that succeed and companies that fail in the modern environment. Because things are changing and becoming more competitive in every sector of business, and the benefits of business intelligence and a proper use of data analytics is key to outperform competition. The methodology of "test, look at the data, adjust" is at the heart and soul of business intelligence. It's all about using data to get a clear understanding of reality, so that your company can make more strategically sound decisions (instead of relying only on gut instinct or corporate inertia). Because ultimately, business intelligence and analytics are about much more than the technology used to gather and analyze data. They're about having the mindset of an experimenter, and being willing to let data guide a company's decision making process. The major benefits of applying BI and BA are listed as below,

1. Understand the customer effectively. The needs, preferences and the relationship with the customers can be improved by having an insight to the business processes that are directly connected to the customer satisfaction and benefit to the customers.
2. Allows to organizations to control the cost and identify the efficient ways to increase the profit. Businesses often fail because of poor financial management strategy or a lack of planning. For your business success, developing and implementing financial and management systems is vital. It is important to keep updating the original business plan.
3. Faster and smart decision making. The organization if able to get a hold of correct and clean data, it would most definitely be able to take accurate decisions, thereby aiding it in leveraging businesses. Analytics provides useful data which can be further analyzed by a major group of people and thus be analyzed for maximum benefit.
4. Business Analytics helps to quantify the business values. The organizations can quantify their business values into numbers, thus when numbers are involved the organization mission statements can be quantified and this can thereby focus on their operating processes.
5. Producing a single, unified view of enterprise information helps to synchronize the financial and operational strategy which can lead to increase in the revenues. With the use of business intelligence and analytics, the organizations can implement business processes and take necessary measures to improve efficiency in various areas of their operations. An organization may also identify new business opportunities and expand accordingly to facilitate its best practices as mentioned by Phillips-Wren et al (2015).

Need for Handling Big Data

In early days before the use of computers, the data was organized in the form of records in the physical files. With the rise in the use of computers, internet and technology to capture the data have increased the amount of data that can be generated in any organization as mentioned by Jin, Wah, Cheng and Wang (2015). By the use of database and spreadsheets the data are organized and stored in an easy accessible way. The data stored and accessed by 2000, is increasingly changed in the amount and is continuously increasing rapidly by 2020. The amount of digital information available will have frown from around 5 zettabytes today to 50 zettabytes. Nowadays, almost every action we take leaves a digital information. We generate data whenever we go online, we use the smartphones, we communicate with our friends on the social media or chat applications, etc. We leave a digital information with everything we do that involves a digital action, which is almost everything.

The amount of machine-generated data is rapidly growing too. Data is generated and shared when our "smart" home devices communicate with each other or with their home servers. Industrial machinery in plants and factories around the world are increasingly equipped with sensors that gather and transmit data.

The term "Big Data" refers to the collection of all this data and our ability to use it to our advantage across the business as mentioned by Kakhani, Kakhani & Biradar (2015). So, 'Big Data' is also a data but with a huge size. 'Big Data' is a term used to describe collection of data that is huge in size and yet growing exponentially with time. In short, such a data is so large and complex that none of the traditional data management tools are able to store it or process it efficiently. For example, The New York Stock Exchange generates about one terabyte of new trade data per day. Statistic shows that 500+ terabytes of new data gets ingested into the databases of social media site Facebook, every day. This data is mainly generated in terms of photo and video uploads, message exchanges, putting comments etc. Single Jet engine can generate 10+ terabytes of data in 30 minutes of a flight time. According to Gantz & Reinsel (2012) IDC report, the volume of data will reach to 40 Zeta bytes by 2020 and increase of 400 times by now. With many thousand flights per day, generation of data reaches up to many Petabytes as mentioned by Monash (2008).

Forms of Big Data

Big data could be found in any of these three forms, Structured, Unstructured and Semi-structured.

1. Structured

Any data that can be stored, accessed and processed in the form of fixed format is termed as a 'structured' data. Over the period of time, talent in computer science have achieved greater success in developing techniques for working with such kind of data where the format is well known in advance and also deriving value out of it. However, now days, we are foreseeing issues when size of such data grows to a huge extent, typical sizes are being in the range of multiple zettabyte.

2. Unstructured

Any data with unknown form or the structure is classified as unstructured data. In addition to the size being huge, un-structured data poses multiple challenges in terms of its processing for deriving value out of it. Typical example of unstructured data is, a heterogeneous data source containing a combination of simple text files, images, videos etc. Now a day organizations have wealth of data available with them but unfortunately they don't know how to derive value out of it since this data is in its raw form or unstructured format.

3. Semi-Structured

Semi-structured data can contain both the forms of data. We can see semi-structured data as a structured in form but it is actually not defined e.g. a table definition in relational DBMS. Example of semi-structured data is a data represented in XML file.

Characteristics of Big Data

1. *Volume*

Size of data plays very crucial role in determining value out of data. Also, whether a particular data can actually be considered as a Big Data or not, is dependent upon volume of data. Hence, 'Volume' is one characteristic which needs to be considered while dealing with 'Big Data'.

2. *Variety*

Variety refers to heterogeneous sources and the nature of data, both structured and unstructured. During earlier days, spreadsheets and databases were the only sources of data considered by most of the applications. Now days, data in the form of emails, photos, videos, monitoring devices, PDFs, audio, etc. is also being considered in the analysis applications. This variety of unstructured data poses certain issues for storage, mining and analyzing data as mentioned by Dietrich (2012).

3. *Velocity*

The term 'velocity' refers to the speed of generation of data as mentioned by Elgendy & Elragal, (2014). How fast the data is generated and processed to meet the demands, determines real potential in the data. Big Data Velocity deals with the speed at which data flows in from sources like business processes, application logs, networks and social media sites, sensors, Mobile devices, etc. The flow of data is massive and continuous.

4. *Variability*

Variability refers to the dynamic, evolving, spatiotemporal data. Multiple disparate data types and sources cause a multitude of data dimensions, contributing to the variability of big data. Big data is also variable because of the multitude of data dimensions resulting from multiple disparate data types and sources. Variability can also refer to the inconsistent speed at which big data is loaded into your database. This type of data can be based on time series, it can be seasonal, and non-static data.

5. *Veracity*

Veracity pertains to the provenance or reliability of the data source as mentioned in the article The Four V's of Big Data (IBM, 2018), its context, and how meaningful the data is to the analysis based on it. Knowledge of the data's veracity in turn helps in better understanding of the risks associated with analysis and business decisions based on a particular data set. It includes the necessary and sufficient data to test many different hypotheses, vast training samples for rich micro-scale model-building and model validation, micro-grained "truth" about every object in your data collection to empower data analysis.

6. *Validity*

Validity refers to how accurate and correct the data is for its intended use. It is concerned with the correctness or accuracy of data used to extract result in the form of information According to Forbes Press (2016), approximately 80 percent of a data scientist's time is expended cleansing the data before being able to do any analysis. The benefit from big data analytics is only as good as its underlying data, so one needs to adopt good data governance and master data management (MDM) practices to ensure consistent data quality, common definitions, and metadata on massive, diverse, distributed, heterogeneous, "unclean" data collections as suggested by Shafer, (2017).

7. *Vulnerability*

Big data brings new security concerns as a data breach with big data is a big breach. Unfortunately there have been numerous big data breaches. For example a data breach with big data is a colossal breach, as can be exemplified by the infamous Ashley Madison hack in Basu, (2015). Another example, as was reported by Greenberg, (2016), "a hacker called Peace posted data on the dark web to sell, which allegedly included information on 167 million LinkedIn accounts and 360 million emails and passwords for MySpace users".

8. *Volatility*

Volatility refers to the duration of usefulness of big data as mentioned by Shafer, (2017), it refers to how long the stored data is useful to the user. It is concerned with how old does data need to be before it is considered irrelevant, historic, or not useful any longer and how long does data need to be kept. Before big data came into being, organizations tended to store data indefinitely. A few terabytes of data would not lead to high storage expenditure; it could even be kept in the live database without hindering performance. In a classical data setting, data archival policies may not even be in place. Due to the velocity and volume of big data, however, the volatility of the data needs to be carefully considered. It will be required to establish rules for data currency and availability as well as ensure rapid retrieval of information whenever it is required. It must be ensured that these are clearly tied to the business needs and processes; with big data the complexity and costs of a storage and retrieval process are magnified.

9. *Visualization*

Visualization refers to the ability of presenting the data as mentioned by Shafer (2017). Due to limitations of in-memory technology and poor scalability, functionality, and response time, current big data visualization tools face technical challenges. One can't rely on traditional graphs when trying to plot a billion data points, so different ways of representing data such as data clustering or using tree maps, sunbursts, parallel coordinates, circular network diagrams, or cone trees are needed. Considering this along with the multitude of variables resulting from big data's variety and velocity and the complex relationships between them, one can see that developing a meaningful visualization is not that easy.

10. *Value*

Vales refers the importance of data as mentioned by Shafer (2017), it represents the business value to be derived from big data. The other characteristics of big data are meaningless if one doesn't derive business value from the data. Substantial value can be discovered from big data, including understanding customers better, targeting them accordingly, optimizing processes, and improving machine or business performance. One needs to understand the potential, along with the more challenging characteristics of big data, before embarking on a big data strategy. It is concerned with providing ever-increasing value to the users as more data is available and new techniques are developed.

11. *Venue*

It is concerned with the distributed, heterogeneous data from multiple platforms, from different owners' systems, with different access and formatting requirements, private vs. public cloud. Various types of data arrived from different sources via different platforms like customer workstations or cloud and the work takes place in different locations and under different arrangements as mentioned by Shafer, (2017),.

12. *Vocabulary*

Vocabulary refers to different data terminology likes data model, schema, semantics, ontologies, taxonomies, and other content and context-based metadata that describe the data's structure, syntax, content, and provenance as mentioned by Shafer, (2017).

13. *Vagueness*

The meaning of found data is often very unclear, regardless of how much data is available. It refers to the confusion over the meaning of big data, in terms of what is new in the data, which tools are available, which tools are useful particular to a specific business, etc as mentioned by Shafer, (2017).

14. *Vastness*

With the advent of the Internet of Things (IoT), the "bigness" of big data is accelerating as mentioned by Shafer, (2017).

15. *Vivify*

Data science has the potential to animate all manner of decision making and business processes, from marketing to fraud detection.

16. *Virality*

It is determined with the spreading speed. It is defined as the rate at which the data is broadcast /spread by a user and received by different users for their use as mentioned by Shafer, (2017).

17. *Vibrant*

A thriving data science community is vital, and it provides insights, ideas, and support in all of our endeavors as mentioned by Shafer, (2017).

18. *Viability*

It is difficult to build robust models, and it's harder still to build systems that will be viable in production as mentioned by Shafer, (2017).

19. *Veer*

With the rise of agility, we should be able to navigate the customer's needs and change directions quickly when called upon as mentioned by Shafer, (2017).

20. *Versed*

Data scientists often need to know a little about a great many things mathematics, statistics, programming, databases, etc as mentioned by Shafer, (2017),.

Due to these characteristics it is difficult to manage the data it the traditional way as earlier it was done using database and spreadsheets.

Significance of Big Data

Big Data works on the principle that the more you know about anything or any situation, the more reliably you can gain new insights and make predictions about what will happen in the future. By comparing more data points, relationships begin to emerge that were previously hidden, and these relationships enable us to learn and make smarter decisions. Most commonly, this is done through a process that involves building models, based on the data we can collect, and then running simulations, altering the value of data points each time and monitoring how it impacts our results. This process is automated, today's advanced analytics technology will run millions of these simulations, altering all the possible variables until it finds a pattern or an insight that helps solve the problem it is working on. Until relatively recently, data was limited to spreadsheets or databases and it was all very ordered and neat. Anything that wasn't easily organized into rows and columns was simply too difficult to work with and was ignored. Now though, advances in storage and analytics mean that we can capture, store and work with many, many different types of data. As a result, "data" can now mean anything from databases to photos, videos, sound recordings, written text and sensor data. To make sense of all of this messy data, Big Data projects often use cutting-edge analytics involving artificial intelligence and machine learning. By teaching computers to identify what this data represents– through image recognition or natural language processing, for example, they can learn to spot patterns much more quickly and reliably than humans. This ever-growing stream of sensor information, photographs, text, voice and video data means we can now use data in ways that were not possible even a few years ago. This is revolutionizing the world of business across almost every industry. Companies can now accurately predict what specific segments of customers will want to buy, and when, to an incredibly accurate degree. And Big Data is also helping companies run their operations in a much more efficient way.

Even outside of business, Big Data projects are already helping to change our world in a number of ways, such as:

1. Improving healthcare. Data-driven medicine involves analyzing vast numbers of medical records and images for patterns that can help find diseases early and develop new medicines as mentioned by Mayer &, Cukier (2013).
2. Predicting and responding to natural and man-made disasters. Sensor data can be analyzed to predict where earthquakes are likely to strike next, and patterns of human behavior give clues that help organizations give relief to survivors. Big Data technology is also used to monitor and safeguard the flow of refugees away from war zones around the world.
3. Preventing crime. Police forces are increasingly adopting data-driven strategies based on their own intelligence and public data sets in order to deploy resources more efficiently and act as a deterrent where one is needed as mentioned by Russom (2011).

The need for Big data handling is increasing to provide a better and efficient way to organize the data for any organization.

Application of Big Data

The influence of big data is prominent on all the types of modern organizations. While understanding the value of big data continues to remain a challenge, other practical challenges including funding and return on investment and skills continue to remain at the forefront for a number of different industries that are adopting big data. With that said, a years. Generally, most organizations have several goals for adopting big data projects. While the primary goal for most organizations is to enhance customer experience, other goals include cost reduction, better targeted marketing and making existing processes more efficient. In recent times, data breaches have also made enhanced security an important goal that big data projects seek to incorporate.

VIRTUAL ORGANIZATIONS

Virtual organizations are distributed 'business processes'. These processes may be 'owned' by one or more organizations acting in partnership. For a specific project, resources are assembled to perform a business process on behalf of the project owner(s), and then disassembled on completion of the contract as mentioned by Wolff (1995). When a business opportunity is prominent, a need for planning and developing a virtual organization, developing an agreement or cooperation contracts among members or good participants and adjusting and arranging the desirable base in order to run the operations according to the agreement is appeared to expand the business opportunities as mentioned by Mowshowitz (2001).

A virtual organization is a "business without walls", not physically existing as such but made and connected by software. The need to remain competitive in the open market forces companies to concentrate on their core competencies while searching for alliances when additional skills or resources are needed to fulfill business opportunities. The changing business situation of companies and customer needs have motivated the introduction of Virtual Organization (VO). A Virtual Organization is always a form of partnership and managing partners and handling partnerships are crucial. Virtual organizations are defined as a temporary collection of enterprises that cooperate and share resources, knowledge, and competencies to better respond to business opportunities. A temporary network of independent companies, suppliers, customers, linked by information technology to share skills, cost, and access to one another's markets. Its goal is to deliver highest-quality product at the lowest possible cost in a timely manner. Virtual organizations work on the idea of outsourcing, groupware use of technology with an intense to improve, and trust the environment with no borders and no clear identity, to increase the business opportunity. The ultimate goal of the virtual organization is to provide innovative, high-quality products or services instantaneously in response to customer demands. Other critical dimensions of Virtual Organization could include, purpose, connectivity, technology, boundary, business process and people as mentioned by Yuan, Lee, & Liao, (2000). Some popularly known virtual organizations include, Wikipedia, Amazon.com, General Motors, Nike, etc as suggested by Sawar (2012).

Virtual organizations offer the following advantages:

1. It saves time, travel expenses and eliminates lack of access to experts.
2. Virtual teams can be organized whether or not members are in reasonable proximity to each other.
3. Use of outside experts without incurring expenses for travel, logging and downtime.
4. Dynamic team membership allows people to move from one project to another.
5. Employee can be assigned to multiple, concurrent teams.
6. Teams' communication and work reports are available online to facilitate swift responses to the demands of the (global) market.
7. Employees can accommodate both personal and professional lives.
8. Virtual teams allow firms to expand their potential labor markets enabling them to hire and retain the best people regardless of their physical locations.

Technologies Used to Support Virtual Organizations

New technology has transformed the traditional ways of working. In particular, the worlds of computing and telephony are coming together to open up a whole new range of responsibilities. Computer Telephony Integrations (CTI) will usher in a new revolution to the desktop. The CTI has traditionally been used in all call centre applications.

1. E-Mail Integration

Integrating Short Message Service (SMS) into the existing e-mail infrastructure allows the whole organization to take advantages of SMS products such as 'Express Way'.

2. Office System Integration

SMS technology can greatly enhance the existing or new office systems, e. g., phone messages can be sent via SMS rather than returning it in a message book.

3. Voice Mail Alert

SMS technology added to the existing voice mail system builds an effective method of receiving voice mail alerts.

4. Mobile Data

This enables a laptop to retrieve information anywhere through the mobile phone network. Mobile data communications revolutionize where and how work is done. In the past, corporate information has been inaccessible from many places where it is needed. One's ability to link laptop to mobile phone keeps one connected to his/her virtual organization from anywhere.

With the use of these technologies lots of digital data is generated, and big data tools and technologies can be applied to different types of organizations in various businesses.

Big Data Usage in Various Industry Sectors

Below is the list of various industries which can utilize the concept of big data in their working culture.

1. Education

Big data is used quite significantly in higher education. Massive Open Online Courses (MOOCs) and related educational technologies offer opportunities to capture massive amounts of real-time data to expand research opportunities in learning as mentioned by Dede (2016), Learning and Management Systems are developed that can be used to track, when a student logs onto the system, how much time is spent on different pages in the system, as well as the overall progress of a student over time. In a different use case of the use of big data in education, it is also used to measure teacher's effectiveness to ensure a good experience for both students and teachers. Teacher's performance can be fine-tuned and measured against student numbers, subject matter, student demographics, student aspirations, behavioral classification and several other variables. Big data can help to improve students' performance and learning abilities making the lessons more personal. The courses can be adjusted from the teachers with the help of analytics. Open Data are able to help parents and students to find the best school or educational program. Companies and candidate employees can discover alternative and more effective tools to use open data to qualify their skills with the needed skills. Also students can find and make applications for jobs which can match with their abilities, more efficient than before as mentioned by West (2012). The major challenge is to integrate data from different sources, on different platforms and from different vendors that were not designed to work with one another. Another issue is of privacy and personal data protection associated with big data used for educational purposes. Big Data Providers in this area include: Carnegie Learning as shown in Explore Our Products, Knewton (2016) and Naviance (2018) as mentioned in Connecting learning to life.

2. Banking and Securities

The Securities Exchange Commission (SEC) is using big data to monitor financial market activity. They are currently using network analytics and natural language processors to catch illegal trading activity in the financial markets. Retail traders, Big banks, hedge funds and other so-called 'big boys' in the financial markets use big data for trade analytics used in high frequency trading, pre-trade decision-support analytics, sentiment measurement, Predictive Analytics etc. This industry also heavily relies on big data for risk analytics including; anti-money laundering, demand enterprise risk management, Know Your Customer, and fraud mitigation. The major challenges in banking sector include securities fraud early warning, tick analytics, card fraud detection, archival of audit trails, enterprise credit risk reporting, trade visibility, customer data transformation and social analytics for trading. Big Data providers specific to this industry include Panopticon Software as mentioned in Datawatch (2018), Streambase Systems mentioned by Ozcan (2018), Nice Actimize as mentioned by Hoboken, (2018) and Atos (2016).

3. Healthcare Providers

The concept of Big Data can be used for better health planning. Its methodologies can be used for healthcare data analytics which helps in better decision making to increase the use of eHealth services. The services may include indications of health levels, Digital Imaging and Communications in Medicine, Health Insurance Portability and Accountability, etc. Big Data techniques can be applied to develop systems for the early diagnosis of diseases, and understand connection between various diseases and also to develop integrated data analytics platforms as mentioned by van Rijmenam (2018). The healthcare sector has access to huge amounts of data but has been plagued by failures in utilizing the data to curb the cost of rising healthcare and by inefficient systems that stifle faster and better healthcare benefits across the board. This is mainly due to the fact that electronic data is unavailable, inadequate, or unusable. Additionally, the healthcare databases that hold health-related information have made it difficult to link data that can show patterns useful in the medical field. Big Data Providers in this industry include: Recombinant Data,

Humedica as mentioned by Research and Markets (2015). Explorys and Cerner as mentioned by Cloudera, Inc. Cloudera (2012).

4. Communications, Media and Entertainment

Organizations in this industry simultaneously analyze customer data along with behavioral data to create detailed customer profiles that can be used to create content for different target audiences, recommend content on demand, and measure content performance. Spotify as mentioned by Mark van Rijmenam (2018), an on-demand music service, uses Hadoop big data analytics, to collect data from its millions of users worldwide and then uses the analyzed data to give informed music recommendations to individual users. Amazon Prime as mentioned by Wills (2016), which is driven to provide a great customer experience by offering, video, music and Kindle books in a one-stop shop also heavily utilizes big data. Since consumers expect rich media on-demand in different formats and in a variety of devices, some big data challenges in the communications, media and entertainment industry include, collecting, analyzing, and utilizing consumer insights, leveraging mobile and social media content and understanding patterns of real-time, media content usage. Big Data Providers in this industry include Splunk, Pervasive Software, Infochimps, and Visible Measures.

5. Manufacturing

Big data allows for predictive modeling to support decision making that has been utilized to ingest and integrate large amounts of data from geospatial data, graphical data, text and temporal data. Enhanced manufacturing quality & higher yield and reduced support costs are central to driving profitability and customer experience for any major manufacturer. Big data technologies can enable improved analysis of yield and quality data, combined with customer rejects/returns, supplier's quality data, and other critical measures for a rich and thorough root-cause analysis resulting in actions for enhanced quality and reduced overall cost as mentioned in Oracle enterprise architecture white paper (2015). Areas of interest where this has been used include; seismic interpretation and reservoir characterization. Increasing demand for natural resources including oil, agricultural products, minerals, gas, metals, and so on has led to an increase in the volume, complexity, and velocity of data that is a challenge to handle. Similarly, large volumes of data from the manufacturing industry are untapped. The underutilization of this information prevents improved quality of products, energy efficiency, reliability, and better profit margins. Big data challenges is in implementing Smart Factory, Smart Supply Chain, Smart Product Lifecycle, Hyper connected Factories, Autonomous Factories and Collaborative

Product-Service Factories as mentioned by Big Data Value Association (2018). Big Data Providers in this area include Liaison, Ingram micro advisor and nist.

6. Government

The big data phenomenon is growing throughout private and public sector domains. Profit motives make it urgent for companies in the private sector to learn how to leverage big data. However, in the public sector, government services could also be greatly improved through the use of big data. Big data can result in transformational government through increased efficiency and effectiveness in the delivery of services. For citizen's improvements the e-participation processes, government innovations, and citizen satisfaction governments need to enhance the collaboration and engagement as mentioned by Zaher & Laith (2017). Big data is being used in the analysis of large amounts of social disability claims, made to the Social Security Administration, that arrive in the form of unstructured data. The analytics are used to process medical information rapidly and efficiently for faster decision making and to detect suspicious or fraudulent claims. The Food and Drug Administration is using big data to detect and study patterns of food-related illnesses and diseases. This allows for faster response which has led to faster treatment and less death. In governments the biggest challenges are the integration and interoperability of big data across different government departments and affiliated organizations. Big Data Providers in this area include e-Zest as mentioned in Big Data Solutions for Government, DLT, informatica in Informatica Corporation (2013).

7. Insurance

Insurance companies are founded on estimating future events and measuring the risk/value of these events. With new data sources such as telematics, sensors, government, customer interactions and social media, the opportunity to utilize big data is more appealing across new areas of this industry nowadays. Big Data technologies are used comprehensively to determine risk, claims and enhance customer experience, allowing insurance companies to achieve higher predictive accuracy. Major uses of big data and its technologies in the insurance industry include risk assessment, fraud detection as mentioned in Ana-Ramona BOLOGA (2010), customer insights, marketing and obtaining customer experience. The major challenges in this area include lack of personalized services, lack of personalized pricing and the lack of targeted services to new segments and to specific market segments.Big Data Providers in this industry include: exastax as mentioned in Exastax (2017), tibco as mentioned in Spotfire Blogging Team (2015), octo telematics as in OctoTelematics (2015).

8. Retail and Whole Sale Trade

Big data from customer loyalty data, POS, store inventory, local demographics data continues to be gathered by retail and wholesale stores. The major concerns in this area are optimized staffing through data from shopping patterns, local events, timely analysis of inventory and reduce fraud. From traditional retailers and wholesalers to current day e-commerce traders, the industry has gathered a lot of data over time. This data, derived from customer loyalty cards, POS scanners, RFID etc. is not being used enough to improve customer experiences on the whole. Social media use also has a lot of potential use and continues to be slowly but surely adopted especially by small scale stores. Social media is used for customer prospecting, customer retention, promotion of products, and more. Big Data Providers in this industry include tableau as mentioned in Tableau (2018), cubeware as mentioned in Business intelligence & performance management solution wholesale trade, First Retail, First Insight, Fujitsu as mentioned by Helsinki, May 30, Fujitsu (2018).

9. Transportation

Transportation, as a means for moving goods and people between different locations, is a vital element of modern society as mentioned in Robert et al (2016). The use of big data in transportation include, traffic control, route planning, intelligent transport systems, congestion management by predicting traffic conditions, revenue management, technological enhancements, logistics and for competitive advantage by consolidating shipments and optimizing freight movement, route planning to save on fuel and time, for travel arrangements in tourism etc. In recent times, huge amounts of data from location-based social networks and high speed data from telecoms have affected travel behavior. Big Data Providers in this industry include, intersec in Intersec (2018), AndSoft as suggested by Clementine & Víctor (2018), omnitracs as mentioned by Lacombe (2018).

10. Energy and Utilities

Energy and Utilities are turning knowledge into power by using big data & analytics to better understand and shape customer usage, improve service levels and availability, and detect and prevent energy theft. Major areas include Grid Operations, Smart meters, Asset and workforce management as suggested by Clementine & Víctor (2018). Smart meter readers allow data to be collected almost every few minutes as opposed to once a day with the old meter readers. This granular data is being used to analyze consumption of utilities better which allows for improved customer feedback and better control of utilities use. In utility companies the use of big data also allows for better asset and workforce management which is useful for recognizing errors and correcting them as soon as possible before complete failure is experienced. Big Data Providers in this area include, epam as mentioned by Transforming the Energy Business with a Digital Services Platform & Data Intelligence (epam,2018), cloudera as mentioned in Smart utilities use smart data (Cloudera, 2018).

DIFFERENT APPROACHES OF MANAGING BIG DATA

One of the major issues in handling Big Data is to store and query the data. In this section we present some of the top tools used to store and analyze Big Data.

1. **Apache Hadoop:** Apache Hadoop is a java based free software framework that can effectively store large amount of data in a cluster (Apache Hadoop, 2018)). This framework runs in parallel on a cluster and has an ability to allow us to process data across all nodes. Hadoop Distributed File System (HDFS) is the storage system of Hadoop which splits big data and distribute across many nodes in a cluster. This also replicates data in a cluster thus providing high availability.

2. **Microsoft HD Insight:** It is a Big Data solution from Microsoft powered by Apache Hadoop which is available as a service in the cloud. HD Insight as mentioned by Chauhan et al(2014) uses Windows Azure Blob storage as the default file system. This also provides high availability with low cost.

3. **NoSQL:** While the traditional SQL can be effectively used to handle large amount of structured data, we need NoSQL (Not Only SQL) to handle unstructured data. NoSQL databases store unstructured data with no particular schema. Each row can have its own set of column values. NoSQL gives better performance in storing massive amount of data. There are many open-source NoSQL DBs available to analyze Big Data.

4. **Hive:** This is a distributed data management for Hadoop. This supports SQL-like query option HiveSQL (HSQL) to access big data. This can be primarily used for Data mining purpose. This runs on top of Hadoop.

5. **Sqoop:** This is a tool that connects Hadoop with various relational databases to transfer data. This can be effectively used to transfer structured data to Hadoop or Hive.

6. **PolyBase:** This works on top of SQL Server 2012 Parallel Data Warehouse (PDW) and is used to access data stored in PDW. PDW is a data warehousing appliance built for processing any volume of relational data and provides integration with Hadoop allowing us to access non-relational data as well.

7. **Big Data in EXCEL:** As many people are comfortable in doing analysis in EXCEL, a popular tool from Microsoft, you can also connect data stored in Hadoop using EXCEL 2013. Hortonworks, which is primarily working in providing Enterprise Apache Hadoop, provides an option to access big data stored in their Hadoop platform using EXCEL 2013. You can use Power View feature of EXCEL 2013 to easily summarize the data.

Similarly, Microsoft's HDInsight allows us to connect to Big data stored in Azure cloud using a power query option.

8. **Presto:** Facebook has developed and recently open-sourced its Query engine (SQL-on-Hadoop) named Presto which is built to handle petabytes of data. Unlike Hive, Presto does not depend on MapReduce technique and can quickly retrieve data. The organization can select the tool based on their requirement to handle the data and business processes.

BENEFITS OF BIG DATA PROCESSING

The big data processing offers various benefits like,

1. Businesses can not only consider internal factors but also external factors while taking decisions. Access to social data from search engines and sites like Facebook, twitter are enabling organizations to fine tune their business strategies.
2. Improved customer service. Traditional customer feedback systems are getting replaced by new systems designed with 'Big Data' technologies. In these new systems, Big Data and natural language processing technologies are being used to read and evaluate consumer responses.
3. Early identification of risk to the product/services, if any as mentioned by Cebr (2012).
4. Better operational efficiency.

Big Data technologies can be used for creating staging area or landing zone for new data before identifying what data should be moved to the data warehouse. In addition, such integration of Big Data technologies and data warehouse helps organization to discharge infrequently accessed data.

CHALLENGES OF APPLYING BIG DATA

Big Data is a term used for a collection of data sets so large and complex that it is difficult to process using traditional applications/tools. It is the data exceeding Terabytes in size. Because of the variety of data that it encompasses, big data always brings a number of challenges relating to its volume and complexity. A recent survey says that 80% of the data created in the world are unstructured. One challenge is how these unstructured data can be structured, before we attempt to understand and capture the most important data. Another challenge is how we can store it. Apart from these aspects Big Data gives us unprecedented insights and opportunities, but it also raises concerns and questions that must be addressed:

1. **Data Privacy:** The Big Data we now generate contains a lot of information about our personal lives, much of which we have a right to keep private. Increasingly, we are asked to strike a balance between the amount of personal data we divulge, and the convenience that Big Data-powered apps and services offer.
2. **Data Security:** Even if we decide we are happy for someone to have our data for a particular purpose, it is difficult to trust them to keep it safe.
3. **Data Discrimination:** When everything is known, will it become acceptable to discriminate against people based on data we have on their lives? We already use credit scoring to decide who can borrow money, and insurance is heavily data-driven. We can expect to be analyzed and assessed in greater detail, and care must be taken that this isn't done in a way that contributes to making life more difficult for those who already have fewer resources and access to information.

Facing up to these challenges is an important part of Big Data, and they must be addressed by organizations who want to take advantage of data. Failure to do so can leave businesses vulnerable, not just in terms of their reputation, but also legally and financially.

Data is changing our world and the way we live at an unprecedented rate. If Big Data is capable of all this today – just imagine what it will be capable of tomorrow. The amount of data available to us is only going to increase, and analytics technology will become more advanced. For businesses, the ability to leverage Big Data is going to become increasingly critical in the coming years. Those companies that view data as a strategic asset are the ones that will survive and thrive. Those that ignore this revolution risk being left behind.

REFERENCES

Agrifoglio, R. (2015). *Knowledge Preservation through Community of Practice.* Springer International Publishing. doi:10.1007/978-3-319-22234-9

Apache Hadoop. (2018). Retrieved from http://hadoop.apache.org

Atos. (2016). *Atos and Quartet FS launch a Big Data appliance that facilitates compliance with the future FRTB banking regulations.* Retrieved from https://atos.net/en/2016/press-release/general-press-releases_2016_02_22/pr-2016_02_22_01

Bergeron, B. (2000). Regional business intelligence: The view from Canada. *Journal of Information Science, 26*(3), 153–160. doi:10.1177/016555150002600305

Big Data Value Association. (2018). *Big data challenges in smart manufacturing.* Retrieved from http://www.bdva.eu/sites/default/files/BDVA_SMI_Discussion_Paper_Web_Version.pdf

Blackman, B. (2008). Uniquely Barbara. *Compass.*

Bologa, A., Bologa, R., & Florea, A. (2010). Big Data and Specific Analysis Methods for Insurance Fraud Detection. Database Systems Journal, 1(1).

Carnegie Learning. (2018). *Explore Our Products.* Retrieved from https://www.carnegielearning.com/products/our-products/overview/

Cebr. (2012). *Data equity, Unlocking the value of big data.* SAS Reports.

Chauhan, A., Fontama, V., Hart, M., Hyong, W., & Woody, B. (2014). Introducing Microsoft Azure HDInsight, Technical Overview. Microsoft Press.

Cloudera. (2012). *Explorys Medical: Improving Healthcare Quality & Costs Using a Big Data Platform.* Retrieved from http://blog.cloudera.com/wp-content/uploads/2012/05/Cloudera-Explorys-case-study-final.pdf

Cloudera. (2018). S*mart utilities use smart data.* Retrieved from https://www.cloudera.com/solutions/energy-and-utilities.html

Cubeware. (2018). *Business intelligence & performance management solution wholesale trade.* Retrieved from https://www.cubeware.com/en/solutions/industries/wholesale-and-retail-trade/

Cui, Z., Damiani, E., & Leida, M. (2007). Benefits of Ontologies in Real Time Data Access. *Digital Ecosystems and Technologies Conference, DEST '07,* 392-397. 10.1109/DEST.2007.372004

Cyber security Lessons Learned From the Ashley Madison Hack. (2015). Retrieved from https://www.forbes.com/sites/ericbasu/2015/10/26/cybersecurity-lessons-learned-from-the-ashley-madison-hack/#32870cf14c82

Datawatch. (2018). *Imagine Software Incorporates Panopticon Dashboards into its Real-Time Portfolio, Risk and Compliance Management Solutions*. Retrieved from, http://www.panopticon.com/2018/02/07/imagine-software-incorporates-panopticon-dashboards-real-time-portfolio-risk-compliance-management-solutions/

Dede, C. (2016). Next steps for "Big Data" in education: Utilizing data-intensive research. *Educational Technology*, *56*(2), 37–42.

Dietrich, D. (2012). *EMC: Data Science and Big Data Analytics*. EMC Education Services.

E-Zest. (2018). *Big Data Solutions for Government*. Retrieved from https://www.e-zest.com/big-data-solutions-for-government

Elgendy, N., & Elragal, A. (2014). Big Data Analytics: A Literature Review Paper. LNAI, 8557, 214–227.

Epam. (2018). *Transforming the Energy Business with a Digital Services Platform & Data Intelligence*. Retrieved from https://www.epam.com/our-work/customer-stories/transforming-energy-business-with-digital-services-platform-and-data-intelligence

Exastax. (2017). *Top 7 big data use cases in insurance industry*. Retrieved from big data https://www.exastax.com/big-data/top-7-big-data-use-cases-in-insurance-industry/

Firestone, J. M., & McElroy, M. W. (2003). *Key issues in the new knowledge management*. New York: Routledge.

Fujitsu. (2018). *Fujitsu Receives Extended Managed IT Infrastructure and Data Center Services Contract from Orion*. Retrieved from http://www.fujitsu.com/in/

Gantz, J., & Reinsel, D. (2012). *IDC, The digital universe in 2020: big data, bigger digital shadows, and biggest growth in the Far East*. Retrieved from http://www.emc. com/ leadership/ digital-universe/index.htm

Gartner, R., & Gartner, V. (2015). *Gartner Survey Shows More Than 75 Percent of Companies Are Investing or Planning to Invest in Big Data in the Next Two Years, Skills, Governance, Funding and ROI Challenges Set to Increase*. Retrieved from https://www.gartner.com/newsroom/id/3130817

Gasteau, C., & Vilas, V. (2018). *Transportation & Logistics Software And Soft: Technology e-TMS – A web based Transportation Management System.* Retrieved from https://transporttmsandlogisticstms.com/big-data-and-e-tms-software-andsoft/

Greenberg. (2016). *Hack Brief: Yahoo Breach Hits Half A Billion Users.* Retrieved from https://www.wired.com/2016/09/hack-brief-yahoo-looks-set-confirm-big-old-data-breach

Howson, C. (2006). *Seven Pillars of BI Success, Information Week.* Retrieved from http://www.informationweek.com/software/business-intelligence/the-seven-pillars-of-bisuccess/191902420

Hwang, H.-G., Ku, C.-Y., Yen, D. V., & Cheng, C.-C. (2004). Critical factors influencing the adoption of data warehouse technology: A study of the banking industry in Taiwan. *Decision Support Systems, 37*(1), 1–21. doi:10.1016/S0167-9236(02)00191-4

IBM. (2018). *The Four V's of Big Data.* Retrieved from http://www.ibmbigdatahub.com/infographic/four-vs-big-data

Informatica Corporation. (2013). *Big Data for Government.* Retrieved from https://www.informatica.com/content/dam/informatica-com/global/amer/us/collateral/executive-brief/big_data_government_ebook_2340.pdf

Inmon, W. H. (2005). *Building the Data Warehouse* (4th ed.). Indianapolis, IN: Wiley & Sons.

Intersec. (2018). Retrieved from https://www.intersec.com/refgb/big-data-analytics-application-in-transportation.html

Jin, X., Wah, B. W., Cheng, X., & Wang, Y. (2015). Significance and challenges of big data research. *Big Data Research, 2*(2), 59–64. doi:10.1016/j.bdr.2015.01.006

Kakhani, M. K., Kakhani, S., & Biradar, S. R. (2015). Research issues in big data analytics. *International Journal of Application or Innovation in Engineering & Management, 2*(8), 228–232.

Kntonew. (2016). *Knewton to Accelerate Personalized Learning for Students Worldwide With $52M in Financing.* Retrieved from https://www.knewton.com/resources/press/67525/

Kohavi, R., Rothleder, N. J., & Simoudis, E. (2002). Emerging Trends in Business Analytics. *Communications of the ACM, 45*(8), 45–48.

Lacombe, A. (2018). *Transform Your Fleet with Big Data*. Retrieved from https://www.omnitracs.com/solutions/data-analytics

Laudon, K. C., & Laudon, J. P. (2002). *Essential of management information systems* (5th ed.). Englewood Cliffs, NJ: Prentice Hall.

Leading Core Banking Provider Serving Thousands of Customers Selects NICE Actimize as its Integrated Cloud Financial Crime and Compliance Solution. (2018). Retrieved from https://www.niceactimize.com/press-releases/Leading-Core-Banking-Provider-Serving-Thousands-of-Customers-Selects-NICE-Actimize-as-its-Integrated-Cloud-Financial-Crime-and-Compliance-Solution-209

Levy, M., & Powell, P. (1998). SME flexibility and the role of information systems. *Small Business Economics*, *11*(2), 183–196. doi:10.1023/A:1007912714741

Liu, W., & Park, E. K. (2014). *Big Data as an e-Health Service*. IEEE Electronic. doi:10.1109/ICCNC.2014.6785471

Mayer, V. V., & Cukier, K. (2013). *Big Data: A Revolution That Will Transform How We Live, Work and Think*. John Murray Press.

Mohapatra, S., Agrawal, A., & Satpathy, A (2016). *Designing Knowledge Management-Enabled Business Strategies A Top-Down Approach*. Springer International Publishing.

Monash, C. (2008). *The 1-petabyte barrier is crumbling*. Retrieved from http://www.networkworld.com/community/node/31439

Mowshowitz, A. (2001). Virtual organization: The new feudalism. *Computer*, *34*(4), 100–111. doi:10.1109/MC.2001.917551

Naviance. (2018). *Connecting learning to life*. Retrieved from https://www.naviance.com/

Negash, S. (2004). Business Intelligence. *Communications of the AIS*, *13*, 177–195.

OctoTelematics. (2015). *The promise of insurance telematics*. Retrieved from https://www.octotelematics.com/news/the-promise-of-insurance-telematics

Oracle Enterprise Architecture White Paper. (2015). *Improving Manufacturing Performance with Big Data Architect's Guide and Reference Architecture Introduction*. Retrieved from http://www.oracle.com/us/technologies/big-data/big-data-manufacturing-2511058.pdf

Ozcan, A. (2018). *Senior Trader*. Retrieved from https://www.tibco.com/customers/kuveytturk-bank

Phillips-Wren, G., Iyer, L. S., Kulkarni, U., & Ariyachandra, T. (2015). Business Analytics in the Context of Big Data: A Roadmap for Research. *Communications of the Association for Information Systems, 37*, 23.

Press, G. (2016). *Cleaning Big Data: Most Time-Consuming, Least Enjoyable Data Science Task, Survey Says*. Retrieved from https://www.forbes.com/sites/gilpress/2016/03/23/data-preparation-most-time-consuming-least-enjoyable-data-science-task-survey-says/#7955038a6f63

Quitzau, A. (2014). *Big Data & Analytics*. Retrieved from https://www.slideshare.net/AndersQuitzauIbm/big-data-analyticsin-energy-utilities

Research and Markets. (2015). *Global Big Data in Healthcare Study 2015-2020 Featuring Explorys, Humedica, InterSystems, Pervasive, Clinical Query, GNS Healthcare, OmedaRX, and Sogeti Healthcare*. Retrieved from https://www.prnewswire.com/news-releases/global-big-data-in-healthcare-study-2015-2020-featuring-explorys-humedica-intersystems-pervasive-clinical-query-gns-healthcare-omedarx-and-sogeti-healthcare-300104781.html

Robert, P. B., Weng, T. K., & Simon, F. (2016). Big data analytics for transportation: Problems and prospects for its application in China. *2016 IEEE Region 10 Symposium (TENSYMP)*.

Russom, P. (2011). Big Data Analytics. TDWI Best Practices Report.

Sawar, A. (2012). *Virtual organizations*. Retrieved from https://www.slideshare.net/aijazansf/virtual-organisations

Scott Morton, M. S. (1991). *The Corporation of the 1990s: Information Technology and Organizational Transformation*. New York: Oxford University Press.

Shafer, T. (2017). *The 42 V's of Big Data and Data Science*. Retrieved from https://www.elderresearch.com/blog/42-v-of-big-data

Shanmugam, C. G. (2002). The Need for Knowledge Management in Special Libraries. In *Proceedings of the National Conference on Information Management in e-Libraries (ImeL)*. New Delhi: Allied Publishers.

Shao, Y., Lee, M., & Liao, S. (2000). Virtual organizations: the key dimensions. *Proceedings Academia/Industry Working Conference on Research Challenges '00. Next Generation Enterprises: Virtual Organizations and Mobile/Pervasive Technologies.*

Sharma, R., Yetton, P. W., & Zmud, R. W. (2008). Implementation Costs of IS-Enabled Organizational Change. *Information and Organization, 18*(2), 73–100. doi:10.1016/j.infoandorg.2007.09.001

Sivasubramanian, S. (2016). *Process Model for Knowledge Management* (Doctoral thesis). CMU-LTI-16-003 Language Technologies Institute School of Computer Science Carnegie Mellon University. Retrieved from www.lti.cs.cmu.edu

Spotfire Blogging Team. (2015). *4 Ways Big Data Is Transforming the Insurance Industry.* Retrieved from https://www.tibco.com/blog/2015/07/20/4-ways-big-data-is-transforming-the-insurance-industry/

Stackowiak, R., Rayman, J., & Greenwald, R. (2007). *Oracle Data Warehousing and Business Intelligence Solutions.* Indianapolis, IN: Wiley Publishing, Inc.

Tableau. (2018). *Retail and Wholesale Analytics.* Retrieved from https://www.tableau.com/solutions/retail-and-wholesale-analytics

Tvrdikova, M. (2007), Support of Decision Making by Business Intelligence Tools. *Computer Information Systems and Industrial Management Applications, 2007. CISIM '07. 6th International Conference*, 368.

van Rijmenam, M. (2018). *How Big Data Enabled Spotify To Change The Music Industry.* Retrieved from https://datafloq.com/read/big-data-enabled-spotify-change-music-industry/391

Virkus, S. (2014). *Theoretical Models of Information and Knowledge Management.* Retrieved from http://www.tlu.ee/~sirvir/IKM/Theoretical_models_of_Information_and_Knowledge_Management/the_von_krogh_and_roos_model_of_organizational_epistemology.html

West, D. M. (2012). *Big Data for Education: Data Mining, Data Analytics, and Web Dashboards.* Gov. Stud. Brook. US Reuters.

Wills, J. (2016). *7 Ways Amazon Uses Big Data to Stalk You (AMZN)*. Retrieved from, https://www.investopedia.com/articles/insights/090716/7-ways-amazon-uses-big-data-stalk-you-amzn.asp

Wixom, B., & Watson, H. J. (2001). An empirical investigation of the factors affecting data warehousing success. *Management Information Systems Quarterly*, *25*(1), 17–41. doi:10.2307/3250957

Wolff, M. (1995*). Ki-Net - New Organizational Structures for Engineering Design*. Retrieved from http://www.ki-net/part1.html

Zaher, A. A., & Laith, M. A. (2017). Big data and E-government: A review. *2017 8th International Conference on Information Technology (ICIT)*, 580-587.

Chapter 2
Analysis of the 5Vs of Big Data in Virtual Travel Organizations

Serkan Polat
Istanbul Medeniyet University, Turkey

Fevzi Esen
Istanbul Medeniyet University, Turkey

Emrah Bilgic
Mus Alparslan University, Turkey

ABSTRACT

Virtual travel organizations, one of the most effective actors of tourism marketing, use information technology-based systems in parallel with the increasing use of information technologies. The competition in the tourism industries pushes virtual travel organizations to remain dynamic. Thus, customers can demand affordable and qualified tourism products. For this reason, it is inevitable for virtual travel organizations to use information technologies, in order to meet customers' demands efficiently and cost-effectively. Due to its nature, tourism products cannot be experienced before the sale. In order to analyze the expectations of the tourism customers, big-data-related technologies are valuable assets to the virtual travel organizations. From this point of view, managing massive data generated by tourism consumers is vital for the tourism supply chain. To the best of the authors' knowledge, there is no study relating big data and virtual travel organizations. In this chapter, the importance of five key concepts of big data have been discussed in terms of virtual travel organizations.

DOI: 10.4018/978-1-5225-7519-1.ch002

INTRODUCTION

Technological developments have created a significant increase in the size and variety of data. It has been reported that 90% of the available data stacks in the world has been produced in the last two years until 2013 (Dragland, 2013). Mobility and widespread use of internet has played an important role in the size and diversity of data. According to IDC, big data production is projected to increase by nearly 20% annually until 2025 and the global datasphere is expected to be 163 zettabytes which is ten times bigger than the data generated in 2016 (IDC, 2017).

Tourism industries cover a wide range of operations as transactions, events and activities. The types of big data stem from users (user generated content such as online textual and social media data), devices (Wi-Fi, RFID, Bluetooth, GPS, roaming data, etc.) and operations (online booking, web search, consumer cards, attractions sales, visitors traffic, tourists consumption and stay data). Therefore, the systems integrated with virtual businesses such as mobile applications, smart readers, sensors, social media, website usage, customer relationship management systems and enterprise resource planning systems are crucial to understand and manage for many industries as well as for the tourism industries.

Information and communication technologies (ICTs) are important tools of tourism and hospitality business (Law et al., 2009). The aims of adopting ICTs include productivity and efficiency, enhanced customer services and cost reduction (Singh & Kasavana, 2005). Buhalis and O'Conner (2005) state that ICTs introduce to consumers tourism products and encourage consumers to purchase products. In the '90s, acquisitions, market alliances and the systems opening to other suppliers such as hotels, car rental agencies, visitor information centers and inbound tour operators resulted in the formation of four global distribution systems: SABRE, Amadeus/System One, Galileo/Apollo and Worldspan (Gretzel & Fesenmaier, 2009). These systems can link products and services across various sectors based on up-to-date information and this is also an attempt to transfer knowledge among service providers, computers and people.

To discover valuable knowledge from meaningless big data is a focal point for businesses. Traditional data systems and analysis techniques have failed to manage and scale big data. This makes big data management and its applications even more important. Businesses and consumers create structured and unstructured data resulting from their daily activities such as sales-bookings, web sites, call centers, social network interactions, blog posts, etc. Thus, ICTs have became a partner for a broad range of industries especially for big data and its applications in tourism field. For example, a travel agency is trying to collect information about a client's basic identity as well as his cultural characteristics and socio-economic status. The agency intends to carry out promotional activities by this information in the future.

In order to handle the complexities of various types and volumes of data, businesses need to create information technologies infrastructure that keeps business operations running smoothly.

Due to the nature of products and services of tourism industries, customers cannot experience tourism product before purchasing and they want to obtain detailed information about the product. This enables tour operators to execute their activities without a physical location, through online services. For this reason, tourism products and services are offered online through tour operators and travel agencies. According to American Society of Travel Agents (ASTA) report of 2017, digital travel sales amounted to $564.8 billion worldwide and it is expected to be $817.5 billion by 2020. Moreover, virtual travel organizations generated revenues of about $166 billion in 2016. Also, the number of customers, who managed their reservations through online services, reached 64 million in 2016 (ASTA, 2017).

A virtual organization requires an integrated information management system which supports operational efficiency with downstream and upstream tourism product information sharing. The establishment of an efficient big data explanation in tourism sector will provide a dynamic and deep understanding for knowledge sharing between tourism supply chain parties. This also helps to manage the services which are supplied by virtual tour operators and travel agencies.

In tourism industries, a tour operator is engaged in assembling and operating tour packages including transportation, accommodation, guides and meals once the customer purchase the tour package by a booking channel such as online or walk–in agents, and, besides, a travel agency provides tourism products and services to customers on behalf of operators by making reservations and coordinating the needs of customers. Virtual travel organizations play an important role between tour operators which offer their products, and the tourism costumers (Ling et al., 2014).

Prior a purchase, customers use virtual travel organizations (travel agencies, travel portals or tour operators) via websites and specifies their needs onto the digital system through a user interface. It is aimed to be able to program travels or trips in accordance with the needs of customers. Once the customer entered his/her requests here, ontology and search engine help travel agencies provide access to products and services that are available to her/him. On the other hand, the supplier of tourism products is tour operators. A large amount of data including user requests, product-service–company information are collected and processed by all cooperating parties.

This chapter is organized as follows: Section 1 gives information about tourism products/services and focuses on virtual organizations in terms of tourism industries. Section 2 explains online travel agencies and tour operators. Section 3 discusses the importance of 5v's of big data within the virtual organizations of tourism industries. Finally, Section 4 concludes the chapter and give some ideas for further researches.

BACKGROUND

Tourism is a social complex phenomenon. Due to its complex structure, many academic disciplines such as economics, psychology, geography, sociology, management, marketing, planning and statistics are utilized. The industrial revolution has caused a significant shift in the travel industry. People have started to move faster and in large numbers to places where they do live and work (Jayapalan, 2001).

In tourism, intangible services are usually produced. There is no physical product to be stored or transferred from one intermediary to another. For example, a hotel room as "product" can only be available for a certain day. If this room is not sold, the revenue will be lost forever (Leuterio, 2007). In Table 1, main differences between products and services are summarized.

The distinction between travel and tourism is certainly not clear and two often coalesce. Some claim that travel is part of tourism; others argue that travel is a key component or part of the definition of tourism. Travel, tourism and hospitality businesses operate in the service sector. These businesses are known in the following five specialties (Robinson, 2009):

1. **Intangibility:** Services are not tangible, they cannot be touched or sensed. For example, the holiday package cannot be looked out and tested before the customer experiences it.
2. **Heterogeneity:** Every experience is different to different individuals. Two people in the same restaurant may have very different ideas about the level and quality of service, based usually on their previous experiences which can be used to measure the experience.
3. **Perishability:** Services cannot be stockpiled. A holiday that is available from 1 April to 1 May cannot be kept and sold on 5 May because there are spaces left on the aircraft.

Table 1. The differences between products and services

Product	Service
One can own a product.	One experiences a service.
Products are the result of a physical process.	Service is the result of a "people" process.
Products are tangible – a "thing".	Service is intangible – a "performance".
Needs are satisfied through the consumption of mainly one product.	Service is essentially a bundle of activities consisting of a "core" product plus "supplementary" services.
Production and consumption are separate: goods are produced away from the consumer.	Production and consumption are inseparable: consumers use the service at the point of production.

Source: Lubbe, 2000

4. **Inseparability:** The service has to be used where it is bought – it cannot be taken home for later.
5. **Lack of Ownership:** Because of the intangible nature of the industry, services which are bought do not confer ownership. A hotel customer who books a room does not own the bed or the room, just the opportunity to use it and to except to receive a certain level of service.

Archer et al. (2004) state that a country can achieve positive results in economic, social, cultural and environmental issues through tourism. On the other hand, Goeldner and Ritchie (2009) point out the following positive and negative aspects of tourism by expressing that tourism has some costs as well as economic and non-economic benefits for local people as given in Table 2.

Businesses need to be flexible in order to keep up with changing customer and business environments. Collaborative agreements, such as establishing strategic alliances and networking allow organizations to assess market opportunities, have new capabilities, and respond to customer requests more quickly. With technological developments, global competition and changes in environmental factors, businesses have made innovations and created new ways of business for continuous improvement and growth. The common feature of these innovations is the intensive use of communication and computer technologies and the creation, use and representation of information. The emergence of virtual organizations has been realized in parallel with these innovations.

Virtual organizations can be defined as businesses of the future and are separated from traditional businesses with a cost-effective but more functional operating structure. Metzger and Flanagin (2008) point out that a virtual organization is an electronically unified organization that coordinates its work via ICT. Koçel (2015) identifies virtual organization as being connected through communication technologies for specific production purposes and working harmoniously with other organizations as if there is a single business. Virtual organizations provide a responsive and interactive place that allows multi-way communications to consumers, producers, suppliers, and all of the parties that add value to the production altogether. Bringing the resources and skills of the organizations together for a common purpose is a crucial element of virtual organizations.

Virtual organizations are based on a network of people who are the experts in this field while guiding and adapting information technologies according to the priorities and objectives of organization. Generally, they do not have a traditional office except for tax payment purposes. They operate in virtual offices or virtual workplaces, where employees can reach the common network. This ensures a highly agile, cost-effective, reconfigurable and functionalized business structure. They are also built with dynamic technologies that cannot be managed by traditional

Table 2. Positives and negatives of tourism products and services

Positives of Tourism	Negatives of Tourism
Provides qualified and unqualified employment opportunities due to the fact that it is labour intensive industry.	Causes excessive demand for resources.
Provides the foreign exchange. Increases revenues, national income and government revenues.	Causes inflation and seasonality problems
Can be built on top of existing infrastructure.	May cause unbalanced economic growth.
Develops an infrastructure that will stimulate local trade and industry.	Causes social problems.
Can be developed with local products and local resources. It spreads development and the multiplier effect is high.	Damages the natural physical environment and causes pollution.
Helps diversify the economy. It may be one of the most appropriate economic activities complementary to other economic activities in a region.	Damages the cultural environment.
Develops cultural and educational horizons with personal values. Improves quality of life for high income and improved living standards.	Causes increases in crime, prostitution and gambling incidents.
Supports the preservation of cultural heritage and traditions.	Increases sensitivity to economic and political changes.
Supports environmental improvement and protection.	Threatens the family structure.
Provides employment for painters, musicians and other performing artists.	Commoditizes culture, religion and art.
Allows local people to use tourist facilities and removes language, socio-cultural, race, political and religious obstacles.	Causes conflicts in the host society or misunderstandings
Creates a positive image on a global scale for a destination and promotes global society, contributes to international peace.	Causes illnesses, economic fluctuation and transportation problems.

Source: Goeldner and Ritchie, 2009

business structures such as closed and vertical management systems and sell–or–die environment supported by limited information flow. It is a temporary collaboration of multiple organizations which aim to reach common goals by sharing ICTs (Unver & Sadigh, 2013). In this way, organizations are able to produce high value added products with financial benefits of using ICTs via a secured collaboration platform.

ICT is a key element of a virtual organization for providing flow of data within the system. For example, a tourist connects to the web site of a virtual travel agency through the user interface. Once he/she types his/her requests here, they provide access to products and services that are offered to them by the tour operators via ontology and search engine. Besides, the tourists' data are being processed (including collecting, preservation, organization, deletion, etc.) under the general principles of relevant legal acts and principles.

In order to achieve an efficient and dynamic information flow between consumers and businesses in a virtual environment, an efficient organizational structure should be designed. Dimensions constituting the structure of a virtual organization as follows (Matos & Afsarmanesh, 2006):

1. **Target Specificity:** The relationships among the members are harmonized to achieve specific goals. The objectives are comprehensive and clearly shown.
2. **Formalization:** The cooperation between the members of organization is realized consciously. The structure of relations is deliberately determined, reconstructed, and openly established.
3. **Mutual Dependency:** It is the whole of elements or attributes that create interrelated changes in business processes.
4. **Space and Time Diffusion:** It refers to the size of organizational elements spread over time and place.
5. **Modularity:** Virtual organizations include customer integration and related processes. This is achieved by gathering manageable units.
6. **Consistency:** Overcoming obstacles and removing the constraints of organizations in virtual environment.
7. **Limits:** This term points out the absence of physical boundaries amongst the organizations/parties.
8. **Complexity or Diversity:** This is a term that results from the interactions of components of a system. Virtual organizations have a continuous change in components such as business processes, objects, and responsibilities.

Tourism industries have dynamic and inter-organizational environments that require a close cooperation between the service providers in tourism value chain. These environments contribute to competitive advantage of tourism businesses and the value of tourism experiences and also create sustainable operational excellence for service providers. In this sense, there is a need of a virtual structure grounded on Web that organizes the relationships between tourism service providers, suppliers and customers; and ensures efficient flow of information between the parties.

Tourism products and services are offered online through commercial enterprises. The main parties of tourism industries are the suppliers such as travel agencies, tour operators or other businesses. Airline companies, hotel chains and travel agencies use the ICT products or services for global marketing and distribution. At this point, a virtual tourism organization can be defined as a business which executes its operations independently of a physical location, and carries out all business processes and activities on the internet. Business processes include the marketing of products, payments, finance, administration and customer relationship management.

In tourism industries, the sale of tourism products and services are actually the knowledge about the product (Medlik, 2016). They are heavily dependent on up-to-date information. Since the product is seen as a sale, there is a need for a wide range of bits of information–data, and experiences of tourists and consumers. The relationship between tourism suppliers and customers is sustained not only by goods but mostly by flow of data. The data regarding flights, hotel reservations, transfers, tariffs and confirmations are available to all parties of tourism industry at any time. For instance, as shown in Figure 1, the data regarding check-in, baggage, special requests, service availability, charges and changes of a flight have multi-stream flows from airlines to travel agencies or vice versa. The same system is also eligible for hotels, resorts, museums, sea and land transports and other tourism related suppliers even restaurants.

Tourism industry is one of the main contributors of ICTs and the foundation of tourism industry is data. It has an unifying role in different parties within tourism industries such as travel agencies, tour operators, online travel services, airlines, hotels, and other suppliers. Data also have been at the center of global travel distribution. Global distribution systems integrate multiple services such as flight reservation, hotel reservation, car rental, online ticketing and transfer systems by providing up-to-date information to all customers. All of these services produce enormous quantity of data which are either structured, semi-structured or unstructured.

ICTs are the main tools that capture big data. Increasing use of ICTs is directly linked to the emergence of big data in many forms. The main objectives of businesses are to create value and establish competitive advantage using new generation information technologies and sharing them with stakeholders. In order to extract valuable information from various data sources in terms of socio-economic sense, there is a need for collecting, storing and analyzing data. This revealed some big data characteristics (5Vs) such as velocity, variety, value, veracity and volume (Fosso et al., 2015).

Figure 1. Data and information flow of the tourist trade
Source: This figure is formed by authors

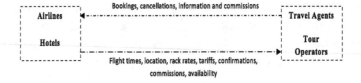

A tourism product sale is conducted through a distribution system controlled by travel agencies and tour operators and they use ICTs in several fields (Bhatia, 2006). In order to confirm sale of tourism products, gather and manage customer data and ensure optimal designs of fares, journey times and costs, computerized devices and systems that connect all of the parties and retrieve data from users, operations and transactions in tourism industries, are in use.

Today, most of the travel agencies and tour operators use big data related technologies to distribute all types of services. They also provide data about planning trips, ticketing, quotes and schedules through a global interconnected distribution system. Lubbe (2000) divides the use of information systems into three categories: front-office, back-office and middle-office systems. The information regarding clients (occupation, gender, address, etc.), bookings, the availability and use of facilities, ordinary travel transactions, special fares or requirements are in the flow of data, as well as itineraries, payments, cheques and other travel expenses information via these systems.

As stated in Table 3, communication in virtual organizations takes place electronically. For this reason, face-to-face communication is not easily seen in virtual organizations. Moreover, in traditional businesses, knowledge accumulation which can be converted into investments within an organization is important, but sharing the knowledge is more important than accumulating the knowledge in virtual organizations. Also, the existence of physical objects has a crucial role in traditional businesses, whereas electronic information management which has been

Table 3. Processing information in traditional and virtual tourism organizations

Traditional Travel Agencies and Tour Operators	Virtual Travel Agencies and Tour Operators
All of the sources are brought together	Dispersed sources with connected devices
Serial processing of data	Parallel processing of data
Data management is performed periodically on a routine basis	Data management is performed continuously
Physical objects	Virtual objects and virtual environments
Distribution of data	Accessing to data and knowledge
Information is on the paper	Information is in the electronic environment
Sharing the workloads in the groups	Dynamic sharing of workloads in virtual environments
Transparent physical processes	Processes followed on computers
Focus on top-down or bottom-up business processes	Focus on the whole processes
Hard to create prototypes	Easy to create prototypes and simulations.

Source: This table is formed by authors

passed through both electronic and manual record generating, keeping and analyzing processes are the main tools of virtual organizations.

It is no longer sufficient to operate tourism industries and drive value from tourism customers by using traditional data sources such as reservation books, receipts, customers' feedback forms, etc. Mobile devices, web searches and social media are at the center of technological developments that accelerate the development of virtual organizations. Even the sub-industries of tourism are connected with competitors and customers via internet–enabled devices and online applications. They use digital platforms that coordinate operations such as reservations, room rates and billing, catering, food and beverage operations, rooms and facilities maintenance, revenue management, customer relations, marketing and so on (Table 4). This means that the usage of ICTs which are capable of processing (batch, real-time or stream) and storing various types of data, are vital assets that create business value for companies. However, according to McKinsey (2011) tourism services face barriers due to the lack of IT intensity (it refers to the benefits of a company from its IT structure) and analytical-managerial talent (it refers to being talented and having a depth of expertise in statistics and big data analytics).

VIRTUAL TRAVEL AGENCIES AND TOUR OPERATORS

The travel industry uses data technologies more than twenty years. It has become inevitable in the areas of reservation, accounting, management, customer service improvement, human resources management, and financial management to reduce

Table 4. Data sources of tourism in different environments

Traditional Data Sources of a Tourism Environment	Web 3.0 and Web 4.0 Age
Reservation Books for Hotels, Meetings and Luncheons	Global Distribution Systems
Guest List Management Sheets	Guest and Property Management Systems
Reservation Receipts	Online Accounting Systems
Customer Feedback Forms	Customer relationship management
Verbal, Auditory and Visual Materials for Marketing	Websites, social media, informational digital videos, interactive online advertisements
Face-to-face communication	Real-time online communication
Daily prices of hotel and other related services	Online pricing and Hotel Ads and APIs
-	Crowd sourcing
-	Sensors and communication systems

Source: This table is formed by authors

operating processes and costs. Even though information technology is a key competitive weapon in the travel industry, it is the biggest threat to a travel agency's operating method and even its existence. Travelers, instead of going to the travel agency, have started making their own reservations electronically (Lubbe, 2000).

Developments in information technology, services and applications are effective in tourism industry, which is in the increasingly competitive environment. Due to the change of global distribution channels and new improved communication opportunities with business partners, every actor in the travel industry, such as suppliers, tour operators, travel agencies and travelers, is under the influence of big data and related technologies. Besides, up-to-date information has a crucial role in marketing of tourism products and services. For this reason, big data are at the center of global travel distribution system.

In the 1970s, airline computer reservation systems and travel agencies were provided access to electronic distribution channels. Subsequent company mergers, market alliances and opening of the systems to other suppliers (hotel, car rental, etc.); led to the birth of four global distribution systems such as SABRE, Worldspan, Galileo/Apollo and Amadeus/System One (Kuom & Oertel, 1999). These systems are extended for use of tourism businesses to manage tourism related data flows from various service providers and incorporates most of tourism services as shown in Figure 2. The systems enable the necessary information to be delivered to the people in convenient place and on time. In addition, it allows customers to make reservations and purchase the desired tourism products/services.

Figure 2. Data flow of virtual travel agencies and tour operators
Source: This table is formed by authors

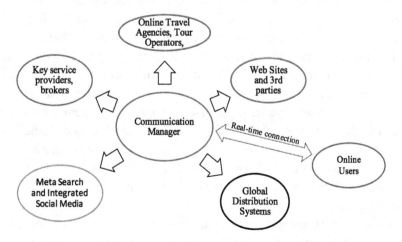

Tourism knowledge and decision making are increasingly influenced by online sources, online trade, business to business, and business to consumer communications and marketing. Virtual connectivity is essential for all businesses to reach potential and existing tourists and to influence the businesses' ability to improve their competitiveness and to achieve greater socio-economic benefits. A fast and reliable virtual connectivity is a vehicle for business expansion, investment incentives and reaching potential markets. Countries with extensive super-fast broadband connections have a competitive advantage due to increased demand for social media and internet access. Internet plays an important role in awareness building, branding and purchasing decision-making process for tourists (Dupeyras & MacCallum, 2013).

1. **Target Specificity:** Tourism systems are dynamic. It involves continuous interaction of different market actor groups. Each actor group has different and potentially conflicting goals. Visitors are subject to personal and societal trends that affect their motivation to travel and their perception of new, interesting and satisfying goals that meet their needs. Travel distribution channel members (wholesalers and retailers) want to make a profit. Because of this, they try to balance their income and costs through promotion and marketing of alternative trips.

2. **Formalization:** The process of electronic business systems is realized at four levels. At the first level, which is referred to as the initiation, businesses recognize the importance of virtual systems and implement applications on their web sites. At this level, internet is used to access information. The following level represents a remarkable investment in the company's virtual infrastructure. Then, at the third level, which is the level of interactions within or among the organizations (i.e. travel agency adopts online communication to stay in touch with its main indirect tour operator, which provides products and services, or with other suppliers). The top level "virtual business system" is the entire organizational business model (Andreu et al., 2010).

3. **Mutual Dependency:** In tourism industries, close cooperation and partnership is needed to take advantage of the benefits of information technology. The necessity of this cooperation is to improve tourism services and to provide the seamless travel experiences. In addition, modern economic developments, such as globalization and deregulation, require this close cooperation. Airline companies, hotels, intermediaries and tourism operators have started to restructure their organizations in accordance with ICTs.

4. **Space and Time Diffusion:** Technological advances have caused the collapse of space and time. People and organizations are no longer restricted by space and time to work and stay connected. Work can be done at the desired place and at any time. It is common today for people and businesses in different parts of

the world to hold meetings via smartphones, tablets, and laptops (Benckendorff et al., 2014).

5.   **Modularity:** Every tourist is different and every tourist has different experiences and motivations. In the pre-Internet period, customers had no choice but to have capacities of the travel agencies and tour operators. Therefore, customers are dependent on the intermediaries. The Internet enabled businesses to deliver their products directly to their customers through a number of distribution channels. Online tourism agencies and search engines have succeeded in accessing information and providing information. Virtual communities are becoming more and more effective in the field of tourism. Customers make choices based on the trustworthiness of communities instead of marketing messages given by the organizations. Businesses can learn the expectations, needs and behaviors of customers by analyzing virtual communities. Thus, businesses can have the opportunity to offer products and services that match the expectations of their customers (Condratov, 2013).

6.   **Consistency:** In the online tourism market, many hotels cooperate with virtual travel organizations to expand market shares. In the meantime, hotel web sites and online travel agencies offer the same prices as a result of addressing the same customer pool. For this reason, it is necessary to establish a balance between hotels and online travel agencies in context of cooperation and competition (Guo et al., 2014).

7.   **Limits:** Apart from face-to-face, catalog and telephone sales, internet offers a new distribution channel. Nowadays, internet users are making their own searches, comparisons, and reservations whenever they want in any region of the world. This means that travel agencies and tour operators are no longer required to wait for potential tourists to reach them. The success of the Internet has created new and up-to-now non-existent forms of intermediaries. Travel meta-search engines and "infomediaries", which collect and filter the necessary and relevant information from the data stack, have emerged (Buhalis & Egger, 2008). This shows that one of the obstacles for parties and businesses to reach each other has been overcome through information technology.

8.   **Complexity or Diversity:** In addition to having lots of information the nature of tourism is very diverse. It is necessary to require information about destinations, transportation, activities, facilities, availability, prices, border controls, geography, and climate for travelers; information about market trends, destinations, transportation, activities, facilities, availability, prices, border controls, geography, climate, suppliers, and competitors for the intermediaries; information about the company, consumer behavior, intermediaries, and competitors for suppliers; information about the trends in industry, the size

and nature of flow of tourism, marketing, influences, policies, planning, and development for destinations (Benckendorff et al., 2014).

New technologies offer an efficient and flexible organizational structure, the creation of new products and services, long-term relationships with corporate businesses and global marketing opportunities offered by Internet (Kuom & Oertel, 1999).

As shown in Figure 3, there are many components of an online holiday. In an online market, firstly products, services, reservation and booking services are required. The advertising of these services provides additional information such as tourism destination and weather. Smart search options must be available for customers to be able to access these services easily and effectively. In the next step, customers will be provided with the ability to prepare payment for the service they will purchase and travel documents. In addition, there should be an online support service where customers can be provided with information on any topic they may need. In many stages of this online holiday process, customers' data are collected.

Figure 3. Functions of an electronic marketplace
Source: Kuom and Oertel, 1999

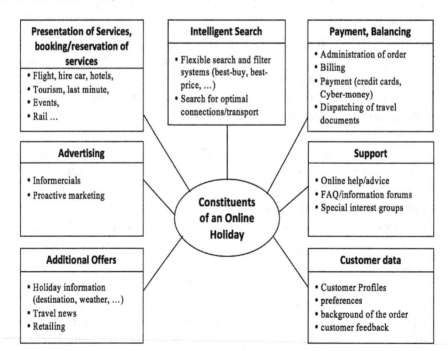

Law et al. (2004) have conducted a study. In the study, the perceptions of tourists towards the potential for elimination of travel agencies due to the internet were researched. The survey was conducted on 413 tourists using both traditional distribution channels and online distribution channels. The survey represents that tourists use the services and recommendations provided by travel agencies. Moreover, tourists acknowledge that more information will be available via the internet. Based on the research results, it can be said that in the future there will be a combination of online and traditional distribution channels.

Tourism related products and services are very well adapted to the internet. The fast-growing internet has an impact on the distribution of travel services. On the other hand, it has caused speculation that no longer need for travel agencies as intermediary. The effects of technology and the rapid development of virtual travel agencies operating in Taiwan have been researched. The research was conducted on 438 travel agencies using quantitative questionnaires and in-depth interviews. According to the results of the research, travel agencies view the internet as an effective tool to conduct their business. Although travel agencies are influenced by e-commerce services, the impact is not significant. Also, this effect is not significant, depending on the size and type of travel agencies. On the other hand, travel agencies consider the decreasing of the commission made by the suppliers as a threat, but this does not mean that there is no need for the travel agencies as intermediaries (Bennett & Lai, 2005). According to the results of the research conducted by Card et al. (2003), the distribution of travel products purchased online is given in Table 5.

Airline tickets are among the first to be purchased online. This result will not be surprising because of the fact that airline operators are at the top of the areas where centralized reservation systems are applied first. On the other hand, the purchase of accommodations, which is an important element for tourists, at a rate of 63.5% can be considered as an important progress in e-tourism.

Table 5. Percentage of travel products purchased online (N=252)

Travel Product	Percentage (%)
Airline tickets	82.4
Accommodations	63.5
Travel information	61.5
Car rentals	50.4
Tickets for events	44.1
Tickets for rail, bus	15.5
Package tours	13.9

Source: Card et al., 2003

Today, consumption habits also change with technological developments. The travel and tourism industry is also affected by this change. For example, people can experience tourist attractions via 2D or 3D applications. This experience shows that, with the help of technology, mental trips can be carried out outside of physical travels. Therefore, this situation, which is referred to as hyper-reality, means that tourism activities can be done anytime and anywhere independently of time and space (Aktaş-Polat, 2015). Moreover, Schuler (2010) argues that until 2030, people can experience all kinds of travel experiences through virtual reality, without being physically present in a destination. This shows that there are many big data generating mechanisms which consist of tons of structured and unstructured data in all fields of tourism.

THE IMPORTANCE OF 5VS OF DATA IN VIRTUAL TRAVEL ORGANIZATIONS

Virtual organizations manage a huge diversity of data types every day. In big data era, companies can obtain data from different kind of sources such as web, GPS technology, social networks, smart tools, etc. These data have nominal, ordinal, interval and ratio measurement scales. For instance, while a transaction data have 0's and 1's, the price of an product/service differs from cents to thousand dollars. Furthermore, in the past, the companies mostly focused on structured data which were on tables such as customers' demographic data or sales data; however, the generated data are now unstructured. Just depending on the number of photos, video sequences or social media updates shared in each second by approximately two billion smart phone users around the world, there is an increasing need of big data ecosystems that can simultaneously collaborate and co-create service or product within a virtual environment especially in tourism industries (Esen & Turkay, 2017).

With the rapid developments in technology and science during the past decades, the data started to grow exponentially. The data are still flowing and the experts estimate 4300% increase in annual data generation by 2020 (Reddy, 2016). For this reason, data collection, data storage, data management and data analytics steps of big data are the hottest agenda for healthcare, management, education and business.

In tourism industries, as shown in Table 6, big data are derived from sales-booking processes and traditional distribution channels such as web sites, call centers, press releases, and customer relationship management systems. In addition, unstructured data such as search records, location data, social media messages, photographs, and videos, GPS signals, sensor data, and tourists' behavior and movement data during their visits, constitute about 80% of the data used in tourism planning. The remaining data come from the sources such as hotel management, customer relationship

Table 6. Big data sources for virtual travel agencies and tour operators

Data Type	Analytics	Applications
Text data (Twitter, Facebook, forums, Yelp, TripAdvisor, Expedia)	Text mining, Sentiment Analysis, Opinion Mining, Latent Dirichlet Allocation Algorithms, Association rule mining, Social network analysis,	Measuring tourists' satisfaction, Hospitality management, Recommender systems, Topic identifying,
Photos (Flickr, Instagram, Panoramio) with embedded meta-data such as photo ID, user ID, date, geo-tags, descriptions etc.	Data mining for meta-data, Text mining for meta-data,	Analyzing tourist behavior, Recommender systems, Discovering popular destinations, Promote tourism marketing, Discovering tourism spots,
GPS data (longitude, speed, etc.)	Statistical analysis Frequent pattern mining Clustering Graph mining	Tracking tourists movements Visitor behavior Segmentation of visitors Recommender systems
Mobile roaming data	Econometric modelling Statistical analysis Data mining	Tracking tourist location Analyzing tourist flow Analyzing travel distances Measuring destination loyalty
Bluetooth data	Data mining	Tracking event tourism activities Tracking tourist movements
RFID data	Qualitative analysis Data mining	Hospitality management Recommender systems Guiding and informing tourists
Wi-Fi data	Data mining	Analyzing tourist behavior
Transaction data	Data mining Statistical analysis	Recommender systems Purchasing behaviors

Source: This table is formed by reviewing the paper by Li et al. (2018)

management, and blog content management systems (Xiang & Fesenmaier, 2016). This brings new challenges and dimensions for the nature of big data characteristics. These characteristics can be described by following:

1. **Volume:** Refers to the huge amounts of data which is being generated every minute, every second even every milliseconds. Many companies collect and process large amounts of data.
2. **Velocity:** Refers to the increasing speed at which new data is being generated and the speed at which data moves around. For being competitive, corporations/companies need to analyze the flowing data in near real time, even without saving the data in their databases.

3. **Variety:** Relates to the different types and ranges of data. This includes data with usable formats and incompatible types.
4. **Veracity**: Is the quality or trustworthiness of data. Companies face different types of data, including fake social media accounts, online rumors, typos, frauds, etc. These data require verification since it is an essential process in big data management. Poor quality of data may cause faulty decision making (Akter & Wamba, 2016).
5. **Value:** Refers to the extraction of economic benefits by analyzing big data. However, not always there is value in Big Data, sometimes bad data would obstruct adding business value. According to NewVantage Partners (2018), more than 80% of executives states that big data investments are successful and have value for their companies. Li et al. (2018) indicate that the types of big data used in tourism research are mainly derived from three data sources:
    a. *Users (47%),*
    b. *Devices (36%),*
    c. *Operations or transaction data (17%).*

The data generated by *users* are mostly from user-generated content (UGC) which includes online data such as texts, photos, and videos. The *device data* are being obtained from tools such as GPS, Wi-Fi, sensors, RFID, bluetooth and the *transaction data* are continuously coming from web clicks, web searches, online bookings and online purchasing data. Virtual travel organizations generally use the data from all three data sources. For instance, computerized information systems (CRS) virtually distributes tourism services and products to all sales offices by gathering all requests, reviews, deals, complaints and other UGCs from both customers and other parties. The system provides the best prices and tariffs for the goods or services that consumers are prepared to purchase. In addition, hundreds of airline agencies, millions of different prices, thousands of hotels and car rental companies, tours, cruise lines, etc. can be ordered through GDS in accordance with customers' and companies' data. Let's say, a tourist from US, plans to visit Spain. He reads positive/ negative reviews or likes/dislikes a shared photo or video of another travelers from various countries visiting Spain at social media or other virtual communities. This targeted advertising helps tour operators to protect or allocate its resources to the same or another destination.

UGC data have mixed types of data, mostly have categorical variables such as textual data, which can be analyzed with Sentiment Analysis and Opinion Mining and can help in predictive analytics (Guo et al., 2017). UGC data seem problematic since the accounts on social media platforms, forums and blogs may be fake. However, researchers/practitioners can still follow the updates of registered customers' sharings and by mining those data for different issues such as exploring tourist behavior and attitudes, improving CRM, recommending services, promoting marketing, etc. can be supported (Miah et al., 2017).

Device data are mostly derived from devices such as GPS, sensors, bluetooth, RFID, and Wi-Fi. In parallel to the development of Internet of Things (IoT) these devices are being used not just in production systems and also in areas such as marketing, health care, agriculture, tourism, logistic, finance, etc. These devices can simply track movements of tourists and support tourism management. For example, *GPS data* may give an opportunity to understand tourist behaviors (East et al., 2017; Tchetchik et al., 2009). *Roaming* service is a continuous data service that mobile phone receives when one goes outside of mobile operator's cellular network. These kind of data can be used to track tourists' behaviors and allow identifying tourists' locations. Raun et al. (2016) used roaming data to econometrically model the tourist flows and travel distances. *Bluetooth* is used in event tourism activities such as festivals, trade fairs and other indoor organizations. For example, Versichele et al. (2012) tracked over 80K visitors in a festival with bluetooth for counting visitors. *Radio-Frequency Identification* (RFID) has been used in a wide range of applications where the devices are converted into smart objects. This environment consists of enormous big data and it is a great potential for customer analytics. In retailing, RFID tags on items are used to avoid theft or for marketing purposes. For tourism industries, RFID tags are being used in hotels, resorts and parks. The technology is also used to connect databases or software systems of virtual travel agencies with real-time integration. Tsai et al. (2017) used RFID systems in recreation parks to find group members. *Wi-Fi* is also a facility allowing computers, smartphones, tablets, machines, etc. to connect to internet or communicate with one another wirelessly within a particular area. Chilipirea et al. (2016) proposed a scheme which uses Wi-Fi to automatically capture users' locations and track behaviors. Thron et al. (2017) used sensor networks for tracking Wi-Fi users in outdoor urban environments.

Transaction data are another data source for virtual travel agencies and tour operators. In fact, all kinds of web search data, such as page views, clicks, durations in web sites, traffic data, online booking data, etc. have valuable information for tourism management. Transaction data are generated every millisecond by internet users from all around the world. Tourism prediction (tourism demand, tourist volume, hotel demand) is the most popular topic which uses web search data (Song & Liu, 2017). A travel agency such as booking.com may easily promote and better advertise its services by analyzing its web site visits. The company may discover which services (hotels, cities, places, etc.) are hot or not and may deliver a personalized web experience for its users. In addition to web sites searches and web visits data, the data which are obtained by booking different kind of services (hotel, car rental, tickets of parks museums, etc.) are also valuable for both virtual tourism agencies and tour operators, even regulatory authorities. Booking and purchasing data from web also support decision making processes such as hospitality management. As some other case studies indicate how companies turn big data to business value, Amadeus should be given first for tourism sector. Amadeus, the largest technology solution company for tourism industries, meets agencies and operators on a virtual platform. The company uses big data analytics effectively to offer the best service to its customers which increases satisfaction, loyalty, and revenues. The Big Data Report by Amadeus indicates that big data helps tourism companies for decision support, customer relationship and data processing. It also offers an extreme search facility according to budgets, trip characteristics and the needs of customers. The search tool returns best proposals for that trip (Amadeus, 2013).

Another example is from Kayak.com facing over a billion searches each year also uses big data analytics to gain business value. The company offers different tailored services to its customers using searching data of its web-site and competitors web sites. Another example is Marriott also takes advantage of big data which are created by its web site. The company predicts the optimal prices, tries to fill its rooms by offerings and it improves its revenue management by taking advantage of Big Data Analytics. Hipmunk is also designed with special algorithms to rank flights and hotels for its customers by using price, customer ratings and services providers' properties. These virtual travel platforms can offer tailored services, enhanced pricing strategies, create effective CRM and so increase profits through big data analytics which is highly related with value of big data's 5V.

Table 7 indicates the opportunity of performing big data analytics for a virtual travel agency, booking.com. Approximately 443 million people have visited the website on 2017. People locate in the site about eight minutes in average and search eight pages during a session. All of these data consist valuable information about purchasing behaviors of customers. This enables decision makers how to promote marketing strategies and how to design web sites effectively and so on.

Types of experiences created in social media include three different categories for tourism industries. These can be listed as past experiences, during the travel or accommodation experiences and after travel or stay experiences. In the first experience, tourism consumers plan to travel using the content that they created. For the second type of experience, consumers create content by sharing experience, especially with mobile applications. In the third type experience, new content is created by comments and evaluations through social media platforms after the experience. Customer comments are the contents that are shared with positive or negative thoughts about tourism products and services and they give ideas to potential customers.

Customers rely on reviews as an important data source for their decisions (Jang et al., 2012). Researches show that the feedbacks of customers are a credible metric contributing to consumers' purchase decision making (Schindler & Bickart, 2012). The need of extracting meaningful information from massive volume of consumers'

Table 7. Web analytics of Booking.com on as of December 2017

Total Visits	443 million	Source of traffic to website	Access directly: 35,2% Access with a search engine:34,6% Access with Reference web sites:18,8%
Average Visit Duration	8,13 minutes	Reference sources	Tripadvisor.com - 3,42% Trivago.com – 2,52% Webbooks.site – 2,40% Kayak.com - 1,91%
Average Number of Page Visited During a Session	8,1	Goal site	Facebook.com – 10,77% Google.com – 5,48% Gmail.com - 4,49%
Proportion of Leaving Web Site Straight Away (Bounce Rate)	32,92%	Most visited pages	Booking.com 75,30% secure.booking.com 17,62% admin.booking.com 6,67%
Highest Traffics		8,4% - Russia 6,93%- Germany 6,65%- US	

Source: analytics.google.com

Table 8. Customer reviews on virtual travel agencies on 2017

	Hotels.com	Booking.com	Tripadvisor
Associated object (total)	>150 thousands	>1,18 million	>7 million
User reviews (total)	>7 million	>116 million	>465 million
Using info	Ratings and reviews		
User info	Location based user	Location based user	Forum messages and review lists

Source: Hotels.com & Booking.com & Tripadvisor.com

reviews introduced text mining methods and machine learning techniques to optimize operational and decision processes of tourism organizations. The data collected from online reviews are often unstructured and need verification and compliance with quality and security standards. Sources of big data and its characteristics in popular virtual travel agencies are given in Table 8.

CONCLUSION

Some of the characteristics of the products and services produced by tourism businesses are unique. Customers who want to purchase tourism products and services do not have a trial opportunity before purchasing. Accommodation businesses, travel agencies and tour operators, airline companies, restaurants and entertainment businesses cannot store goods and services that they offer. For example, if a restaurant cannot sell a table for four, it will suffer a loss of revenue that is irreversible. Therefore, effective use of resources is essential both for customers and for enterprises. In this context, the effective use of information technology provides customers with time-saving and comparison opportunities, while also providing direct access to customers for businesses. In addition, businesses have the opportunity to market their products and services on a global scale at a lower cost using information technologies.

Those who have experienced tourism products and services share their positive and negative experiences online via internet. For this reason, many internet sites and travel forums have been created. Through these sites, people are influencing potential and current tourists' buying decision processes. In addition, there are directories about places to go, hotels to stay, restaurants to eat, places to visit, and other tourist activities. These developments in information technologies have emerged as virtual organizations in terms of tourism businesses.

The Internet, which is used so intensely by the customers, offers many opportunities for tourism enterprises as well. One of them is that potential and existing tourists can be reached very quickly. In addition, tourism products and services can be offered from many nations on a global scale. By following the expectations and wishes of the customers, appropriate products and services can be developed. An online travel agency can provide customers with all kinds of information about their products and services very quickly. Nevertheless, trust stands out as the most important problem on the internet in terms of both customers and tourism enterprises. The sharing of all kinds of personal information over the internet, such as people's identity, marital status, family structure, educational status, credit card information, preferences, locations and communication information, is one of the reasons behind skepticism about virtual organizations.

Due to the developments in information technologies and its impact on virtual travel organizations, the amount of big data is increasing. There are tremendous opportunities for these organizations to use big data resulting in higher profits. Big data aim to provide meaningful knowledge from meaningless data and provide better service to customers. This allows multi-dimensional analysis for economic, social and psychological digital traces left by customers and it can be used as an alternative and adaptive technology for cost-effective and long-term field investigations of tourism businesses. Thus, data from different geographies and samples can be simultaneously obtained and analyzed at lower costs. The use of big data also allows the monitoring and measurement of travelers' wishes, needs, and behaviors.

Every customer leaves a digital trace about his/her characteristics from booking, searching, reviewing, comparing, etc. through devices. For virtual travel portals and other service providers, this is a big challenge to utilize the digital trace to create a business value with their customers. The potential benefits of managing 5Vs of big data in virtual travel organizations include:

1. Providing better decision support and improving tourism industries' decisions,
2. Innovative, data-derived tourism products and services,
3. Better customer relationship, better targeted products and services, enhancing experiences for each customer,
4. Reliable, cheap and faster data management for enormous amounts of data,
5. Dynamic and optimized pricing strategies (including competitors' pricing trends and future demand patterns) with real-time data from various data sources.

It is very important for service providers to improve the physical infrastructure for obtaining and storing large amounts of data. At this point, creating virtual and physical sources that centralize data life cycle phases and ensuring the employment of skilled personnel to make big data available for virtual travel organizations are crucial. Big data management tools, semantics, privacy and confidentiality, adaptation of business policies, and policy enforcements are needed to maintain big data's 5v properties and its related components. Also, transformation of the products, services and operational processes of virtual travel organizations into completely digital form which allows travel services adaptation and composition, will provide intended data value for a better decision making and innovative insights for the organizations.

Big data is complex and it is in a massive-scale. In tourism applications, there is still a high proportion of traditional methods which are not able to handle 5Vs of big data and its analysis fast and easy. Data types such as audio, video, multi-type or cross-domain data from external sources are potential field of interest that needs to be studied in virtual travel organizations. In addition, due to its virtual, adaptable, flexible and powerful structure, cloud architectures with numerous parallel operations for processing very big data sets can be used in virtual travel organizations.

REFERENCES

Aktaş-Polat, S. (2015). Üstgerçeklik ve turizmin sonu. *Celal Bayar Üniversitesi Sosyal Bilimler Dergisi, 13*(1), 120–137.

Akter, S., & Wamba, S. F. (2016). Big data analytics in E-commerce: A systematic review and agenda for future research. *Electronic Markets, 26*(2), 173–194. doi:10.100712525-016-0219-0

Amadeus. (2013). *Amadeus Global Report of 2013*. Retrieved from: https://amadeus.com/

American Society of Travel Agents (ASTA). (2017). *How America travels-sheds light on America's perceptions of travel and better enables ASTA and the travel agent community*. Retrieved from: https://www.asta.org/

Andreu, L., Aldas, J., Bigne, J. E., & Mattila, A. S. (2010). An analysis of e-business adoption and its impact on relational quality in travel agency-supplier relationships. *Tourism Management, 31*(6), 777–787. doi:10.1016/j.tourman.2009.08.004

Archer, B., Cooper, C., & Ruhanen, L. (2004). The positive and negative impacts of tourism. In W. F. Theobald (Ed.), *Global Tourism* (3rd ed.; pp. 79–102). Elsevier.

Benckendorff, P. J., Sheldon, P. J., & Fesenmaier, D. R. (2014). *Tourism information technology* (2nd ed.). CAB International. doi:10.1079/9781780641850.0000

Bennett, M. M., & Lai, C. K. (2005). The impact of the internet on travel agencies in Taiwan. *Tourism and Hospitality Research, 6*(1), 8–23. doi:10.1057/palgrave. thr.6040041

Bhatia, A. K. (2006). *The business of tourism: Concepts and strategies*. New Delhi: Sterling Publishers.

Buhalis, D., & Egger, R. (2008). *Intermediaries*. In R. Egger & D. Buhalis (Eds.), *eTourism case studies: Management and marketing issues* (pp. 83–87). Oxford, UK: Butterworth-Heinemann.

Buhalis, D., & O'Connor, P. (2005). Information communication technology revolutionizing tourism. *Tourism Recreation Research, 30*(3), 7–16. doi:10.1080/ 02508281.2005.11081482

Card, J. A., Chen, C. Y., & Cole, S. T. (2003). Online travel products shopping: Differences between shoppers and nonshoppers. *Journal of Travel Research, 42*(2), 133–139. doi:10.1177/0047287503257490

Chilipirea, C., Petre, A. C., Dobre, C., & Van Steen, M. (2016). Presumably simple: Monitoring crowds using WiFi. In *2016 IEEE 17th international conference on mobile data management (MDM)*. Porto, Portugal: IEEE.

Condratov, I. (2013). E-tourism: Concept and evolution. *Ecoforum, 2*(1), 58–61.

Dragland, A. (2013). *Big data–for better or worse*. SINTEF Report. Retrieved from: https://www.sintef.no/en/latest-news/big-data-for-better-or-worse/

Dupeyras, A., & MacCallum, N. (2013). Indicators for measuring competitiveness in tourism: A guidance gocument. In *OECD Tourism Papers*. OECD Publishing.

East, D., Osborne, P., Kemp, S., & Woodfine, T. (2017). Combining GPS & survey data improves understanding of visitor behavior. *Tourism Management*, *61*, 307–320. doi:10.1016/j.tourman.2017.02.021

Esen, M. F., & Turkay, B. (2017). Big data applications in tourism industries. *Journal of Tourism and Gastronomy Studies*, *5*(4), 92–115. doi:10.21325/jotags.2017.140

Fosso Wamba, S., Akter, S., Edwards, A., Chopin, G., & Gnanzou, D. (2015). How 'big data' can make big impact: Findings from a systematic review and a longitudinal case study. *International Journal of Production Economics*, *165*, 234–246. doi:10.1016/j.ijpe.2014.12.031

Goeldner, C. R., & Ritchie, J. R. B. (2009). *Tourism: Principles, practices, philosophies* (11th ed.). Wiley.

Gretzel, U., & Fesenmaier, D. R. (2009). Information technology: Shaping the past, present, and future of tourism. In T. Jamal & M. Robinson (Eds.), *The SAGE Handbook of Tourism Studies* (pp. 558–580). London: Sage. doi:10.4135/9780857021076.n31

Guo, X., Zheng, X., Ling, L., & Yang, C. (2014). Online coopetition between hotels and online travel agencies: From the perspective of cash back after stay. *Tourism Management Perspectives*, *12*, 104–112. doi:10.1016/j.tmp.2014.09.005

Guo, Y., Barnes, S. J., & Jia, Q. (2017). Mining meaning from online ratings and reviews: Tourist satisfaction analysis using latent dirichlet allocation. *Tourism Management*, *59*, 467–483. doi:10.1016/j.tourman.2016.09.009

IDC. (2017). *Data age 2025: The evolution of data to life-critical.* IDC White Paper by Seagate. Retrieved from: https://www.seagate.com/tr/tr/www-content/our-story/trends/files/

Jang, S., Prasad, A., & Ratchford, B. (2012). How consumers use product reviews in the purchase decision process. *Marketing Letters*, *23*(3), 825–838. doi:10.100711002-012-9191-4

Jayapalan, N. (2001). *An introduction to tourism.* New Delhi, India: Atlantic Publishers and Distributors.

Koçel, T. (2015). *İşletme Yöneticiliği.* İstanbul: Beta Basım Yayım Dağıtım.

Kuom, M., & Oertel, B. (1999). Virtual travel agencies. *NETNOMICS: Economic Research and Electronic Networking*, *1*(2), 225–235. doi:10.1023/A:1019114208191

Law, R., Leung, K., & Wong, R. J. (2004). The impact of the internet on travel agencies. *International Journal of Contemporary Hospitality Management, 16*(2), 100–107. doi:10.1108/09596110410519982

Law, R., Leung, R., & Buhalis, D. (2009). Information technology applications in hospitality and tourism: A review of publications from 2005 to 2007. *Journal of Travel & Tourism Marketing, 26*(5), 599–623. doi:10.1080/10548400903163160

Leuterio, F. C. (2007). Introduction to Tourism. Manila, Philippines: Academic Press.

Li, J., Xu, L., Tang, L., Wang, S., & Li, L. (2018). Big data in tourism research: A literature review. *Tourism Management, 68,* 301–323. doi:10.1016/j.tourman.2018.03.009

Ling, L., Guo, X., & Yang, C. (2014). Opening the online marketplace: An examination of hotel pricing and travel agency on-line distribution of rooms. *Tourism Management, 45,* 234–243. doi:10.1016/j.tourman.2014.05.003

Lubbe, B. (2000). *Tourism distribution: Managing the travel intermediary.* JUTA.

Matos, L. M., & Afsarmanesh, H. (2006). Creation of virtual organizations in a breeding environment. *Proceedings of INCOM, 6,* 595–603.

McKinsey. (2011). *Big Data: The next frontier for innovation, competition, and productivity.* Retrieved from: https://www.mckinsey.com/

Medlik, S. (2016). *Managing tourism.* Butterworth-Heinemann.

Metzger, M. J., & Flanagin, A. J. (2008). *Digital media, youth, and credibility.* Cambridge, MA: MIT Press.

Miah, S. J., Vu, H. Q., Gammack, J., & McGrath, M. (2017). A big data analytics method for tourist behaviour analysis. *Information & Management, 54*(6), 771–785. doi:10.1016/j.im.2016.11.011

NewVantage Partners. (2018). *Big data executive survey of 2018.* Retrieved from: http://newvantage.com/

Raun, J., Ahas, R., & Tiru, M. (2016). Measuring tourism destinations using mobile tracking data. *Tourism Management, 57,* 202–212. doi:10.1016/j.tourman.2016.06.006

Reddy, T. (2016). *5 ways to turn data into insights and revenue in 2016.* Retrieved from: https://www.ibm.com/blogs/watson/2016/02/5-ways-to-turn-data-into-insights-and-revenue-in-2016/

Robinson, P. (2009). Travel and management: An introduction. In P. Robinson (Ed.), *Operations management in the travel industry* (pp. 1–13). Cambridge, UK: CAB International. doi:10.1079/9781845935030.0001

Schindler, R. M., & Bickart, B. (2012). Perceived helpfulness of online consumer reviews: The role of message content and style. *Journal of Consumer Behaviour, 11*(3), 234–243. doi:10.1002/cb.1372

Schuler, B. (2010). *Virtual travel: Embrace or expire*. iUniverse.

Singh, A. J., & Kasavana, M. L. (2005). The impact of information technology on future management of lodging operations: A delphi study to predict key technological events in 2007 and 2027. *Tourism and Hospitality Research, 6*(1), 24–37. doi:10.1057/palgrave.thr.6040042

Song, H., & Liu, H. (2017). Predicting tourist demand using big data. In *Analytics in smart tourism design* (pp. 13–29). Springer.

Tchetchik, A., Fleischer, A., & Shoval, N. (2009). Segmentation of visitors to a heritage site using high-resolution time-space data. *Journal of Travel Research, 48*(2), 216–229. doi:10.1177/0047287509332307

Thron, C., Tran, K., Smith, D., & Benincasa, D. (2017). Design and simulation of sensor networks for tracking Wifi users in outdoor urban environments. *Proceedings of SPIE.*

Tsai, C. Y., Chang, H. T., & Kuo, R. J. (2017). An ant colony based optimization for RFID reader deployment in theme parks under service level consideration. *Tourism Management, 58*, 1–14. doi:10.1016/j.tourman.2016.10.003

Unver, H., & Sadigh, B. L. (2013). Small and medium enterprises: Concepts, methodologies, tools, and applications. In *An agent-based operational virtual enterprise framework enabled by RFID* (pp. 198–215). IGI Global.

Versichele, M., De Groote, L., Bouuaert, M. C., Neutens, T., Moerman, I., & Van de Weghe, N. (2014). Pattern mining in tourist attraction visits through association rule learning on bluetooth tracking data: A case study of Ghent, Belgium. *Tourism Management, 44*, 67–81. doi:10.1016/j.tourman.2014.02.009

Xiang, Z., & Fesenmaier, D. R. (2016). *Analytics in smart tourism design: Concepts and methods*. Springer.

KEY TERMS AND DEFINITIONS

5Vs: 5V is the basic components of big data covering the terms: volume, velocity, variety, value, and veracity.

Big Data: The data which are not possible to be stored in relational databases at low cost and cannot be analyzed by classical methods, due to its volume and characteristics.

Tour Operator: A tour operator is a manufacturer that combines two or more tourism products and then develops travel packages according to customers' needs and interests.

Tourism Organization: Economic units that provide the production and marketing of goods and services to meet travel, accommodation, and other related needs to customers.

Tourism Product: Tourism product is the combination of accommodation, food and beverage, transportation, entertainment, and many other goods and services that are used throughout the trip.

Travel Organization: The organization that sells travel services to consumers, places reservations for these services, gives tickets, and accepts payments in return.

Virtual Organization: It is an organization that has the ability to respond to customers' needs and expectations in the shortest time, regardless of time and space through the possibilities provided by ICTs.

Chapter 3

Integrating Heterogeneous Enterprise Data Using Ontology in Supply Chain Management

Kamalendu Pal
City, University of London, UK

ABSTRACT

Many industries prefer worldwide business operations due to the economic advantage of globalization on product design and development. These industries increasingly operate globalized multi-tier supply chains and deliver products and services all over the world. This global approach produces huge amounts of heterogeneous data residing at various business operations, and the integration of these data plays an important role. Integrating data from multiple heterogeneous sources need to deal with different data models, database schema, and query languages. This chapter presents a semantic web technology-based data integration framework that uses relational databases and XML data with the help of ontology. To model different source schemas, this chapter proposes a method based on the resource description framework (RDF) graph patterns and query rewriting techniques. The semantic translation between the source schema and RDF ontology is described using query and transformational language SPARQL.

DOI: 10.4018/978-1-5225-7519-1.ch003

INTRODUCTION

A supply chain is a network of business facilities and distribution options that performs key functions: raw material procurement, transformation of these materials into intermediate and finished products, and distribution of these finished products to customers (Pal, 2017). In a typical supply chain, raw materials are purchased from different vendors and products are manufactured at one or more manufacturing plants, shipped to warehouses for intermediate storage, and then shipped to retailers or customers. All supply chains share the following characteristics: (i) in an enterprise all business activities are focused to supply products and/or services to its customers; (ii) any number of supply chain business-partners can be linked in the supply chain; (iii) a customer can be a supplier to another customer within the supply chain, which means that the total network of activities can consists of a number of supplier/customer relationships; (iv) the path from supplier to customer, can include a number of intermediaries (distributors) such as wholesalers, warehouses, and retailers, depending on the products and markets. Associated information flows among different supply chain business-partners. In this way, a supply chain creates a complex set of networked business processes, which need to be optimized for organizational profit. The core business processes of modern supply chains are: procurement, production, and sales. Moreover, these business activities need to consider scheduling, delivery, inventory planning, distribution, and understanding market conditions. Market specific supply and demand information, and warehousing facilities along the supply chain, are highlighted in Figure 1.

Figure 1. A diagrammatic representation of supply chain business processes

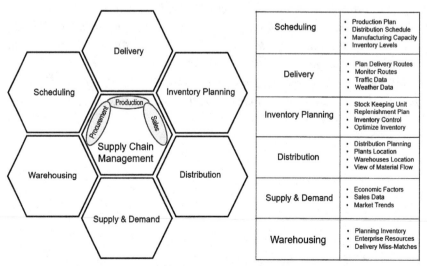

Managing a supply chain involves numerous decisions about the flow of information, product, funds, and coordination. Supply chain management (SCM) has been instrumental in connecting and smoothing business activities as well as forming various kinds of business relationships e.g., Customer Relationship Management (CRM), Supplier Relationship Management (SRM), among supply chain stakeholders. In this way, SCM is an integrative mechanism to manage the total flow of a distribution channel from supplier level to production, distribution and then ultimately to the end customer. The aim is to achieve goals related to total system performance rather than optimization of a single phase in a logistics chain. The ultimate aim for SCM is to enhance productivity by reducing total inventory level and cycle time for orders. It is important for supply chain business-partners to create a network that is agile and able to respond rapidly to unpredictable changes in demand. To achieve these objectives close cooperation among business partners is essential.

SCM systems utilize modern Information and Communication Technologies (ICT) to acquire, interpret, retain, and distribute information. The software applications of SCM are ready-made packages, usually targeting a certain set of tasks, e.g. tracking product related information during the transportation process. These ready-made package-software applications are mass-customized products that ignore the specific requirements of a certain business sector, and so they are quite problematic. The problem of the appropriate IT solutions for supporting collaboration between supply chain business-partners is not new and it has been approached with several standards and protocols implemented in numerous enterprise information systems. The application like ERP (Enterprise Resource Planning), CRM (Customer Relationship Management), and WMS (Warehouse Management System) contains valuable data that can be utilized by the decision support systems (DSS), however, information integration problems often exist. Specifically, this problem is often attributed to heterogeneous hardware, different data formats, and pressure to improve a system's performance, as shown in Figure 2. The problem with information interchange is related to issues of data exchange between business-partners operating independently-designed information systems. From a logistics point of view the key issues in Supply Chain Visibility (SCV) is the ability of parts, components or products in transit to be tracked from the manufacturer to their final destination, and traced from the customer to the manufacturer.

The aim of enhancing SCV is to improve the traceability of business process actions and reactions along the global supply chain. Innovative SCV technology promotes near real-time response to global supply chain business environments; and it improves operational performance of many high-tech industries (e.g. pharmaceutical, automotive, apparel). The objective of such data collection and analysis in the supply chain is to provide greater visibility of business operations. In other words,

Figure 2. Heterogeneous data sources in a global supply chain

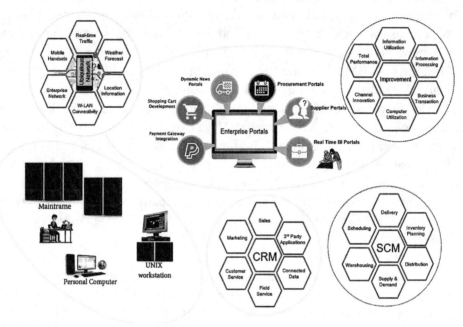

this greater visibility can be interpreted as "the ability of supply chain mangers to know exactly where things are at any point in time, or where they have been, and why". Collection of this data is not enough; the enterprises need new software tools, business process management practices, and properly trained personnel to interpret the contextual hidden meaning in the data.

The important challenges in supporting huge heterogeneous data integration in global supply networks are: (i) increasing number of business alliance partners due to globalization of business processes, (ii) different business practice and infrastructure facilities within participating business-partners, and (iii) differences in data exchange formats and standards among business-partners. Moreover, data capture and transmission mechanisms (e.g. bar coding, radio frequency identification technique, electronic data interchange, wireless networking infrastructure and protocols, global positioning system's capability) produce huge amounts of supply chain transportation data that, if properly controlled and shared, can enhance performance and agility of global supply chain networks. To harness this value-added service of data to global enterprises, a single representation data format is very essential. The global standardization organizations (e.g. Global Standardization 1 – GS1) provides a partial solution to the problem of heterogeneous data formats. These organizations have defined a detailed Global Product Classification system

(GPC) that can be used to identify products that match criteria. The example of a standard, which reasonably facilitates information exchange in SCV is the Global Trade Item Number (GTIN). There are also other operational standards (e.g. Global Data Synchronization Network) available for improving trading partnerships.

However, this unique codification of products (e.g. GETIN) are not enough for transferring knowledge from the producer all the way to the ultimate customer. The main issue of providing detailed information on the product and its history (such as when, where and by whom it was produced, packaged, and transported) can be crucial to supply chain operational management. However, integrating data from multiple heterogeneous sources requires dealing with different data models, schemas, and query languages. The semantic web has provided several new methods for data integration. This chapter provides an integration of relational database and XML data with the help of ontology.

This chapter describes a framework which will help query rewriting, and query answering, using views. The semantic mappings between source schema and RDF ontology are used with a query rewriting algorithm. Ontology provides a shared vocabulary for the specification of the semantics. To implement the integration, the meaning of the source schemas must be understood. A source describing method, based on RDF graph patterns, is proposed to specify the semantic mapping between ontology and source schemas. The semantic of query rewriting is further discussed, and a query rewriting algorithm is presented to reformulate a SPARQL query into source specific queries (e.g. SQL, XQuery). This helps SPARQL access heterogeneous data sources without converting the data into physical triples.

Section 2 of the chapter outlines the background of data integration problem. Section 3 describes the structure of a data integration framework. Section 4 presents different concepts of semantic mapping; it includes an RDF graph model, relational data model, and XML data model. In addition, some principles for semantic mapping between data source schemas and ontology have been introduced. After this, an algorithmic semantic query rewriting and optimization techniques are discussed. Section 6 concludes the chapter with summary remarks.

BACKGROUND OF DATA INTEGRATION PROBLEM

In today's digital age, data is the supply chain operation's lifeblood. Whether recruiting new staffs in London or New York, gaining new customers, or closing the accounting books at the end of every day, data keeps everything running smoothly. It enables business organizations to innovate, make smart and timely decisions, and maintain a quality level of supply chain operational service. To provide certain level of operational service, business needs to capture data, clean them if it is appropriate, integrate different business activities data, and process them to make corporate decisions. Therefore, database management system is an essential part of supply chain's day-to-day operations.

Modern database management systems are heavily influenced by relation database model (Codd, 1970). In this model, a *database schema* represents the logical configuration of all or part of a relational database. It can exist both as a visual representation and a set of operational conditions known as integrity constraints that govern a database. These constraints are expressed in a data definition language, such as SQL (Structured Query Language). As part of a central repository all the data and metadata, a database schema keeps track of the classes of objects (or entities) that make up the database, including tables or relations, different *views*, *stored procedures*, and more.

Typically, a database schema conveys – the logical constraints that apply to the stored data in the database. The mechanism of creating a database schema is called data modelling. When following the three-schema approach to database design, this step would follow the certain of a conceptual schema. Conceptual schemas focuss on an organization's information. There are two main kinds of database schema:

1. A logical database schema conveys the logical constraints that apply to the stored data. It may define integrity constraints, views, and tables.
2. A physical database schema lays out how data is stored physically on a storage system in terms of files and indices.

At the most basic level, a database schema indicates which tables or relations make-up the database, as well as the attributes including on each table. Thus, database schema is an essential part of heterogenous information system.

Database technology was introduced in business communities since the late 1960s to support (initially rather simple using third generation procedural programming languages - e.g. COBOL and RPG) business information providing applications. The software of the day provided a *'file-oriented record processing'* model. Typical programs sequentially read several input files and produced new files as output. COBOL and several other programming languages were designed to make it easy to define these record-oriented sequential tasks. As the number of business applications and data repositories rapidly grew, the need for integrated data became apparent. Consequently, first integration approaches in the form of multi-database systems (Hurson & Bright, 1991) were designed around 1980s – e.g. MULTIBASE (Landers & Rosenberg, 1982). This was a first exemplar in a notable history of research in data integration. The development continued over mediators (e.g., Garlic (Carey et al., 1995)) and agent systems (e.g., InfoSleuth (Bayardo et al., 1997)), to ontology-based (e.g., OBSERVER (Mena et al., 1996)), peer-to-peer (P2P) (e.g., Piazza

(Halevy et al., 2003)), and web service-based integration approaches (e.g., Active XML (Abiteboul et al., 2002); SWSDF (Pal, 2017)).

In many supply chain business applications, the number of data providers and amount of available data is increasing. Heterogenous data integration is now a very commonly used notion in supply chain operation management research. However, it appears that the problem of data integration resided initially in the lack of formalisms for representing data, and subsequently in the lack of standardization in the use of data formalism representing the same datasets. This latter case is known as *logical heterogeneity* (Hull, 1997) or *semantic heterogeneity* (Ceri & Widom, 1993) and stems from the fact that the same information resided in multiple overlapping data storages represented with different formats or different instance values.

Structured datasets from supply chain business customers can be used to explore some of the research issues in data heterogeneity. General concepts like *name* and *surname* may be represented by two *attributes* by some information system developers. Others may represent them in one unique attribute *Name+Surname*. The two cases highlight how even a simple and well understood concept can result in different representations. It is worth noting that the conceptual, logical and physical representation of data and related information is obtained after the requirements and specifications pass through users, business analysts, data specialists, systems developers and other software project workers, each having their own level of knowledge and preference for data representation. In this way, different representations are possible for the same conceptual pieces of data; and all of them could be accurate and complete. This highlights the standardization problem in data representation.

In this way, there is a spectrum of approaches for resolving the problems arising from semantic heterogeneity. One key method is to standardize databases and data representations through the development of a global data model. Many practitioners and academics have provided detailed discussions on various aspects of semantic heterogeneity (Kim et al., 1993; Hammer & McLeod, 1993; Batini et al., 1986; Kim & Seo, 1991) for database systems. Most of these discussions highlight one crucial point that the types of heterogeneity between data sources to be integrated is a first step in developing an integration solution. Many other issues were identified e.g., (i) getting an integrated view of overlapping data sets; (ii) identification and specification of the relationship between replicated data; and (iii) keeping replicated data '*synchronized*'.

Given that the schemas and instances of data sources to be integrated are usually different, any integration system must also handle instance inconsistency. This is generally achieved using two components: *wrapper* (Wiederhold, 1992) and *mediator* (Ullman, 1997). A wrapper is a tool that can access a local data source, and then extract and translate data from the local schema to an external global schema. An integration system is usually composed by two or more wrappers. They feed data to a mediator that reconciles and presents the local data to the final user, or to other systems as a unified view. The unified view is the only point of access for the final users who see the unified view independent of the integrated sources. This provides simplicity to the end user who can better focus on integration and manipulation of the repositories, rather than on the integration process.

The relation between the global schema and local schemas is characterized mainly by two types of approaches: *Local As View* (LAV) or *Global As View* (GAV) (Lenzerini, 2002). The first asserts that each local schema is a view over the global schema and can be used whenever there is a global reference model for the local repositories. The second considers the global schema as a view over the local schemas (Halevy, 2001). The global schema is obtained by analyzing, mapping and synthesizing the local schemas into a unique reference model that can simultaneously express the concepts of each independent data source, and offer users a transparent, unified overview.

A *Global-Local As View* (GLAV) approach (Friedman, Levy, & Millstein, 1999) has also been proposed to combine the advantages of the previous approaches. Without analyzing the approaches further, it must be said that the type of approach changes the semantics of the querying and integration processes.

One other important aspect of data integration is the architecture of the integration framework. Simplifying the numerous types of proposed architectures, one may conclude that the most frequently adopted solution for data integration is a central integration repository, federation approaches, and data exchange scenarios for distributed networks.

In the first case, a global point of reference is considered for integrating data from various sources (Beneventano et al., 2000; Chawathe et al., 1994; Carey et al., 1995; Roth et al., 1996), either through a materialized view, or through a mediator that accesses the individual data sources and extracts it from subsequent reconciliation and integration. A federation approach is like the first case but is focused on maintaining the physical division of the data sources. In distributed networks (think data sources in peer-to-peer networks) data is exchanged between single data sources (Arenas et al., 2013; Fagin et al., 2005b).

One of the main differences between building a central integration repository and data exchange is that, in the first case a single point of access is offered to the user who can seamlessly access the combined data sources through the interface (known as global schema architecture). In the second case, data is exchanged directly between two points of interest through a series of mappings and translation rules that convert data from the source schema to the target schema for critical discussion (Fagin et al., 2005a; Fagin et al., 2005b).

The different kinds of integration architecture radically change the semantics of the integration process. Without extending the discussion to the rigors of critical analysis, it must be emphasized that the main advantage of a mediator architecture is the unified global view through which the users have the possibility of accessing all data sources contemporaneously with a single query. The main disadvantage is the complexity required to analyze and synthesize a global scheme, as in real-life cases data integration systems need to combine a multitude of sources. Such systems rely on wrappers that can interface the mediator to each local source for rewriting the global query into a local query that is compatible to the schema of the local source and converting the result to the schema required by the mediator. The process introduces an overhead in accessing the data sources, both when rewriting the global query, as well as when translating and integrating data from all the data sources into a unified answer.

In this way, the reason for integration is twofold: First, given a set of existing information systems, an integrated view can be created to facilitate information access and reuse through a single information access point. Second, given a certain information need, data from different complementing information systems is combined to gain a more comprehensive basis to satisfy the need (Ziegler & Dittrich, 2007).

The other issue of heterogeneous data integration is *data cleaning*, also known as *data cleansing* or *scrubbing*, deals with detecting and removing errors and inconsistencies from data to improve the *quality of data*. These problems are present in single data collections, such as files and databases, and it can be due to misspellings during data entry, missing information or other invalid data. When multiple data sources need to be integrated, for example, in data warehouses, federated database systems or global web-based information systems, the need for data cleaning increases significantly. This is because the sources often contain redundant data in different representations. To provide access to accurate and consistent data, consolidation of different data representations and elimination of duplicate information become necessary. Data warehouses (Chaudhuri & Dayal, 1997) (Jarke et al., 2000) require and provide extensive support for data cleaning. They load and continuously refresh huge amounts of data from a variety of sources so the probability that some of the sources contain "*dirty data*" is high. Furthermore, data warehouses are used for decision making, so that the correctness of their data is vital to avoid wrong conclusions.

In the database design, semantics can be considered as end-user's interpretation of data and schema items according to their conceptualization of the worlds in a problem. In heterogeneous data integration, the type of semantics discussed is almost always real-world semantics that are involved with the mapping of entities in the model or computational world onto the real world; and it concern human interpretation of purpose and use of data and information. In this context, semantic integration is the activity of grouping, combing or completing data from various sources by considering explicit and precise data semantics to avoid that semantically incompatible data is structurally merged. That is, semantic integration must ensure that only data related to the same or very closely similar real-world object or concept is merged. A precondition for this is to resolve semantic ambiguity regarding integratable data by explicit metadata to find-out all relevant implications assumptions and underlying context information.

In one way to resolve semantic heterogeneity in the supply chain database research is to exhaustively specify the intended real-world semantics of all data and schema elements. However, it is impossible to completely define what a data or schema element denotes or means in the database world (Sheth et al., 1993). Therefore, database schemas do typically not provide enough explicit semantics to interpret data always consistently and unambiguously (Sheth & Larson, 1990). These difficulties are further worsened by the fact that semantics may be embodied in data models, conceptual schemas, application programs, the data itself, and the minds of users. Moreover, there are no absolute semantics that are valid for all potential users; semantics are relatives ((Garcia-Solaco et al., 1996). These problems regarding semantics are triggering many heterogeneous data integration important research challenges.

An important step during database integration is to determine relations between schema elements from different local databases. Finding meaningful relations is in turn based on a sound understanding of the meaning of the schema elements, that is, their semantics. To that end, one can rely on formal ontologies (Gruber, 1993) available for local schemas. In simple, ontology can be defined as explicit, formal descriptions of concepts and their relationships that exist in a certain universe of discourse, together with a shared vocabulary to refer to these concepts – can contribute to solve the problems of semantic heterogeneity. Compared with other classification schemes, such as taxonomies, thesauri, or keywords, ontologies allow more complete and more precise domain models (Huhns & Singh, 1997). With respect to an ontology a particular user group commits to, the semantics of data provided by data sources for integration can be made explicit. Based on this shared understanding, the danger of semantic heterogeneity can be reduced. For instance, ontologies can be applied in the application of the Semantic Web to explicitly connected information from web documents to its definition and context in machine-processable form; therefore, semantic services, such as semantic document retrieval, can be provided.

In database research, single domain models and ontologies were first applied to overcome semantic heterogeneity. AS in SIM (Abiteboul & Polyzotis, 2007), a domain model is used as a single ontology to which the contents of data sources are mapped. Thus, queries expressed in terms of the global ontology can be asked. In general, single-ontology approaches are useful for integration problem where all information sources to be integrated provide nearly the same view on a domain

(Wache et al., 2001). In case the domain views of the sources differ, finding a common view becomes difficult. To overcome this problem, multi-ontology approaches (e.g. OBSERVER (Mena et al., 1996)) describes each data source with its own ontology; then, these local ontologies have to be mapped, either to a global ontology or between each other, to establish a collective understanding. This concept is changing the state of art of heterogenous database integration, in real-world applications.

DATA INTEGRATION FRAMEWORK

The proposed data integration framework is shown in Figure 3. The framework consists of four distinct components: application layer, mediating layer, wrapper layer, and heterogeneous data source layer. The application layer communicates with end-users; mediating layer contains a mediator which allows integration; wrapper layer contains software-based wrappers for each data resource; and source layer contains a set of heterogeneous data sources. The data integration system has a set of source descriptions that specify the semantic mapping between the mediated schema and the source schemas. It uses these source descriptions to reformulate a user query into a query over the source schemas.

- **Query Processor:** A database system needs to respond to requests for information from the end-user; and the dedicated software component which deals with the user-request to produce the required output is simply known as *query processor*. A *database query* is the vehicle for instructing a database management system (DBMS) to update or retrieve specific data to/from the physically stored medium. The actual updating, and retrieval of data is performed through various "*low-level*" operations. Examples of such operations for a relational DBMS can be relational algebra operations (e.g. select, project, join, and so on). How a DBMS processes queries, and the methods it uses to optimize their performance, are topics that will be covered in the later part of this chapter in the context of semantic data storage and querying facilities. There are three phases that a query passes through during the DBMS' processing of that query: *parsing and translation*, *optimization*, and *evaluation*.

Most queries submitted to a DBMS are in a high-level language such as SQL. During the parsing and translation stage, the human readable form of the query is translated into forms usable by the DBMS. These can be in the forms of a *relational algebra expression, query tree,* and *query graph* (Beg & Connelly, 2017).

The system in discussion parses, translates, rewrites and dispatches the user query to related data sources. When users pose their queries expressed in SPARQL (Ducharme, 2013) using terms from mediated schema, the parser analyzes the query, verifying if it is in accordance with SPARQL system. Rewrite implements the query rewriting work with reference to source descriptions.

- **Mediated Schema:** In the present framework, the mediated schema has two roles: (i) it facilitates the end-user access to the data with a uniform query interface to serve the formulation of a query on all sources; (ii) it provides a shared vocabulary set for wrappers (i.e. a software system working with a data source responsible for querying, processing the results and mapping them in the global schema according to the metadata from the data dictionary) to describe the content in every data sources. The mediated schema is expressed using RDFS (Resource Description Framework Schema). Moreover, ontology has been used in the mediated schema.
- **Semantic Module:** The queries are posed in terms of the mediated schema. To answer a query, the rewriter needs descriptions that relate the content of each data source to the classes, attributes and relations in the mediated schema. Each data source is described by one or more SPARQL queries. These semantically rich descriptions help the rewriter to form queries and direct the query dispatcher to distribute queries to specific data sources.
- **Wrapper Layer:** Initial work on data integration predates the recent efforts to standardize data exchanges. Thus, every data source might have its own format for presenting data (e.g. object database connectivity from relational databases, HTML from web servers, binary data from an object-oriented database). As a result, one of the major issues was the "wrapper creation problem".

In the present framework, the wrapper module provides an SPARQL view representing a data source, and a means to access and to query the data source. It translates the incoming queries into source-specific queries executable by the query processor of the corresponding sources.

- **Data Storage Layer:** The data storage layer, in this framework, is a conglomeration of pre-existing, heterogeneous, autonomous data sources.

Figure 3. Diagrammatic representation of the proposed framework

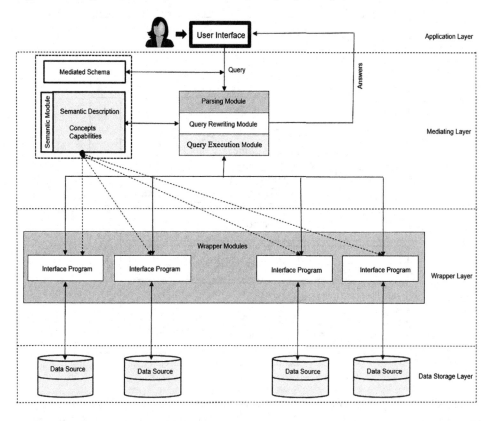

SEMANTIC MAPPING

Everything on the web can be expressed in terms of object or resource: a webpage, a profile, person's name, a piece of content like *raw material price*, *global trade item number* (GTIN), and so on. In semantic web, each of these resources can be described using standard framework called *resource description framework* (RDF). One can think semantic web as a stack of different technologies, from the simplest to most powerful and expressive; RDF is in the medium level, just above XML and XML schemas (Lassila & Swick, 1998) as shown in Figure 4. RDF is a language for creating data model for expressing statements about objects and their relations. Statements are defined by triples that are composed of *subject*, *predicate* and *values*. Triples are used to store data and make it easier for machines to process and understand the data. Subject refers to a resource; predicate denotes the relationship between the subject and the object, where object is the value (Antoniou & Harmelen, 2004).

Figure 4. Semantic web layer stack

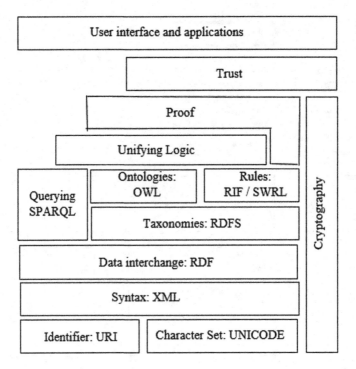

However, only describing resources is not enough; the relationship between resources and types of relations are important to make sense. Both syntax (structure) and semantics (meanings) need to be considered. RDF is represented in XML form. The RDF model consists of three things: resource, property and statements, as shown in Figure 5. Each resource has properties and resource represented by a class or a type. Like a website, URL represents a document of class (webpage) and has properties like created date, creator, language of the page, type of content, and so on. The values of the properties represent the current state of the resource. It is like an object (instance of a class) in object-oriented programming. Figure 7 shows the possible representation of resource. This is shown in Figure 6 in XML.

There are various names used in XML document for tags and attributes. Depending upon the domain, the names can have different meanings. For example, the tag '*title*' may represent *book name* in an XML document that contains book details. The same tag may represent *name of firm* when information about the firms is stored in XML format. An XML spaces names to avoid element name conflicts. The primary use of such names in XML documents is to enable identification of logical structures in documents by software modules such as query processors, stylesheet-driven rendering engines (to convert into HTML), and schema-driven validators (to conform to structure). Multiple namespaces can be used in the same XML document.

RDF Schema is a vocabulary description language that extends RDF in order to include some basic features for defining application specific classes and properties. It enables definition of sub classes, sub properties and domain and range restrictions on properties (Antoniou & Harmelen, 2004).

RDF statements show relationships between resources and properties. The RDF statement has a form called triple: subject-property-object (as shown in Figure 5c). For example, RDF statement '*English is the language of web page* http://www.abc.co.uk/intro.htm'. In this statement, http://www.abc.co.uk/intro.htm is a resource (subject), language is the property (predicate) of the resource, whose value is English (object). The example in Figure 6a represents statements: URL http://www.abc.co.uk/intro.htm represents a web page; which is *created by John Smith*; *it is created on 4 July 2018*; *the language of the webpage is English.* As in natural language, composite sentences are possible. A statement itself can be the object for a composite statement. For example, the statement: *web page* http://www.abc.co.uk/intro.htm *is created by John Smith who is a 34 years old teacher.* In this example, [*John Smith-age-34, John Smith-Occupation-Teacher*] is object/value for property: creator of resource: http://www.abc.co.uk/intro.htm as shown in Figure 6c.

RDF statement in the form of subject-predicate-object is more general purpose or represents a meta-model. It just defines the structure in general. To model meaningful composite statements, RDF schemas are defined. The RDF schema

Figure 5. Generic resource structure

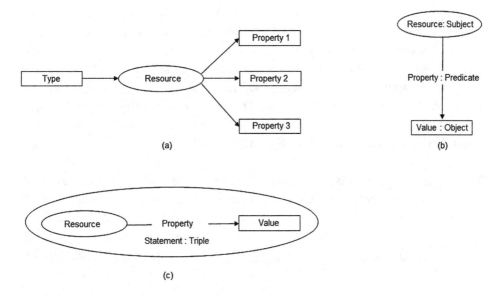

provides information about the interpretation of the RDF statements and the relationships with other resources. It can be treated as a template to create similar kind of statements (Antoniou & Harmelen, 2004).

However, RDF lacks more advanced capabilities in defining the relationships. For example, it does not provide set cardinality, equality, disjointedness, and so on (Cure & Blin, 2015). These capabilities emerge in the semantic web world with the advance of Web Ontology Language by W3C, which is briefly explained below.

Web Ontology Language (OWL)

Due to the limitations of RDF, the semantic web technology needed a more expressive ontology language through the end of 1990s. There were several proposals for the new language such as Simple HTML Ontological Extensions (SHOE), the Ontology Inference Layer (OIL) and DML+OIL (Antoniou & Harmelen, 2004). Moreover, W3C launched the standard for a Web Ontology Language that is called OWL. W3C organization expanded the earlier work of OIL and improved the integration of it with RDF. OWL solves the deficiencies of RDFS by providing additional vocabulary like relations between classes (e.g. disjointedness), conjunction of classes, property characteristics (e.g. symmetry), cardinality (e.g. one or more, at most one), and so on (Cure & Blin, 2015).

RDF Graph Model

The RDF is a standard for representing knowledge on the web. It is particularly designed for building the Semantic web and has been widely adopted in database and data mining communities. The simple model of assertions leads to a network of information resources, interrelated by properties which establish relationships between resources and property values. In this way, RDF models a fact as a triple which consists of a *subject* (s), a *predicate* (p), and an *object* (o). The value of a statement is captured by URI references. Thus, one can intuitively understand a collection of information resources and RDF statements depicting them in a graph. To emphasize this characteristic, the term RDF Graph is defined as a set of RDF triples; hence, any collection of RDF data is an RDF Graph.

Definition 1 - RDF Terms, Triples, and Variables: Formally, any RDF dataset is a set of RDF triples. One can consider an RDF triple <s, p, o> from the RDF triple-set <S, P, O>. Let us assume there are a pair of wise disjoint infinite sets I, B, and L (IRIs, Blank nodes, literals). A *tuple* (s, p, o) $\in$ $(I \cup B) \times I \times (I \cup B \cup L)$ is called an RDF triple. In this tuple, s is the subject,

Figure 6. Sample resource and schema

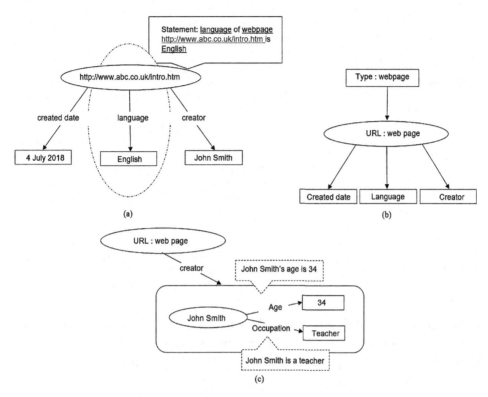

p the predicate and o the object. We denote the union $I \cup B \cup L$ by T (RDF terms). Assume additionally the existence of an infinite set V of variables disjoint from the above sets.

Definition 2 - RDF Graph: An RDF graph is a set of RDF triples. Figure 7 shows a part of RDF ontology. In this diagram, there is a relation "write" between concepts "Manager" and "Publication", indicating the relationship between authors and their works. The relation "belong to" between "Manager" and "Organization" indicate what organizations manager belongs to. The relation "man-name" and "man-email" point a manager's name and email. The same applies to "pub-title", "pub-year" and "org-name".

As RDF databases increase in size to approach tens of thousands of triples, sophisticated graph matching queries expressible in language like SPARQL (Prud'hommeaux & Seabornr, 2013) become increasingly important. As more and more RDF database systems come 'online' and as RDF gets emphasized by both established companies (e.g. Oracle, Hewlett Packard), as well as from a slew of

Figure 7. Part of RDF ontology

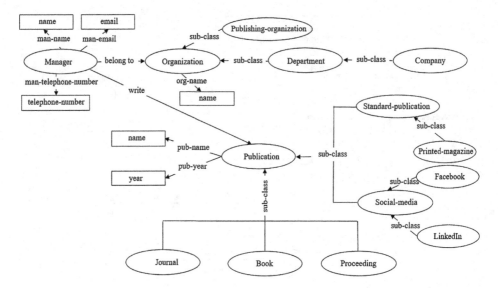

startups, the need to store and efficiently query massive RDF datasets is becoming increasingly important. Moreover, large parts of query languages like SPARQL increasingly require that queries (which may be viewed as graphs) be matched against databases (which may also be viewed as graphs) – the set of all possible "*matches*" is returned as the answer. The formal concepts of query graph and subgraph follow.

SPARQL Protocol of RDF Query Language (SPARQL)

After the improvements in Semantic Web during the last decade, there was a need to create a query language to process data that are stored in RDF format, as XML query language did not satisfy the needs (Antoniou & Harmelen, 2004). Although there were other query languages before, in 2008 W3C announced the standard for ontology query language, which is SPARQL (Prud'hommeaux & Seabornr, 2013). It is a simple query language that resembles SQL and extracts information from RDF graphs. A query can consist of triple patterns that the RDF graph is composed of, and conjunctions and disjunctions (Prud'hommeaux & Seabornr, 2013).

Table 1 is a small example of a SPARQL query, which is supposed to return all creators and their corresponding dates.

An SPARQL query usually contains a set of triple patterns, much like RDF triples, except that any of the subject, predicate and object may be a variable, whose bindings are to be found in the RDF data. This chapter addresses the SPARQL queries with 'SELECT/WHERE' option, where the predicate is always instigated as

Table 1. SPARQL example

```
PREFIX archive: <http://www.abc.co.uk/archive >
SELECT ?date ?language ?creator
WHERE
{ ?creator archive:has-created ?date }
```

an URI (Uniform Resource Identifier). The SELECT clause identifies the variables to appear in the query results, while the WHERE clause provides triple patterns to match against the RDF data.

Overview of Query Graph and Subgraph

A network can be modeled as a graph $G = \{V, E, \sum, \natural\}$ where V is a set of vertices and $E \subseteq V \times V$ is a set of edges. $\sum$ is a vertex label set and $\natural: V \rightarrow \sum$ denotes the vertex labelling function. For each notation, the vertex set of G is denoted as V(G) and its edge set is denoted as E(G). The *size* of G is defined as $|V(G)|$, the size of its vertex set. Analogously, the graph queries posed upon the network can be modeled as a graph as well. This chapter focuses on the case of connected, undirected simple graphs with no weights assigned on edges.

A graph G' is a subgraph of G, denoted as $G' \subseteq G$, if $V(G') \subseteq V(G)$, $E(G') \subseteq$ E(G), and $\forall (u, v) = E(G'), u, v \in V(G')$. In other words, one can say that G is a supergraph of G' and G contains G'.

Definition 3 - Graph Query: *Given a network G and a query graph Q, the graph query problem is to find as output all distinct matching of Q in G.*

Figure 8. A Network G and a Query Graph Q

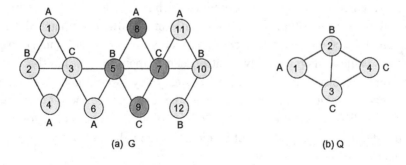

(a) G   (b) Q

Example: Figure 8(a) and Figure 8(b) show a network sample G and a query graph sample Q, respectively. Here the *numeric identifiers* have been used to distinguish different vertices in a graph. A subgraph G' of G with V(G') = {8,5,7,9} coloured in grey is isomorphic to Q and hence return as an answer to the graph query. It is worth noting that there exists multiple matching of Q in G. For example, given a triangle graph Q with A, B, C as the label for each vertex, respectively. All the matchings of Q in G, as shown in Figure 9(a), are {1,2,3}, (6,5,3}, {8,5,7} and {11,10,7}.

Relational Model

The relational model (Codd, 1970), built on a mathematical basis, provided the foundation for current relational database systems. A query language is a language in which a user requests information from the database. One can categorize query languages as being either procedural or non-procedural (Silberschatz, Korth, & Sudarshan, 1997). The difference lies in their approach to obtain the result. When a user wants to obtain a result using a procedural language, they need to instruct the system to perform a specific sequence of tasks on the database. In a nonprocedural language, the user only needs to describe the desired information without giving the system a specific procedure.

Relational algebra is a good example of procedural language, while relational calculus is representative of non-procedural languages (Silberschatz, Korth, & Sudarshan, 1997). However, most query languages used in current relational database systems combine elements of both the procedural and non-procedural approaches. The relations are stored in a database and the results from a database can be obtained by using database queries. In the field of relational databases, SQL became a standard that is now being used worldwide.

The term relation is used here in its accepted mathematical sense. Given sets D_1, D_2, ..., D_n, R is a relation on these n sets if it is a subset of the *cartesian product* $D_1 \times D_2 \times ... \times D_n$. R is said to have degree n, often called n-ary. An n-ary relation R can be represented as a table with n column, which has the following properties: (i) each row represents an n-tuple of R; (ii) the ordering of rows is immaterial; and (iii) all rows are distinct. Normally, one column (or combination of columns) of a given relation has values which uniquely identify each element (n-tuple) of that relation. Such a column (combination) is called a primary key. A common requirement is for elements of a relation to cross-reference other elements of the same relation or elements of a different relation. We shall call a column of relation R a foreign key if it is not the primary key of R, but its elements are values of the primary key of some relation, S.

In the later part of this chapter, various concepts will be illustrated with reference to two example databases. Some of the relations in those databases, are managers and proceedings. These relations are shown in Table 2. Each manager and proceeding are unique; each manager can have *zero* or *more* papers in a proceeding. A manager can write and publish multiple papers.

The Relational Data-Base Management Systems (RDBMS) uses SQL (Standard Query Language) as the vehicle for instructing its database to update or retrieve specific data to/from the physically stored storage. The actual updating, and retrieval of data is performed through various 'low-level' operations. Examples of such operations for a relational DBMS can be relational algebra operations such as project, join, select, cartesian product, and so on (Silberschatz, Korth, & Sudarshan, 1997). With this back-ground information, it is worth considering the specific implementation issues for the proposed framework.

As shown in Figure 9(a), suppose there are two heterogeneous relational databases, each has several tables containing information about authors and papers.

XML Model

Extensible Markup Language (XML), a W3C recommendation, emerged as a standard for data representation and interchange among various web-applications, providing a simple means for more meaningful and understandable representation of web-contents. An XML document need only be well-formed, i.e., its tags be properly nested, but need not conform to a particular *document type definition* (DTD) or *Schema*. Hence, it is a variation of *semi-structured data* – data which may be varied and not restricted to any particular-schema. Management of semi-structured data by highly-structured modelling techniques, such as relational and object-oriented models, not only leads to a very complicated logical schema, but also demands much effort and frequent schema modifications, and thus obstructs

Table 2. Manager and proceeding relations

Attribute	Length	Key
The Manager Relation		
ManagerID	10	YES
Name	30	NO
The Proceeding Relation		
ProceedingID	15	YES
Year	8	NO
ISBN	13	NO

Figure 9. Two heterogeneous data sources: (a) The relational tables; (b) The XML tree

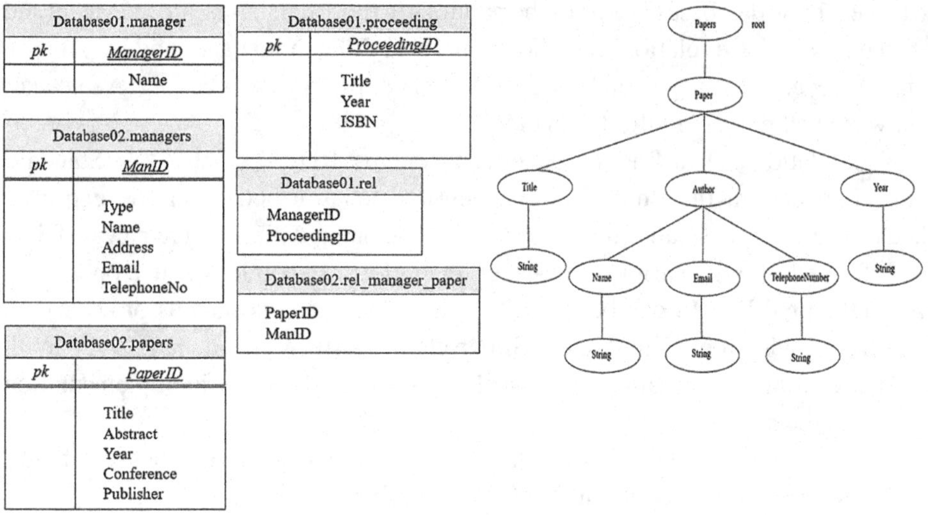

(a)　　　　　　　　　　　　　　　　　(b)

the use of such approaches in modelling XML data. Consequently, development of an appropriate and efficient data model for XML documents has become an active research area with major current models based on directed, edge-labeled graphs, and Description Logic.

In addition, some systems offer XML views of non-XML data sources such as relational databases, allowing XML-based processing of data that are not physically stored as XML. The basic characteristic of the XML Schema is that it can define element attributes that can appear in a document, define which elements are child elements, the order of these elements, and their cardinality. XML Schema provides the user with ability to define an element or an attribute as a specific scope. The User can define complex or simple elements (depending on whether they have further structure on not) and cardinalities for them. Figure 9 (b) shows an XML tree, which describes the schema of an XML document about papers and their authors.

Mapping Relational Schemas to Ontology

To solve the heterogeneity problem, the meaning of the relational schema must be well described, which is called "source description". Before presenting how source descriptions are defined, it is worth considering how, in general terms, relational schema can be mapped to RDF ontology.

Figure 10. Semantic mapping between relational schemas and ontology

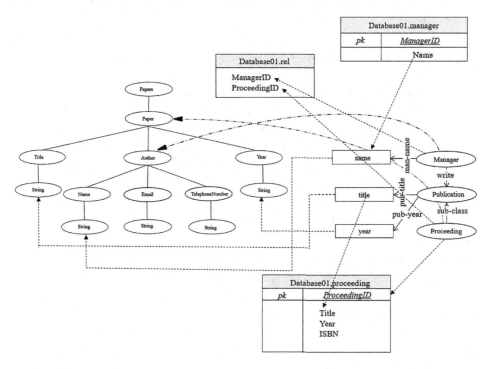

As mentioned above, RDF describes resources using a graph model. RDF Schema (RDFS) provides modelling primitives for defining classes and properties, range and domain constraints on properties, and subclass and sub-property relations.

The relational schema is based on entity-relationship diagram (ERD). Typically, each entity is represented as a database table, each attribute of the entity becomes a column in that table, and relationships between entities are indicated by foreign keys. Each table typically defines a particular class of entity, each column one of its attributes. Each row in the table describes an entity instance, uniquely identified by a primary key. The table rows collectively describe an entity set.

There are some similarities and differences between RDF and the ER model. Basically, ERD RDF Graphs have much in common. RDF can be viewed as a member of the Entity-Relationship model family. Class in RDFs corresponds to entity in ERD; property is kind of binary relationship; subclass and sub-property are subsumption relations. Therefore, some principles for semantic mapping between relational schema and RDF ontology are: (i) primary key of table is mapped to class, (ii) columns in table are mapped to properties, (iii) column value is mapped to property value, (iv) each row key corresponds to an instance, (v) each row is represented in RDF by a collection of triples with a common subject. As shown in Figure 10, the semantic mapping between relational schemas and ontology are marked by arrows with broken line.

Mapping XML Schemas to Ontology

In the present framework, RDF metadata needs to be defined here because RDFS Class and RDF Property are enough for the specifications of classes and properties. Considering XML elements, attributes and their relationships, the proposed architecture proposes some principles below for semantic mapping between XML schema and RDF ontology: (i) attributes are mapped into properties, (ii) simple-type elements are mapped into properties, (iii) complex-type elements are mapped into classes.

As shown in Figure 10, the semantic mappings between XML schemas and ontology are marked by arrows with solid lines. In this example, attributes (e.g. title, name, year) are mapped into properties in ontology. And, complex-type elements (e.g. author, paper) are mapped into RDFS classes.

Source Description

After being mapped to ontology, source schemas have to be described so that the query rewriting algorithm can use them to generate executable query plans efficiently. The functionality of SPARQL is used here.

Definition 4 - Source Description: Given a data source P, its source description D_p is a tuple (Q_p, μ), where Q_p is a SPARQL query and μ is a mapping from variables appeared in Q_p to corresponding columns in P.

Each relational table is described by a SPARQL query over domain ontology. The semantic of the databases are thus explicitly defined, and it is easy to add and delete sources. Some of the relevant queries are presented in Table 3.

SEMENTAIC QUERY REWRITING AND OPTIMIZATION

The problem of query rewriting considers how to reformulate a query from the mediated schema to the underlying relational database. A survey and analysis of different algorithms to solve the problem is given in (Pottinger & Halevy, 2001). In this chapter, an algorithm is used to execute the query rewriting over the RDF Graph model.

Table 3. Different SPARQL queries used in the framework

database01.manager	database01.proceeding
(SELECT ?name WHERE {?X man_name ? name}, { ?name → Name}).	(SELECT ?title, ?year WHERE {?X pub_title ?title. ?X pub_year ?year}, {?title → Title, ?year → Year}).
database01.rel	**XML tree in Figure 9(b) described**
(SELECT ?manager, ?proceeding WHERE (?person Write ?proceeding}, {?manager → ManagerId, ?proceeding → ProceedingId}).	(SELECT ?title, ?name, ?year WHERE {?X man_name ?name. ?Y pub_title ?title. ?Y pub_year ?year. ?X Write ?Y}, {?name → /papers/paper/author/name, ?title → /papers/paper/title, ?year → /papers/paper/year}).

The SPARQ query language is based on matching graph patterns. The Graph pattern contains triple patterns that are like RDF triples, but with the option of query variable in place of RDF terms in the subject, predicate or object positions.

Definition 5 - Minimal Connectable Units (MCU): Given a SPARQL query Q, a data source P and its source description $D_p = (Q_p, \mu)$, a MCU m for P is a tuple of the form (Y, μ') where: Y is a subset of triple patterns in Q_p, and μ' is a partial mapping from variables appeared in Q_p to corresponding component in P.

In the current system, as shown in Algorithm 1, an algorithm has been used to find minimal connectable units and joining them. This algorithm consists of two parts: *find* and *join*. It helps to reduce the number of rewritings in the heterogenous data integration process.

CONCLUSION

It is typical that global supply chain businesses run different but coexisting information systems. Using these information systems, supply chain organizations try to realize business opportunities in highly competitive markets. In this setting, the integration of existing information systems is becoming more and more indispensable to dynamically meet business and customer needs while leveraging long-term investments in

Algorithm 1.

```
// Find minimal connectable units part - FindMCUs //
// Q is a SPARQL query, D is the source description of a data
    source P has the form (Q_p, μ), where. μ is a subset. //
FindMCUs (Q, D_p)
Initialize M = Ø;
For each triple pattern t in Q, do
For each triple pattern t' in Q_p do
    If exist a mapping ┌ that map t to t', then
    Find the minimal subset (denoted by Y) of triple
    pattern of Q_p that is connectable.
    Find the subset (denoted by μ) of μ that relative to Y.
      M = M U <Y, μ'>;
End for
End for
Return M
// Join minimal connectable units part - JoinMCUs //
// Q is a SPARQL query, M is a set of MCUs, M = {m_1, … m_n },
    where m = (Y_i,, μ_i'), A is a set of rewritings. //
Initialize A = Ø;
For each minimal subset {m_1, .. m_k}of M such that Y_1 U Y_2 U Y_k
cover all triple patterns of Q.
 Create the conjunctive rewriting Q' contain all relative table
to {m_1, .. m_k}
 Add Q' to A
End for
Return A
```

existing information systems infrastructure. For example, in business intelligence (BI), integrated information can be used for querying and reporting on business activities, for statistical analysis, online analytical processing (OLAP), and data mining to enable forecasting, decision making, enterprise-wide planning, and, in the end, to gain sustainable competitive advantage. For CRM, integrated information on individual customers, business environment trends, and current sales can be used to improve customer services. Enterprise information portals preset integrated company information as personalized web sites and presents single information access points primarily for employees, but also for customers, business partners, and the public. Moreover, in e-commerce and e-business, integrated information enables and facilitates business transactions and services.

In addition, within this ambitious and broad aim, this chapter work focused on two related but independent aspects: semantic integration and query interoperability. Within the semantic integration problem, this chapter focused on XML-RDF integration, and the use of ontology. Within the query interoperability problem, the chapter queried restricted and heterogenous data interfaces with XML technologies.

The main problem highlighted is that integrating data from multiple heterogeneous sources needs to deal with different data models, database schema, query languages, and the chapter presents a framework. In this framework, ontology has been used as the mediated schema to represent data source semantics. It is also describing a method based on resource description framework graph patterns and query rewriting techniques.

The proposed solution first analyzes the similarities and differences among RDF schema, relational model and XML schema. It then discussed how to map relational schema and XML schema to ontology. A data source describing method based on SPARQL was defined. Heterogeneous data source schemas were described using queries defined by SPARQL. Based on an RDF Graph model, the semantic of query rewriting was defined, and a query rewriting algorithm is presented.

REFERENCES

Abiteboul, S., Benjelloun, & Milo, T. (2002). Web Services and Data Integration. In *Third International Conference on Web Information Systems Engineering (WISE 2002)*. IEEE Computer Society.

Abiteboul, S., & Polyzotis, N. (2007). The Data Ring: Community Content Sharing. *Third Biennial Conference on Innovative Data Systems Research (CIDR 2007)*.

Antoniou, G., & Harmelen, F. V. (2004). *Semantic Web Primer*. MIT Press.

Batini, C., Lenzerini, M., & Navathe, S. B. (1986). A Comparative Analysis of Methodologies for Database Schema Integration. *ACM Computing Surveys*, *18*(4), 323–364. doi:10.1145/27633.27634

Bayardo, R. J., Bohrer, B., Brice, R. S., Cichocki, A., Fowler, J., Helal, A., ... Woelk, D. (1997). InfoSleuth: Agent-Based Semantic Integration of Information in Open and Dynamic Environments. *1997 ACM SIGMOD International Conference on Management of Data (SIGMOD 1997)*, 195-206. 10.1145/253260.253294

Beneventtano, D., Bergamaschi, S., Castano, S., Corni, A., Guidetti, R., Malvezzi, G., ... Vincini, M. (2000). Information Integration: the MOMIS Project Demonstration. *Proceeding of the 26th Very Large Database Conference*, 611-614.

Carey, M., Haas, L., Schwarz, P., Arya, M., Cody, W., Fagin, R., ... Wimmers, E. (1995). Towards Heterogeneous Multimedia Information Systems: The Garlic Approach. *5th International Workshop on Research Issues in Data Engineering-Distributed Object Management (RIDE-DOM 1995)*, 124-131. 10.1109/RIDE.1995.378736

Ceri, S., & Widom, J. (1993). Managing Semantic Heterogeneity with Production Rules and Persistent Queues. *Proceedings of the 19th Very Large Data Base Conference*, 108-119.

Chaudhuri, S., & Dayal, U. (1997). An Overview of Data Warehousing and OLAP Technology. *SIGMOD Record*, 26(1), 65–74. doi:10.1145/248603.248616

Chawathe, S. GarciaMolina, H., Hammer, J., Ireland, K., Papakonstantinou, Y, Ullman, J., & Widom, J. (1994). The TSIMMIS Project: Integration of Heterogeneous Information Sources. *Proceeding of the 1000th Anniversary Meeting of the Information Processing Society of Japan (IPSJ)*, 7-18.

Codd, E. F. (1970). *The Relational Model for Database Management*. Addison Wesley.

Cure, O., & Blin, G. (2015). *RDF Database Systems Triples Storage and SPARQL Query Processing*. Waltham, MA: Morgan Kaufmann.

DuCharme, B. (2013). *Learning SPARQL: Querying and Updating with SPARQL 1.1*. Sebastopol, CA: O'Reilly Publishing Company.

Fagin, R., Kolaitis, P. G., Miller, R. J., & Popa, L. (2005a). Data Exchange: Semantics and Query Answering. *Theoretical Computer Science*, 336(1), 89–124. doi:10.1016/j.tcs.2004.10.033

Fagin, R., Kolaitis, P. G., Popa, L., & Tan, W. (2005b). Composing schema mappings: Second-order dependencies to the rescue. *ACM Transactions on Database Systems*, 30(4), 994–1055. doi:10.1145/1114244.1114249

Friedman, M., Levy, A., & Millstein, T. (1999). Navigational plans for data integration. In *Proceedings of AAAI* (pp. 67–73). Menlo Park, CA: AAAI Press/MIT Press.

Garcia-Solaco, M., Saltor, F., & Castellanos, M. (1996). Semantic Heterogeneity in Multidatabase Systems. In O. A. Bukhres & A. K. Elmagarmid (Eds.), Object-Oriented Multidatabase Systems, A Solution for Advanced Applications (pp. 129-202). Prentice-Hall.

Gruber, T. R. (1993). A translation approach to portable ontology specifications. *Knowledge Acquisition*, *5*(2), 199–220. doi:10.1006/knac.1993.1008

Halevy, A. Y. (2001). Answering queries using views: A survey. *The VLDB Journal*, *10*(4), 270–294. doi:10.1007007780100054

Halevy, A. Y. (2003). Data Integration: A Status Report. *Datenbanksysteme in Business, Technology and Web (BTW 2003), 26*, 24-29.

Hammer, J., & Mcleod, D. (1993). An Approach to Resolving Semantic Heterogeneity in a Federation of Autonomous, Heterogeneous Database Systems. *International Journal of Intelligent and Cooperative Information Systems*, *2*(1), 51–83. doi:10.1142/S0218215793000046

Huhns, M. N., & Singh, M. P. (1997). Agents on the Web: Ontologies for Agents. *IEEE Internet Computing*, *1*(6), 81–83. doi:10.1109/4236.643942

Hull, R. (1997). Managing semantic heterogeneity in databases: A theoretical perspective. *Proceedings of the sixteenth ACM SIGACT-SIGMOD-SIGART symposium on Principles of database systems*, 51-61. 10.1145/263661.263668

Hurson, A. R., & Bright, M. W. (1991). Multidatabase Systems: An Advanced Concept in Handling Distributed Data. *Advances in Computers*, *32*, 149–200. doi:10.1016/S0065-2458(08)60247-8

Jarke, M., Lenzerini, M., Vassiliou, Y., & Vassiliadis, P. (2000). *Fundamentals of Data Warehouses*. Springer. doi:10.1007/978-3-662-04138-3

Kim, W., Choi, I., Gala, S., & Scheevel, M. (1993). On Resolving Schematic Heterogeneity in Multidatabase Systems. *Distributed and Parallel Databases*, *1*(3), 252–279. doi:10.1007/BF01263333

Kim, W., & Seo, J. (1991). Classifying Schematic and Data Heterogeneities in Multidatabase Systems. *IEEE Computer*, *24*(12), 12–18. doi:10.1109/2.116884

Landers, T., & Rosenberg, R. L. (1982). An Overview of MULTIBASE. *Second International Symposium on Distributed Data Bases (DDB 1982)*, 153-184.

Lenzerini, M. (2002). Data integration: A theoretical preceptive. *Proceedings of Twenty-first ACM SIGACT-SIGMOD-SIGART Symposium on Principles of Database System*, 1-14.

Mena, E., Kashyap, V., Sheth, A. P., & Illarramendi, A. (1996). OBSERVER: An Approach for Query Processing in Global Information Systems based on Interoperation across Pre-existing Ontologies. *First IFCIS International Conference on Cooperative Information Systems (CoopIS 1996)*, 14-25. 10.1109/COOPIS.1996.554955

Pal, K. (2017). Supply Chain Coordination Based on Web Service. In H. K. Chan, N. Subramanian, & M. D. Abdulrahman (Eds.), *Supply Chain Management in the Big Data Era* (pp. 137–171). Hershey, PA: IGI Global Publishing. doi:10.4018/978-1-5225-0956-1.ch009

Pottinger, R., & Halevy, A. (2001). MiniCon: A Scalable Algorithm for Answering Queries Using Views. *The Very Large Dabase Journal, 10*, 182–198.

Prud'hommeaux, E., & Seaborne, A. (2013). *SPARQL Query Language for RDF*. Retrieved from http://www.w3.org/TR/rdf-sparql-query

Sheth, A. P., Gala, S. K., & Navathe, S. B. (1993). On Automatic Reasoning for Shema Integration. *International Journal of Intelligent and Cooperative Information Systems, 2*(1), 23–50. doi:10.1142/S0218215793000034

Sheth, A. P., & Larson, J. A. (1990). Federated Database Systems for Managing Distributed, Heterogenous, and Autonomous Databases. *ACM Computing Surveys, 22*(3), 183–236. doi:10.1145/96602.96604

Silberschatz, A., Korth, H. F., & Sudarshan, S. (1997). *Database System Concepts*. McGraw-Hill.

Ullman, J. D. (1997). Information integration using logical views. *Proceedings of International Conference on Database Theory*, 19-40.

Wache, H., Vogele, T., Visser, U., Struckenschmidt, H., Schuster, G., Neumann, H., & Hubner, S. (2001). Ontology-Based Integration of Information – A Survey of Existing Approaches. *IJCAI-2001 Workshop on Ontologies and Information Sharing*, 108-117.

Wiederhold, G. (1992). Mediators in the architecture of future information systems. *IEEE Computer,* 38-49.

Ziegler, P., & Dittrich, K. R. (2007). *Data Integration – Problems, Approaches, and Perspectives, Database Technology Research Group*. Department of Informatics, University of Zurich.

KEY TERMS AND DEFINITIONS-

Linked Data: An approach taken to linking data such that it becomes more useful/accessible than it would be in isolation.

Ontology: Information sharing among supply chain business partners using information systems is an important enabler for supply chain management. There are diverse types of data to be shared across supply chain, namely order, inventory, shipment, and customer service. Consequently, information about these issues needs to be shared in order to achieve efficiency and effectiveness in supply chain management. In this way, information-sharing activities require that human and/ or machine agents agree on common and explicit business-related concepts (the shared conceptualization among hardware/software agents customers, and service providers) are known as explicit ontologies; and this help to exchange data and derived knowledge out of the data to achieve collaborative goals of business operations.

Relational Database: Relational database systems support processing of tuples of relations to generate a single result as a set of tuples. Relational algebra, relational calculus and structured query language (SQL) are used to specify queries on relational databases.

Resource Description Framework (RDF): The RDF is a standard for representing knowledge on the web. It is primarily designed for building the semantic web and has been widely adopted in database and datamining communities. RDF models a fact as a triple which consists of a subject (s), a predicate (p), and an object (o).

SPARQL: The SPARQL query language is a structured language for querying RDF data in a declarative fashion. Its core function is subgraph pattern matching, which corresponds to finding all graph homomorphism in the data graph for a query graph.

SPARQL Query: A SPARQL query usually contains a set of triple patterns, much like RDF triples, except that any of the subject, predicate and object may be a variable, whose bindings are to be found in the RDF data.

SQL: Structured query language (SQL) – a commonly-used language for querying relational database systems.

Structured Data: Data are stored in accordance with a strict schema for database management purpose.

Supply Chain Management: A supply chain consists of a network of key business processes and facilities, involving end users and suppliers that provide products, services, and information. In this chain management, improving the efficiency of the overall chain is an influential factor; and it needs at least four important strategic issues to be considered: supply chain network design, capacity planning, risk assessment and management, and performances monitoring and measurement. Moreover, the details break down of these issues need to consider in the level of individual business processes and sub-processes; and the combined performance of this chain. The coordination of these huge business processes and their performance improvement are the main objectives of a supply chain management system.

XML: Extensible markup language (XML) is a simple, very flexible text format derived from SGML (standard generalized markup language). While XML was originally designed to meet the challenges of large-scale electronic publishing, it plays an increasingly significant role in the exchange of a wide variety of data on the web.

Chapter 4
About Digital Avatars for Control Systems Using Big Data and Knowledge Sharing in Virtual Industries

Vardan Mkrttchian
HHH University, Australia

Leyla Gamidullaeva
Penza State University, Russia

Ivan Palatkin
K. G. Razumovsky Moscow State University of Technologies and Management, Russia

Svetlana Panasenko
Plekhanov Russian University of Economics, Russia

ABSTRACT

The authors in this chapter show the essence, dignity, current state, and development prospects of avatar-based management using blockchain technology for improving implementation of economic solutions in the digital economy of Russia. The purpose of this chapter is not to review the existing published work on avatar-based models for policy advice but to try an assessment of the merits and problems of avatar-based models as a solid basis for economic policy advice that is mainly based on the work and experience within the recently finished projects Triple H Avatar, an avatar-based software platform for HHH University, Sydney, Australia. The agenda of this project was to develop an avatar-based closed model with strong empirical grounding and micro-foundations that provides a uniform platform to address issues in different areas of digital economic and creating new tools to improve blockchain technology using the intelligent visualization techniques for big data analytics.

DOI: 10.4018/978-1-5225-7519-1.ch004

INTRODUCTION

The model of teaching students in an environment enabled by the evolutions in modern virtual industry software tool is in need of a new paradigm for solving problems of human-computer interaction. This is especially so if Block chain technology is to be adopted in order to implement human-computer interaction in the education sector in an economically viable way. The purpose of this chapter is not to consider existing literature on avatar-based models for the purpose of providing policy advice. Rather, the purpose is to attempt to evaluate the merits and problems of avatar-based Electronic/Ubiquitous/pervasive learning (E/U-learning 4.0) models as a solid basis for economic policy recommendations that are mainly based on performance The scope of performance covered in this chapter is the reflexive adaptability of the E/U learning software system.

The chapter is organized as follows. The introduction is followed by the inspiration for the chapter; a background highlighting software adaptivity of E/U-learning software; an analysis on the reflexive adaptation of E/U-learning software; solutions and recommendations to attaining reflexive adaptation of E/U learning software; and a conclusion.

INSPIRATION FOR THE CHAPTER

The chapter is written based on the reflections on the experiences in a recently completed project at the HHH University, Sydney, Australia. In this project christened the "Triple H Avatar", an Avatar-based Software Platform was developed for HHH University, Sydney, Australia. The agenda of this project was to create a closed model based on avatars supported with strong empirical grounding and micro levels. The avatars will provide a single platform for solving problems in the educational sector and it also has the potential to address various areas of the digital economy. It will also create new tools for improving upon Block chain technology using Intelligent Visualization technologies for Big Data Analysis and Knowledge sharing in virtual industries as well. (Mkrttchian, and Aleshina, 2017). In this section, an overview of the Triple H Avatar and its implications on E/U learning software systems will be discussed.

Triple H Avatar and E/U Learning

This approach adopted by the HHH University, Sydney, Australia to the learning model using Block chain technology led to the creation of Electronic / Ubiquitous Learning - pervasive e-learning (E/U-Learning 4.0)-) or new tools for improving upon

Block chain technology being used for Intelligent Visualization technologies for Big Data Analysis and Knowledge sharing in virtual industries. E/U-Learning 4.0 and the newer tools are based on the interface of very advanced information technologies, such as distributed computer systems, service-oriented Internet technologies, cloud technologies, mobile personal devices and telecommunications, artificial intelligence systems and means of virtual reality using all the technical and software achievements of the virtual industry. The introduction of E / U-Learning technologies has elevated the modern educational system to a new stages of education delivery, contributing to the processes of internationalization and the intellectualization of education.

Emerging Challenges to E/U Learning Software Implementation

However, despite the introduction of the E/U-Learning, a fundamentally new scientific problem has arisen. This is the need to create a unified interstate intellectual environment for managing the transfer of knowledge and the provision of electronic educational services, which will include heterogeneous forms of knowledge representation, interstate standards and forms of education, international teaching and student/- staff relationship (Mkrttchian et al., 2015).

Potential Solutions to E/U Learning Software Implementation

The solution to this fundamental problem requires the formulation of solutions on a number of more specific technical problems. Such solutions will require:

1. Ensuring the autonomy of the life cycle of the software components of the electronic educational environment due to multi-level self-organization without the unnecessary processes of recompiling the source code. In particular, the problems of the software components that are not adaptable to changes in the scope and quality of knowledge in subject areas; changes in the requirements of society to the knowledge and skills of specialists; changes in the forms and methods of training and education delivery; changes in the technical means of training and communications can be solved with this proposed solution.

2. The provision of cross-platform compatibility through the support of a wide variety of desktop computers and personal mobile devices, as well as the compatibility of wireless communication protocols. In this scenario, the user should be granted permanent presence in the educational cloud without being tied to specific geographical territories, life circumstances or software and hardware platforms.

3. Ensuring flexible personalization due to adaptive adjustment of electronic educational services to the requirements of each individual (psychophysical,

intellectual, technical), as well as the efficient usage of distributed educational resources.

Properties of E/U Learning Systems

These solutions to the aforementioned problems reveals three important properties of modern E / U Learning systems. These properties are: autonomy, pervasive accessibility and adaptability. Adaptability as a property should be considered from three main points of view:

1. The adaptability of the educational system to the constantly changing level of knowledge of the learner;
2. The adaptability of the educational system to the changing course materials within the framework of each individual training course;
3. The adaptability of the educational system to changing requirements from employers and labor markets.

Pervasive accessibility as a property implies the continuous transfer of knowledge and the provision of reference and educational services in initially uncertain conditions for previously uncertain groups of users. At the same time, in a forced way, the concept of the life cycle of the electronic educational system is changing. This is because:

1. It is no longer advisable to provide adaptability as a property through the release of chains of updated software versions. The developer simply does not have the right amount of time to recompile, debug and verify each new version of the system or training course, therefore distance education services software must be provided continuously and with an equally good level of quality.
2. The E / U Learning system requires a self-tuning that is transparent to the user, without recompiling the source code as mentioned earlier. Therefore, the architecture of such a system should initially be based on variability models (VMs) controlled by feedback loops with the trainee, the teacher and the employer (that is, taking into account all three of the above points of view on adaptability) (Mkrttchian et al., 2015).

In order to implement this property of adaptation (or rather, self-adaptation), it is advisable to use the methods currently used in the field of Engineering Product Lines (SPLE). In particular, the paradigm for reusing software products through the dynamic reconfiguration of their software code as developed within the framework of DSPL technologies (Dynamic Software Product Lines). In addition, the structure of the E / U Learning system should have a distributed modular appearance with clearly defined autonomous services and flexible algorithms for their interaction. To date, one of the best approaches to solving these problems is service-oriented technology. Here the architecture of the system is built on the basis of an autonomous, jointly functioning web-services. This architecture is called Service-Oriented Architecture (SOA) (Mkrttchian et al., 2015).

Practical Implications of the Triple H Avatar

The aggregate of various E / U Learning web services makes sense because it is functionally classified and grouped, thus creating intelligent software agents capable of adapting to, the current knowledge level of the learner; the environmental requirements (for example, labor markets); to specific teaching methods and forms training; and to various the national educational systems and standards (Mkrttchian et al., 2015).

Goals of the Chapter

Concluding the description of the general point of view of this chapter, you can identify specific goals:

1. To evaluate the merits and problems of models based on avatars as a solid basis for recommendations on economic policy;
2. Creation of a closed model based on avatars with strong empirical grounding and micro levels, which provide a single platform for solving problems in various areas of the digital economy;
3. Create new tools to improve Block chain technology using Intelligent Visualization for Big Data Analysis for Knowledge sharing in virtual industries.
4. Develop a method of structural and parametric synthesis of adaptive software components of the environment for Knowledge sharing in virtual industries.

BACKGROUND

The existing tools used in the modern learning environment, to improve upon Block chain technology, with the aid of Intelligent Visualization for Big Data Analysis for knowledge sharing in virtual industries is a complex system. The complex system includes didactic and methodical components, as well as information and software components. As program components may include various interactive simulators and testing programs with adaptive properties, an important thing to consider is the development of methods of synthesis of these components (Czarnecki, et al., 2012).

Apart from the complexity of the system, in recent years, technology tools that utilize intelligent visualization to analyze big data to facilitate knowledge sharing in virtual industries to improve Block chain technology are being developed rapidly. As a result, issues related to improving the quality of software of virtual systems are becoming more relevant. There is an increasing focus on the continuous operation of programs. There is also a demand on the increase in their reliability and flexibility. These characteristics are directly dependent on the ability of the software system to adapt to changes in the subject area, environmental conditions and user characteristics.

Currently, among specialists there is no single definition of the concept of software adaptability. The situation is such that for different types of software systems adaptability can be determined in various ways. For information systems, adaptability primarily means that the system has reactions to changes in the subject area; for virtual simulators, adaptability is most often the program's ability to change its structure and behavior depending on the user's actions and personality characteristics. Views on the implementation of the adaptation process may also vary within the consideration of one class of systems and that strongly depends on the chosen design methodology.

Nevertheless, despite seemingly significant differences in definitions and approaches, one can identify one common property of all systems that can be referred to as adaptive. These properties include: the ability of the system to self-modify (at the level of the structure of the system as a whole or at the level of individual components). The requirements imposed by the external environment, the characteristics of users and the subject area, are usually such that it is impossible to adequately adapt to them without making changes to the architecture. However, for each type of software system, the restructuring process will continue to be carried out in its own way and depend on various factors. The analysis of adaptive software made it possible to distinguish 4 main adaptation mechanisms in software systems.

1. **Runtime Adaptation:** Runtime adaptation is carried out by a software system in the course of its operation and it is characterized by the relative speed in the process of program restructuring. Most often, adaptation by runtime type is characterized by simulator systems which collects data about the learner in the process of execution; form an individual trajectory without significant delays in the functioning of the program for Knowledge sharing in virtual industries.

2. **Self-Healing Systems:** Another area of possible use of runtime models is the construction of so-called self-healing systems. Such systems must control their own reliability and security, as well as be able to automate tasks that often lead to system failures and require the attention of specialists. Self-

healing software systems should provide maximum resistance to deviations in operating conditions. The implementation of large virtual environments (virtual, universities, laboratories, technology parks) requires increased fault tolerance, and, therefore, the inclusion of self-healing mechanisms in them.

3. **MAPE-K:** IBM's approach to organizing a runtime adaptation is widely known. The approach was called MAPE-K (from the English Monitor, Analyze, Plane and Execute with a Knowledge), and it is based on the specific architecture of the software system that implements the adaptation cycle, which consists of 4 main stages. The stages are: the observation and collection of the necessary information; the analysis of the obtained information; the planning of program behavior and the performance of planned operations. A number of other approaches to the implementation of runtime adaptation, in particular, approaches, are built on the integration of the principles of software engineering and control theory.

4. **Domain Adaptation:** Adaptation of the domain is used primarily in information systems and decision support systems. It differs from runtime adaptation, firstly, by the obligatory participation of the user (designer or expert) when making changes to the domain models, and secondly, by the need to temporarily decommission the modified system. The adaptation of the domain was first implemented in ERP-systems. ERP-system is a software product that implements the principles of the ERP concept (from the English. Enterprise Resource was planning, enterprise resource planning). The concept of ERP determines the organizational strategy for the integration of production. The basis of ERP-systems is the principle of creating a single data warehouse containing all corporate business information, to which simultaneous access of a certain number of company employees with different levels of authority should be ensured. Since the subject areas of ERP-systems are rapidly changing, the need to endow such systems with adaptive properties arose rather quickly. Two approaches towards adaptation were developed namely, the original and model design. The original design is based on the use of CASE-technology (for example, SilverRun) and involves the generation (re-creation) of the information system whenever the need for change arises. The basis of a typical design is the component design systems (R/3, BAAN, Prodis, etc.), and instead of regeneration, the configuration (adaptation to the features of an economic object) of software systems is carried out. At the heart of both approaches lies the principle of a constantly evolving domain model, for the storage of which a special knowledge base is used - the repository. It is on the basis of the data stored in the repository that the program is generated or configured. Adaptation in such systems is reduced to the timely adjustment of the domain model, for

the construction and subsequent modification of which special software tools are used.

MAIN FOCUS OF THE CHAPTER

Issues, Controversies, Problems

The approaches developed initially for Enterprise Resource Planning (ERP) systems are now part of information systems used in many areas of human activity. Some of these approaches can be used to address the major goal of this chapter as mentioned in the introduction. This goal was the development and implementation of new technologies that can deliver new tools for improving Block chain technology. These new technologies will utilize Intelligent Visualization technologies for the purpose of analyzing Big Data and enable Knowledge sharing in virtual industries. In our case in the education sector. As inspired by the Triple H Avatar project, we realized the need to, find the cause of reflex adaptation; create non-removable hardware and software; and create suitable products for its implementation.

Reflexive adaptation is characterized by the presence and combination of features of the adaptation mechanisms of the previous types considered in the previous section. Like the runtime adaptation, it does not require the substantial participation of an expert for either in the self-modification of the system or in the decommissioning of the modified system. However, as in the case with the adaptation of the subject area, it needs some time to analyze the current state of the program and prepare recommendations for its subsequent restructuring. Unlike runtime adaptations, reflexive adaptations do not lead to automatic self-modification during execution. Its main purpose is the "offline" analysis of the system's behavior by using information about its internal structure and making decisions about possible restructuring on that basis. Information of this kind may include protocols on system behavior over a sufficiently long period of time or protocols on procedures for dynamic analysis of the source code.

Reflexive adaptation can be implemented in training systems, in particular, virtual simulators. Logging the behavior of different users for a certain period of time and the subsequent analysis of the obtained data will allow the elimination of the problematic points from the behavior of the simulator. The problematic points are understood to be those inaccuracies made during the design of the simulator, which, according to the results of the analysis, reduces the effectiveness of its operation when working with a large number of students. These may include, excessive complexity or ease of implementation of individual stages of the simulator operation; excessive concentration at some stages to the detriment of others; and poor organization of the interface, resulting in an unjustified increase in the time to master the program, etc.

The purpose of reflexive adaptation is the search by the system in its own program code for fragments that can lead to malfunctions or inefficient functioning (the task of dynamic analysis of program code). In addition to the ability to find problem areas in the community structure, an ideal adaptive system must also have the ability to eliminate them. This property is especially relevant for systems organized according to a service-oriented principle: adding an incorrectly written module to the general structure of a workable system as a whole can lead to unforeseen disruptions in its functioning.

SOLUTIONS AND RECOMMENDATIONS

Elements of reflexive adaptation were successfully implemented in the WebCT e-learning system developed and first introduced at the University of British Columbia. WebCT implements a Web Mining mechanism - optimizing the interface in accordance with user requests. However, adaptation based on observation of the information environment is still a poorly developed mechanism for implementing adaptive behavior in software systems. And most of the work in this area are mainly devoted to the prospects of using Big Data technology in constructing adaptive systems of this kind. The basic idea underlying this adaptation mechanism is the use of various methods of collecting and analyzing a large amount of data related to the subject area of the software system, and subsequent restructuring the system based on the findings of the analysis.

Furthermore, the global information network can serve as an information medium from which the necessary information can be gathered. This type of adaptation is in many ways similar to the adaptation of the subject area, but differs from the latter by a significant decrease in human participation in the process of forming and making a decision on restructuring the program.

FUTURE RESEARCH DIRECTIONS

The question about the successful implementation of the adaptation mechanism in the systems of the virtual industry is currently debatable. The influence of models on the level of reflexive adaptation; the level of observation of the information environment on domain models and the execution time in such systems are, at first glance an obvious fact. But this fact is currently not studied sufficiently and it is a serious issue that warrants further research. Another issue of interest to researchers is the integration of the considered adaptation mechanisms within a single software system.

CONCLUSION

In order to create a closed model based on avatars with strong empirical grounding and micro levels, which can provide a single platform for solving problems in various areas of the digital economy and creating new tools for improving Block chain technology using Intelligent Visualization technologies for Big Data Analysis and Knowledge sharing in virtual industries, a system has been developed and implemented on avatars for reflexive adaptation. This system is an effective mechanism for self-optimization of a software system. The ability of the system to self-observe and the subsequent formation of decisions on restructuring is a feature whose presence allows you to maximize the participation of developers in the maintenance of the program and increase the time of its continuous operation.

The developed method of structural-parametric synthesis of adaptive software components of the virtual environment allows you to formalize a complex mathematical procedure for defining variability in a visual, simple and intuitive way using visual design tools. The use of the method in practice will increase the life of systems and reduce the resource costs of their creation. It will also support the mobility of electronic education, improve the adaptive properties of software for Knowledge sharing in virtual industries.

REFERENCES

Baresi, L., & Quinton, C. (2015). Dynamically Evolving the Structural Variability of Dynamic Software Product Lines. *Proceedings of the 10th International Symposium on Software Engineering for Adaptive and Self-Managing Systems*, 57–63. 10.1109/SEAMS.2015.24

Bershadsky, A. M., & Krevsky, I. G. (1996). The Organization of Distance Education in Penza Region of Russian Federation. *Proceedings of the Second International Conference on Distance Education in Russia: Open and Distance Learning as a Development Strategy*, 174-176.

Big Data in eLearning: The Future of eLearning Industry. (n.d.). Retrieved from https://elearningindustry.com/big-data-in-elearning-future-of-elearning-industry

Bjork, E., Ottosson, S., & Thorsteinsdottir, S. (2008). E-Learning for All. In *E-Learning: 21st Century Issues and Challenges* (pp. 49–69). Nova Science Publishers Inc.

Czarnecki, K., & Helsen, S. (2006). Feature-based survey of model transformation approaches. *IBM Systems Journal, 45*(3), 621–646. doi:10.1147j.453.0621

Finogeev A. A., Finogeev A. G., Nefedova I. S. (2016). Izvestiya vysshikh uchebnykh zavedeniy. Povolzhskiy region. Tekhnicheskie nauki. *University Proceedings. Volga Region. Engineering Science, 2*(38), 49–60.

Hellerstein, J., Diao, Y., & Parekh, S. (2004). *Feedback control of computing systems*. Hoboken, NJ: Wiley Interscience. doi:10.1002/047166880X

Iglesia, D. G. (2014). MAPE-K Formal Templates for Self-Adaptive Systems: Specifications and Descriptions. Smaland: Linnaeus University.

Keromytis, A. D. (2007). *Characterizing Software Self-healing Systems. In Computer Network Security* (pp. 22–33). Berlin: Springer.

Kumunzhiev, K. V. (2003). Teoriya sistem i sistemnyy analiz: ucheb. Ulyanovsk: UlGU.

Mkrtchian, V., Bershadsky, A., Bozhday, A., & Fionova, L. (2015). Model in SM of DEE Based on Service-Oriented Interactions at Dynamic Software Product Lines. In Identification, Evaluation, and Perceptions of Distance Education Experts (pp. 231-248). Hershey, PA: IGI Global.

Mkrttchian, V. (2011). Use 'hhh" technology in transformative models of online education. In G. Kurubacak & T. V. Yuzer (Eds.), *Handbook of research on transformative online education and liberation: Models for social equality* (pp. 340–351). Hershey, PA: IGI Global. doi:10.4018/978-1-60960-046-4.ch018

Mkrttchian, V. (2012). Avatar manager and student reflective conversations as the base for describing meta-communication model. In Meta-communication for reflective online conversations: Models for distance education (pp. 340–351). Hershey, PA: IGI Global.

Mkrttchian, V. (2014). Modeling using of Triple H-Avatar Technology in online Multi-Cloud Platform Lab. In M. Khosrow-Pour (Ed.), *Encyclopedia of Information Science and Technology* (3rd ed.; pp. 116–141). Hershey, PA: IGI Global.

Mkrttchian, V., & Aleshina, E. (2017). *Sliding Mode in Intellectual Control and Communication: Emerging Research and Opportunities*. Hershey, PA: IGI Global. doi:10.4018/978-1-5225-2292-8

Mkrttchian, V., Kataev, M., Hwang, W., Bedi, S., & Fedotova, A. (2014). Using Plug-Avatars "hhh" Technology Education as Service-Oriented Virtual Learning Environment in Sliding Mode. In G. Eby & T. V. Yuzer (Eds.), *Emerging Priorities and Trends in Distance Education: Communication, Pedagogy, and Technology* (pp. 43–55). Hershey, PA: IGI Global. doi:10.4018/978-1-4666-5162-3.ch004

Mkrttchian, V., & Stephanova, G. (2013). Training of Avatar Moderator in Sliding Mode Control. In Enterprise Resource Planning: Concepts, Methodologies, Tools, and Applications (pp. 1376-1405), Hershey PA: IGI Global.

Munster W. W. U. OpenUSS. (n.d.). Retrieved from https://www.uni-muenster.de/studium/orga/openuss.html.

Papazoglou, M. P., & Heuvel, W.-J. (2007). Service oriented architectures: Approaches, technologies and research issues. *The VLDB Journal, 16*(3), 389–415. doi:10.100700778-007-0044-3

Pelyushenko, A. V. (2006). Izvestiya Volgogradskogo gosudarstvennogo tekhnicheskogo uni-versiteta, *University proceedings. Volga region. Engineering and Science*, (8): 48–50.

Schobbens, P. E., Heymans, P., & Trigaux, J. C. (2011). 14th IEEE International Requirements Engineering Conference (RE'06). *Computers & Society, 2011*, 139–148.

Smartsparrow. (n.d.). Retrieved from https://www.smartsparrow.com/

The Next Evolution of ERP. (n.d.). *Adaptive ERP // ERP the Right Way: Changing the game for ERP Cloud implementations*. Retrieved from https://gbeaubouef.wordpress.com/2012/09/05/adaptive-erp/

Villegas, N. M., Muller, H. A., Tamura, G., Duchien, L., & Casallas, R. A. (2011). Framework for evaluating quality- driven self-adaptive software systems. *Proceeding of the 6th International Symposium on Software Engineering for Adaptive and Self-Managing Systems*, 80-89. 10.1145/1988008.1988020

WebC. T. (n.d.). Retrieved from http://www.cuhk.edu.hk/eLearning/c_systems/webct6/

Younis O., Ghoul S., Alomari M. H. (2013). Systems Variability Modeling: A Textual Model Mixing Class and Feature Concepts. *International Journal of Computer Science & Information Technology, 2013*(5), 127–139.

ADDITIONAL READING

Mkrttchian, V. (2015). Modeling using of Triple H-Avatar Technology in online Multi-Cloud Platform Lab. In M. Khosrow-Pour (Ed.), *Encyclopedia of Information Science and Technology* (3rd ed., pp. 4162–4170). Hershey, PA, USA: IGI Global. doi:10.4018/978-1-4666-5888-2.ch409

Mkrttchian, V. (2015, January-June). Use Online Multi-Cloud Platform Lab with Intellectual Agents: Avatars for Study of Knowledge Visualization & Probability Theory in Bioinformatics. *International Journal of Knowledge Discovery in Bioinformatics*, 5(1), 11–23. doi:10.4018/IJKDB.2015010102

Mkrttchian, V., Aysmontas, B., Udin, A., Andreev, A., & Vorovchenko, N. (2015). The Academic Views from Moscow Universities on the Future of DEE at Russia and Ukraine In Gulsun Eby, Volkan Yuser (Eds.) Identification, Evaluation, and Perceptions of Distance Education Experts, (pp.32- 45), Hershey, PA, USA: IGI Global.

Mkrttchian, V., Bershadsky, A., Bozhday, A., Kataev, M., & Kataev, S. (Eds.). (2016). *Handbook of Research on Estimation and Control Techniques in E-Learning systems*. Hershey, PA, USA: IGI Global. doi:10.4018/978-1-4666-9489-7

Mkrttchian, V., Bershadsky, A., Bozhday, A., Noskova, T., & Miminova, S. (2016). Development of a Global Policy of All-Pervading E-Learning, Based on Transparency, Strategy, and Model of Cyber Triple H-Avatar. In G. Eby, T. V. Yuser, & S. Atay (Eds.), *Developing Successful Strategies for Global Policies and Cyber Transparency in E-Learning* (pp. 207–221). Hershey, PA, USA: IGI Global. doi:10.4018/978-1-4666-8844-5.ch013

Mkrttchian, V., Kataev, M., Bershadsky, A., & Volchikhin, V. (2015). Use Triple H-AVATAR Technology for Research in Online Multi-Cloud Platform Lab, In A. Kravets (Eds.), *Proceedings of CIT&DS 2015* (pp. 58–67). Springer International Publishing.

Mkrttchian, V., Kataev, M., Hwang, W., Bedi, S., & Fedotova, A. (2016). Using Plug-Avatars "hhh" Technology Education as Service-Oriented Virtual Learning Environment in Sliding Mode. Leadership and Personnel Management: Concepts, Methodologies, Tools, and Applications (4 Volumes), Information Resources Management Association (IRMA), (pp.890-902), Hershey, PA, USA: IGI Global.

Mkrttchian, V., Kataev, M., Shih, T., Misra, K., & Fedotova, A. (2014, July-September). Avatars "HHH" Technology Education Cloud Platform on Sliding Mode Based Plug- Ontology as a Gateway to Improvement of Feedback Control Online Society. *International Journal of Information Communication Technologies and Human Development*, 6(3), 13–31. doi:10.4018/ijicthd.2014070102

KEY TERMS AND DEFINITIONS

Assessment of Institutional Effectiveness: Is application of the multivariate analysis conformity for the structural analysis of the pedagogical staff of the research university use tools of virtual industries.

Education Technology in Virtual Industries: Are technical, biological, and engineering systems for education whose components are combined, controlled, and generated using the aligned single processing core. All the components at all levels of interaction are combined in the network infrastructure. All components include built-in calculators, providing data processing in real-time and in virtual industries.

Functional Modeling Software Platform: A specification software designed to be used modeling of the risk management process of enterprise resource planning on lab multi-cloud platform has allowed us to solve the problem of compliance, as well as to identify modern and future issues, concepts, trends and solutions IS&T throughout the software lifecycle.

Moderator, Researcher, Teacher, Student Avatars: Personalized graphic file or rendering that represents a computer user used to represent moderator, researcher, teacher, student in an online environment of virtual industries.

Multimedia Online Teaching: Is recently been revolutionized by the recent development in information and communication technologies in virtual industries.

Online Multi-Cloud Platform Lab: Is laboratory on the internet that is available on the multi-cloud platform and intended for research, training, and development of forecasting use tools of virtual industries.

Triple H-Avatar Technology: Is the technology of modeling and simulation based on known technology of Avatar used in the HHH University since 2010.

Virtual Research and Study Environment: Is the space where with the help of virtual reality creates a special environment for research and study.

Chapter 5

Rife Information Pollution (Infollution) and Virtual Organizations in Industry 4.0:
Within Reality Causes and Consequences

Qaisar Iqbal
Universiti Sains Malaysia, Malaysia

Rashid Nawaz
University of Education, Pakistan

ABSTRACT

Information pollution, which usually refers to the overabundance of irrelevant, unsolicited, unwanted messages, is a major cause of concern for practitioners and academic researchers. Advances in the information and communication technologies has proliferated the production of information. Consequently, people are suffering from information pollution. Information pollution has made it difficult for employees and individuals to find the quality information quickly and conveniently from diverse information sources including print and electronic sources. This chapter sheds light on the relevant literature of information pollution and analyzes its causes in the Industry 4.0 era and puts forward suggestions for tackling this problem. This chapter emphasizes the significance of concrete efforts from computer scientists, academic professionals, and information professionals to devise strategies and techniques for refuting the effects of information pollution.

DOI: 10.4018/978-1-5225-7519-1.ch005

INTRODUCTION

Industries are undergoing a historic turning point (Laudante, 2017). People, machines, and products are now communicating with one another via the internet within the context of industry 4.0. Industry 4.0 refers to the convergence between industries and the Internet technology (Fernández-Miranda, Marcos, Peralta, & Aguayo, 2017). Industry 4.0 offers opportunities in the form of resource efficiency, energy efficiency, and increased productivity. It also solves industry challenges by shortening the innovation creation process; and time-to-market cycles, facilitated through horizontal integration, vertical integration and end-to-end digital integration (Kagermann, Helbig, Hellinger, & Wahlster, 2013). For the most part, both manufacturers and technology suppliers do have a very positive outlook towards industry 4.0 (de Sousa Jabbour, Jabbour, Godinho Filho, & Roubaud, 2018).

Industry 4.0 is made up of different components which includes, 3D printing, big data, Internet of Things (IoT), and the Internet of Services (IoS). These components individually and collectively facilitate smart manufacturing and logistics processes (Kagermann et al., 2013). These components enable and support the management and the production processes within Industry 4.0. The industry 4.0 context in this chapter is its managerial aspect and not the technical and automation process. The managerial aspect is discussed within the context of virtual organizations.

Industry 4.0 is driven by big data generated and used in the processes within this industry. Therefore the prospect of managing big data is this industry becomes challenging. However, currently new ways of managing big data are now evident in Industry 4.0. But these new approaches towards managing big data are not sufficient. This is because most of the information harvested from the big are not credible and useful to the management and administrative employees in virtual organizations utilizing industry 4.0. What makes big data challenging are its characteristics. Big data is made up of the 4Vs, i.e. velocity, veracity, volume, and variety of information. The 4Vs have increased significantly in the contemporary age resulting in increased information pollution or infollution. *Information pollution refers to the information that is irrelevant, outdated, inaccurate, hidden and unsolicited.* How infollution is handled in an industry is important to the value derived from big data in the context of industry 4.0. Therefore, the successful realisation of benefits associated with virtual organizations in industry 4.0 relies on how a firm's Research and Development (R&D) process is directed towards the reduction or mitigation of infollution caused by the 4Vs. This idea is supported by Prause (2015), who based on the glueing function, emphasised the management of the 4Vs to reduce information pollution or infollution within the context of industry 4.0 (see (Jay Lee, Kao, & Yang, 2014)).

The focus of this chapter is on how infollution could affect the decision makers and administrative employees working in a virtual organization delivering an industry 4.0 service. The chapter is designed in a progressive manner. Here the discussion begins with general overview of the central concepts of the chapter. This is followed by how these concepts are seen within virtual organizations and Industry 4.0. The chapter is designed as follows. The first section is the introduction. This is followed by an overview of the concept of infollution. As industry 4.0 is an ICT enabled industry, the next discussion is on the influence of ICT on infollution. This is followed by a discussion on infollution and Industry 4.0; a discussion on the interplay between infollution, virtual organizations and industry 4.0; and the conclusion of the chapter. In this chapter the words "information pollution" and "infollution" are used interchangeably.

INFORMATION POLLUTION: NATURE AND SIGNIFICANCE

In this section, a general overview on infollution as a concept and how it impacts organizations in general is discussed. The context of the discussion in this section is broad, because information pollution is assumed to emerge from divergent sources. This includes online and offline sources.

Overview on Information (Infollution)

Presently, information is increasing exponentially while quality information is increasing linearly (Kirsh, 2000). Based on this fact, polluted information also increases exponentially (Iqbal et al., 2018) (See Figure 1).

The increasing quantity of information has an influence on the information processing behaviour of individuals (Swar, Hameed, & Reychav, 2017), and it also

Figure 1. Graph-01

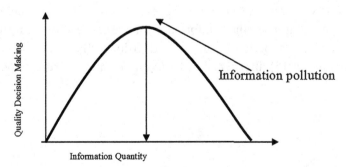

has an influence on the managerial and operational processes within an organization. Yet, the amount of information that is credible is not much because there is a great deal of polluted information available compared to quality information. These polluted information are often *irrelevant, outdated, inaccurate, hidden and unsolicited*. This actually becomes problematic when dealing with Big data.

Therefore in ordinary lingo, information pollution refers to the situation where individuals receive irrelevant, useless and outdated supply of information, resulting in dysfunctional consequences and diminished decision quality (Eppler & Helfert, 2004).

Nature of Information Pollution

Information pollution has an effect on decision makers and employees in an organization. Furthermore, it has an effect on individuals working in the organization and the organization as a whole.

1. **Individual Level:** On an individual level, once, the information supply exceeds the information processing capacity; individuals start facing problems in the sifting of relevant and updated information. Information imbibed by the individual therefore becomes overtly selective which means that it becomes incomplete. A large amount of polluted information makes it hard for people to understand the association between details and the overall perspective (Eppler & Helfert, 2004). Therefore, with increasing infollution, efforts to secure quality information is also on the increase. But the information processing capacity and response rate of humans are not always efficient resulting in a failure to secure quality information (Chen, Shang, & Kao, 2009).

2. **Organizational Level:** The effect of infollution on the organizational level stems from a spill over effect from the individual level. This is because, information acquired at the individual level is used for decision making, which affects the organizational level. The adoption of lack of credible information will result in bad consequences for the organization. These effects are discussed in the next sub-section. Literature suggests that information quantity, quality decision-making and polluted information move in one direction up to a certain point. Beyond that point the quality of decision will decline (Sasaki, Kawai, & Kitamura, 2015) after which infollution becomes a critical concern (See Figure 2).

Figure 2. Graph-02

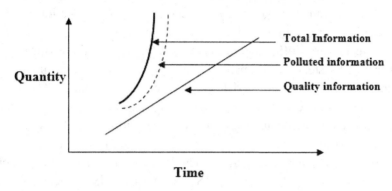

Effect of Information Pollution on Organizations

As mentioned in the previous sub-section, information pollution has an effect on the organization level. When information pollution exists, it affects the opportunity cost of the company; it affects the accuracy of the information used for decision making; it affects the organization's ability to forecast in its processes and it magnifies the downside organizations experience with imperfect information. Let's look at each effect, one by one.

1. **The Effect of Infollution on Opportunity Cost:** From an organizational perpective, infollution causes organisations to incur substantial costs. Employees waste a lot of time searching for and sorting irrelevant information into meaningful knowledge (Kutty, 2006). Managers have also reported delays in quality decision-making processes due to *"analysis paralysis"* or the presence of too much-polluted information (Jackson & Farzaneh, 2012). Infollution distracts employees from their core job responsibilities and employees and makes it hard to develop effective organisational strategies (Kutty, 2006).

2. **The Effect of Infollution on Information Accuracy:** Information pollution has been investigated in a substantial body of literature. More than 60% of 500 medium-size firms have been found suffering from infollution (Han, Pei, & Kamber, 2011). 1% to 10% of organisational information are inaccurate (Nelson et al., 2005; Klein 1997). The 30% error rate within industrial information is typical and that can rise up to 75% (Zaveri et al., 2016). 70% of orders in the manufacturing sector are based on polluted information (Preece, Missier, Embury, Jin, & Greenwood, 2008). 40% of the credit-risk management database in a New York bank was found to be incomplete (Ge & Helfert, 2008). Between 50% and 80% of computerised U.S. criminal records are estimated

to be incomplete, inaccurate and ambiguous (Strong, Lee, & Wang, 1997). The above literature suggests that the pervasiveness of infollution has made it difficult for organisations and individuals to make quality decisions.

3. **The Effect of Infollution on Forecasting:** Infollution facilitates the likelihood of harmful disasters. Across many organisations, many business initiatives have been delayed or even cancelled due to poor information quality (Ge & Helfert, 2008). In other areas of life, the same trend can be identified. On January 28, 1986, seven astronauts were killed in the explosion of the space shuttle challenger soon after lift-off (Madnick et al., 2009). Seventeen years later, seven other astronauts were killed when the space shuttle Columbia exploded (Mahler, 2009). In July 1988, the U.S. Navy Cruiser USS Vincennes had shot down an Iranian Airbus killing all 290 people aboard. On September 11, 2001, 19 hijackers entered an airport and converted four commercial passenger jets into guided missiles where approximately 3000 people were killed (Kean, 2011). These events occurred because they were difficult to predict due to infollution.

4. **The Effect of Infollution on the Consequences of Imperfect Information:** Infollution magnifies the consequences of imperfect information. Decision-making based on polluted information is associated with high costs. In an Australia hospital, inadequate prognostic information resulted in the fatal overdose of a paediatric patient (Madnick et al., 2009). An eyewear company faced a 15% lens grinding rework rate because of information errors that cost them at least $1 million annually (R. Y. Wang, 1998). One healthcare organisation that had consistently overpaid $4 million per annum in claims to non-eligible patients (Levis, 2011). Organisations fail to make an adequate profit due to incomplete information (Alenezi, Tarhini, & Sharma, 2015). They also lose clients because of infollution on their website (Jumin Lee, Park, & Han, 2008). A telecommunication company lost $3 million because of wrong financial analysis based on polluted information in customer bills (Kurniati & Surendro, 2010). Decisions based on poor information results in 8% to 12% loss of revenue in a typical enterprise. Service organisations bear from 40% to 60% of their expenses because of low-quality decision-making (Madnick et al., 2009). Some 599 surveyed organisations lose more than $1.4 billion annually because of infollution(Ge & Helfert, 2008). Hence, managing polluted information is beneficial to organisations.

Overall, infollution causes damages that amount to billions of dollars annually. It sometimes results in either loss of live or permanently altered life. Hence, the pervasiveness of infollution is evident (Wang et al. 2001). It is costly (Eppler &

Helfert, 2004) and even disastrous (Madnick et al., 2009). The common thread in all these events is poor information quality or infollution.

In the next section, the discussion is on how Information and Communication Technologies (ICT) affect infollution. This discussion is important because, Industry 4.0 and virtual organizations are enabled by ICT.

INFORMATION POLLUTION (IP) AND INFORMATION AND COMMUNICATION TECHNOLOGIES (ICT)

ICT has a general effect on infollution. Information and Communication Technologies (ICT) is now one of the major conduits of information globally. Organizations and individuals are now depending on information extracted from ICT informational applications and services. Due to the geographical coverage of ICT, tons of information are available now than it has ever been. This has given rise to big data. Unfortunately, ICT informational services are a major source of infollution (Pandita, 2014) (Bawden & Robinson, 2009). In this section, the discussion is on the effect of ICT on infollution generally. This is followed by the effect of ICT on infollution and how it affects decision making in an organization.

Effect on ICT on Infollution

ICT has its various subcategories, contributing to information pollution. However, a major sub-category with a significant infollution problem is the World Wide Web. The World Wide Web is one of the largest sources of information. Most of the information it contains are unstructured and unsolicited. However, what constitute infollution on the World Wide Web is the low level of relevant information delivered either structurally or unstructurally to end users. In the case of this chapter, organization and virtual organizations in the industry 4.0. On the World Wide Web, the irrelevant information could be on Social media and via spam electronic messages etc. Spam is defined as electronic messages received from unknown senders. The abundance and frequent delivery of junk emails undermine the merits of email communication.

It is important to note that irrelevant information could result in health problems for employees which could in turn affect the organization. As an example, irrelevant information on social media has a significant association with certain chronic diseases (Soucek & Moser, 2010). Therefore the authenticity of information in cyberspace is a major concern for researchers (Iqbal et al., 2018). And this has led researchers to emphasise on individuals and organization checking on the reliability and validity of information they consume (Kelton, Fleischmann, & Wallace, 2008).

Effect of ICT on Infollution in Organizations

In an organizational context, decision makers and employees are exposed to varied channels of information delivered via ICT. In the presence of this excessive supply of information, employees find it difficult to identify the relevant information (Ozdemir, 2016). These employees and decision makers are bombarded with information from all corners. These information are presented in different format. This implies that infollution constantly takes on new shapes and manifestations, making it increasingly difficult to find the right information at the right time in the right format. What makes the matter worse is the fact that employees working with computers suffer from cognitive loads and are therefore more susceptible to interference from interruptions. These problems affects the manner in which they sift through the needed information, turning ICT into a source of interruption and distraction. As the distraction increases, there is a high probability in the decrease in decision accuracy. Such interruptions are detrimental to decision-making processes (Ou & Davison, 2011). Given the above, Eppler & Helfert (2004) identified five factors of information overload that contribute to the infollution as shown in Figure 3.

The existence of multiple information sources, over-abundance of information, inefficient information management, irrelevant information, and scarcity of time on the part of information users are factors that enable information pollution.

A solution to the problem would be that decision makers and employees in an organization possess information literacy skills. In a case where the information literacy skills are lacking, it is hard for the individual to manage the ever-increasing quantity of information acquired.

Figure 3. Diagram: Causes of information pollution

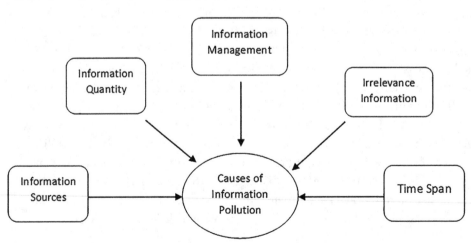

Infollution has been categorised into that which provokes disruption and those that affect the quality of information. Disruption infollution constitutes unsolicited messages and instant messages particularly in the context of a workplace (Wardle & Derakhshan, 2017). Mobile phones also contribute to this category (Neilson & Chadha, 2008). Reduction in the quality of information is considered infollution because information is inaccurate and outdated (Widen, Steinerová, & Voisey, 2014).

Now as Industry 4.0 is ICT driven and the amount of information available constitutes Big data, how does Infollution affect industry 4.0. That is the discussion of the next chapter.

INFOLLUTION AND INDUSTRY 4.0

In the previous 2 sections, a general overview of Infollution and how it affects organizations and how ICT enables infollutions in organizations were discussed. In this section infollution is contextualized within the context of organizations and virtual organizations operating in industry 4.0 sector. For starters, it is important to note that infollution is not the only challenge facing Industry 4.0. The top five barriers towards the implementation of industry 4.0, as seen by manufacturers, are exhibited in figure 4, highlighted in blue. However, advanced manufacturers have added three more issues to the context of industry 4.0 as shown in figure 4, highlighted in red.

Figure 4.
Source: (McKinsey Digital, 2016)

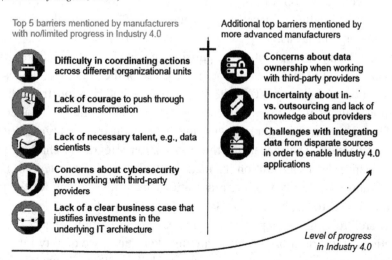

Despite these major challenges, the challenges caused by Infollution cannot be ignored. Industry 4.0 is enabled by ICT, it is data driven both in its management and operational aspects. Consequently there is a dramatic increase in the variety of information sources in industry 4.0, resulting in big data. Hence there is an increase in the risk and uncertainty associated with the quality of information available in this industry. As this industry is data driven the credibility of the information quality becomes paramount (Iqbal, Hassan, & Ahmad, 2018). Having realised this problem, academic researchers have recommended the need for an effective evaluation of information sources and information assessment (Flanagin, Metzger, Pure, Markov, & Hartsell, 2014).

In the context of virtual organizations, the credibility of the information in industry 4.0 becomes critical. Before industry 4.0, information credibility was a function of face-to-face interaction. In that setting in an organization, employees depended on diverse sources of information. They even solicited personal advice from friends and family members (Samadi & Yaghoob-Nejadi, 2009) as well as rely on information channels predating the internet such as books, television, and radio. But in virtual organizations, although these functions still exist, there is a greater need to acquire credible information from remote teams. This is because, a team could constitute remote employees working together. And if the virtual organization is an industry 4.0 organization, then this becomes challenging. This is because in industry 4.0, information sources vary. Similarly, the perception on the credibility of information sources also varies along with categories of information in industry 4.0 (Iqbal et al., 2018). An information category could be that needed for machine-to-machine communication, machine-to-human communication, human-to-human communication etc. Despite the diverse perception of credibility in the Industry 4.0 context, the credibility of information sources still plays a vital role in the persuasion of quality information (Flanagin et al., 2014). And this is especially so for virtual organizations.

As most industry 4.0 applications require information from disparate information sources (mentioned in the previous paragraph), one of the major challenges in the implementation of industry 4.0 is the integration of information from disparate information sources with the prevalence of information pollution (Bauer et al., 2016). This also becomes more challenging if the industry 4.0 organization is a virtual organization. The reason for the information integration challenge is the exponential increase in infollution, resident in the big data generated an industry 4.0 organization. Currently virtual organizations are still searching for the perfect means for sifting through big data for credible information needed by virtual teams. Therefore with the exponentially increasing infollution, employees in the organizations and virtual organization are unable to integrate quality information into their decision-making processes (Eppler & Helfert, 2004). Thus, infollution is a critical problem in today's world and industry 4.0 (Iqbal et al., 2018). This is more so as organisations become more and more dependent on information to achieve their objectives. (Iqbal et al., 2018).

In conclusion to this section, poor information quality is pervasive and costly. Information within organisational stores are neither entirely accurate nor complete (Nelson, Todd, & Wixom, 2005). Error rates up to 75% are being reported, while error rates up to 30% are customary (Batini, Cappiello, Francalanci, & Maurino, 2009). Infollution may lead to real losses both economically and socially. When people select alternatives based on limited resources (information), these misinformed individuals are more likely to make poor decisions (Madnick et al., 2009). Decisions based on low-quality information can cost organisations billions of dollars (Madnick, Wang, Lee, & Zhu, 2009).

Now, let's narrow down the discussion specifically to how Infollution affects Virtual organizations in industry 4.0. So far, the aim has been to build a preamble to this discussion.

INFOLLUTION, VIRTUAL ORGANIZATIONS AND INDUSTRY 4.0

In this section, the discussion will be on how infollution affects virtual organizations in the industry 4.0 sector. The discussion begins with the description of a virtual organization. This is followed by the impact of big data on industry 4.0 virtual organizations and how infollution affects virtual organization in industry 4.0.

Virtual Organizations

Virtual organizations are made up of virtual teams or group of employees in an organization dispersed geographically, organisationally and across time zones. These teams and their employees work together collaboratively using ICT to complete one or more assignments (Corvello & Migliarese, 2007). Advances in ICT sector, have enabled the organisations to operate virtually (Chumg, Seaton, Cooke, & Ding, 2016) to achieve a common goal through the flexible allocation of resources. In the same vain, virtual teams exist in industry 4.0 organizations. These teams could be part of the management, administrative or production processes. It is important to note that the context of this chapter is not in the production processes. However, there are more virtual organizations today due to the advancement in ICT. And researchers are now recommending the establishment of more flexible organisational structures, such as virtual organisations, in order to adapt to the technological changes in the business environment (W. Y. Wang & Chan, 2010). Never the less, as industry 4.0

is driven by big data, what do virtual industries use big data for? This is discussed in the next section.

Industry 4.0 Virtual Organizations and Big Data Usage

Virtual organizations also exist in the industry 4.0 context as alluded to in the previous section. These organizations utilize a big data for their management, administrative and production processes. Big data in Industry 4.0 virtual organizations has an impact on the decision making process in the area of the organization's management, organisational structure, and the evolutionary game theory processes used in the organization. In addition, it also enables virtual organizations to identify new business opportunities. Therefore the big data creates the possibility for the virtual organisation to find more suitable partners; use technology effectively; enable industry integration; and search for business cooperation benefits. Let's take the finding of new partners as an example. The quick identification of potential partners with required competencies from a broad spectrum of possible partners is vital for any organization. This is not different in the case of an industry 4.0 virtual organization. Such a virtual organisation may use coping strategies such as filtering, and withdrawal strategies, based on the criteria of information required and the reduced number of information sources respectively, to deal with the big data. Now knowing what we know now about infollution and big data. The next question is how does infollution affect virtual organizations? This is discussed in the next section.

Virtual Organisation and Information Pollution in Industry 4.0

As organizations generate big data, information pollution becomes a problem. As mentioned in the previous section, industry 4.0 facilitate exponential infollution. Nevertheless, industry 4.0 virtual organisations may not suffer the adverse effect as other organizations. This is because these virtual organizations may easily get quality information in the presence of proliferating infollution, since they themselves are producing big data themselves. They will have a mechanism for filtering the data. The challenge for them will arise in a situation where the data is externally generated and delivered to them.

In the same vain, smaller industry 4.0 virtual organizations may also fell a lesser effect of infollution. This is because they might be concerned with the organisational structure where enhanced effectiveness and efficiency of the management practices are promoted by handling them in a flexible way (Ferreira, de Lima, & da Costa, 2012). However in a larger industry 4.0 virtual organization, there are bound to be challenges due to the complexities of their internal procedure and operations.

Although infollution will affect different industry 4.0 virtual organizations in different ways, it is likely that Industry 4.0, which is advanced ICT, will further enhance some positive transformation in virtual organizations with respect to dealing with infollution. As new tools and applications are being developed, it is likely that the transformation will be focused on the delivery of more enhanced value, credible and quality information. This transformation will enhance internal operations as well as enhance the external operations of the virtual organization. It will also solidify external partnerships between virtual companies which will enable access quality information; acquisition and jointly building of information sources and risk sharing in decision-making. The internal transformation will enable the adoption of internal processes that will enable the ability to gather quality information; and the promotion of knowledge sharing activities - where employees share information through email and sometimes opt for video conferencing, thereby facilitating the redistribution of credible information within the organization.

Although certain industry 4.0 virtual organizations are expected to fare better when it comes to dealing with infollution, this does not imply that there will be no challenges. A challenge that could degrade the quality of information shared in any virtual organization could be the trust deficit among staff members (McCarter & Northcraft, 2007). Another challenge is that the internal competition among stakeholders in a virtual organisation could raise further objection about information quality. This requires balancing the self-interest of different stakeholders which can be achieved by effectively managing infollution.

CONCLUSION

The preceding discussion depicts that infollution is here to stay. As big data is generated in industry 4.0 virtual organizations, it is likely that infollution will be on the increase. This chapter focused on the managerial significance of Infollution in such organizations. However, infollution will also affect the technical aspect of virtual organizations in industry 4.0, since they are data driven as well. But as that is not the scope of the chapter, nothing is mentioned about it. However, there are a need for information professionals, academicians, computer scientists, and knowledge management specialists to develop strategies to keep the adverse effects of infollution to a minimum. This will provide new effective and innovative techniques for information seekers to manage infollution and secure, reliable information.

REFERENCES

Alenezi, H., Tarhini, A., & Sharma, S. K. (2015). Development of quantitative model to investigate the strategic relationship between information quality and e-government benefits. *Transforming Government: People, Process and Policy, 9*(3), 324–351.

Association, A. L. (2008). *Presidential committee on information literacy.* Retrieved from http://www. ala. org/ala/acrl/acrlpubs/whitepapers/presidential. cfm

Batini, C., Cappiello, C., Francalanci, C., & Maurino, A. (2009). Methodologies for data quality assessment and improvement. *ACM Computing Surveys, 41*(3), 16. doi:10.1145/1541880.1541883

Bauer, H., Baur, C., Mohr, D., Tschiesner, A., Weskamp, T., Alicke, K., & Kelly, R. (2016). *Industry 4.0 after the initial hype–Where manufacturers are finding value and how they can best capture it.* McKinsey Digital.

Bawden, D., & Robinson, L. (2009). The dark side of information: Overload, anxiety and other paradoxes and pathologies. *Journal of Information Science, 35*(2), 180–191. doi:10.1177/0165551508095781

Chen, Y.-C., Shang, R.-A., & Kao, C.-Y. (2009). The effects of information overload on consumers' subjective state towards buying decision in the internet shopping environment. *Electronic Commerce Research and Applications, 8*(1), 48–58. doi:10.1016/j.elerap.2008.09.001

Chumg, H.-F., Seaton, J., Cooke, L., & Ding, W.-Y. (2016). Factors affecting employees' knowledge-sharing behaviour in the virtual organisation from the perspectives of well-being and organisational behaviour. *Computers in Human Behavior, 64*, 432–448. doi:10.1016/j.chb.2016.07.011

Corvello, V., & Migliarese, P. (2007). Virtual forms for the organization of production: A comparative analysis. *International Journal of Production Economics, 110*(1-2), 5–15. doi:10.1016/j.ijpe.2007.02.006

Coult, G. (2008). Managing the 'information pollution'. *Managing Information, 14*(10), 10-12.

de Sousa Jabbour, A. B. L., Jabbour, C. J. C., Godinho Filho, M., & Roubaud, D. (2018). Industry 4.0 and the circular economy: A proposed research agenda and original roadmap for sustainable operations. *Annals of Operations Research*, 1–14.

Edmunds, A., & Morris, A. (2000). The problem of information overload in business organisations: A review of the literature. *International Journal of Information Management, 20*(1), 17–28. doi:10.1016/S0268-4012(99)00051-1

Eppler, M., & Helfert, M. (2004). *A classification and analysis of data quality costs.* Paper presented at the International Conference on Information Quality.

Fernández-Miranda, S. S., Marcos, M., Peralta, M., & Aguayo, F. (2017). The challenge of integrating Industry 4.0 in the degree of Mechanical Engineering. *Procedia Manufacturing, 13*, 1229–1236. doi:10.1016/j.promfg.2017.09.039

Ferreira, P. G. S., de Lima, E. P., & da Costa, S. E. G. (2012). Perception of virtual team's performance: A multinational exercise. *International Journal of Production Economics, 140*(1), 416–430. doi:10.1016/j.ijpe.2012.06.025

Flanagin, A. J., Metzger, M. J., Pure, R., Markov, A., & Hartsell, E. (2014). Mitigating risk in ecommerce transactions: Perceptions of information credibility and the role of user-generated ratings in product quality and purchase intention. *Electronic Commerce Research, 14*(1), 1–23. doi:10.100710660-014-9139-2

Ge, M., & Helfert, M. (2008). *Data and information quality assessment in information manufacturing systems.* Paper presented at the International Conference on Business Information Systems. 10.1007/978-3-540-79396-0_33

Han, J., Pei, J., & Kamber, M. (2011). *Data mining: concepts and techniques.* Elsevier.

Hoq, K. M. G. (2016). Information Overload: Causes, Consequences and Remedies-A Study. *Philosophy and Progress, 55*(1-2), 49–68. doi:10.3329/pp.v55i1-2.26390

Huang, G. Q., Zhang, Y., & Jiang, P. (2007). RFID-based wireless manufacturing for walking-worker assembly islands with fixed-position layouts. *Robotics and Computer-integrated Manufacturing, 23*(4), 469–477. doi:10.1016/j.rcim.2006.05.006

Iqbal, Q., Hassan, S. H., & Ahmad, N. H. (2018). The assessment of perceived information pollution in banking sector: A scale development and validation study. *Business Information Review, 35*(2), 68–76. doi:10.1177/0266382118772891

Jackson, T. W., & Farzaneh, P. (2012). Theory-based model of factors affecting information overload. *International Journal of Information Management, 32*(6), 523–532. doi:10.1016/j.ijinfomgt.2012.04.006

Kadiri, J. A., & Adetoro, N. A. (2012). Information Explosion and the Challenges of Information and Communication Technology Utilization in Nigerian Libraries and Information Centres. *Ozean Journal of Social Sciences, 5*(1), 21–30.

Kagermann, H., Helbig, J., Hellinger, A., & Wahlster, W. (2013). *Recommendations for implementing the strategic initiative INDUSTRIE 4.0: Securing the future of German manufacturing industry; final report of the Industrie 4.0 Working Group.* Forschungsunion.

Kean, T. (2011). *The 9/11 commission report: Final report of the national commission on terrorist attacks upon the United States.* Government Printing Office.

Kelton, K., Fleischmann, K. R., & Wallace, W. A. (2008). Trust in digital information. *Journal of the American Society for Information Science and Technology, 59*(3), 363–374. doi:10.1002/asi.20722

Kirsh, D. (2000). A few thoughts on cognitive overload. *Intellectica, 1*(30), 19–51.

Koh, S., Gunasekaran, A., & Rajkumar, D. (2008). ERP II: The involvement, benefits and impediments of collaborative information sharing. *International Journal of Production Economics, 113*(1), 245–268. doi:10.1016/j.ijpe.2007.04.013

Kurbanoglu, S., Grassian, E., Mizrachi, D., Catts, R., & Spiranec, S. (2013). *Worldwide Commonalities and Challenges in Information Literacy Research and Practice: European Conference, ECIL 2013, Istanbul, Turkey, October 22-25, 2013. Revised Selected Papers* (Vol. 397). Springer. 10.1007/978-3-319-03919-0

Kurniati, A. P., & Surendro, K. (2010). *Designing IQMM as a maturity model for information quality management.* Paper presented at the Informing Science & IT Education Conference (InSITE).

Kutty, A. D. (2006). *Managing Information Overload for Effective Decision-Making: An Empirical Study on Managers of the South Pacific (Master of Arts).* The University of the South Pacific.

Laudante, E. (2017). Industry 4.0, Innovation and Design. A new approach for ergonomic analysis in manufacturing system. *The Design Journal, 20*(sup1), S2724-S2734.

Lee, J., Kao, H.-A., & Yang, S. (2014). Service innovation and smart analytics for industry 4.0 and big data environment. *Procedia Cirp, 16*, 3–8. doi:10.1016/j.procir.2014.02.001

Lee, J., Park, D.-H., & Han, I. (2008). The effect of negative online consumer reviews on product attitude: An information processing view. *Electronic Commerce Research and Applications, 7*(3), 341–352. doi:10.1016/j.elerap.2007.05.004

Levis, M. (2011). *Information quality training requirements analysis guideline demonstrated in a healthcare context.* Dublin City University.

MacDonald, J., Bath, P., & Booth, A. (2011). Information overload and information poverty: Challenges for healthcare services managers? *The Journal of Documentation, 67*(2), 238–263. doi:10.1108/00220411111109458

Madnick, S. E., Wang, R. Y., Lee, Y. W., & Zhu, H. (2009). Overview and framework for data and information quality research. *Journal of Data and Information Quality*, *1*(1), 2. doi:10.1145/1515693.1516680

Mahler, J. G. (2009). *Organizational learning at NASA: The Challenger and Columbia accidents*. Georgetown University Press.

McCarter, M. W., & Northcraft, G. B. (2007). Happy together? Insights and implications of viewing managed supply chains as a social dilemma. *Journal of Operations Management*, *25*(2), 498–511. doi:10.1016/j.jom.2006.05.005

McKinsey, D. (2016). Industry 4.0 after the initial hype. Retrieved from McKinsey&Company: https://www.mckinsey.com/~/media/mckinsey/business%20functions/mckinsey%20digital/our%20insights/getting%20the%20most%20out%20of%20industry%204%200/mckinsey_industry_40_2016.ashx

Neilson, L. C., & Chadha, M. (2008). International marketing strategy in the retail banking industry: The case of ICICI Bank in Canada. *Journal of Financial Services Marketing*, *13*(3), 204–220. doi:10.1057/fsm.2008.21

Nelson, R. R., Todd, P. A., & Wixom, B. H. (2005). Antecedents of information and system quality: An empirical examination within the context of data warehousing. *Journal of Management Information Systems*, *21*(4), 199–235. doi:10.1080/07421222.2005.11045823

Ou, C. X., & Davison, R. M. (2011). Interactive or interruptive? Instant messaging at work. *Decision Support Systems*, *52*(1), 61–72. doi:10.1016/j.dss.2011.05.004

Ozdemir, Ş. (2016). Individual contributions to infollution (information pollution): Trust and share. *International Journal on New Trends in Education and Their Implications*, *7*(3), 23–33.

Pandita, R. (2014). Information pollution, a mounting threat: Internet a major causality. *Journal of Information Science Theory and Practice*, *2*(2), 49–60. doi:10.1633/JISTaP.2014.2.4.4

Prause, G. (2015). Sustainable business models and structures for Industry 4.0. *Journal of Security & Sustainability Issues*, *5*(2), 159–169. doi:10.9770/jssi.2015.5.2(3)

Preece, A., Missier, P., Embury, S., Jin, B., & Greenwood, M. (2008). An ontology-based approach to handling information quality in e-Science. *Concurrency and Computation*, *20*(3), 253–264. doi:10.1002/cpe.1195

Reedy, K., Mallett, E., & Soma, N. (2013). iKnow: Information skills in the 21st century workplace. *Library and Information Research, 37*(114), 105-122.

Samadi, M., & Yaghoob-Nejadi, A. (2009). A survey of the effect of consumers' perceived risk on purchase intention in e-shopping. *Business Intelligence Journal*, *2*(2), 261–275.

Sasaki, Y., Kawai, D., & Kitamura, S. (2015). The anatomy of tweet overload: How number of tweets received, number of friends, and egocentric network density affect perceived information overload. *Telematics and Informatics*, *32*(4), 853–861. doi:10.1016/j.tele.2015.04.008

Soucek, R., & Moser, K. (2010). Coping with information overload in email communication: Evaluation of a training intervention. *Computers in Human Behavior*, *26*(6), 1458–1466. doi:10.1016/j.chb.2010.04.024

Stover, A., & Nielsen, J. (2002). *E-mail newsletter usability: 79 design guidelines for subscription, newsletter content and account maintenance based on usability studies*. Fremont, CA: Nielsen Norman Group.

Strong, D. M., Lee, Y. W., & Wang, R. Y. (1997). Data quality in context. *Communications of the ACM*, *40*(5), 103–110. doi:10.1145/253769.253804

Swar, B., Hameed, T., & Reychav, I. (2017). Information overload, psychological ill-being, and behavioral intention to continue online healthcare information search. *Computers in Human Behavior*, *70*, 416–425. doi:10.1016/j.chb.2016.12.068

Wang, R. Y. (1998). A product perspective on total data quality management. *Communications of the ACM*, *41*(2), 58–65. doi:10.1145/269012.269022

Wang, W. Y., & Chan, H. K. (2010). Virtual organization for supply chain integration: Two cases in the textile and fashion retailing industry. *International Journal of Production Economics*, *127*(2), 333–342. doi:10.1016/j.ijpe.2009.08.006

Wardle, C., & Derakhshan, H. (2017). *Information Disorder: Toward an interdisciplinary framework for research and policymaking*. Council of Europe report, DGI(2017), 9.

Widen, G., Steinerová, J., & Voisey, P. (2014). Conceptual modelling of workplace information practices: a literature review. *Information Research, 19*(4).

Zaveri, A., Rula, A., Maurino, A., Pietrobon, R., Lehmann, J., & Auer, S. (2016). Quality assessment for linked data: A survey. *Semantic Web, 7*(1), 63–93. doi:10.3233/SW-150175

Zhang, Y., Qu, T., Ho, O. K., & Huang, G. Q. (2011). Agent-based smart gateway for RFID-enabled real-time wireless manufacturing. *International Journal of Production Research*, *49*(5), 1337–1352. doi:10.1080/00207543.2010.518743

Zhang, Y., Zhang, G., Wang, J., Sun, S., Si, S., & Yang, T. (2015). Real-time information capturing and integration framework of the internet of manufacturing things. *International Journal of Computer Integrated Manufacturing*, *28*(8), 811–822. doi:10.1080/0951192X.2014.900874

Chapter 6

Generating Big Data:
Leveraging on New Media for Value Creation

Ezer Osei Yeboah-Boateng
Ghana Technology University College, Ghana

ABSTRACT

Big data is characterized as huge datasets generated at a fast rate, in unstructured, semi-structured, and structured data formats, with inconsistencies and disparate data types and sources. The challenge is having the right tools to process large datasets in an acceptable timeframe and within reasonable cost range. So, how can social media big datasets be harnessed for best value decision making? The approach adopted was site scraping to collect online data from social media and other websites. The datasets have been harnessed to provide better understanding of customers' needs and preferences. It's applied to design targeted campaigns, to optimize business processes, and to improve performance. Using the social media facts and rules, a multivariate value creation decision model was built to assist executives to create value based on improved "knowledge" in a hindsight-foresight-insight continuum about their operations and initiatives and to make informed decisions. The authors also demonstrated use cases of insights computed as equations that could be leveraged to create sustainable value.

DOI: 10.4018/978-1-5225-7519-1.ch006

INTRODUCTION

Social media gives everyone - not only B2B companies but also consumer brands, consultants, non-profits, and even rock bands, churches, and colleges - a tremendous opportunity to reach people and engage them in new and different ways. Now we can earn attention by creating something interesting and valuable and then publishing it online for free: a YouTube video, a blog, a research report, photos, a Twitter stream, an e-book, a Facebook page. Those measurements, which seemed so great in an offline world, are wholly inadequate online. But what should we do instead? A debate has raged in recent years. On one hand, people tried to adapt old (but successful) offline measurements to the social media world. David Meerman Scott, (culled from the Foreword of (Sterne, 2010, p. x))

The above quote can be said to be a synopsis of this book chapter on Leveraging on New Media for Value Creation. New Media and its associated infrastructure of Information Systems play crucial roles in businesses today. Businesses have become dependent on Information systems, and indeed, the survival of businesses is hinged on the importance placed on information systems.

As technology becomes more pervasive, flexible and easier to use, the issues of globalization affect every business (Piccoli, 2013). The market place has expanded from hitherto local economies to a global space. To compete effectively and efficiently, decision-makers require secured, relevant and accurate information or data. The size of data, as well as its mostly unstructured complex nature, and coupled with the rate at which data is generated – Big Data – is the object of this study.

Traditionally, in industrial economies, there have been three (3) factors of production until in recent times. The Financial Times, in its December 27, 2012 edition, posited that "Big Data" has assumed the 4th factor of production, considering its pivotal role in business decision-making (Jones, 2012). Big data appeals to corporate executives and business leaders, with such intuition and creative thinking – that are unexpectedly emanating from data patterns (Dunlop, 2015). In terms of value creation, Big Data could be harnessed for value creation or competitive advantage, especially when an increased range of data sources are employed. Jones (2012) posits that Big Data can be harnessed for value creation by employing both subjective and objective decision-making approaches, i.e. "intuitive and analytical thinking".

Big Data can be used to manage the limited government resources to the right people at the right time. For example, Predictive Policing uses data to predict where crimes might occur, so that police can deploy its limited resources efficiently (Dunlop, 2015). That is, Big Data is used to identify people and locations at risk of crime.

Big Data is basically "large datasets (with vast amounts of data) with an irregular structure" involving high storage of data. Big Data is about the customer behavior, rather than the transactions carried out (Chen, Mao, & Liu, 2014). Big Data finds various uses from social media user generated data (Baker, 2013) (Dunlop, 2015) (Cerrato, 2012).

Big data is usually multivariate in nature – and in enterprises, must, should and ought to fit into the key processes and more importantly, to create value for the business. Big Data – should, must and ought – NOT to be:

1. Disorganized;
2. Dysfunctional and unusable;
3. Disconnected from business strategy; and
4. Denying business leaders the needed intelligence to make key informed decisions.

In discussing Big Data value creation, Preator (2018) avers that there needs to be organizational clarity and alignment with the business strategy. In essence, Big Data value creation must, necessarily:

1. Connect the overall corporate critical data to the Big Data strategy. He goes on to define Critical Data as the business side data and which represents less than 10% of the total data that the business generates or consumes;
2. Drive key business decisions using critical data, that is used or relied on heavily by business leaders;
3. Monitor key processes, leading to product development and delivery; and to harness Big Data to generate profits;
4. Generate insights for business leaders from the critical data used;
5. Ensure significant rigor and governance with the Big Data generated.

Some attributes or criteria for high quality critical data are:

1. Critical to business operations;
2. Critical for benchmarking;
3. Critical for regulatory compliance, governance and standardization;
4. Critical for key business decisions;
5. Crucial source of security intelligence;
6. Critical to intelligence sharing; i.e. security intelligence involving utilizing and sharing information, such as domain name; URL patterns; filenames; malicious attachments; etc.

Using the Scrum methodology and scraping, we gleaned through extensive literature of key articles, online databases, and authorities, towards improving the value creation with Big Data strategies and appropriating or sustaining the gains made (Yeboah-Boateng, 2017). Typically, the agile development model requires extreme agility with benchmarking the metric for new media and its associated computations.

This study is an exploratory data analytics of Big Data and value creation aspects of knowledge management practices employed in new media. Sources of data have been employing use cases of domestic, transnational and global literature on Big Data value creation focusing on new media. In this adapted approach, a variety of techniques are employed to optimize the insights into datasets, to extract important variables or constructs (presented in equations), and to develop a parsimonious model (Aarts, 2007). It is hinged on the use of simplest assumption of creating value from Big Data, using case examples of social media, to gain insights into new media generated Big Data.

A conceptual decision model depicting the flow processes of Big Data multivariate datasets is modeled against various levels of value creation required for decision-making. The decision model shows the value creation processes using Big Data generated from new media data acquisition, processing, analysis and utilization. The abscissa represents the various processing phases of multivariate datasets from its capturing through analysis to utilization. The ordinate represents values created from gleaning through raw datasets to information and subsequently the knowledge gained. The model shows the flow control throughout the predictive and prescriptive analytics, as the values derived from knowledge are utilized for decision-making.

Problem Formulation

First of all, the problem with data, which ought to be dealt with, is that it exceeds the ability of traditional tools to manipulate them. The term "Big Data" refers to datasets so large and complex that traditional tools, like relational databases, are unable to process them in an acceptable timeframe or within reasonable cost range.

Some of the problems associated with Big Data are enumerated below:

1. Sourcing;
2. Moving;
3. Searching;
4. Storing;
5. Analyzing the data, etc.

The problems manifest with the following characteristics and categories (Firican, 2017) (Thomas, Therlal, & Danytel, 2015):

1. **Volume:** The overall size of the datasets, with the possibility of storing the same data (e.g. photos) across multiple platforms; i.e. characteristically the data is co-evolutionary – interactivity produces new patterns and structures of data;
2. **Velocity:** The rate at which the data arrives (either generated or produced or created or refreshed) and also how fast it needs to be processed; i.e. characteristically the data is non-linear – with unpredictable data flow and in any direction;
3. **Variety:** The wide range of data that the database may contain – i.e. web logs, audio, images, sensor or device data, and unstructured text, among many other types; i.e. characteristically the data is dynamic – changing continuously and at different rates and times;
4. **Veracity:** The reliability of data source, its context and associated meaning; i.e. characteristically the data exhibits uncertainty – with unpredictable but expected interactive outcomes;
5. **Value:** Implies the business value derived from the data; i.e. characteristically the data is emergent – with diverse interactions producing new patterns, ideas or knowledge and highly context-dependent.

Peter Drucker has said that "you can only manage what can measure". Social Media analytics ought to define succinctly the metrics being employed or deployed. For example, how does the organization classifies a podcast that has been accessed a million times? Does it suffice to represent an awareness created, or a mere engagement and/or interaction?

The problems reside with the stakeholders; implying, the users do not want to undertake the measurement process (Sterne, 2010). So, we need to be creative in order to, first achieve the business objectives and then, to align them to the business strategy – i.e. sustaining the gains or appropriating value creation.

It must be noted that with the right tools these problems can be overcome.

Key Research Questions and Objectives

Based on innovative parsimonious methodology, and cognizance of criterion for model specification, which "… is just one of several quality criteria that should be observed in empirical research" (Aarts, 2007, p. 4), key research questions and objectives for this study are presented hereunder:

1.   How can knowledge capturing and utilization activities be harnessed for best-value decision-making?
2.   What are the computational tools and concerns for capturing new media based Big Data?
3.   What are the strategies employed to harness new media for Big Data value creation?

The objectives of the study are as follows:

1.   To design a value-creation based Big Data generated model to utilize actionable information for decision-making;
2.   To assess some computational formulae used in benchmarking new media based Big Data;
3.   To explore some strategic approaches needed to enhance new media generated Big Data.

Highlights of Findings

Key findings are the catalogue of computational equations used in benchmarking the new media analytics utilized by corporate executives for competitive advantage. Similarly, an intuitive strategic Big Data based Multivariate Value Creation (MVC) decision model aimed at assisting stakeholders as a guide in gathering, processing, analyzing and utilizing actionable information that could be harnessed to formulate appropriate competitive advantage strategy is proposed.

Significance of the Chapter

The study's appeal with perspectives from Big Data and knowledge management – from datasets generated, captured and processed, analyzed and utilized, to create value. It presents knowledge levels needed by corporate executives to make important strategic decisions towards competitive advantage. The treatise is enhanced with diverse discourse on discovery informatics and new media analytics leveraged to position the organization, especially SMEs, to leapfrog the competition using social media metrics and computations. In spite of the nascent literature on Big Data and Value Creation, this study seeks to contribute to the body of knowledge with the strategic decision model of intuitive reasoning applied to enhance competitive advantage within one's market, using social media.

Outline of the Chapter

This introductory section dealt with overview of Big Data and new media aspects of knowledge management generation and utilization. Followed by related works on knowledge-based modeling, Big Data, new media metrics and datasets, approaches employed in processing Big Data generated. Agile techniques employed to source data are discussed. By intuitive deductions and critical thinking the model is designed and its implications for strategic value creation based on Big Data decision making follows, and then conclusion and recommendations.

LITERATURE REVIEW

This section deals with the key thematic areas of the study. It commences with the knowledge-based system modeling, dealing with social media domain-specific facts and rules as the fundamental knowledge elements upon which the conceptual knowledge-based value creation decision model is built.

Then, the concept of Big Data is discussed in respect of challenges and prospects and its life-cycle. Various approaches necessary for dealing with Big Data are also discussed.

The concept of new media follows. Social media as a form of new media, with its class of tools and technologies employed to create value are discussed. The foundational social media metrics that organizations use to measure the value contributions of social media are also discussed extensively. Social media analytics and sample computations are illustrated.

Finally, value creation strategies, with emphasis on social media generated Big Data, are presented.

Knowledge-Based Modeling

Traditionally, Knowledge-based systems were developed to argument the scarcity of human expertise. The systems elicited expert opinions, then captured expert problem-solving skills and translated them into computational rules that can be implemented in knowledge-based systems. The computerized system has the advantages of being consistent and accurate in performance, once the system is trained with the acquired datasets.

It must be noted that the general purpose system (GPS) theory of knowledge-based systems, reckons that domain-specific datasets are necessary in resolving real-life corporate problems (Ericsson & Smith, 1991) (Witteman & Krol, 2005). In essence, in this study social media datasets, comprising facts and rules (which could be manifested as metrics, and presented herein as equations) are acquired for the conceptual value creation model. These knowledge-based elements are combined to formulate various metrics or computational equations or logical sets.

The notion of knowledge-based value creation model is such that datasets generated and captured are not merely to be stored, but also to process them to provide needed advice or aids, in guiding corporate executives in decision-making. Furthermore, it is noted that the knowledge elements (i.e. facts and rules) are encoded separately so that problem-solving models can be applied to similar domains, without necessarily re-modeling the entire knowledge-based system. For example, though this study hinges on social media, the main datasets are gathered from Twitter specific domain, but the model must be applicable to Facebook and/or other social media platforms.

Typically, knowledge-based systems modeling involves task analysis, knowledge acquisition, modeling and knowledge representation, implementation and testing (Witteman & Krol, 2005). In this study, the task analysis and knowledge acquisition are combined as the Big Data acquisition phase, whilst the modeling involves Big Data processing and analysis. Ultimately, the knowledge representation is the Big Data utilization as it's only a conceptual model rather than a typical knowledge-based system.

Big Data

Big Data is often perceived as the storage, processing and analysis of large and diverse datasets emanating from disparate sources. Typically, Big Data computations are employed whenever traditional storage, processing and analytical techniques are unsuitable to process large multivariate datasets, usually gleaned or combined from different and diverse sources, and with time-sensitive or streaming-centric processing demands imposed (Erl, Khattak, & Buhler, 2016).

Big Data is at the inception of the problem with Data. Datasets that are so large and complex such that traditional tools, e.g. relational databases, are unable to process them "in an acceptable time frame or within a reasonable cost" (Frampton, 2015).

There are some problems associated with data in respect of sourcing, moving, storing, searching, and analyzing the data. Some initiatives aimed at addressing the problems with data, include Big Data manipulation (Frampton, 2015, p. 3):

1. A method of collecting and categorizing data;
2. A method of moving data into the system safely and without data loss;

3. A storage system that
    a. Is distributed across many servers;
    b. Is scalable to thousands of servers;
    c. Will offer data redundant and backup;
    d. Will offer redundancy in case of hardware failure;
    e. Will be cost-effective;
4. A rich tool set and community support;
5. A method of distributed system configuration;
6. Parallel data processing;
7. System-monitoring tools;
8. Reporting tools;
9. ETL-like tools (preferably with a graphic interface) that can be used to build tasks that process the data and monitor their progress;
10. Scheduling tools to determine when tasks will run and show task status;
11. The ability to monitor data trends in real time;
12. Local processing where the data is stored to reduce network bandwidth usage.

Big Data reports or results generated, must communicate to the organization; how do customers or partners think, act or use the services or products – that the organization wasn't aware of previously? The data must tell a story. The results must transform the data from numbers to impressionable information or actionable information, which is knowledge. It must deliver some context around the data; thus, humanizing the information for its targeted audience.

The definitions attributed to Big Data could be time-dependent. For example, 40 Gigabytes of data in the 1970's was "Big Data" at that time, whereas the same size of data in 2018 could be processed and stored by possibly a Smartphone.

"Data Analysis is the process of examining data to find facts, relationships, patterns, insights and/or trends" (Erl, Khattak, & Buhler, 2016, p. 21). Data Analysis encompasses the complete data life-cycle, consisting of data collection, data cleansing, data organization, data storage, data analysis and data governance (Erl, Khattak, & Buhler, 2016).

Big Data Analytics involves the identification, procurement, preparation and analysis of large datasets of raw, unstructured data to extract meaningful information (or insights) that could be used as inputs for pattern identification, enrichment of existing datasets, and performance of large-scale searches (Erl, Khattak, & Buhler, 2016).

Big Data analytics herein take various phases and are basically summed up as follows:

1. **Descriptive Analytics:** Used to resolve or address events that have already occurred. For example, what is the number of distress or emergency calls received as categorized by severity and base stations or cell sites? It is noteworthy, that descriptive analysis provide the least worth value and required a relatively basic skillset, usually presented in data grids or charts.
2. **Diagnostic Analytics:** Used to determine the cause of a phenomenon that occurred in the past using questions that focus on the reason behind the event. For example, why have there been more calls originating from the business district than from the free-zone enclave? It is noted that, Diagnostic analytics provide more value than descriptive analytics, but require a more advanced skillset.

Diagnostic analytics usually require collecting data from multiple sources and storing it in a structure that lends itself to performing drill-down and roll-up analysis; presented using interactive visualization tools that enable users to identify trends and patterns.

3. **Predictive Analytics:** Used to determine the outcome of an event that might occur in the future. It is used with enriched information; i.e. the strength and magnitude of associations form the basis of models that are used to generate future predictions based on past events. It is usually formulated using a what-if rationale statements; e.g. what are the chances that a customer will default on a loan if they have missed a monthly payment?

Predictive analytics predicts the outcomes of events, and predictions are made based on patterns, trends and exceptions found in historical and current data. It is often used to identify risk and opportunities.

4. **Prescriptive Analytics:** Used to build upon the results of predictive analytics by prescribing actions that should be taken. It provides results with embedded elements of situational understanding. It is used to gain an advantage or mitigate a risk. For example, among three (3) mobile network operators in the rural area, which one provides the best quality connections?

It is noted that, prescriptive analytics provide more value than any other type of analytics, and require the most advanced skillset. Various outcomes are calculated and the best course of action for each outcome is suggested. It also incorporates both internal and external data sources. The internal data is from internal sources within the organization; such as current and historical sales data, customer information, product data, business rules, etc. External data, on the other hand, are from external sources outside of the organization; such as social media data, weather forecast, government produced demographics data, etc.

Typically, prescriptive analytics utilizes business rules and large amounts of internal and external data to simulate outcomes and prescribe the best course of action.

New Media

New Media is a relative term. It refers to those digital media that are highly interactive, incorporate two-way communications and involves some form of computing. New Media is native to computers. Social Media is a form of new media that relies heavily on the participation of users to provide value. They are present with mobile Apps, video, Podcasts, e-books, Blogs, emails, etc. These media create what is known as findable media object of value.

New Media metrics include visitors, visits, page views, and increasingly, events that are so widely used in online marketing and digital business functions; these have become a common currency against which all efforts are judged.

Social Media is a class of tools and technologies used to describe media that drives its value from social interactions. It is about formulating and enhancing relationships. This characteristics render social media adept for value creation strategies through customer intimacy.

In systems analysis, the social media relationship is characterized by both one-to-many and many-to-many relations. That is, a social media platform may be able to generate many data sources, such as real-time feeds, raw datasets, historic datasets, cleaned datasets, as well as value-added datasets (Batrinca & Treleaven, 2015). Similarly, different social media platforms could also generate similar datasets as above.

Social Media Analytics metrics include:

1. Interaction
2. Engagement
3. Influence
4. Advocates
5. Impact

Foundational measures can be used across any social media channel and the individual inputs should be modified to fit each distinct channel. By calculating the measures in the same way, you can create consistency across different platforms and channels (Lovett, 2011, p. 172).

There is the need to establish a baseline first before building the key performance indicators (KPIs) or assigning values to specific metrics (Lovett, 2011).

In this study, we herewith adapt the following baseline metrics from (Lovett, 2011) as the basis for computations and discussions of measures through which business values are created, or as the case may be, strategies are developed.

1. Interaction must be measured against a specific marketing initiative. It's evaluated within specific channels or across multiple channels for comparison. It's a composite measure of number of views, unique visitors, shares, conversions surrounding an initiative. The organization can evaluate the percentage of interactions against a benchmark of all visitors. It is given by

$$Interaction = \frac{Conversions}{Activity}$$

It must be noted that Interaction is active, not passive, and it requires sharing, submitting or transacting with the social media channel.

2. *Engagement:* (Lovett, 2011, p. 173) posits that "numerous engagement calculations exist, some of which are as simple as $(time + pageviews)$, and others are extremely complex". The organization is enjoined to find a measure that works for its business needs and which can be explained to its stakeholders. It is computed as a relative score from 1 to 100, whereby numbers below 50 indicate less engaging topics or initiatives, and numbers greater than 50 indicate highly engaging topics or initiatives. It can also be weighted; e.g. comments and shares are more valuable than time. It is given by

$$Engagement = Visits * Time * Comments * Shares$$
$$\forall \, less \, engaging \, topic \leq 50 \, \& \, more \, engaging \, topic > 50$$

It involves read, converse, comment, and participate.

3. Influence is a relative power to affect other people regarding a specific brand, topic or field of expertise. It is not measured by sheer volume of fans or followers a person has, but rather a demonstration of expertise to sway others into action. It is a measure of authority and it is given by:

$$Influence = VolumeofRelevantContent * Comments * Shares * Reach$$

It must be noted that Reach represents potential, which is akin to the impressions metric in advertising (c.f. impressions in Twitter, for example).

4. Advocacy (Advocates) is concerned with a person who acts as a proponent for a brand or cause. Often, advocates act independently of the organizations. It is measured using a combination of sentiment analysis, influence, and commitment to the brand. Advocacy is a measure of positive Influence. It fosters interaction, engagement and impact. It is given by:

$$Advocacy = Influence * PositiveSentiment$$

5. Impact is the ability of a person to guide the outcome of derived events as measured against specific goals, a.k.a. campaign return on investment (ROI). It answers the return of investment questions within social media.

It is a measure of success towards desired outcomes. It is measured in terms of tangible results against expectations set forth when determining business objectives. For example, if the goal of a specific marketing campaign is to acquire a thousand new customers, Impact should be measured as total exposure divided by total new customer acquisitions.

$$Impact = \frac{TotalExposure}{TotalNewCustomersAcquisitions}$$

Organizations can measure Impact using purely digital metrics and attribution tactics or with a mix of qualitative metrics and anecdotal evidence. It is a critical component of gauging the overall success of organization's social media activity. It is given by:

$$Impact = \frac{Outcomes}{(Interactions + Engagement)}$$

6. Exposure is the 21st century equivalent of brand marketing because it is a measure of how far and wide the organization's message travels via social media channels. It's usually about Awareness, which is a precursor to starting

a dialogue, engaging consumers, or encouraging interactions. Exposure is given by the following metrics:

$$Reach = SeedAudience * SharedNetworkAudience$$

$$Velocity = Reach * Time$$

$$ShareofVoice = \frac{BrandMentions}{TotalMentions\left\{Brand + \sum_{i=1}^{n} Competitor\right\}}$$

Practically, the organization can reach more targeted audience using the boosting feature in Facebook Page, for example.

7. Other supporting computations are used, such as the following:

$$IssueResoultionRate = \frac{Total\,\#\,IssuesResolvedSatisfactorily}{Total\,\#\,ServiceIssues}$$

$$ResolutionTime = \frac{TotalInquiryResponseTime}{Total\,\#\,ServiceInquiries}$$

$$SatisfactionScore = \frac{CustomerFeedback\left\{\sum_{i=1}^{n} Input\right\}}{AllCustomerFeedback}$$

Social Analytics and Computations

Most of the social media datasets are unstructured data. Typically, unstructured data doesn't conform to a data model or data schema. It is mostly textual or binary in form, it may be self-contained or non-relational. For example, a text file containing various tweets or blog postings. A binary file may be the media file containing image, audio or video data. It requires a special purpose logic to process and store data. For example, to play a video file, the correct codec (coder-decoder) is required.

Metadata provides information about the dataset's characteristics and structure. It is often machine-generated and its' appended to the data. It's crucial to the storage and processing of the Big Data. For example, XML tags providing the author and creation date of document, attributes providing the file size and resolution of a digital photograph.

In furtherance of actionable information or knowledge, the social media datasets collected can be correlated, consolidated and contextualized to create value. Various data sources are herein considered, including logs, network packets, Likes, Engagement, Reach, Demographics, Page Views, Posts, Actions on page, events, videos, people or visitors, messages, promotions, branded content, etc. The metrics depict how the content or initiative is resonating with the targeted audience, and can offer overviews or insights of social media strategy.

The strategic value-added, notwithstanding, the social media metrics can assist in measuring, managing, improving on the metrics themselves, and to improve on the measurement system (Lovett, 2011).

It must be noted that the key objectives of social media analytics are:

1.   To have an understanding of preferences and onsite behavioral patterns of patrons and/or visitors to social media campaigns through baselining;
2.   To inform on future campaigns and product development and delivery;
3.   To correlate social media metrics and campaign performance metrics, interactions and impact of social media channels.

For example, Twitter datasets (as monitored within 6 minutes after Tweet) are presented hereunder to buttress the essence of creating value using social media. It could be deduced that social campaigns seem to have more influence or impact than technology and political issues.

Creating value with social media could be involving and the metrics sometimes may be fuzzy. Merely having more friends and followers in social media doesn't imply that the product is superior per se. Admittedly, this could be harnessed to create value. Some important metrics, according to (Sterne, 2010, p. 107) are as follows:

1.   How many shared a link to the product's content, for example?

Table 1. Twitter datasets (monitored 6 minutes after tweet)

Metrics	Descriptors	Social	Technology	Political
Impressions	# times people saw this Tweet on Twitter	118	24	19
Total Engagements	# times people interacted with this Tweet	12	8	3
Details Expands	# times people viewed the details about this Tweet	8	7	2
Replies	# replies to this Tweet	4	3	1
Likes	# times people liked this Tweet	5	3	1

2. How many links have been shared?
3. How many people clicked through to it in a given time span?

Consolidating the issues emanating from the above, a given metric towards creating value may be given by:

$$ConversionsRate = \frac{\# \, of Visitors Comments}{\# \, of Posts}$$

In order to create value using social media initiatives or campaigns, the desired business outcomes must be measurable. These may include metrics or measures such as awareness, comments, posts, engagement and interactions (e.g. sign-ups, navigation, persuasion, conversions, web-hits, purchases, referrals, submissions, etc.) (Sterne, 2010).

According to Sterne (2010) irrespective of the metrics or computations adapted, the most important measures are those that drive the "business-critical action" (p.187).

Value Creation

Value is anything that is useful to the organization. It could tangible as well as intangible. Often, the tangible assets can easily be estimated in monetary value, whereas the intangible may be fuzzy, vague or uncertain and usually estimated by its utility value. Value is also associated with the quality, integrity and fidelity of the data or business assets.

Value as it pertains to Big Data has the following attributes (Erl, Khattak, & Buhler, 2016):

1. How well has the data been stored?
2. Were valuable attribute of the data removed during data cleansing?
3. Are the right types of questions being asked during data analysis?
4. Are the results of the analysis being accurately communicated to the appropriate decision-makers?

McKinsey& Co. (2011) recommends the following five (5) ways in which Big Data can create value:

1. Big Data can unleash significant value by making information transparent and usable in much higher frequency;

2. Organizations create and store more transactional data in digital form; they collect more accurate and detailed performance information on everything from product inventories to sick days, and these boost performance;
3. Big Data allows ever narrower segmentation of customers and, therefore, much more precisely tailored products or services;
4. Sophisticated analysis can substantially improve decision making;
5. Big Data can be used to improve the development of the next generation of products and services.

In creating value, for example for SMEs in developing economies, we recommend the use of Microsoft PowerPivot in Excel to facilitate the building up of data models with multivariate datasets using multiple tables. PowerPivot in Excel is capable of handling diverse data formats. Based on their file extensions used in storing the data or file, conversions may be necessary to facilitate PowerPivot to process the datasets. For example, the .XLSX extension format is the format that works with the PowerPivot, used in building Big Data models. Excel workbooks prior to 2007 Excel, had .XLS file extension; whereas later versions use the .XLSX extension, with second X indicating that the data is stored in XML format.

Conventionally, Excel functions as a database, with tables consisting of rows and columns. As a Schema, each row has a record, which includes its attributes, and each column is a field or attribute. Excel supports the importation of various data types and sources, such as text files, tables in a website, data in XML files and in JSON format (Dunlop, 2015).

It must be noted that Excel does not read the JavaScript Object Notation (JSON) format directly. Most data on NoSQL are stored in the JSON format; so in order to work with Excel it is converted into XML format and subsequently read.

The PowerPivot data model for Excel 2013 is built on the platform of tabular engine of SQL server Analysis Services 2012 running inside Excel. The data model facilitates the relating of multiple tables, which can run or process millions of rows of datasets (Dunlop, 2015).

Big Data initiatives are strategic in nature and should be business-driven. The adoption of Big Data can be transformative but is more often innovative. Transformation activities are typically low-risk endeavors designed to deliver increased efficiency and effectiveness, whereas, innovation requires a paradigm shift. Innovation alters the structure of a business in its products, services or organization.

Big Data analytics lifecycle involves identifying, procuring, filtering, extracting, cleansing, and aggregating of data.

Big Data builds upon business intelligence (BI) by acting upon cleansed, consolidated enterprise-wide data (with semi-structured and unstructured) sources (Dunlop, 2015). It utilizes both predictive and prescriptive analytics to create business value. The business value created is seen in patterns and anomalies, leading to discovery of insights. That is, acting upon multiple data sources simultaneously, with a variety of data formats (unstructured, semi-structured and structured).

In presenting the business value created (i.e. hindsight, foresight and insights), we note that traditional data visualization such as charts (static), maps, data grids, infographics and alerts, are usually not interactive. However, with Big Data visualization, the solutions have features which incorporate, predictive, prescriptive and transformative tools, with reduced latency (Erl, Khattak, & Buhler, 2016).

Some of these features include (Erl, Khattak, & Buhler, 2016, p. 97):

- **Aggregation:** Provides a holistic and summarized view of data across multiple contexts;
- **Drill-Down:** Enables a detailed view of the data of interest by focusing in on a data subset from the summarized view;
- **Filtering:** Helps focus on a particular set of data by filtering away the data that is not of immediate interest;
- **Roll-Up:** Groups data across multiple categories to show subtotals and totals;
- **What-If Analysis:** Enables multiple outcomes to be visualized by enabling relating factors to be dynamically changed.

Big Data analytics requires a shift from batch processing to real-time computation. It actually combines both statistical and computational approaches.

Firstly, from statistical approaches – there is a focus on quantifying the patterns and correlations found in the data. Here, the value is created from the datasets. Then, there is a re-focus on describing various data qualities using words. It must be noted that the value so generated herein is often fraught with human data interpretations or subjectivity. Next, we employ automated algorithms to sift through massive datasets to identify and extract hidden patterns and trends. Indeed, the value created herein forms the basis for predictive analytics and business intelligence.

With regards to the social media datasets –which are often in textual, image, audio and video formats – semantic analysis is employed to extract the valuable information from the datasets. Unstructured textual datasets are mined and discovered, then searched and analyzed to create value. In fact, the textual analytics involves two main steps (Erl, Khattak, & Buhler, 2016):

1. To parse text within documents to extract (e.g. named entities – person, group, place, company; pattern-based entities – social security number, Zip code; concepts – an abstract representation of an entity; facts – relationship between entities;));
2. To categorize documents using these extracted entities and facts.

The textual analytics is often enhanced with the support of sentiment analytics – which focuses on determining the bias or emotions of individuals and their feelings and extent of feelings. The value created is used in decision-making such as customer satisfaction determinants.

It must be noted that in Big Data, correlation assumes that the variables are independent and have no causation. It suggests that there is the possibility of the causative agent, known as the Confounding Factor. On the other hand, regression assumes that there's some dependency amongst the dependent and independent variables. So, in Big Data, correlation can be employed to identify the existence of a relationship, and then regression is used to explore the extent of the dependency.

METHODOLOGY

The notional objective of employing mathematical or computational approaches to problem-solving is to present accurate, precise and concise concepts or discoveries (Bindner & Ericsson, 2011). By extension, applying these principles to this study and adapting the Agile Scrum approach, the Big Data life cycle serves as the key model in developing a knowledge-based decision-making strategies. Here, we emphasize on the Big Data acquisition, Big Data processing, Big Data analytics and Big Data utilization or presentation.

Depending on the strategic abstraction of a particular knowledge-based model, Big Data and its associated value creation could be perceived as either a product or a service facilitated by the use cases of social media interactions.

Sources of data employed are some domestic, transnational and global literature on Big Data value creation. In this study, we carried out site scraping or web data extraction, which involved collecting online data from social media and other web sites in the form of unstructured text (Batrinca & Treleaven, 2015). We also conducted extensive literature review of key articles, databases, repositories, and authorities, with the view to examining value creation approaches when using social media networks and platforms.

Also, cognizance of the agile requirements in respect of benchmarking, we adapted (Lovett, 2011) (Erl, Khattak, & Buhler, 2016) and (Frampton, 2015) social media metrics as the basis for developing the computational equations. Indeed, the data sources are varied; that is, collecting structured, semi-structured and unstructured datasets. The scope of the datasets gathered is based on the dynamic, interactivity and impression uncertainty characteristics of social media.

In view of the above, and cognizance of the fuzzy nature of the social media metrics, decision-makers perceptions are factored into the treatment in computing for value-added in all cases (McFadzean, Ezingeard, & Birchall, 2007). In essence, or the key objective is to develop a model that will utilize the experts' opinions to connect the organization's product and services to their customers through customer intimacy programs (Piccoli, 2013).

Theoretically, systems thinking models can be employed to evaluate or assess the utility and reach of social media campaigns, and to explore users' interactions and preferences (Norman, 2009). In assessing social media metrics with evaluation models, (Norman, 2009) recommends Developmental Evaluation (DE), whereby the outcomes or value created are those of enhancing program development and strategic learning. The approach is said to be apt for innovation and dynamic applications, such as the social media.

As an illustration, social media interactions can be assessed by the outcomes or value created, as per the following (Norman, 2009):

1.   How does the users benefit from the interactions?
2.   What lessons were learned from the interactions?
3.   Was the interaction considered engaging, impactful or influential?
4.   What sort of decisions could be derived from the interactions?

The development evaluation is augmented with reflective practice to optimize the value creation as insights are deduced from either the activity (or interactions) and the learning that occurs during the interaction.

Indeed, the value created as in lessons learnt or best practices could influence both present and future decisions.

Some Examples of Pseudo-Codes

First of all, the equations are metrics depicting the acquired knowledge representations that can be modeled to create value. Indeed, in terms of computational programming, these knowledge elements captured would have been modeled with specific notations that can easily be encoded into a particular computer program. Indeed, these are simple techniques suitable for SMEs, especially in developing economies. For the purposes of this study, we demonstrate with pseudo-codes to emphasize the points.

So, for example in computing the metric Interaction (equation (1.1)) using pseudo-codes as follows:

Declare Interaction

Declare Conversions

$*//\{$the number of times some interactions are made with social media Activity$\}$

$*//\{$i.e. shares,submit,re-submit,transacting,etc.$\}$

Declare Activity

$*//\{$assumed to be a non-zero$\}$

if Activity is not null and Conversions is greater than zero

let Conversions $= 0$ and Interaction $= 0$

for i from 0 to $(\text{Activity} - 1)$

$Conversions = Conversions + Activity(i)$

$*//\{$Activity is an array,with (i) being the index$\}$

$end(for)$

$$Interaction = \frac{Conversions}{Activity}$$

$end(if)$

end of algorithm

Big Data Based Multivariate Value Creation (MCV) Model

The Big Data based Multivariate Value Creation (MCV) model is an algorithmic decision model, depicting the flow processes of Big Data multivariate datasets generated and the levels of value creation required for corporate decision-making. The model is aimed at facilitating decision-making through understanding and analysis of social media metrics. The model shows the various levels of value creation processes, using social media based Big Data generated, which datasets are acquired, processed, analyzed and utilized based on systematic intuitive procedures to identify optimal solutions.

Value creation is the process of driving or conceiving business objectives, exhibited in data (critical data) into knowledge and insight. Traditionally, businesses had relied upon their own internal data to create value. Today, most businesses have reckoned the need to utilize both internal and external data, which are exhibited as Big Data datasets (Erl, Khattak, & Buhler, 2016).

The Multivariate Value Creation (MVC) model was developed based on the knowledge value creation from the Data-Information-Knowledge-Wisdom concepts (Erl, Khattak, & Buhler, 2016). They espouse that business events or activities generate data, which in turn becomes Information when data is in a given context; Information becomes Knowledge upon given meaning; which ultimately metamorphosed into Wisdom upon given understanding. They are however, quick to disclaim that they "Wisdom" is not generated through the use of ICT technologies. Indeed, "Big Data enhances value as it provides additional context through integration of external perspectives to help convert data into information and provide meaning to generate knowledge from information" (Erl, Khattak, & Buhler, 2016). Taking cues from (Aarts, 2007), any inferences on the basis of the social media generated Big Data (sets), we endeavor to account for some explanatory constructs in the model.

The horizontal axis, also known as the abscissa, represents the various processing stages of the social media based multivariate datasets, from its acquisition through analysis to utilization. The vertical axis, also known as ordinate, represents the values created from gleaning through raw datasets to information and subsequently the knowledge gained. The model also shows the flow control throughout the predictive and prescriptive analytics, as the values derived from knowledge are utilized for corporate decision-making.

Figure 1. Big data based multivariate value creation (MVC) model

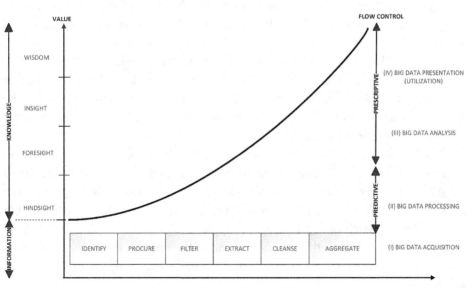

It must be noted that the model serves as a support or guide in decision-making tasks associated with social media analytics. It serves as a guide in value creation, but doesn't in anyway invalidate the user's perceptions nor prejudices (c.f. (Yeboah-Boateng, 2013a)).

The characteristics of the model is premised upon the facts and rules embedded within the gathered datasets, For instance, attributes such as being dynamic or static, as well as the correlations between the facts and the rules are important.

The Big Data Analytics involves the utilization of data analyzed and computed to assist corporate executives to create value based on improved insight about their business operations and initiatives, and to make fact-based and informed decisions (Evans, 2013). It must be noted that the Value Creation model is pertinent to improved revenue mobilization and profitability, as well as enhancing the understanding of critical data (in this case, the data the business collects and use) and necessary for competitive advantage.

The model is built upon various analytics; key amongst them are both predictive and prescriptive analytics. Using a hypothetical scenario to explain the utility of the Value Creation model; we consider datasets gathered by an online store in reaching at the decision to reduce or discount prices of items.

First, the datasets are analyzed using merely descriptive analytics to examine both past and present sales and interactions to these products. Informed data on prices of products, number of products sold, number of visitors who interacted with the products, number of visitors to the website, etc. Then, we carry out predictive analytics based on past performance datasets to predict sales of those products and pricing scheme. It must be noted that, predictive analytics have inherent uncertainties which is associated with risk management, and the intuitive experiences of the decision-maker.

Lovett (2011) posits that social media metrics are "malleable and adapt to change with human behavior" (p.224). Relying on the utility of predictive and prescriptive analytics during decision-making, social media metrics "optimization offers the potential to deliver continually" (p.224) optimal experiences aimed at creating sustained growth or value-added.

This is followed by the prescriptive analytics based on some optimization techniques (Evans, 2013) to decide on the best pricing scheme necessary to achieve the set target revenue and profit. In essence, based on the insights gained, the decision-makers (corporate executives) are aided into identifying the best possible value-added approach or decisions.

Based on the above, the executives can differentiate customers or visitors using some reward-based campaigns or techniques to encourage more visitors and interactions.

CONCLUSION

Generally, Big Data is characteristic of data generated at a fast rate (such as a live streaming), in unstructured, semi-structured and structured data formats, with inconsistencies in datasets and its associated disparate data types and sources.

Social Media based Big Data have been harnessed to better understand the organization's customers, to design targeted campaigns, to optimize business processes and to improve business performance.

This study has demonstrated that social media could be harnessed as business motivation and driver towards Big Data adoption amongst SMEs in developing economies, for example.

Corporate executives ought to appreciate that Big Data isn't just about emerging technologies but also about how the insights derived from these datasets can be harnessed to leverage the business performance and to create value (Erl, Khattak, & Buhler, 2016).

Business delivers value to customers through the execution of their business processes. In essence the business objectives are use cases with the executives, customers and partners as the actors. For example, employees as well as customers are co-creators of the product brands and corporate reputation; such as using social media to provide unique and differentiating value propositions. Furthermore, businesses leverage on innovative cloud computing capabilities and resources to provision Big Data solutions using external datasets. That is, leveraging on social media data, businesses can rent and/or provision scalable processing facilities and available huge storage opportunities to create value (Erl, Khattak, & Buhler, 2016).

Future studies would dwell on harnessing the Facebook Page Insights as value propositions and other related metrics to carry out experiments to ascertain the extent of value-added from social media.

REFERENCES

Aarts, K. (2007). Parsmony Methodology. *Methodological Inovations Online, 2*(1), 2-10. Retrieved October 1, 2018, from http://journals.sagepub.com/doi/pdf/10.4256/mio.2007.0002

Baker, E. W. (2013). Relational Model Bases: A Technical Approach to Real-Time Business Intelligenec and Decision making. *Communications of the Association for Information Systems, 33*(1).

Batrinca, B., & Treleaven, P. C. (2015). Social Media Analytics: A Survey of Techniques, Tools and Platforms. *AI & Society, 30*(1), 89–116. doi:10.100700146-014-0549-4

Bindner, D., & Ericsson, M. (2011). *A Student's Guide to the Study, Practice and Tools of Modern Mathematics*. CRC Press.

Cerrato, P. (2012, July 31). Is Population Health Management the Latest Health IT Fad? *Information Week*. Retrieved from www.informationweek.com/healthcare/clinical-systems/is-population-health-management-ltest-h/240004578

Chen, M., Mao, S., & Liu, Y. (2014). Big Data: A Survey. *Mobile Networks and Applications, 19*(2), 171–209. doi:10.100711036-013-0489-0

Department of Defence (DoD). (2000). *Doctrince for Intelligence Support to Joint Operations, Joint Publications 2-0*. Washington, DC: GPO.

Dunlop, N. (2015). *Beginning Big Data with Power BI & Excel 2013*. Apress. doi:10.1007/978-1-4842-0529-7

Ericsson, K. A., & Smith, J. (1991). *Toward a General Theory of Expertise: Prospects and Limits*. Cambridge, UK: Cambridge University Press.

Erl, T., Khattak, W., & Buhler, P. (2016). *Big Data Fundamentals: Concepts, Drivers & Techniques*. Prentice Hall.

Evans, J. R. (2013). Business Analytics: Methods, Models & Decisions. Pearson Education, Inc. (Prentice Hall).

Firican, G. (2017, February 8). *The 10 V's of Big Data*. Retrieved July 4, 2018, from Transforming Data with Intellignce (TDwI): www.tdwi.org/articles/2017/02/08/10-vs-of-big-data.aspx

Frampton, M. (2015). *Big Data Made Easy: A Working Guide to the Complete Hadoop Toolset*. Apress. doi:10.1007/978-1-4842-0094-0

Jones, S. (2012, December 27). Why 'Big Data' is the Fourth Factor of Production. *Financial Times*. Retrieved July 5, 2018, from https://www.ft.com/content/5086d700-504a-11e2-9b66-00144feab49a

Lovett, J. (2011). *Social Media Metrics Secrets*. Wiley Publishing, Inc.

McDowell, D. (2009). *A Handbook for Practitioners, Managers and Users: Strategic Intelligence*. The Scarecrow Press, Inc.

McFadzean, E., Ezingeard, J.-N., & Birchall, D. (2007). *Perception of Risk & the Strategic Impact of existing IT on Information Security Strategy at the Board level.* Academic Press.

McKinsey & Co. (2011). *Big Data: The Next Frontier for Innovation, Competition and Productivity.* McKinsey & Co.

Norman, C. D. (2009). Health Promotion as a Systems Science and Practice. *Journal of Evaluation in Clinical Practice, 15*(5), 868–872. doi:10.1111/j.1365-2753.2009.01273.x PMID:19811602

Piccoli, G. (2013). *Information Systems for Managers: Text & Cases* (2nd ed.). John Wiley & Sons, Inc.

Preator, B. (2018, June). Delivering Big Data Expectations. *CIO Review.* Retrieved July 24, 2018, from www.bigdata.cioreview.com

Rocha, L. (2015, August 15). *The 5 Steps of the Intelligence Cycle.* Retrieved from Security Monitoring, Threat Intelligence: www.countuponsecurity.com/2015/08/15/the-5-steps-of-the-intelligence-cycle/

Sager, T. (2014). *An Intelligent Approach to Attack Prevention.* SANS Institute.

Sterne, J. (2010). *Social Media Metrics: How to Measure and Optimze Your Marketing Investment.* Hoboken, NJ: John Wiley & Sons, Inc.

Thomas, D., Therlal, G., & Danytel, J. (2015). Worldwide Big Data Technology and Services: 2012-2015 Forecast. *Clinical Pharmacology and Therapeutics, 92*(1), 77–95.

Witteman, C., & Krol, N. (2005). Knowledge-Based Systems: Acquiring, Modeling, and Representing Human Expertsie for Information Systems. In *Creation, Use, and Deployment of Digital Information* (pp. 177–198). Mahwah, NJ: Lawrence Erlbaum Associates, Inc.

Yeboah-Boateng, E. O. (2013). *Cyber-Security Challenges with SMEs in Developing Economies: Issues of Confidentiality, Integrity & Availablity (CIA).* Aalborg University.

Yeboah-Boateng, E. O. (2017). Cyber-Security Concerns with Cloud Computing: Business Value Creation & Performance Perspectives. In A. K. Turuk, B. Sahoo, & S. K. Addya (Eds.), Resource Management & Efficiency in Cloud Computing Environment (pp. 106-137). IGI Global Publishers.

Chapter 7
Big Data, Privacy, and Healthcare

Nirav Bhatt
Charotar University of Science and Technology, India

Amit Thakkar
Charotar University of Science and Technology, India

ABSTRACT

In the era of big data, large amounts of data are generated from different areas like education, business, stock market, healthcare, etc. Most of the available data from these areas are unstructured, which is large and complex. As healthcare industries become value-based from volume-based, there is a need to have specialized tools and methods to handle it. The traditional methods for data storage and retrieval can be used when data is structured in nature. Big data analytics provide technologies to store large amounts of complex healthcare data. It is believed that there is an enormous opportunity to improve lives by applying big data in the healthcare industry. No industry counts more than healthcare as it is a matter of life and death. Due to rapid development of big data tools and technologies, it is possible to improve disease diagnosis more efficiently than ever before, but security and privacy are two major issues when dealing with big data in the healthcare industry.

DOI: 10.4018/978-1-5225-7519-1.ch007

INTRODUCTION

Due to the growth of the healthcare industry, a lot of data is generating. There are massive problems presented in modern healthcare including high cost, high waste, and low quality. But the hope of big data is lead to better care and lower cost. There is massive amount of data which gives analytical algorithms or systems a lot to act on Figure 1 shows characteristics of Big Data.

Characteristics of Big Data

1. **Volume:** There is a massive amount of data which gives analytics algorithms or systems a lot to act on. For example, for genomic data each human genome requires 200 gigabyte of raw data, or 125 megabyte if store only snips. For medical imaging data, single FMRI is about 300 gigabyte.
2. **Variety:** There is a variety of data which connect lots of information sources together. For example, clinical informatics such as patients diagnosis, procedure, meditation, lab results and clinical notes. Patient generated data, such as the information coming out of on-body sensors and other devices that patients wear. Real-time data sources such as blood pressure measures, temperature heart rate, drug dispensing levels at intensive care units.
3. **Velocity:** Often data is coming in live and need to be processed and analyze live.
4. **Veracity:** There is a lot of noise, missing data, errors and a lot of false alarms.

Figure 1. Characteristics of Big Data

Challenges for Big Data and Health Analytics

1. Incorporating new information, such as biomedical data, and new technologies into electronic health records that store big data. Text data require special algorithms; generic data may be voluminous, and continuously monitored.
2. Harnessing the potential of unstructured data for analysis, such as medical imaging and text.
3. Building a culture of data sharing and architecture, including interoperability, to meet health system needs, including future meaningful use requirements.
4. Building data systems that meet requirements of accountable care organizations and other types of payment reforms.

HEALTHCARE APPLICATIONS

1. **Predictive Modeling:** Predictive Modeling is about using historical data to view the model for predicting future events. We have millions of patients we want to analyze and their diagnosis information, medication information, and so on. So all these data combined together, create a big challenge. The second challenge in predictive modeling is there are so many models to be built. Predictive model is not a single algorithm. It is a sequence of computational tasks.
2. **Computational Phenotyping:** The input to Phenotyping is raw patient data. It consists of many different sources, such as demographic information, diagnosis, medication, procedure, lab tests and clinical notes. And phenotyping is process of turning the raw patient data into medical concepts or phenotypes.

BIG DATA ALGORITHMS

1. **Classification Algorithms:** Classification algorithm takes that input X which is in matrix and for example every row in this matrix represents a patient and every column of this matrix represents a feature. And the classification algorithm will map this input feature matrix X into a set of discrete outcome Y. For example, these Y vectors indicate whether the patient had a heart attack or not. So we want to learn this function that maps input X to the target outcome variable Y, this is classification Examples for classification algorithms include Decision tree for Big Data, k-nearest neighbor for Big Data, Naïve Bayes for Big Data, Random forest for Big Data, Support vector machine for Big Data.

2. **Clustering:** Clustering is about taking an input matrix X, each row is a patient and every column is a feature. Need to learn a function that partitioned matrix into multiple clusters X_1, X_2, X_3. Each cluster consists of set of patients and those patients are similar to each other, and those patients within a cluster will be different patients in a different cluster. Examples of clustering algorithms include partitioning based clustering for Big Data; Hierarchical based clustering for Big Data, High-dimensional clustering for Big Data.

3. **Dimensionality Reduction:** The input is the matrix X, every row is a patient and every column is a feature. Need to learn a function that will turn this matrix X into a smaller matrix with fewer features.

4. **Graph Analysis:** Graph is a very important data structure that represents the relationships. Suppose there are two patients and connected through different disease and the relationship between diseases is given as a Graph. A graph algorithm can help us to figure out what are the important nodes of a graph and their relationship between those nodes.

BIG DATA SYSTEMS AND HEALTHCARE

In order to deal with big data set and for implementation of the algorithm, there is a need to have big data systems. There are many popular big data systems like Hadoop, Spark, etc. Hadoop is a distributed disk-based big data systems that all the data are stored in disk while Spark is a distributed in-memory big data systems that most of the data store in memory (Abouelmehdi, K., Beni-Hssane, A., Beni., Khaloufi, H., & Saadi, M.,2017). So Spark is faster than Hadoop but both are popular big data systems that people are using.

Tool for Processing Big Data

1. **Hadoop and Map Reduce:** Map Reduce is a powerful system that can perform that can perform on big data using distributed environment. Hadoop is the java implementation of MapReduce. There are many software tools have been developed to facilitate development effort for data science tasks such as data processing, extraction, transform and loading process. In a nut shell, Hadoop and MapReduce enable a powerful big data ecosystem by providing the combination of all these things. In fact MapReduce or Hadoop is a big data system that provides following capabilities:
   a. Distributed Storage for large datasets through Hadoop Distributed File System

b. Distributed computation through programming Interface MapReduce
c. Fault tolerance systems in order to cope up with constant system failures on large distributed systems that are built on top of commodity hardware.

MapReduce is proposed by Jeff Dean and Sanjay Ghemawat from Google in 2004 and was implemented inside Google as proprietary software for supporting many of their search engine activities. Later on, Apache Hadoop is developed which is an open source software that mimin original Google's MapReduce systems. It is written in Java for distributed file storage and distributed processing of very large data set. To program on Hadoop systems, need to use the programming abstraction MapReduce which provides a very limited but powerful programming paradigm for parallel processing on large data set. The entire algorithm running on MapReduce or Hadoop has to be specified as MapReduce programs. The reason for this very constrained programming model is to support super scalable, parallel and fault-tolerance implementation of data processing algorithm that can run on large data set. To utilize Hadoop and MapReduce, need to understand and master common patterns for computation using MapReduce.

Comparisons of tools with some of the case studies are mentioned in Table 1.

The fundamental pattern for writing a data mining or machine learning algorithm using Hadoop is to specify the machine learning algorithms as computing aggregation statistics. So need to implement machine learning algorithms for identifying the most common risk factors of health failure. And need to decompose the algorithm into a set of smaller competition units. For example, we want to extract the list of risk factors related to heart failure appeared in each patient's record. Then result from this map function will be aggregated by a reduce function. For example, instead of listing the risk factors for each patient, we want to compute the frequency of each risk factor over entire population. Then in that case, the entire reduce function would

Table 1. Analysis on top case study and their tools

CASE	Hadoop	MapReduce	Spark	Flink	Strom
JPMorgan	✓				
Cigna	✓	✓			
ING			✓		
Ericsson				✓	
Groupon					✓
Cloudera	✓				
Intel	✓				
IBM	✓				

do that by performing the aggregation statistic on result from the map function. This process is quite abstract.

Map Reduce Abstraction

Assume we have a large database of patients stored in Hadoop Distributed File System. Each patient is stored as a separate record and each record consists of the history of this patient encounter. Goal is to write MapReduce programs to compute the number of cases in each disease. To do this in MapReduce, first specify the map function that going through each patient record and extracting the disease mentions and output that. All the outputs from the map function will be processed internally by Hadoop. In particular, all those outputs will be shuffled and aggregated. Intermediate result will be the input to the reduce function. So in order to write MapReduce program, we need to specify the map function and the reduce function.

Real world dataset is too big to be stored and processed on a single machine. So we have to split that data into two partitions, so that each partition can be stored and processed in parallel on multiple machines. So MapReduce systems have two components which are Mappers and Reducers. So all this data will be partitioned and processed by multiple mappers and each mapper deals with a partition which is a subset of records in entire dataset. In Figure 2 mapper one processes three records, mapper two processes another three records, and mapper three processes another three records. Then we have reducer and they are divided the work by processing the intermediate results. In below figure, there are two reducers, reducer 1 and reducer 2. For example Reducer 1 will be in charge of the heart disease and Reducer 2 will be in charge of Cancers. So in the map phase, each mapper will iteratively apply the map function on the data that they are in charge of. And they will prepare the output that will be sent to the corresponding reducer. For example, we have a set of intermediate result are prepared for reducer one and we have a set of intermediate results are prepared to be sent to the reducer two. And across different mappers, the processes are happening in parallel. This process is iteratively going through all the records and all that intermediate result will be processed internally throughout combination and shuffling process. So combine the values for the same disease at each mapper then send out all intermediate results to the corresponding reducers. So at the reducer site, once they receive those records, they can start generating the final output by applying the reuse function. So MapReduce system has three different phases. The map stage, where we perform the map function and the pre-aggregation and combination function. Then we have shuffle stage, all the intermediate results will be stamped to the corresponding reducers and we have the final reducer stage, where the final output is generated.

Figure 2. Map Reduce Stages

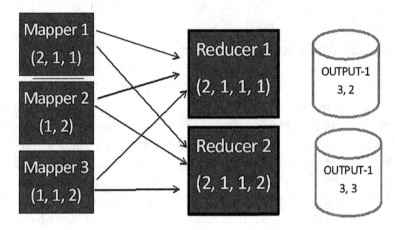

One of the key functionality that MapReduce or Hadoop system provides is fault tolerance. On a large cluster environment, many things can fail at any given times. So, failure recovery is very costly and often times data scientists, do not want to deal with failure recovery when implement algorithms. Assume that mapper 2 can fail during execution of the MapReduce program from fig 2. In this time, the MapReduce system will restart mapper two then go through the same workload again by generating the intermediate result. Then all intermediate result will be sent to the corresponding reducers and the final output is generated. Similarly, reducer can also fail. For example, if reducer two failed, then MapReduce system will automatically restart Reducer two, and extract the corresponding intermediate result again, back from the Mappers and recomputed all those reduce functions. Ideally when a component fails, only that component should be re-computed. For example, when Reducer two fails, Reducer one should not be impacted at all. So MapReduce systems are designed in a way that such optimization is taking place and all those re-computations is minimized.

Hadoop Distributed File Systems

Large file is impractical to store the whole file on a single machine. So we split the whole file into different partitions and we store those partitions on different machines which are called workers and we store multiple copy of the same partition on different workers. In order to access large file, we can retrieve those different partitions many different ways. There are two advantages of it. One is we can access the multiple partitions in the single file concurrently so the root speed is actually faster than accessing the single file on a single machine. Second, if any of those workers fail, we still can retrieve a larger file. So HDFS is the backhand file system to store all the data using MapReduce program.

Security for Hadoop

Security measure which is built on Hadoop is Kerberos. It relies on encrypted keys that are exchanged back and forth between the client server and the user that is attempting to access the system since trust levels are defined within the system. This can be useful if Hadoop is running on a secured network. However, most big data processes are being conducted in the cloud because it is a cost effective storage option for most organizations. Cloud storage generally accessed over the internet which is a public network. It would therefore not allow for this type of authentication with Kerberos. As a result, organizations using Hadoop for big data analysis need to use other methods to secure the information as it is open source. Many different researchers, programmers and network administrators have contributed their own efforts towards making Hadoop and related systems better.

The Impact of Big Data in Healthcare Sector

The healthcare industry is anticipated to develop at an exceptional rate, and also the data linked with it. It is estimated to generate very large data collected from laboratories, equipment and through the patient itself (Mind Fire solutions, 2018). Hence it becomes difficult and challenging for software industries to analyze such plenty of data. Incorporating these big data securely into effective storage for analysis is very important.

When big data technology enters into medical field it gives new direction. With added big data security mechanism, now health care industry able to upload more information. In the upcoming days, the patient will share health data securely through mobile apps and wearable health devices with the doctor which can be act as an analytical tool to give good treatment speedily.

The difficulty to meet the terms of several laws specifically when data are pooled from different sources increases the possible demand of proper authority and authentication for data access.

Issues of Big Data Privacy in Healthcare

1. The same portion of information is used each to scale back health differences and authorize individuals and to break up privacy.
2. The same piece of data can be used both to reduce health discrepancies and empower people and to violate privacy and cause harm.

3. Focus on utilization and harms more rather than costs and benefits(C&B). Focusing on C&B implies trade-offs. Instead, seek redress via civil rights laws.

4. Universal strategy. Strategies that the technology and services to fulfill the vary of desires while not barriers for a few.

5. Not only agreement but also to Confirm the privacy and security of healthcare data through some standard principal like FIPPs- Fair Information Practices Principles.

6. Standard of preventing misuse of patient information. There are several smart usages of health data; however there should even be certain preventions.

7. Many times there are demands to utilize full identifiable data.

8. Difficult to informed individual personally regarding all usages.

9. There is need of standard that defines: "clearly good/appropriate uses" and "clearly bad/inappropriate uses"

HEALTHCARE QUALITY MEASUREMENT

A phenotyping algorithm is very important for health care quality measures. It is important to compare health quality measures across hospitals. One way for doing that is to have all hospital sending their raw EHR data to the central site which can be an insurance company or public health agency, such as Centers for Disease Controls. Then, this central site has to aggregate all those raw information in order to compute all those health care quality measure. And this becomes a very difficult task because all those hospitals can use very different format to represent their raw data and this central site has to figure out how to process them differently. A more scalable way for dealing with this problem is to process all those raw EHR data through phenotyping first, then obtain high-quality phenotypic information, and then share that to the central site. With those consistent phenotypic information sending from different hospitals, now the central site can aggregate that information to compute the health care quality measures then compare them across the hospitals. So in this case, high-quality and consistent phenotypic data are crucial to enable this health care quality measure comparison across the hospitals.

Following are the few of the reasons why healthcare data difficult to measure (LeSueur, D, 2016):

1. **Majority of the Data is at Various Places:** Health care data are available at different places and distributed location like: HR software, laboratories, pharmacy and radiology. To make data useful, there is requirement to integrate at single data warehouse.

2. **Data is in Heterogeneous Format:** Since many years, healthcare data from different sources are stored with different and most convenient format without taking care of how eventually data will be combined and processed or analyzed. These data may be structured or unstructured. EMRs attempt to standardize the data capture process, but care providers are reluctant to adopt a one-size-fits-all approach to documentation (Haselton,M, G., Nettle, D., & Andrews, P,W, 2005).

3. **Non-Unified Definition for Health Care Information:** Different definitions are available for healthcare data as different opinion exist. As the new research in the same area is coming day by day, our thoughts continue to be changed for "what is important", "what to measure", "how and when to measure it".

4. **Complexity of the Data:** As there is no uniformity, there is no standardize data available or it may be incomplete in nature. Altering those data into the format which can be measured is very difficult.

5. **Fluctuating Controlling Requirements:** In order to provide the transparent quality and best price, regulatory requirements are changing frequently which can lead to difficulty in specifying unique measure for healthcare data.

PRIVACY AND SECURITY OF HEALTHCARE DATA

The healthcare business is observing a rise in large volume of regarding complication, variety and correctness (Abouelmehdi, K., Beni-Hessane. A, & Khaloufi, H.,2018). With the inclusion of the influence of big data in healthcare, issue of security & privacy is the crucial fact as evolving threats and susceptibilities increase more and more. Patient's medical information is very personal and required to be safe and secured against loss and theft. As the computing technology enhanced and allowed big data in health care, these issues of privacy can be deal with major priority.

Also the Patient's data are stored with variable stages of security. Furthermore, many healthcare data storage has HIPAA, but that accreditation doesn't assure patient record privacy, because the HIPAA is more concentrated on confirming security rules & regulations rather than implementing them (Patil, H, K., and Ravi, S, 2014).

Three major and important concepts which are related with each other, frequently used while talking about security of healthcare information:

6. **Confidentiality:** Confidentiality issue in health care considered to be the responsibility of professionals. These professionals are one who has right to use to patient records and to keep that information confidential. Now this is also to be found to medical professionals' guidelines for confidentiality (McWay, 2010,

p. 174). Confidentiality is standardizing by law as confidential communication between the two in a professional connection, for example with a patient and a doctor or a nurse.

7. **Privacy:** Privacy is different from confidentiality in a view as, it is the property of the patient to take decisions regarding how to share personal information (Brodnik, 2012). "We are not unaware of the threat to privacy implicit in the accumulation of vast amounts of personal information in computerized data banks. "The right to collect and use such data for public purposes is typically accompanied by a concomitant statutory or regulatory duty to avoid unwarranted disclosures." (Cate, F. H., & Cate, B. E., 2012) (Gayton, C. M.,2006).

8. **Security:** Security brings up the protection and moreover related to protection to the privacy of healthcare data and holding that information in confidence. It is traditionally related to the concept of security in a paper format like protected file cupboards. With the growth of utilization of electronic health record systems and communication of healthcare data to various medical activities, there is need for controlling strategies to electronic healthcare information. The HIPAA Security Regulation is the 1st nationwide criteria for protecting of healthcare data. The HIPAA Security Rule's stated goal is: "To protect individually identifiable information in *electronic* form—a subset of information covered by the Privacy Rule—while allowing healthcare providers appropriate access to information and flexibility in adoption of technology" (HHS, 2003b).

At present, health care trade is observing a overflow of subtle attacks starting from DDoS-"Distributed Denial of Service" to silent malware. Moreover, occurrences threats related to social media activity is increasing and therefore the risks related to same attack is tough to forecast while not considering human psychological feature.

Figure 3. Privacy and Security of Healthcare

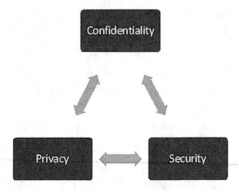

Psychological feature bias, as an example, will inherit play, particularly within the case of older patients. "Cognitive bias is a pattern of deviation in judgment, whereby influences about other people and situations may be drawn in an illogical manner" (Haselton, M, G., Nettle, D., & Andrews, P,W.,2005). Big data indeed act as an important role in the incorporation of new treatments and medicines along with maintaining the privacy & security.

Healthcare groups depend primarily on policies as shown in Figure 4 (Ponemon, Institute Research Report, 2016), more than 60% approve that policy are efficiently protect unauthorized access of patient data or theft. Now here we can see this increment from its last year report and further increased in 2017 also. 57% said that they have the benefit from technical expertise to recognize and solve data breaks having unauthorized access of patient data which is also increase from 53% since its last year report. So concluding remark is here at least 50% have faith in technology to efficiently protect unauthorized access of patient data which is also more compared to its last year 2015. They are also agreed up on the fact that they have resources to prevent or quickly detect unauthorized access of patient data have been increased from 33% to 37%.

As the Healthcare industry have many significant duties to perform on a regular basis, they deliver their patients an extra care, and provide security. Considering all, there is needed to upgrade the resources which provide privacy to healthcare

Figure 4. Healthcare organizations' perceptions about privacy and healthcare data protection

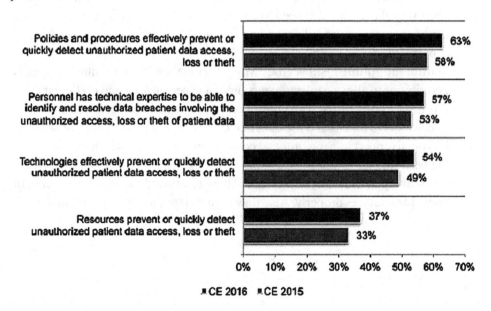

information. However, majority are not being able to upgrade their equipment indeed they wish to secure their information with the upgraded technology. Investing in new resources and/or hardware can cost a bit but at the same time, an attack at the weak point can create a threat which costs higher than it to be invest in resource up-gradation.

STEPS TO PROTECT BIG HEALTHCARE DATA

Following are the ways to protect the sensitive big healthcare data (Schott .W, 2017).

1. **Drain the Open Incoming Ports:** There is continuous need of open incoming port to receive information from server which may possibly the attack about to happen. Alternate solution to the same is to use a safe network which creates outgoing connections. For the possible implementation of the same, one needs to have publish/subscribe connection strategy which is based on protocols like: "CoAP", "MQTT", "Web Sockets" & "HTTP 2.0" w/o open ports.
2. **Provide "end-to-end" Encryption:** SSL-Secure Sockets Layer & Transport Layer Security is still practical for regular data transmission. However, when moving healthcare information and communications among embedded devices, it needs a more security. "End-to-end" security can be provided through AES-Advanced Encryption Standard.("Only devices with encryption keys can decrypt AES data when it's pushed and received, providing full end-to-end security").
3. **Implement Token Based Control for Access:** Although data encryption is a good step ahead, one still need to control regarding who can access and what can be accesses, instead of depending on devices to filtering which they haven't subscribed to.
4. **Within the "publish/subscribe" Model:** Even token based control for access permits one to allocate tokens to resources and permit access to particular data, this model gives us the well control on tokens, which are created the devices which receive tokens and the data that tokens permit to access. Network then be effectively act as a monitor and controlling the devices which can deal with the network.
5. **Regular up-Gradation of Devices:** There is demand to install and maintain embedded devices properly. Also they required frequently updating firmware.

REFERENCES

Abouelmehdi, K., Beni-Hessane, A., & Khaloufi, H. (2018). Big healthcare data: Preserving security and privacy. *Journal of Big Data*, *5*(1).

Abouelmehdi, K., Beni-Hssane, A., Khaloufi, H., & Saadi, M. (2017). Beni., Khaloufi, H., & Saadi, M.(2017). "Big data security and privacy in healthcare: A Review. *Procedia Computer Science*, *113*, 73–80. doi:10.1016/j.procs.2017.08.292

Cate, F. H., & Cate, B. E. (2012). The Supreme Court and information privacy. *International Data Privacy Law*, *2*(4), 255–267. doi:10.1093/idpl/ips024

Gayton, C. M. (2006). Beyond terrorism: Data collection and responsibility for privacy. *Vine*, *36*(4), 377–394. doi:10.1108/03055720610716647

Haselton, M. G., Nettle, D., & Andrews, P. W. (2005). The evolution of cognitive bias. In *The Handbook of Evolutionary Psychology*. John Wiley & Sons Inc.

LeSueur, D. (2016). *Reasons Healthcare Data Is Unique and Difficult to Measure*. Health Catalyst.

Mind Fire Solutions. (2018). *The impact of Cloud and Big Data on Healthcare Sector*. Retrieved from,https://medium.com/@mindfiresolutions.usa/the-impact-of-cloud-and-big-data-on-healthcare-sector-e26509a01071

Patil, H. K., & Ravi, S. (2014). Big data security and privacy issues in healthcare. *Big Data (BigData Congress), 2014 IEEE International Congress on. IEEE*. 10.1109/BigData.Congress.2014.112

Ponemon, Institute Research Report. (2016). *Sixth Annual Benchmark Study on Privacy & Security of Healthcare Data*. Author.

Schott, W. (2017). *4 ways to protect information in data-driven healthcare system*. HealthCare Business & Technology. Retrieved from http://www.healthcarebusinesstech.com/protect-data-healthcare-system/

ADDITIONAL READING

York, T. W., & MacAlister, D. (2015). *Hospital and Healthcare Security*. Butterworth-Heinemann.

Chapter 8
What Are Basketball Fans Saying on Twitter?
Evidence From Euroleague Basketball's Final Four Event

Burçin Güçlü
Universitat Romon Llull, Spain

Marcela Garza
Universitat Ramon Llull, Spain

Christopher Kennett
Universitat Ramon Llull, Spain

ABSTRACT

Social media receives growing interest from sports executives. Yet, very little is known about how to make use of such user-generated, unstructured data. By exploring tweets generated during Turkish Airlines Euroleague's Final Four event, which broadcasted the four tournaments of championship among four finalist teams, the authors studied how fans respond to gains and losses and how engaged they were during games through the course of the event. The authors found that favorable reactions were received when teams won, but the magnitude of unfavorable reaction was larger when teams lost. When it came to the organizer rather than the teams, the organizer of the event received most of the positive feedback. The authors also found that main source of tweets was smartphones while tablets were not among real-time feedback devices.

DOI: 10.4018/978-1-5225-7519-1.ch008

INTRODUCTION

Society is connected on a global scale by digital communications. By year 2015, there were 3.5 billion Internet users and over 50% of the adult population around the world are said to be smartphone users (Castells, 2016). By 2017, 31% of the world's population (more than 2.3 billion people) were active social media users (Leaders, 2017).

The global population is consuming media in different ways. For instance, over the past decade the use of computers for internet access has declined rapidly and a shift to instant access through mobile devices like smartphones and tablets has occurred. For this reason, industries are adapting to new distribution channels to keep up with consumer tendencies, including the sports industry. This has led the sports ecosystem to experience dramatic changes, enabling the creation of new communication networks through emerging technologies (De Moragas et al, 2013).

How sport is watched and consumed has been disrupted in the digital era and continues to change due to technology and the emergence of various new direct-to-customer distribution channels. Fans can engage with a sports event without the need to be at venue or even watch it on television. With the advent of live or delayed streaming, instant messaging, the ability to maintain conversations in real time on social media platforms, the opportunity to review large amounts of statistics online and through applications, has created new, more complex multi-directional communication processes. These sports conversations are now happening 'on-the-go' through mobile devices and across geographic boarders on a global scale.

Social media channels receive growing interest from sports executives, politicians, and companies where the opinions of fans, voters and investors matter respectively. Given that social media allow users to build networks in an easy and timely way and to share various kinds of information (photos, videos, texts, links etc), they form an excellent platform for real-time feedback, opinion sharing and to observe fan engagement.

Social media channels have become increasing important for marketing communication because they are instant, have a global reach, are simple to use and require minimal bandwidth and device capability (Abeza et al, 2015). They have become an essential marketing tool in recent years, allowing managers, marketers, and users to interact and share information instantaneously. Advertisers use social media in sport events to generate valuable leads, get immediate feedback, post messages in real time and with the possibility to create viral effects through sharing (Beech et al, 2014). A leading example from sports is the NBA where teams provide information and content through their social media channels, while promoting their team and events, aiming to interact with their fans to receive feedback and increase the probabilities of engagement (Meng, Stavros, & Westberg, 2015).

In collaborative social media platforms such as Facebook, Instagram, Twitter or any other social media platform that allow fans to create, publish, edit or share content. Fans become co-creators of the content that is been shared, generating interactivity and increasing fans' involvement in what is happening at around the live event. Interactive content turns the fan into an active user, increasing the capacity to collaborate and manage the flow of information (Beech et al, 2014; De Moragas et al, 2013; Meng et al., 2015).

Among social media platforms, Twitter is a social networking and micro-blogging service that allows its users post real time messages and multimedia content (Kumar & Kalwani, 2012). Since Twitter was created in 2006 it has been increasingly recognized by marketing and advertisement executives as a key tool in social media-based communication campaigns, embracing the use of hashtags to share thematic content and reach diluted groups of fans with common interests (Delia & Armstrong, 2015).Twitter has become one of the most important social networks for sharing sport stories, enabling customized content to segmented target audiences, connecting fragmented audiences with other users with similar interests, helping disseminate information.

Although Twitter provides an excellent channel for fan engagement, given facilitated opinion creation and presentation, it brings newer and different challenges for researchers analyzing this content and attempting to understand its meaning. At the time of writing the 350m active Twitter users were generating around 6,000 tweets per second, creating large amounts of potential data for analysis.

While several studies explore the use of social media platforms such as Twitter around sports events, there is very limited analysis to date on the meaning of this content. By exploring tweets generated during Euroleague Basketball's Turkish Airlines Final Four event, which includes semi-finals, third and fourth place game and the championship game all played over a single weekend, the authors studied how fans respond to winning and losing, the key content in their conversations and how engaged they are during games through the course of the event. In the next section, the authors conduct a literature review. This is followed by an explanation of the research methods, results and findings, and discuss the implications of their work in the context of big data and virtual organizations. Finally, they discuss the implications and some possible directions for further research.

LITERATURE REVIEW

Fan Engagement

Sports events host an exciting mix of drama, emotion and information that attract very loyal customers: sports fans. The need to engage sports fans in meaningful ways has been an ongoing focus of sports marketing research.

The role of technology in fan engagement has become increasing important in the digital era. Geographical barriers can be crossed by online tools and social media networks creating opportunities for sport marketers to enhance engagement of fans by creating online experiences on a worldwide basis (Parganas, Anagnostopoulos, & Chadwick, 2015).

The Beijing 2008 Olympic Games was one of the first sports event where the use of digital technology enhanced successful engagement of fans from all around the world despite the geographic distance (IOC, 2009). Today, sports events such as the Olympic Games and FIFA World Cup reach large live audiences and clearly defined customer segments as part of wider marketing and communication strategies (Adıgüzel & Kennett, 2017).

Fan engagement can be achieved around a sport event time in several ways such as through the event itself, the players, the club, the venue, the media, sponsors and advertisers, online content such as websites or social media, gambling, fantasy sports, and electronic games (Foster et al, 2016).

Sports events generate conversations and sports fans seek for information and entertainment in online sources. Fans want to be informed of game results, statistics or any sports related news even without watching a game or attending to a venue. Thanks to the fragmentation of the audiences, sport marketers have had enable more choices for following sports events to allow a greater audience viewing and engagement such as watching a game on television, through online streaming or following it in social media networks (Smith & Smith, 2012).

Social media as a platform has been key to engage fans during the last decade. Sports marketers have increasingly invested time and resources to create new strategies to drive online engagement of fans enabling real-time communications and interactions (Meng et al., 2015; Smith & Smith, 2012) transforming their relationship from a passive message communication to an active message consumption, aiming to achieve the highest level of engagement by driving the fans into a participative action where they become co-creators (Vale & Fernandes, 2018) by producing and sharing their own content (Smith & Smith, 2012). Furthermore, thanks to social media networks, fans that are engaged and involved with an event, creating and sharing content, can turn into promoters of the event giving more opportunities for sports marketers to reach a bigger audience. In this matter, sports marketers and advertisers can take advantage of this behavior and communicate directly with different groups of fans through social media.

Twitter as a Fan Engagement Platform

Twitter is a social media tool that allows interaction and conversation in real-time (N. M. Watanabe, Yan, & Soebbing, 2016; Price, Farrington, & Hall, 2013; Smith & Smith, 2012). It is a platform where information such as news, opinions or updates are continuously shared and in a faster way than other media tools (Gibbs, O'Reilly, & Brunette, 2014). Sports leagues, teams, athletes, brands, and media aim to engage fans by developing marketing and communication strategies in Twitter. Fan engagement through Twitter can be achieved and maintained with different strategies such as communicating news, updates, or sharing live content during events (Gibbs et al., 2014), by creating marketing and communication strategies with the use of hashtags (Delia & Armstrong, 2015; Meng et al., 2015) which facilitate fans to filter, follow and participate in conversations by connecting them in virtual communities related to a specific topic but with a wider scope (Smith & Smith, 2012), by having quick interactions from sports social media manages such as click as "favorite" a user's post on Twitter (N. M. Watanabe et al, 2016), or conducting activation activities such as trivia competitions (Meng et al., 2015).

By 2013, Twitter was considered as the "most influential social media platform in sport" (Gibbs & Haynes, 2013). Later, Parganas and colleagues (2015) cite different authors that mention that sports was the highlighted conversation in Twitter with more than 40% of all tweets being sports related, especially during live events. By June 2018, Euroleague Basketball had more than 1.75 million followers in their main social media channels (Facebook, Twitter, Instagram and YouTube), almost 30% (507 thousand followers) from their Twitter account alone.

Twitter gives fans the possibility to have an active role in the online conversation through different actions such as tweeting, re-tweeting, replying, or marking as favorite other people's tweets (Parganas et al., 2015), always with the possibility of sharing their content with fans beyond their network by the use of hashtags (Smith & Smith, 2012). Twitter has become an essential tool for proliferating sports content, multiplying sports consumers' participation thanks to the real-time interaction and access to teams or athletes (N. Watanabe et al., 2015).

Even though sports marketers use Twitter as a strategic platform of engagement to connect with fans having the hashtags as a tool to identify an event or a specific topic, fan engagement strategies can be improved by knowing the fans, their motivations and actions when they actively participate in social media conversations by sharing information, cheering or criticizing a sport event, player or club. The volume of data generated around sports events creates a wealth of data for researchers to analyze and attempt to understand, and has involved the design of new methodologies and research tools amongst scholars.

Tweet Analysis

The most common methods to evaluate tweets are word clouds and sentiment analysis, A word cloud is a visual representation of word frequency (Atenstaedt, 2012). The more commonly a word appears within the raw text being analyzed, the larger the word appears in the image generated. Word clouds are increasingly being employed as a simple tool to identify the core content of, as well as to better understand the themes covered in written material, and to sketch the domains to which they pertain (Halevi & Moed, 2012).

Despite its wide use in text mining, word clouds should be interpreted with certain caveats. They often fail to group words that have the same or similar meaning. As they tend to focus only on single word frequency, they also do not identify phrases, reducing context.

In the current research, word clouds have been applied to analyze the content of tweets with specified hashtags to see whether sufficient attention is being given to the players, coaches, organization, sponsors and games and to identify outstanding factors other than the aforementioned ones.

Besides being a platform where sport marketers and advertisers can share information, Twitter is a tool where people also can share their emotions and opinions or 'sentiment'. In the sports context, Twitter can be considered a repository of emotional exchanges allowing fans to have conversations among other fans, the media or athletes (Smith & Smith, 2012).

Sports events evoke emotions in fans (Gratch et al., 2015), but fans have different levels of fandom and passion that are expressed in different ways. There are fans that cheer for their team attending to their games in a regular basis, others may prefer following their team or athlete by watching the games on television (Samra & Wos, 2014), while others will review stats and comments on social media.

Levels of fandom can be categorized in several rankings, for example Meng and colleagues (2015) mention Sutton et al (1997) who ranked fans by their level of identification in: Social fans, focused fans and vested fans; or Samra and Wos (2014) fan types classification in: temporary fan, devoted fan and fanatical fan. Each rank with specific characteristics and behaviors. It is worth noting, however, that not all sports spectators are as fans.

For sport marketers and advertisers, understanding the fans, their motivations, behavior and how they express their emotions and sentiments, can provide insights that can help to plan and execute a successful marketing campaign in social media.

Several authors agree that the uses and gratification theory is one theory that can be applied as an example to explain why people, in this case fans, use social media as a channel to satisfy human needs such as expressing their feelings and opinions joining conversations that give them the opportunity to interact with a wider audience (Santomier, Hogan, & Kunz, 2016). Other identified reasons of using social media are showing affection or negative feelings, recognition and personal identity, integration, entertainment, information seeking or sharing, and relaxation (Santomier et al., 2016; Vale & Fernandes, 2018).

A highly engaged fan is more likely to adopt an active behavior in social media (Browning & Sanderson, 2012). Twitter is nowadays a key platform where fans can express their identity and sentiment, positive or negative, towards a team, club or a specific athlete. Content in Twitter becomes interactive, co-created by the sports marketers and the fans, establishing a new level of engagement where fans aim to be heard, increasing the possibility of enhancing identification and loyalty with their team or athlete (Meng et al., 2015; Vale & Fernandes, 2018).

Greater reach in sports events is accompanied with greater fan engagement in a larger geographical context, which complicates tracking of fan engagement. Highly involved fans engage with the event experience: they use more media and longer hours to follow the games/league, they attend games more than regular sport audience; they read about sports or they practice sports (Shank & Beasley, 1998). This indicates that highly engaged fans use more social media and dispose more positive sentiments towards their teams and games.

Fan engagement can be measured in different ways and in this study refers to the total sentiments score. More recently, there have been several research projects that apply sentiment analysis to Twitter corpora in order to extract general public opinion (for a recent example, see Kim & Youm, 2017). Sentiment Analysis intends to comprehend these public opinions and distribute them into the categories like positive, negative, neutral with respect to opinion lexicons.

MAIN FOCUS OF THE CHAPTER

Fans in Silicon Valley expect more from their sports venues, and last season we scored big with our fans on innovation and engagement at the highest level. We're looking forward to partnering with Avaya to deliver even more value this season and give fans a connected, social and immersive experience unlike any other. – Dave Kaval, President of the San Jose Earthquakes

Technology is rapidly changing and shaping not only the business practices, but also the daily routines. Media coverage based solely on the game is not enough for demanding fans anymore. Sports facilities adapt to the challenges of big data by enabling more built-in data collection processes, such as high-powered wifi technologies and clouds to gather and store data from sport fans.

Despite the common conception on disruptive use of mobile phones, sports fans make use of their smart phones in order to receive real-time feedback during the different phases of the game (Lisi, 2016). As an example, Avaya Stadium in San Jose has taken a step forward by allowing fans during games the ability to get player stats as well as buy tickets and connect to social media through the Stadium App in their mobile phones (O'Connell, 2016). This is part of a broader trend in smart stadiums and it is a matter of time that the same cloud technology will become the norm at all MLS venues in United States and be exported to other sports facilities and geographic regions.

The Avaya Stadium Mobile app gives fans the opportunity to get connected to the fan experience by providing everything they need to know about their team San José Earthquakes. To be more specific, it provides a digital experience from before the game to all the way through the final seconds of the game. As a part of this unique opportunity, the stadium app contains multiple game day experiences, including a fan engagement wall, which displays fans' social media updates and other content in real time. Moreover, there are live polls and special offers, as well as information about other issues like parking, concessions and merchandise. The app also includes Quakes Digital Player Cards, fan trivia and fun facts, which allow fans to chat and post directly during a game. There are customized social media streams and information about tickets. A Wi-Fi service is powered by Avaya to make sure fans do not run into Internet malfunctions, no matter the size of the crowd. Cloud-based technologies are also implemented with "Fanalytics," a data analytics about fans' interests and activities.

METHODS

The dataset analysed in this study contains 892,852 tweets collected between May 18th and May 22nd 2017, both days inclusive, using hashtags associated with the Turkish Airlines Final Four teams and Euroleague Basketball. The four participating teams were Real Madrid, Fenerbahçe Doğuş, CSKA Moscow and Olympiacos BC, and the Final Four event took place in Istanbul from May 19-21, 2017.

The programming of the data collection and most of the analysis were done by using twitteR package in R, which provides an interface to the Twitter web API. Twitter provides free access to a sample of the public tweets posted on the platform.

The platform's precise sampling method is not known, but the data available through twitteR is a good representative of the overall global public communication on Twitter at any given time (citation needed). In order to get the most complete and relevant data set, we consulted with Euroleague Basketball, and identified relevant hashtags and languages used in tweets. The following hashtags were selected for our analysis: #F4Glory, #Fener4Glory, #WeareOlympiacos, #RMBaloncesto, and #CSKAbasket. Fan engagement and use of native language required a greater variety of hashtags related to particular teams and basketball context. Thus, our sampling strategy might have missed some additional minor hashtags that referred to small or short lived conversations about particular people or issues, including tweets that may not have used our identified hashtags at all.

Selecting tweets based on hashtags has the advantage of capturing the content most likely to be about this important sport event. twitteR yields tweets which contain the keyword or the hashtag. The variables generated automatically by this package are (1) text of the tweet, (2) whether it is favorited or not, (3) number of times the tweet is favorited, (4) posted time, (5) user id, (6) whether the tweet is retweeted, (7) number of times the tweet is retweeted, (8) source of the tweet as an HTTP link, (9) user name, (10) user coordinates as latitude, and (11) user coordinates as longitude.

The method counted tweets with selected hashtags in a simple manner. Each tweet counted as one if it contained one of the specific hashtags that were being followed. If a tweet contained more than one selected hashtag, it was credited to all the relevant hashtag categories.

Contributions using none of these hashtags were not captured in this data set. It is also possible that users who used one or more of these hashtags, but were not discussing the Final Four games, had their tweets captured. Moreover, if people tweeted about the Final Four games, but did not use one of these hashtags or identify a candidate account, their contributions were not analyzed here.

Regarding the sentiment analysis, we used both a corpus based technique and a dictionary based technique (Kumar & Sebastian, 2012). We built a corpus, which is a large and structured set of text data, and preprocessed the corpus using the following standard procedures (Weiss et al., 2005). To be more specific, we first prepared the corpus by cleaning up sentences with R's regex-driven global substitute from punctuation, URLs (www), hashtags (#), targets (@) and Tweeter-specific notation (RT). Later, we converted the entire text to small caps and finally split the corpus into words. This enabled the generation of word clouds without any additional process. In order to rate the sentiment of a tweet, we defined two dictionaries which consisted of positive words and negative words lists respectively (Hu & Liu, 2004; Liu, Hu, & Cheng, 2005). The purpose of the algorithm was to assign 1 if a word was either encountered in positive words dictionary or negative words dictionary, and N/A if otherwise. We finally compared our words to the dictionaries of positive and negative terms and obtained the sum of positive and negative matches respectively. Subtracting the sum of positive matches from negative matches would return the sentiment score, which would be a positive number, negative number, or zero.

RESULTS

The communication carried out on Twitter had important characteristics. First of all, tweets in Turkish exceeded tweets in English, the common language used among basketball fans in Europe. On the other hand, the tweets in other native languages (Greek, Spanish and Russian) were far less in numbers. Consequently, the tweets in Turkish and English accounted for the greatest share of activity. Table 1 summarizes the number of tweets per hashtag in English and native languages per day.

The authors analyzed the discussion on Twitter in terms of (1) number of tweets in native language of Fenerbahçe (Turkish), (2) number of tweets per team in English, (3) number of tweets in native language of Olympiacos, Real Madrid, and CSKA (Greek, Spanish and Russian respectively), (4) the preferred means of communication for Turkish and international fans, and (5) sentiment analysis.

Regarding the number of tweets, the highest number of tweets was extracted from Turkish fans using #Fener4Glory hashtag in Turkish. Overall, Turkish fans tweeted for their team Fenerbahçe 643,433 times in Turkish during the span of the event. Not surprisingly, the second highest number of tweets was also extracted from Turkish fans using #F4Glory hashtag in Turkish. In total, Turkish fans tweeted for Final Four 146,127 times during the span of the event. Figure 1 summarizes the number of tweets for #Fener4Glory and #F4Glory hashtags per day in Turkish.

Table 1. Number of tweets per hashtag in English and native languages per day

Hashtag	Language	May 18th	May 19th	May 20th	May 21st	May 22nd	Total
#F4Glory	Turkish	4323	49946	14614	69037	8207	146127
#Fener4Glory	Turkish	17744	168457	46034	361300	49898	643433
#F4Glory	English	1374	10923	2702	28453	6267	49719
#Fener4Glory	English	2359	9419	1048	23854	2838	39518
#WeareOlympiacos	English	148	486	118	447	43	1242
#RMBaloncesto	English	40	228	85	118	4	475
#CSKAbasket	English	45	116	10	26	2	199
#WeareOlympiacos	Greek	314	3760	538	1976	110	6698
#RMBaloncesto	Spanish	509	3403	637	795	33	5377
#CSKAbasket	Russian	4	32	2	24	5	67

Figure 1. Number of tweets for #Fener4Glory and #F4Glory in Turkish

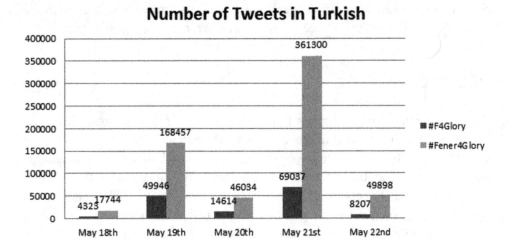

Regarding the number of tweets in English, the highest number of tweets was extracted from #F4Glory hashtag. In the international context, Final Four had been tweeted 49,719 times in English during the span of the event. Not surprisingly, the second highest number of tweets was extracted from #Fener4Glory hashtag with a total of 39,518 times in English during the span of the event. Compared to the aforementioned activities, Twitter activity corresponding to other teams was drastically lower. To be more specific, #WeareOlympiacos, #RMBaloncesto and #CSKABasket had been tweeted only 1242, 475 and 199 times respectively in the international context. Figure 2 summarizes the number of tweets per hashtag per day in English.

Given the low engagement of the international fans, the authors decided to conduct the same analysis for the native language of each team. Regarding the number of tweets in native language, the highest number of tweets was extracted from Greek fans using #WeareOlympiacos hashtag in Greek. Surprisingly, #WeareOlympiacos tweets in Greek outnumbered #WeareOlympiacos tweets in English, such that the former consists of 6696 tweets while the latter consists of 1242 tweets. Twitter activity concerned with #RMBaloncesto in Spanish context was lower with a total of 5377 tweets while Twitter activity concerned with #CSKABasket in Russian was lowest with 67 tweets in total. Figure 3 summarizes the number of tweets per hashtag per day in native languages of the teams.

The authors identified the common means of engagement in social media by looking at the source of the tweet. We found that the engagement pattern was same for both Turkish and international fans: Smart phones (IPhone and Android) apps account for 85% of the sources of tweets, underlining the importance of real-time

Figure 2. Number of tweets per hashtag per day in English

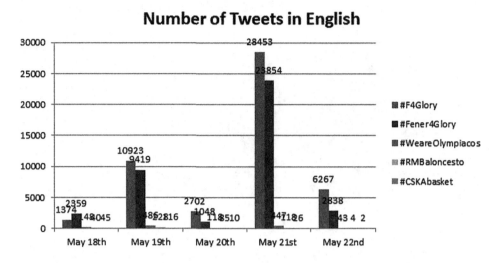

Figure 3. Number of tweets per hashtag per day in native language

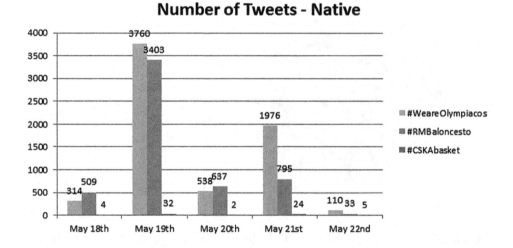

feedback, while the Twitter webpage accounts for 7% to 10% and Ipad app accounts for 1%. Figure 4 depicts common means of engagement in social media by exploring #Fener4Glory tweets in Turkish.

Figure 5, on the other hand, below depicts common means of engagement in social media by exploring #F4Glory tweets in English.

The authors generated word clouds to observe the common conversation about the event. We specifically selected the final game played on May 21st in order to work with the largest number of observations. There were two hashtags of interest

Figure 4. Common means of engagement in social media: Turkish fans

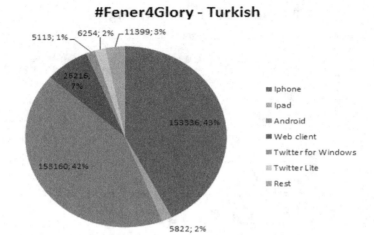

Figure 5. Common means of engagement in social media: International fans

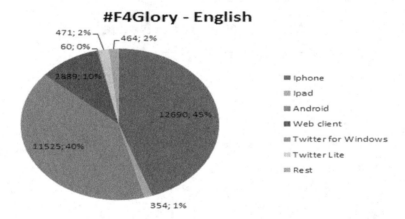

for that particular day, #F4Glory and #Fener4Glory which generated the highest volume of tweets. As seen in Figure 6, Final Four was largely associated with the victory of Fenerbahçe against Olympiacos.

Figure 7, on the other hand, indicates that Fenerbahçe's victory was largely associated with the city where the Final Four tournaments were organized – Istanbul, and the star player Bobby Dixon.

The authors quantified the sentiment inherent in tweets by applying the aforementioned algorithm and accounted for the total sentiment generated per hashtag per day. We found that the highest sentiment was generated #F4Glory hashtag, created by Euroleague Basketball as the event organizers. As seen in Figure 8, a

Figure 6. Word Cloud for #F4Glory

Figure 7. Word Cloud for #Fener4Glory

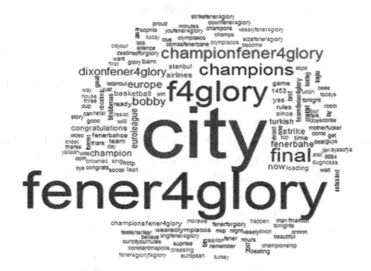

sharp increase in sentiment was observed on the day of the games while a phase-out was observed post-games.

The authors also looked at how positive, negative and neutral sentiments evolved over the course of the game. In order to carry out this analysis, we counted positive, negative and neutral sentiments, and plotted each of these sentiments separately. As seen in Figure 9, the dominant sentiment was neutral in the beginning of the event,

Figure 8. Evolution of #F4Glory sentiment over the event

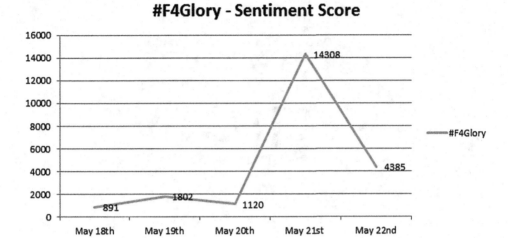

but positive sentiment climbed up drastically during the course of the event. The potential for sports events to generate a 'feel good' factor among fans in general was evident.

When they looked at the sentiments generated from a team-based perspective, the authors observed that the highest sentiment was generated by #Fener4Glory, as Fenerbahçe was the winner of the cup. Second highest sentiment belonged to #WeareOlympiacos as Olympiacos ranked second in Final Four. There was an increase in #RMBaloncesto sentiment on May 20th as Real Madrid won the third-place game on that day. Sentiment score CSKA was low as their fans were not as engaged as other teams' on Twitter. The results can be seen in Figure 10. Therefore, performance on the court directly affected the sentiment of fans.

DISCUSSION

Whilst fan sentiment varies between fan groups depending largely on how their teams are performing, the overall effect of the event is positive and a general 'feel good' factor occurred in Twitter around the event. This is important for all major marketing and communications stakeholders involved in the event. For event sponsors it is important to know that whilst fan rivalries are played out on the court between teams from different geographic markets, the positive sentiment around the event transcends this. Advertisers would be interested to know how the fans are feeling in real time and how this fluctuates during a game and between games. Digital advertising tools enable advertisers to adjust their tactics in response to these

Figure 9. Evolution of #F4Glory sentiment polarity over the event

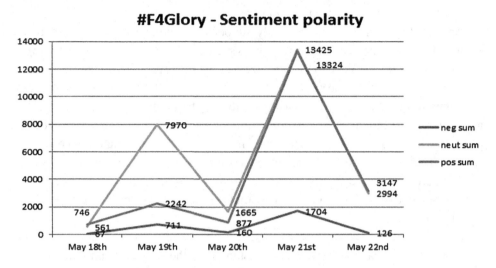

Figure 10. Evolution of team sentiments over the event

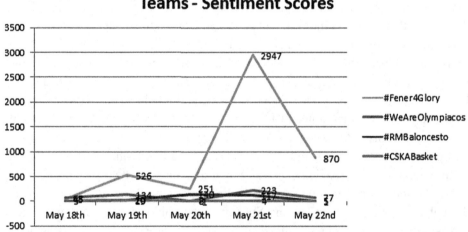

changes, focusing on certain fan groups and adapting their messages accordingly to fit the mood.

The fact that the #F4Glory hashtag was the most active in the English language and was used by fans from all four teams was an important finding for the event organizers, Euroleague Basketball as they created it. The hashtag served to bring together fans from rival teams and create a conversation that the event organizers were at the center of. Again this has interesting implications for events sponsors with whom Euroleague Basketball coordinate their marketing activities as it formed a virtual meeting point that gathered fans.

Another key finding from the study supported existing research was that fan engagement through social media platforms such as Twitter was happening through apps on smart phones. We can hypothesize that the majority of these fans are multi-screening (e.g. watching the game on TV whilst using Twitter on their smart phones) and some were at the event itself, using Twitter on their smart phones whilst at the arena. This is of direct interest to communications stakeholders such as broadcast partners who need to know that their audiences are dividing their attention between screens. This of course has a direct impact on advertisers and sponsors who need to know where the fans' 'eyeballs' are in and around the game, reinforcing the need to multi-channel communication strategies that are adaptable in real-time depending on fan sentiment.

In terms of the most used words and concepts used by fans, a surprising and interesting result was the prevalence of Istanbul as the host city and home to the eventual champions. The importance of place and identity among fans could be linked with pride in this context, and would have clear implications for place marketing (city, region or country) through sports events. This result would also have been of particular interest to the title sponsor of the event, Turkish Airlines, as well as other sponsors interested in geographic marketing. The focus on a player in the word clouds was also interesting and highlights the importance of individual sports stars. Channels such as Twitter become platforms for hero worshiping and yet again, this is of direct interest to the companies that sign endorsement deals with these players and the exposure this may provide not only in terms of the number of times the player was mentioned by fans, but also the ability to link this to sentiment.

Overall, the insights provided by this study reveal several important opportunities for sports event organisers and their marketing and communications partners to monitor not only fan behaviour, such as which social media channels they are using and when, but more importantly their feelings and how these are communicated through interactions with other fans. Such insights enable professionals involved in sports marketing to take better informed decisions and reveal the potential to adapt their digital marketing tactics in real time. For researchers, the increasing use of social media platforms and the growing volume of contents on them represent an unprecedented opportunity to engage in big data analysis in contexts such as sports events, and to better understand the nature and meanings of fan interactions in digital environments. This type of analysis requires new methodologies and the design of new methods to capture and analyse this data, and for researchers to undertake exploratory studies such as the one discussed in this chapter.

FUTURE RESEARCH DIRECTIONS

We see data as inevitable coming into the game. – Jeff Agoos, Vice-President for Competition at Major League Soccer (MLS)

Word cloud and sentiment analysis bring new data to the game. Live sentiment analysis is a future line of practice to check the moods of the fans pre / during / post – game. This motivated us to propose a model that retrieves tweets, calculates the sentiment orientation/score of each tweet and publishes in real-time. This recent trend for research for sentiment analysis in Twitter can be utilized and extended for many practical applications that range from applications in marketing (person marketing, event marketing), customer relationship management (customer segmentation, loyalty tracking), applications in sponsorship (sponsorship effectiveness), applications in digital media (content management, mobile app management). For example, there are new ways for fans to quantify a players' performance such as sharing of data about players in real time, even going far enough to have these data displayed on players' jersey (Lisi, 2016). The model we propose would be just another technological innovation that could make its way to fans when they watch a game on television.

Digitalization and the increasing use of social media by fans means that big data is being generated around sports events, creating an unprecedented opportunity to analyze and understand fan interaction and the nature of fan engagement. The proposed model of live sentiment analysis responds to how to make use of big data in the context of sports management and fan engagement, and how the increasing amount of data improves decision-making and fosters innovation through effective knowledge sharing practices. This model is therefore an answer to how big data in the context of sports management enhances progress and organizational performance.

CONCLUSION

Continuous monitoring is required for a multi-channel strategy, which would need to be channel-specific, team-specific, game cycle-specific and result and performance-specific. Regarding channel-specific, the authors looked at the communication on Twitter only. Regarding team-specific, the authors looked at how the number of tweets and sentimental performance changed for each team. Regarding game cycle-specific, we explored Final Four event-cycle and looked at how the number of tweets and sentimental performance changed with respect to important games. The last but not the least, the authors looked at how game results boost tweets in a performance-specific monitoring.

This comprehensive study aims to be an essential reference source for the use of Twitter data in the context of fan engagement, building on the available literature in the field of sports management while providing for further research opportunities in big data and sports management.

ACKNOWLEDGMENT

The authors thank Turkish Airlines Euroleague Basketball in Barcelona, Spain for guidance in this research project. This research received no specific grant from any funding agency in the public, commercial, or not-for-profit sectors.

REFERENCES

Abeza, G., Pegoraro, A., Naraine, M. L., & Séguin, B., & O'Reilly, N. (2015). Activating a global sport sponsorship with social media: An analysis of TOP sponsors, Twitter, and the 2014 Olympic Games. *International Journal of Sport Management and Marketing*, *154*(34), 184–213. doi:10.1504/IJSMM.2014.072010

Adıgüzel, F., & Kennett, C. (2017). *Sport event sponsorship effectiveness: A cross-cultural study*. Working Paper.

Atenstaedt, R. (2012). Word cloud analysis of the BJGP. *The British Journal of General Practice*, *62*(596), 148. doi:10.3399/bjgp12X630142 PMID:22429422

Beech, J., Kaiser, S., & Kaspar, R. (2014). *The Business of Events Management*. Pearson Education Limited.

Browning, B., & Sanderson, J. (2012). The positives and negatives of Twitter: Exploring how student-athletes use Twitter and respond to critical Tweets. *International Journal of Sport Communication*, *5*(4), 503–521. doi:10.1123/ijsc.5.4.503

Castells, M. (2016). A sociology of power: My intellectual journey. *Annual Review of Sociology*, *42*(1), 1–19. doi:10.1146/annurev-soc-081715-074158

De Moragas, M., Kennett, C., & Ginesta, X. (2013). Football and media in Europe. New sport paradigm for the global era. In Sport and the Transformation of Modern Europe. States, Media and Markets 1950-2010. London: Routledge.

Delia, E. B., & Armstrong, C. G. (2015). #Sponsoring the #FrenchOpen: An examination of social media buzz and sentiment. *Journal of Sport Management*, *29*(2), 184–199. doi:10.1123/JSM.2013-0257

Earthquakes, S. J. (2018). *Avaya Stadium - First cloud-enabled stadium in MLS*. Retrieved from https://sanjose-mp7static.mlsdigital.net/elfinderimages/170712_ avaya_stadium_ infographic_b_print_8-5x11.jpeg

Foster, G., O'Reilly, N., & Davila, A. (2016). *Sports Business Management: Decision Making Around the Globe*. Routledge. doi:10.4324/9781315687827

Gibbs, C., & Haynes, R. (2013). A phenomenological investigation into how Twitter has changed the nature of sport media relations. *International Journal of Sport Communication*, 6(4), 394–408. doi:10.1123/ijsc.6.4.394

Gibbs, C., O'Reilly, N., & Brunette, M. (2014). Professional Team Sport and Twitter: Gratifications Sought and Obtained by Followers. *International Journal of Sport Communication*, 7(2), 188–213. doi:10.1123/IJSC.2014-0005

Gratch, J., Lucas, G., Malandrakis, N., Szablowski, E., Fessler, E., & Nichols, J. (2015). GOAALLL!: Using Sentiment in the World Cup to Explore Theories of Emotion. *International Conference on Affective Computing and Intelligent Interaction (ACII)*, 898-903. 10.1109/ACII.2015.7344681

Halevi, G., & Moed, H. F. (2012, September). *The technological impact of library science research*. Paper presented at the 17th International Conference on Science and Technology Indicators (STI), Montreal, Quebec, Canada.

Hu, M., & Liu, B. (2004). Mining and summarizing customer reviews. *Proceedings of the ACM SIGKDD International Conference on Knowledge Discovery and Data.*

International Olympic Committee (IOC). (2009). *Games of the XXIX Olympiad, Beijing 2008 Global Television and Online Media Report*. IOC.

Kim, E. H., & Youm, Y. N. (2017). How do social media affect analyst stock recommendations? Evidence from S&P 500 electric power companies' Twitter accounts. *Strategic Management Journal*, 38(13), 2599–2622. doi:10.1002mj.2678

Kumar, I., & Sebastian, T. M. (2012). Sentiment Analysis on Twitter. *International Journal of Computer Science Issues, 9*(4-3), 372-378.

Leaders, R. (2017). *OTT - The shifting broadcasting landscape*. Retrieved from leadersinsport.com

Lisi, C. (2016). *Soccer's high-tech future*. Retrieved from https://ussoccerplayers. com/2016/09/soccers-high-tech-future-mls-ifab-video-referee.html

Liu, B., Hu, M., & Cheng, J. (2005). Opinion observer: Analyzing and comparing opinions on the web. *Proceedings of the 14th International World Wide Web conference (WWW 2005)*. 10.1145/1060745.1060797

Meng, M. D., Stavros, C., & Westberg, K. (2015). Engaging fans through social media: Implications for team identification. *Sport, Business and Management. International Journal (Toronto, Ont.)*, 5(3), 199–217.

O'Connell, E. (2016). *Avaya giving San Jose Earthquakes digital boost for in-stadium fan experience*. Retrieved from https://www.sporttechie.com/avaya-giving-san-jose-earthquakes-digital-boost-for-in-stadium-fan-experience/

Parganas, P., Anagnostopoulos, C., & Chadwick, S. (2015). 'You'll never tweet alone': Managing sports brands through social media. *Journal of Brand Management*, 22(7), 551–568. doi:10.1057/bm.2015.32

Price, J., Farrington, N., & Hall, L. (2013). Changing the game? The impact of Twitter on relationships between football clubs, supporters and the sports media. *Soccer and Society*, 14(4), 446–461. doi:10.1080/14660970.2013.810431

Samra, B., & Wos, A. (2014). Consumer in Sports: Fan typology analysis. *Journal of Intercultural Management*, 6(4–1), 263–288. doi:10.2478/joim-2014-0050

Santomier, J. P., Hogan, P. I., & Kunz, R. (2016). The 2012 London Olympics: Innovations in ICT and social media marketing. *Innovation: Management, Policy & Practice*, 18(3), 251–269. doi:10.1080/14479338.2016.1237305

Shank, M. D., & Beasley, F. M. (1998). Fan or fanatic: Refining a measure of sports involvement. *Journal of Sport Behavior*, 21(4), 435–443.

Smith, L. R., & Smith, K. D. (2012). Identity in Twitter's Hashtag Culture: A Sport-Media Consumption Case Study. *International Journal of Sport Communication*, 5(4), 539–557. doi:10.1123/ijsc.5.4.539

Vale, L., & Fernandes, T. (2018). Social media and sports: Driving fan engagement with football clubs on Facebook. *Journal of Strategic Marketing*, 26(1), 37–55. doi:10.1080/0965254X.2017.1359655

Watanabe, N., Yan, G., & Soebbing, B. P. (2015). Major League Baseball and Twitter Usage: The Economics of Social Media Use. *Journal of Sport Management*, 29(6), 619–632. doi:10.1123/JSM.2014-0229

Watanabe, N. M., Yan, G., & Soebbing, B. P. (2016). Consumer Interest in Major League Baseball: An Analytical Modeling of Twitter. *Journal of Sport Management*, 30(2), 207–220. doi:10.1123/jsm.2015-0121

Weiss, S. M., Indurkhya, N., Zhang, T., & Damerau, F. J. (2005). *Text Mining-Predictive Methods for Analyzing Unstructured Information*. Springer Verlag.

KEY TERMS AND DEFINITIONS

Fan Engagement: An engagement, in social media terms, as any deliberate interaction on the fan's part, meaning that something said made them want to spend their time and take an action to show their support for.

Hashtag: A word or phrase preceded by a hash sign (#), used on social media websites and applications, especially Twitter, to identify messages on a specific topic.

Real-Time Feedback: A type of qualitative and/or quantitative data collection, received live from visitors of a website, social media platform, or mobile application.

Sentiment Analysis: A process of computationally identifying and categorizing opinions expressed in a piece of text, especially in order to determine whether the writer's attitude towards a particular topic, product, etc. is positive, negative, or neutral.

Sentiment Polarity: A basic task in sentiment analysis classifying whether the expressed opinion in a document, a sentence or an entity feature/aspect is positive, negative, or neutral.

Social Media Platform: A web-based technology that enables the development, deployment, and management of social media solutions and services. It provides the ability to create social media websites and services with complete social media network functionality.

Word Cloud: An image composed of words used in a particular text or subject in which the size of each word indicates its frequency or importance.

Chapter 9
Developing a Big–Data–Based Model to Study and Analyze Network Traffic

Mahesh Pawar
Rajiv Gandhi Proudyogiki Vishwavidyalaya, India

Anjana Panday
Rajiv Gandhi Proudyogiki Vishwavidyalaya, India

Ratish Agrawal
Rajiv Gandhi Proudyogiki Vishwavidyalaya, India

Sachin Goyal
Rajiv Gandhi Proudyogiki Vishwavidyalaya, India

ABSTRACT

Network is a connection of devices in either a wired or wireless manner. Networking has become a part and parcel of computing in the present world. They form the backbone of the modern-day computing business. Hence, it is important for networks to remain alive, up, and reliable all the time. A way to ensure that is network traffic analysis. Network traffic analysis mainly deals with a study of bandwidth utilization, transmission and reception rates, error rates, etc., which is important to keep the network smooth and improve economic efficiency. The proposed model approaches network traffic analysis in a way to collect network information and then deal with it using technologies available for big data analysis. The model aims to analyze the collected information to calculate a factor called reliability factor, which can guide in effective network management. The model also aims to assist the network administrator by informing him whether network traffic is high or low, and the administrator can then take targeted steps to prevent network failure.

DOI: 10.4018/978-1-5225-7519-1.ch009

INTRODUCTION

Big data is a general term that describes a vast amount of data which can either be in a structured, semi-structured or unstructured form. Such data has the potential to be analysed and subsequently mined to extract useful information. Big data also refers to technologies and tasks that involve data that are extremely diverse in nature, fast-changing or too massive for traditional technologies to handle and analyse efficiently. Big data is characterised, among others, by the three Vs namely, volume, velocity and variety. The 3Vs characteristics of big data accounts for the increasing exponential volume of data being generated. Big data has gained lot of traction in recent years. This is because of the way businesses manage and derive information from the enormous data being generated. Thereby changing the way the world uses data. By analyzing big data in an effective way one can, identify risks, make more informed decisions, and can hence, implement a better system for performing, evaluating and supporting tasks within an organization.

An effective way of analyzing big data is presented in this chapter, based on a proposed model. The proposed model will efficiently facilitate the deployment of big data and its related technologies to perform network traffic analysis. The process will be performed via the collection of data from various connected nodes and studying the different parameters to detect network traffic. A network in the field of IT is a group of computers and associated devices that are connected to each other either in a wired or wireless manner by the means of communications facilities. Networks can also be defined as inter connected collection of autonomous and independent computers or nodes. Computers connected in such a way are capable of sharing not just data but also resources. Networking enables, resource sharing, improved system reliability, cost reduction, fast communication and facillitates file Sharing. In the field of networking, traffic analysis is a very important domain because ever since the internet has become popular, transmission speed and the response time still remain as significant problems. These factors also become decisive because network traffic management as a factor, tends to dominate market share of industries. The model proposed in this chapter, brings forth a method to calculate a factor called- reliability factor. This factor can provide a guide to the efficient and quantitative management of the network. This proposed model has been implemented using tools like netload, iftop, vnstat, bmon. An implementation part has been performed in Python.

RELATED WORK

In a research paper titled, "Network Traffic Analysis Measurement and Classification Using Hadoop (Joshi et al, 2016)" it was discussed that given the increase in Internet users and applications that require higher bandwidth; the quantity of Internet traffic data generated is very huge. In this context, there is the need for an intelligent, highly scalable and efficient technologies to analyze, measure, and classify this data traffic. Traditional tools will not be able to perform this task due to their limited computational capacity and storage capacity. This is why Hadoop exists today.

Hadoop, is a distributed framework which performs big data analysis in a very efficient manner. Hadoop processes this huge amount of traffic data with a Hive and mainly runs on commodity hardware with distributed storage. The main purpose for the invention of Hadoop is to process large data very efficiently. Nowadays, the World Wide Web is generating lots of information on a daily basis. Hence it is extremely necessary and, at the same time, difficult to manage billion of pages of content. The evolution of Hadoop is described in the paper "A Hadoop Framework Require to Process Big data very easily and efficiently" (White, 2008). The paper also described why Hadoop is needed and why it is necessary. There is also detailed study of the Hadoop framework and how it functions as an open source software to support distributed computing. Hadoop also includes a Distributed File System (HDFS), which manages distributed data on different node and Map-Reduce for programming paradigm (Naik & Joshi, 2016). Big data analysis and network traffic analysis are the imperative concepts for effective and efficient data transmission.

However, big data is managed and transported in a networked environment. In today's world, Network systems create huge amount of data of various formats and in various granularities, ranging from statistics to packet level about whole flows. In addition, with the introduction of cloud computing, Content Delivery Networks and mobile Internet usage, the complexity of the Internet has surged rapidly. This complexity is expected to further increase in the future with the increase in the number of Machine-to-Machine communication and ubiquitous wearable devices that have surged in the recent years. Therefore, all the network monitoring frameworks cannot rely only on information or data gathered at a single network interconnection point, but must collect and consolidate information from various vantage points distributed across the network.

In literature, different models have been proposed towards handle the management of big data in a networked environment.

In the paper "DBStream: A holistic approach to large-scale network traffic monitoring and analysis" (Baer et al, 2016) DBStream was compared to MapReduce processing engines and the paper showed how intelligent job scheduling can increase its performance even further. Furthermore, the paper exposed the versatility of DBStream by explaining how it was integrated to import and process data from two passive network monitoring systems.

The another paper titled, "Analysis of high volumes of network traffic for Advanced Persistent Threat (APT) detection (Rinaldi, Himpe & Tampère, 2016)"a presentation is made of a model for network security analysis. The paper further develops a way to discover newer forms of automatic defense mechanisms aimed at quick and early detection of APTs in large and continuously varying networked system via the performance of an experiment based on evaluations in a networked environment.

In another research paper titled "Privacy-aware contextual localization using network traffic analysis"(Morley & Nixon, 2016), the writer introduces a PACL (Privacy-Aware Contextual Localizer) model. This model can discover and identify the user's contextual location just by passively monitoring user's network traffic.

In another research paper titled, "Robust dynamic network traffic partitioning against malicious attacks" (Rinaldi, Himpe & Tampère, 2016), the authors presents a robust dynamic network traffic partitioning scheme to defend against malicious attacks. After introducing the conceptual framework of dynamic network traffic partitioning based on flow tables, the TCP connection management is strengthened by building a half-open connection separation mechanism that will isolate false connections in the initial connection table (ICT) (Xiong, Yang, Zhao & Li, 2017).

The lookup performance of the ICT table is reinforced by applying counting bloom filters to cope with malicious behaviours such as SYN flooding attacks "(Morley & Nixon, 2016). This is an approach adopted in the creation of our proposed model. This was followed by an evaluation of the performance of our proposed traffic partitioning scheme with real network traffic traces and simulated malicious traffic via experimentation. The results in this chapter indicates that, in terms of packet distribution performance especially robustness against malicious attacks, the proposed scheme (model) outperforms the conventional ones.

ARCHITECTURE

To implement traffic analysis using our proposed model, the architecture was created as shown in Figure 1.

The basic architecture of the proposed model as shown in Figure 2 have also been summarized in the form of the flow chart below. The flowchart also depicts the algorithm of the model.

The basic architecture of the proposed model has also been summarized in the form of also depicts the algorithm of the model.

Figure 1. Basic architecture of network traffic analysis

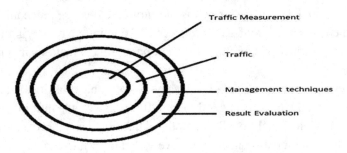

Figure 2. Architecture of the proposed model

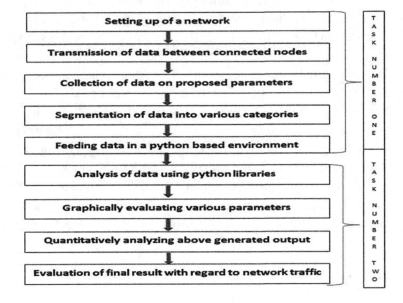

PROPOSED WORK

The model proposes a multi- tool based methodology that resulted in the division of the entire task into two subtasks. The first task was the collection of data and the second task was the analysis of data aimed at achieving traffic management. The first task was performed using these tools: Netload, vnstat, bmon, ifto. The information obtained from these tools on various parameters was fed into a python based environment that generated the reliability factor to quantitatively managed traffic.

The model is based on network analysis and for the network analysis, several tools have been utilized. The data obtained was analysed using several libraries available in python.

The whole architecture is based on python and the underlying hardware used was Ubuntu 17.04 Zesty Zeus (Linux) with the following specifications:

1. **Processor:** Intel i3-4030 @ 1.90 Ghz
2. **Memory:** 3 GB
3. **Hard Disk:** 20 GB

In addition, Windows based laptops were used to create a Local Area network (LAN). The laptos used for the LAN had similar hardware specifications. The LAN was based on wired connection using a D-Link router.

The architecture (methology) was divided into two parts namely data gathering and data analysis.

1. **Data Gathering:** Data gathering was performed using different open source tools available in Linux such as:

BMON, SPEEDOMETER, VNSTAT, IFTOP, and NETLOAD.

Also for programming (coding and its implementation) IPYTHON was used.

2. **Data Analysis:** The data gathered from first step were then analysed using python libraries such as NUMPY, PANDAS and generated as graphs using MATPLOTLIB library.

Based on the result of the network data analysis one can acquire information on, the network status, the Local Area Network, the computers and network devices connected to it. The demo was performed in a small and limited environment consisting of three laptops connected to each other, using wired LAN and files of certain size was sent and received between different laptops. And based on that feedback from that setup, network traffic analysis was performed and the graph was plotted. The analysis helps us in deciding the issues in the network, network consumption and also helps us in localising the fault, if any.

The tools used were:

NETLOAD

Netload is a simple network bandwidth tool. The netload command displays a small report on the current traffic load, and the total number of bytes transferred after the program is started. There is no other feature. It is a part of the netdiag.

As part of netdiag, Netload is available in the default repository. Therefore, we can easily install **netdiag** using **apt** manager using the command given below.

```
$ sudo install netdiag
```

To run netload, we must ensure that a working network interface name like eth0, eh1, wlan0, mon0, etc. And run the following command accordingly in a shell or a terminal as shown in Figure 3.

```
$ netload wlan2.
```

Note: Replace wlan2 with the network interface name you want to use. If you want to scan for your network interface name run ip link show in a terminal or shell.

VNSTAT

Vnstat is bit different than other tools. It actually runs a background service/daemon and keeps recording the size of data transfer all the time. Next it can be used to generate reports of network usage history.

Vnstat is available in the default repository. So, we can run **apt** manager to install it using the following command.

Figure 3. Netload working

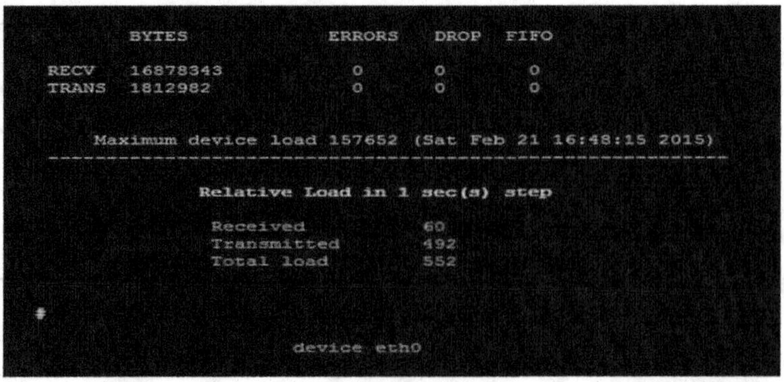

```
$ sudo apt-get install vnstat
$ vnstat
Output:
Database updated: Fri Nov 4 17:05:24 2016
eth3 since 11/04/16
rx: 34.68 MiB tx: 3.45 MiB total: 38.13 MiB
monthly
rx | tx | total | avg. rate
————————+——————-+——————-+————————
Nov '16 34.68 MiB | 3.45 MiB | 38.13 MiB | 0.97 kbit/s
————————+——————-+——————-+————————
estimated 274 MiB | 24 MiB | 298 MiB |
daily
rx | tx | total | avg. rate
————————+——————-+——————-+————————
today 34.68 MiB | 3.45 MiB | 38.13 MiB | 5.08 kbit/s
————————+——————-+——————-+————————
estimated 47 MiB | 4 MiB | 51 MiB |
```

Running vnstat without any options will simply show the total amount of data transfer that took place since the date the daemon is running.

When one runs vnstat first time it gives warning message "eth3: Not enough data available yet" as shown in Figure 4. One can then try this command after some time so the vnstat will gather some details related to network usage.

If one wants to see the current status of network usage then the following command with some options can be used.

```
$ vnstat -l -i wlan2
```

Figure 5 shows a screenshot from the model, depicting the above.

Figure 4. Vnstat working

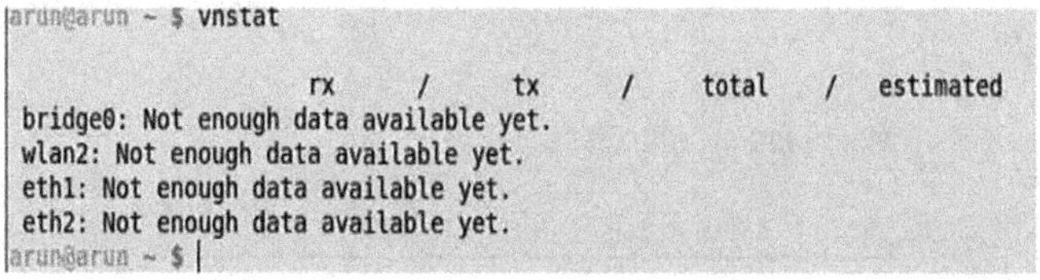

```
arun@arun ~ $ vnstat
                    rx     /     tx     /     total   /   estimated
 bridge0: Not enough data available yet.
 wlan2: Not enough data available yet.
 eth1: Not enough data available yet.
 eth2: Not enough data available yet.
arun@arun ~ $
```

Figure 5. Vnstat output

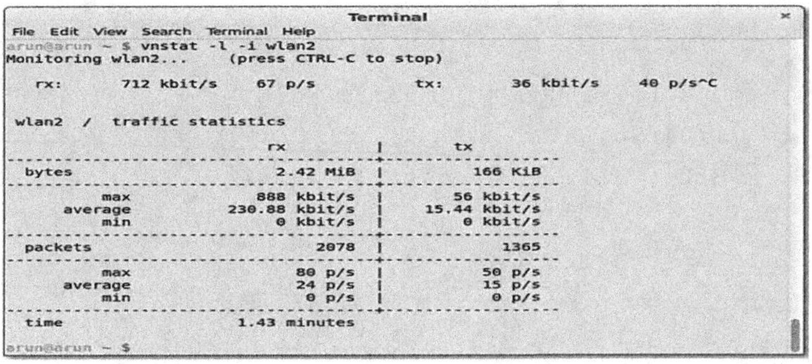

To monitor the bandwidth usage in real time, use the '-l' option (live mode). Then it will show the total bandwidth used by incoming and outgoing data, but in a very appropriate way without any internal details about host connections or processes.

After done, press Ctrl-C to stop which will result the following type (Figures 6 and 7) of output:

```
$ vnstat -l
```

BMON

Bmon (Bandwidth monitor) is similar to netload that shows the traffic load on all the network interfaces on the system but Bmon provides much more details. Bmon is another tool used to monitor bandwidth on a Linux machine. The output is a graph and a section with packet level description. The output of Bmon tool also provides graph and packet details as shown in Figure 8. One can choose the Ethernet option by pressing the arrow up/down to check the bandwidth on the graph. Also, one can choose "d" option for extra details of network usage.

```
$ apt-get install bmon
$ bmon
```

Figure 6. Vnstat options

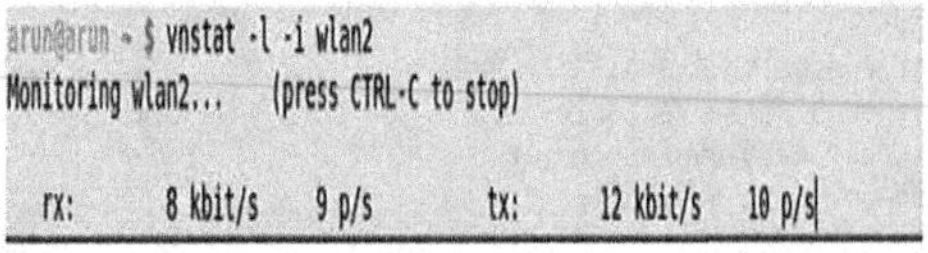

Figure 7. Vnstat report

```
$ vnstat
Database updated: Mon Mar 17 15:26:59 2014

   eth0 since 06/12/13

          rx:   135.14 GiB        tx:   35.76 GiB        total:   170.90 GiB

   monthly
                        rx      |       tx      |      total     |    avg. rate
        -----------------------+----------------+----------------+----------------
         Feb '14      8.19 GiB  |    2.08 GiB    |   10.27 GiB    |   35.60 kbit/s
         Mar '14      4.98 GiB  |    1.52 GiB    |    6.50 GiB    |   37.93 kbit/s
        -----------------------+----------------+----------------+----------------
       estimated      9.28 GiB  |    2.83 GiB    |   12.11 GiB    |

   daily
                        rx      |       tx      |      total     |    avg. rate
        -----------------------+----------------+----------------+----------------
       yesterday    236.11 MiB  |   98.61 MiB    |  334.72 MiB    |   31.74 kbit/s
           today    128.55 MiB  |   41.00 MiB    |  169.56 MiB    |   24.97 kbit/s
        -----------------------+----------------+----------------+----------------
       estimated     199 MiB    |    63 MiB      |   262 MiB      |
```

Figure 8. Bmon working

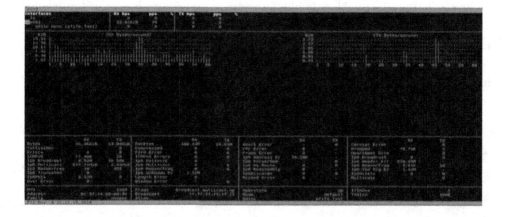

Bmon supports many options as shown in Figure 9 and is able to create reports in html format.

IFTOP

Iftop listens or provide info on network traffic. It will display the traffic by pairs of hosts. Iftop reports a bandwidth on individual connections.

Figure 9. Bmon output

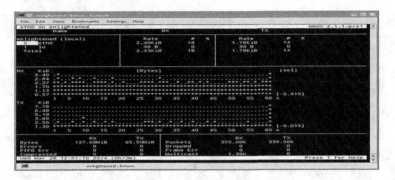

Run below command to install iftop on a Linux machine.

```
$ sudo iftop -n
```

Iftop measures the data flowing through individual socket connections, and it works in a way that is different from Nload. Iftop uses the pcap library to capture the packets moving in and out of the network adapter, and then sums up the size and count to find the total bandwidth under use.

Although iftop reports the bandwidth used by individual connections, it cannot report the process name/id involved in the particular socket connection. But being based on the pcap library, iftop is able to filter the traffic and report bandwidth usage on selected host connections as specified by the filter.

The n option prevents iftop from resolving Internet Protocol (IP) addresses to hostname, which causes additional network traffic of its own.

One can run below command to install iftop on a Linux machine.

```
$ apt-get install iftop
$ iftop -n
```

One can use below options with iftop:

- -h option displays this message
- -n option doesn't do hostname lookups
- -N option don't convert port numbers to services
- -p option run in promiscuous mode (show traffic between other hosts on the same network segment)
- -b options don't display a bar graph of traffic
- -B option display bandwidth in bytes

- -I option interface listen on named interface
- -f option filter code uses filter code to select packets to count
- (Default: none, but only IP packets are counted)
- -F option net/mask show traffic flows in/out of IPv4 network
- -G option net6/mask6 show traffic flows in/out of IPv6 network
- -l option display and count link-local IPv6 traffic (default: off)
- -P option show ports as well as hosts
- -m option limit sets the upper limit for the bandwidth scale
- -c option config file specifies an alternative configuration file

Figure 10 is a screenshot from the model.
Figure 11 is a screenshot of Iftop output from the model.

Figure 10. Iftop working

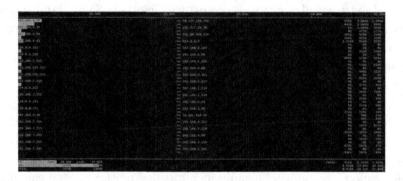

Figure 11. Iftop output

Speedometer

Speedometer is simple network bandwidth tool which draws graphs of incoming and outgoing traffic. Speedometer shows a graph of the speed of your current and past network in your console. It allows you to see the speed and history of your network up and downstream connection at a glance. You can also use the speedometer on a file directly to monitor, the download performance and, a specific download history instead of all network traffic.

Speedometer is written in the Python language and uses the Urwid library to display itself in a terminal. If you are building from source you'll need to install or build Urwid too. Urwid follows the normal Python build and installation using setup.py, as shown below. Speedometer is simply a single Python file and can be directly installed as shown.

```
$ apt-get install speedometer
$ speedometer -r eth0 -t eth0
```

The -tx and -rx command-line options are used to monitor all network traffic transmitted and received respectively on a network interface. Shown in the screenshot is the output of the command speedometer.py -tx eth1 -rx eth1. Speedometer will resize and redraw its display when the terminal window is resized, both when running locally in a gnome-terminal and over SSH.

When you use speedometer to monitor a particular download, it monitors a file rather than the network interface. This makes it useful for all sorts of network transfer monitoring: HTTP downloads from the Web, Samba and NFS file transfers, and scp secure transfer monitoring. One piece of information that is not available from monitoring a file is how large that file should become in the end. Without this information, speedometer happily monitors the transfer rate but can give you no indication of how close to done a transfer is. If you supply the optional size parameter, then it will also display a percentage complete bar at the bottom of the window, letting you quickly see the overall transfer progress.

As the example above shows implicitly, you can monitor multiple things at once with speedometer. That means if you have a multihomed host, you can easily keep an eye on multiple network interfaces at once.

The -f option allows you to monitor a file transfer. One glitch I found when monitoring file transfers is that speedometer waits for a file to be created before starting. This inhibits you from keeping an eye on other network traffic in the meantime. Making speedometer to be able to continuously check whether a file is created in the background, while allowing you to see the other things you wish to monitor, would be a great addition.

When you want to monitor multiple things, you can just keep adding new -tx, -rx, or -f options to the command line, or you can put a -c before the next option to make the graphs stack into columns instead of rows. If you are only monitoring a few things and have a wide screen display, then displaying graphs in columns might be a good idea. You can also create a display with both columns and rows by using -c only where you want to start a new column.

I chose a file with a descriptively long name to see how speedometer handles such cases when monitoring file transfers. It is nice that the graph for the second file transfer retains the same size as the other file transfer graph. Aligned displays like this are usually easier to read.

Speedometer is easy to install and definitely useful if you want to keep an eye on a transfer or network interface on a local or remote machine. Speedometer also plays nicely when you resize your display, in that it not only detects the new size but also redraws the current graph information properly.

1. **Measuring Network Download Speeds:** Before you can measure the speed of the network, first you have to find out the type of connection (the interface's name) you have. If you want to use a Wi-Fi connection (or wireless in general), then the interface name is "wlan0". If you have an Ethernet card, then it is called "eth0".

So, for monitoring the download speed of a Wi-Fi connection for example, use the command given below in your Terminal window.

```
speedometer -rx wlan0
```

If you have an Ethernet card, use one of the following instead.

```
speedometer -rx eth0
```

As stated, it is not a network benchmark tool, but if you want to check your maximum speed of the network, then you can start downloading some files manually (download Firefox for instance, as their servers are always bloody fast! ;-)) and "speedometer" will give you speed graphs with extreme values etc. as shown in the first screenshot.

2. **How to Change the Update Intervals (in Seconds):** If you want, you can easily change the update interval by using the "-i" parameter. So if I wanted change update intervals to 0.5 while monitoring my Wi-Fi connection for example, so I'll use the command given below.

```
speedometer -i 0.5 -rx wlan0
```

3. **Measuring the Upload Speeds:** If you want to measure the speed of the upload, then you can use the above two commands, but replace "rx" with "tx".

For example, if I wanted to measure the upload speed of my Wi-Fi connection, so, I will use something like command below.

```
speedometer -tx wlan0
```

Then, to see the actual speeds, you need to upload a file or two to an online server (such as to "Ubuntu One", Cloud servers for instance).

4. **Measuring the File System Speed:** As mentioned above, "speedometer" can also monitor your HDD speed. To get it, while running it, enter the following command. Basically it will create a new file (RAW) about 1GB in size and while it's creating it, "speedometer" will monitor the HDD and measure the speeds (as shown in Figures 12, 13, 14 and 15).

```
dd bs=1000000 count=1000 if=/dev/zero of=testfile & speedometer
testfile
```

If you want to change the size of the "testfile", then replace the value "1000" (marked in Blue) with your preferred size (in Megabytes).
After running the test, enter the below command to remove the file.

```
rm testfile
Usage
speedometer [options] tap [[-c] tap]...
```

Figure 12. Speedometer working

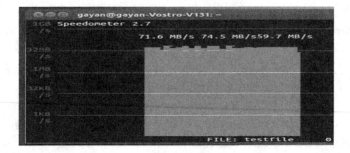

212

Monitor network traffic or speed/progress of a file transfer. At least one tap should be entered. -c starts a new column, otherwise taps are piled vertically.

Taps:

- -f: filename [size] show download speed [with progress bar]
- -r: network-interface show bytes received on network-interface
- -t: network-interface show bytes transmitted on network-interface

Options:

- -p: option use original plain-text display (one tap only)
- -s: option use bits/s instead of bytes/s
- -x: option exit when files reach their expected size
- -z: option report zero size on files that don't exist

Figure 13. Speedometer output

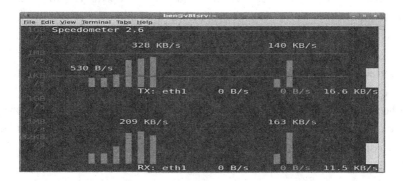

Figure 14. Speedometer graphs

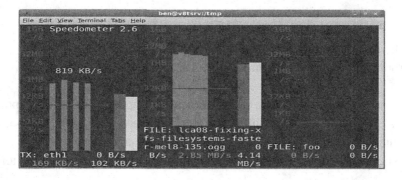

Figure 15. Speedometer report

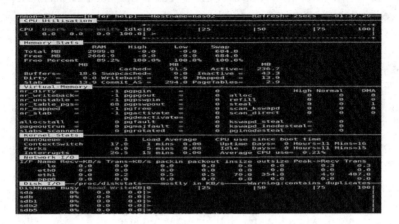

Ipython

It is a tool that supports python based coding; it allows easy text and the implementation of mathematical expressions. It supports inline plots and other media as well. The notebook automatically invokes many python based libraries that may be used for data analysis. It is a GUI based tool and supports graph plotting in a simple manner. This tool was used in the model because it enables to easily evaluate various parameters and also compare them graphically.

IPython is a command shell for interactive computing in multiple programming languages. It was originally developed for the Python programming language that offers introspection, rich media, shell syntax, tab completion, and history. IPython provides the following features:

1. Interactive shells (terminal and Qt-based).
2. A browser-based notebook with support for code, text, mathematical expressions, inline plots and other media.
3. Support for interactive data visualization and use of GUI toolkits.
4. Flexible, embeddable interpreters to load into one's own projects.
5. Tools for parallel computing.

IPython is a growing project, with increasingly language-agnostic components. IPython 3.x was the last monolithic release of IPython, containing the notebook server, qtconsole, etc. As of IPython 4.0, the language-agnostic parts of the project: the notebook format, message protocol, qtconsole, notebook web application, etc.

have moved to new projects under the name Jupyter. IPython itself is focused on interactive Python, part of which is providing a Python kernel for Jupyter.

IPython provides a rich architecture for interactive computing with:

1. A powerful interactive shell.
2. A kernel for Jupyter.
3. Support for interactive data visualization and use of GUI toolkits.
4. Flexible, embeddable interpreters to load into your own projects.
5. Easy to use, high performance tools for parallel computing.

RESULT AND ANALYSIS

The various factors considered for network traffic analysis were:

1. Error rate
2. Transmission rate
3. Reception rate
4. Time
5. Size of file

These are defined as follows:

1. **Error Rate:** The degree of errors encountered during data transmission over a communications or network connection. The higher the error rate, the connection or data transfer will be less reliable.
2. **Transmission Rate:** In networks, the transmission rate is the amount of time from the beginning till the end of a message transmission. In the case of a digital message, it is the time from the first bit until the last bit of a message has left the transmitting node.
3. **Reception Rate:** It is a metric of reliability in computer networks. It signifies the rate at which a node receives packets in a network.
4. **Time and Size of File:** This parameter aimed to calculate time taken to download/upload a file of some constant size.

Platform Used

The whole architecture is based on python and the underlying hardware used was Ubuntu 17.04 Zesty Zeus (Linux) with the following specifications:

1. **Processor:** Intel i3-4030 @ 1.90 Ghz
2. **Memory:** 3 GB
3. **Hard Disk:** 20 GB

And other Windows based laptops were used for connection i.e. LAN having similar hardware specifications. The LAN was based on wired connection using a D-Link router.

Development Environment

Data gathering is done using different open source tools available in Linux such as:

BMON, SPEEDOMETER, VNSTAT, IFTOP, and NETLOAD.

Also for programming i.e. coding and its implementation IPYTHON is used.

The data gathered from first step is then put into this part which analyses the data using python libraries such as NUMPY, PANDAS and made into graph using MATPLOTLIB library.

Implementation Details

The nodes connected to each other gave values of the parameters concerned. 25 different values were collected. The screenshot of the values is shown in Figure 16.

These 25 different values were collected by doing different experiments on machines having different configurations. Data gathering is done using different open source tools available in Linux such as:

1. BMON
2. SPEEDOMETER
3. VNSTAT
4. IFTOP and
5. NETLOAD

The sample data used for data analysis is shown in Table 1.

This data was feed into a python based environment to perform analyses. These screenshots from the model depict the same as in figure: 17, 18 and 19.

This data was analysed to calculate the following:

1. **Network Traffic Factor:** The formula used to calculate network traffic factor was:

Figure 16. Screenshot of data collected

Table 1. Sample data

Network no	Error rate	Transmission rate	Reception rate	Time (in ms)	Size of file (in Kb)
1	10	60	120	20	25
2	9	70	130	18	25
3	18	52	102	25	25
4	25	44	90	30	25
5	8	76	150	16	25

Figure 17. Feeding data in Ipython

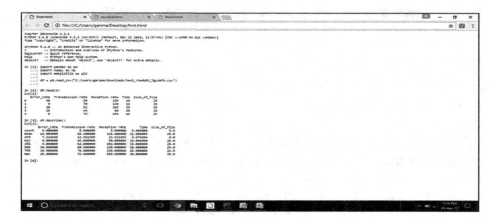

Figure 18. Calculating network analysis factor

Figure 19. Calculating reliability factor

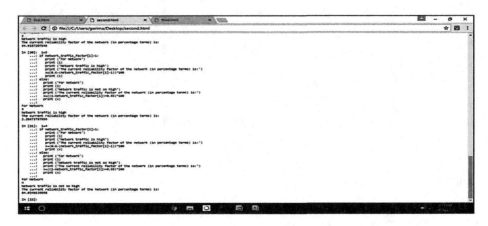

```
network_traffic_factor[i]=((error_rate[i]/error_rate_
avg)*0.8)+((transmission_rate[i]/transmission_rate_
avg)*0.1)+((reception_rate[i]/reception_rate_avg)*0.1)
```

This factor gave a rough idea about network traffic. If the value of this factor is greater than 1 then it indicates that the traffic is high and if it is lower than 1 then it indicated that the traffic is low.

The Table 2 shows network traffic factor for the sample data.

2. **Reliability Factor:** Network traffic factor was used to arrive at reliability factor as shown below:

Table 2. Network traffic Factor

Network number	Network traffic Factor
1	0.77211767112429364
2	0.73997705131811098
3	1.2008127924518655
4	1.5774326242041476
5	0.70965986090158273

The algorithm used to calculate reliability factor was:

```
if network_traffic_factor[i]>1:
    print ('Network traffic is high')
    reliability_factor =(0.6-(network_traffic_factor[i]-1))*100
 else:
    print ('Network traffic is not so high')
    reliability_factor =((1-network_traffic_
factor[i])+0.55)*100
```

Reliability factor (in Table 3) will give a clear idea about network traffic. If reliability factor is low then it is not advisable to use the concerned network for data transmission or reception. In the other case, it is highly recommended to use the associated network.

Graphical analyses of various factors were also done using graphs shown in Figures 20, 21, 22, 23 and 24.

The Graph (Figure 20) does a comparative study of error rates of various networks. The Graph (Figure 21 and 22) similarly compare transmission and reception rates respectively. The Graph (Figure 23) compares the time taken by different networks to process a file of size 25 Kb. Finally (Figure 24), compares the reliability factor of various networks.

Table 3. Reliability Factor

Network number	Reliability Factor
1	77.7882328876 %
2	81.0022948682 %
3	39.9187207548 %
4	2.25673757959 %
5	84.0340139098 %

Figure 20. Error rate Vs network number

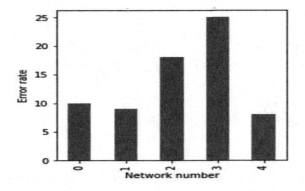

Figure 21. Transmission rate Vs network number

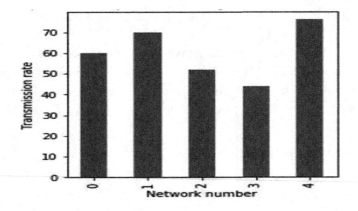

Figure 22. Reception rate Vs Network number

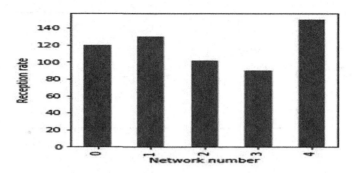

Figure 23. Time taken for file processing Vs network number

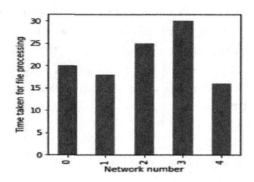

Network Number vs. Reliability Factor

From Figure 24 it can clearly be seen that when time taken for file processing is high, reliability factor is low. It was lowest for network number 3, where time taken was highest.

CONCLUSION

Efficient tools were deployed for data collection and analysis. Nodes connected in the network generated huge amount of network related data. The rate of data generation leads the model to treat the data as big data. Effective big data based analysis tools were deployed. The result of the analysis was quantified in the form of a measurable factor called reliability factor. This quantitative output was cross verified in terms of the time taken for a constant file size to be transmitted. It can be seen that when time taken for file processing is high, reliability factor is low. It

Figure 24. Network number Vs Reliability factor

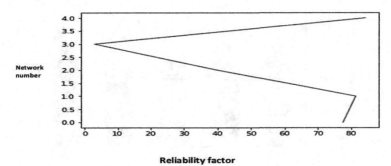

was lowest for network number 3, where time consumed was highest. The reliability factor that is being generated is an indicator for the user to understand whether the concerned network is working efficiently or not and whether the user must transfer files on that network or not. The model can also guide the network administrator to take steps in advance to prevent a network from breaking down to avoid chaos and data loss. Thus, the model can efficiently guide in making conscious decisions to manage network traffic.

REFERENCES

Baer, A., Casas, P., D'Alconzo, A., Fiadino, P., Golab, L., Mellia, M., & Schikuta, E. (2016). DBStream: A holistic approach to large-scale network traffic monitoring and analysis. *Computer Networks*, *107*, 5–19. doi:10.1016/j.comnet.2016.04.020

Joshi, P., Bhandari, A., Jamunkar, K., Warghade, K., & Lokhande, P. (2016). Network Traffic Analysis Measurement and Classification Using Hadoop. *International Journal of Adavanced Research in Computer and Communication Engineering*, *5*(3), 246–249.

Morley, C. K., & Nixon, C. W. (2016). Topological characteristics of simple and complex normal fault networks. *Journal of Structural Geology*, *84*, 68–84. doi:10.1016/j.jsg.2016.01.005

Naik, H. C., & Joshi, D. (2016). A Hadoop Framework Require to Process Bigdata very Easily and Efficiently. *IJSRSET*, *2*(2), 1206–1209.

Rinaldi, M., Himpe, W., & Tampère, M. J. (2016). A sensitivity-based approach for adaptive decomposition of anticipatory network traffic control. *Transportation Research Part C, Emerging Technologies*, *66*, 150–175. doi:10.1016/j.trc.2016.01.005

White, T. (2008). *HDFS Reliability*. Retrieved from www.cloudera.com/HDFS

Xiong, B., Yang, K., Zhao, J., & Li, K. (2017). Robust dynamic network traffic partitioning against malicious attacks. *Journal of Network and Computer Applications*, *87*, 20–31. doi:10.1016/j.jnca.2016.04.013

Chapter 10
Clustering Earthquake Data:
Identifying Spatial Patterns From Non–Spatial Attributes

Cihan Savaş
Kocaeli University, Turkey

Mehmet Samet Yıldız
Kocaeli University, Turkey

Süleyman Eken
Kocaeli University, Turkey

Cevat İkibaş
American University of Malta, Malta

Ahmet Sayar
Kocaeli University, Turkey

ABSTRACT

Seismology, which is a sub-branch of geophysics, is one of the fields in which data mining methods can be effectively applied. In this chapter, employing data mining techniques on multivariate seismic data, decomposition of non-spatial variable is done. Then k-means clustering, density-based spatial clustering of applications with noise (DBSCAN), and hierarchical tree clustering algorithms are applied on decomposed data, and then pattern analysis is conducted using spatial data on the resulted clusters. The conducted analysis suggests that the clustering results with spatial data is compatible with the reality and characteristic features of regions related to earthquakes can be determined as a result of modeling seismic data using clustering algorithms. The baseline metric reported is clustering times for varying size of inputs.

DOI: 10.4018/978-1-5225-7519-1.ch010

INTRODUCTION

Data mining (DM) is an interdisciplinary sub-field of computer science that is closely related to many different areas such as artificial intelligence (AI), machine learning, database systems, computer algorithms and statistics. This technology is widely employed in processes such as problem solving, financial data analysis, telecommunication industry, bio-informatics, learning, and other scientific applications (Pierce et al, 2008;Aydin et.al,2008; Sayer, Pierce & Fox, 2005; Aktas et.al,2006; Aktas et.al, 2005), which provides different approaches and methods. DM is an automated process for discovering patterns, finding association rules, detection of different anomalies structures on large databases.

Clustering analysis aims at creating clusters with the data or objects related to research in question by clustering them based on their similarities. While each created cluster contains objects with maximum similarities, they are least similar compared to data in other clusters. The quality of a clustering method depends on the level of compliance with this rule of thumb. Moreover, clustering approach is chosen based on the type of subject data and the goal of applications.

The main objective of this study is to investigate relationship between spatial and non-spatial data. Seismic Earthquake data of United States Geological Survey (USGS) (Aktas et.al, June 2005) that has multiple factors is chosen to find out this relationship and to graphically represent it. Primarily, normalization and other steps are applied, and then non-spatial data is determined using data mining methods on earthquake data.

After normalization process;

1. Density based clustering is conducted and the results are monitored. DBSCAN (Density Based Spatial Clustering of Applications with Noise) algorithm is applied (United States Geological Survey (USGS), 2015; R language).
2. Dendrogram is created by conducting hierarchical clustering operation. Agglomerative Nesting (AGNES) algorithm is applied (see reference DBSCAN algorithm R packet).
3. k-Means clustering algorithm which aims at grouping the data in k-groups is employed.
4. A method is developed and implemented in R programming language in order to correlate non-spatial features with spatial ones based on the results of clustering algorithms and the data is drawn on the world map in respect to its latitude and longitude, which provides graphical representation of the effects of clustering distribution on the map.

The results of these studies provides a way for comparison of clustering algorithms. Based on the conducted comparisons, it is monitored that whether or not similar features exist for different regions. R Studio platform, providing tools for both statistical calculations and high level graphical language, is used in application development phase. This programing language also provides interface and facilities for eliminating the errors for other high-level programming languages.

The remainder of this article is organized as follows. "Related works" section presents the related work. The proposed framework is given in "Architecture" section. Used algorithms are presented in "Clustering algorithms" section. The performance results and their analyses is given in "Performance tests and evaluation" section. The last section concludes the article.

RELATED WORKS

Spatial studies related to analysis and clustering of earthquake data have been conducted successfully by Morales-Esteban et al. (2010) at Sevilla University in Spain. However, this study is different in terms of time series, and it does not mention specific earthquake characteristics of regions. Our study aims at clustering data without considering latitude and longitude information in any region or city of the World. Moreover, the paper which is related to analysis of spatial data and presented by Shashi Shekhar et al (2011), mathematically questioned the general information in the area. But the study covers general scope rather than specific subjects and it only focuses on how to analyze spatial data. K-Means and DBSCAN algorithms that we also employ in this study, are broadly defined in the paper. Another work related to subject is that Mahdi Hashemi and Hassan Karimi (2011) conducted clustering of seismic data based on non-spatial data in Pittsburgh in USA. But, this study employees SVM and KNN methods as clustering approach. Anderson and Nanjo (2013) clustered the earthquakes according to their distances on space and time proposed using optimal distance and time interval that are obtained *chnology*, *1*(3), 33-37. experimentally in clustering earthquakes. Zmazek et al. (2003) employed a decision tree to estimate the amount of radon, proposed estimating concentration ratio based on environmental variables and duration of earthquakes in seismically inactive periods. On the other hand, Lei (2010) defined earthquake centers as 3D visualization using density-based algorithms. Then, Hinneburg and Keim (1998), who conducted researches on density-based clustering introduced DENsity-based CLUstEring (DENCLUE). This study, which employed Gauss function as density measurement tool, made more progress compared to DBSCAN algorithm. Buscema et al. 2015 performed some researches devoted to estimating the magnitude of earthquake, which employed artificial neural networks. Moreover, Golghate et al.

(2014), conducted studies on parallel clustering based on K-Means algorithm utilizing Hadoop framework. In this study, employing open source R programming language tool, we perform clustering operation on non-spatial data and reveal its relationship with spatial characteristics. In addition to this, we also utilize hierarchical, density based and distance vector-based algorithms together and compare them in terms of efficiency.

ARCHITECTURE

Data preprocessing operation must be performed in order to increase the quality of data in data mining. Otherwise erroneous input may lead us to incorrect outputs. As illustrated in Figure 1, raw data, obtained from USGS, is exposed to preprocessing/ normalization. Then, non-spatial dataset is generated by separating the latitude and longitude characteristics that are called spatial features from data set. Next, k-Means, DBSCAN and AGNES clustering algorithms are applied on the generated data set. After that, the quality of clustering operations is monitored by associating non-spatial data with spatial data and displaying the results on world map.

Properties of Data Set and Normalization

The data set utilized in this study was obtained from United States Geological Survey(USGS).It includes both spatial and non-spatial characteristics/ attributes. Spatial characteristics present latitude and longitude information. Latitude and longitude information is exposed to some operations during the analysis phase since it provides only location information, which cannot be considered as a size or magnitude. Therefore, latitude and longitude characteristics are initially separated from the data set. But this information is preserved due to the fact that it will be correlated later on as seen in Figure 1.

Clustering analysis is separating the data set into groups that contains similar objects. In clustering operation, the similarity of two records is determined based on the distance between them. Hence, spatial characteristics of dataset are separated since clustering operation is to be performed on non-spatial dataset. Numerical and non-spatial instances are separated and a checked to see whether there exists any missing data (NA). (NAs are shown in Table 1). The missing data is identified and completed according to average value method of the relevant characteristics. Thus, preprocessing of data is completed. Then, non-spatial data is utilized by applying normalization method using clusterSim package (n4 type normalization -unitization with zero minimum-) on the data. In this method, range and minimum value of

Figure 1. Target process diagram

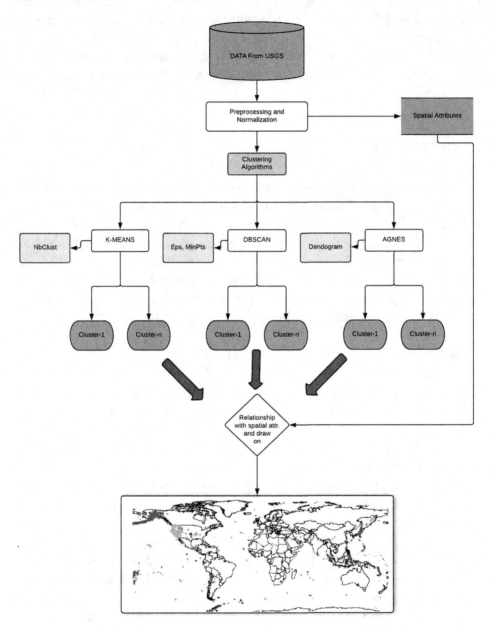

Table 1. Raw non-spatial attributes in dataset

	Depth	Magnitude	Number of Station	Gap	Minimum Distance	Quadratic Mean
1	13.790	0.85	26	50.00	0.05458000	0.2200
3	18.400	1.10	NA	NA	NA	0.2200
4	98.000	1.80	NA	NA	NA	0.7700
5	18.400	1.90	NA	NA	NA	0.6700
6	11.700	0.50	4	141.30	0.07300000	0.0343
7	4.510	0.95	10	85.00	0.03053000	0.0300
8	9.940	1.51	18	79.00	0.08948000	0.0500
9	4.310	0.40	12	131.00	0.07165000	0.1200

the group of data are handled and all of the other data in the group is normalized accordingly. The representation of normalized data set can be seen in Table 2.

CLUSTERING ALGORITHMS

K-Means Algorithm

K-means clustering method aims at clustering p-variant data sets obtained from many different units into k-sets in a way that sum of squares is minimum in the sets. The placements of units into the sets is conducted iteratively. The optimum solution is reached by employing a permutational approach which assigns the units into different

Table 2. Normalized non-spatial attributes

	Depth	Magnitude	Number of Station	Gap	Minimum Distance	Quadratic Mean
1	0.10722524	0.08549223	0.15662651	0.14005052	0.0029502703	0.0118918919
3	0.13658749	1.00000000	0.11144578	0.05164187	1.0000000000	1.0000000000
4	0.13658749	1.00000000	0.11144578	0.05164187	1.0000000000	1.0000000000
5	0.13658749	1.00000000	0.11144578	0.05164187	1.0000000000	1.0000000000
6	0.09419612	0.06735751	0.02409639	0.39629526	0.0039459459	0.0018540541
7	0.04937348	0.09067358	0.06024096	0.23828235	0.0016502703	0.0016216216
8	0.08322424	0.11968912	0.10843373	0.22144260	0.0048367568	0.0027027027
9	0.04812668	0.06217617	0.07228916	0.36738703	0.0038729730	0.0064864865

sets in each iteration. In order to apply k-means method, the variables in data set should at least be in the scaled interval since new set centers are determined based on the averages or variables in each iteration in created set.

Algorithm consists of four main steps;

1. Determine the cluster centers
2. Classify samples outside of the center according to their distances
3. Determine the new centers according to the new classification (or moving the old centers to the new center
4. Repeat step 2 and 3 until stable state is reached.

Hierarchical Tree Algorithm

Agglomerative Nesting (AGNES) hierarchical clustering method follows a bottom up strategy. Every object is considered as a separate set at the beginning. In each of following steps of the algorithm, these separate sets are combined until the similar sets are put in one set or targeted features are provided. Most of the hierarchical clustering methods fall in to this category. On the other hand, Divisive Analysis (AGNES) hierarchical clustering method follows a top down strategy. At the beginning, all data objects are considered to be in one set. In each of following steps of the algorithm, the bigger set is separated in to smaller sets by putting the objects that have maximum similarities in those sets. The clustering operation continues until each object by itself forms a different set or providing a targeted condition. Dendrogram which is a tree structure is employed in order to depict hierarchical clustering processes. Figure 2 demonstrate how dendrogram objects are clustered step by step.

Even though hierarchical clustering method is considered as a simple method, it demonstrates some complexity and hardships in choosing combination or separation points. Choosing these points efficiently is very important since the next steps are carried out on new sets created by combination or separation of an object group. Neither the previous operations nor the objects in the sets can be changed. Therefore, not making decisions on combination or separation in some steps causes the low-quality sets to come into existence.

DBSCAN Algorithm

This algorithm, based on density-based methods which is one of the data mining clustering models, achieves clustering operation by calculating the distance of objects with their neighbors. In this algorithm clustering is done by grouping regions where

Figure 2. Agnes Diagram (Dendrogram)

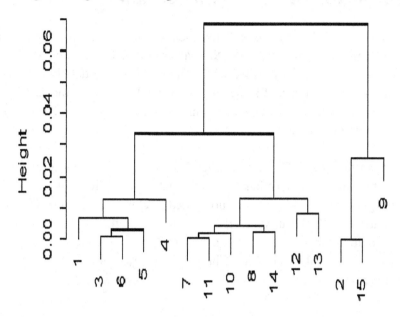

number of objects is higher than the previously determined threshold. There are some terms and approaches related to DBSCAN algorithm. These are:

1. **Seed Object:** If a data object contains more points than previously determined threshold this object is seed object.
2. **Eps:** The distance or closeness that is necessary to determine the neighbors of a data object.
3. **MinPts:** Minimum number of neighbors in Eps neighborhood in order to call a region as dense.
   a. For every object in data base, Neighborhood region with Eps radius is investigated.
   b. In this region, bunches are created in a way that p object that includes more object than MinPts is located as seed object.
   c. Directly reachable objects of seed objects are found out.
   d. Reachable objects of seed objects are found.
   e. Density related bunches are merged.
   f. The process is completed if no new object can be added to a bunch.

PERFORMANCE TESTS AND EVALUATIONS

While blue colored data in Figure 3 represents data without NA values, the red colored values represents data with NA values. Instead of removing data items including NA values, they are filled with average values and data lost is avoided.

The most important step of k-Means clustering algorithms is the determination of parameter "k". silhouette and within sum of square (wss) methods are employed in order to determine k value.

- **Silhouette Index:** This index is used to measure the quality of clustering result. Namely, it determines how well each object in its own set. The higher average width of silhouette shows better clustering result. The average silhouette method calculates the average silhouette for different k values. Optimum number of sets k is the value that maximize the average silhouette through a possible interval. Clustering diagram for Silhouette index is depicted in Figure 4.

Figure 3. Distribution of all instances

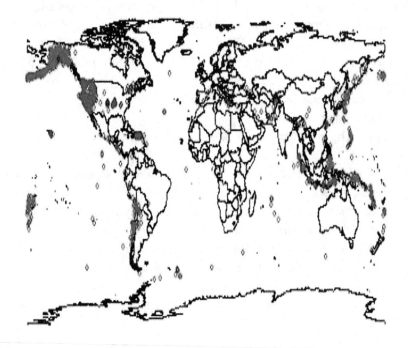

Figure 4. Determination of parameter k using silhouette index

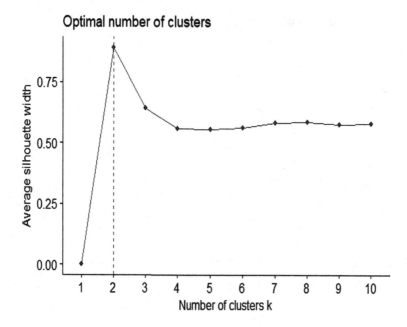

- **Wss Index:** After executing the algorithm on total number of K set centers, quadratic error rate is evaluated by plotting a curve graph. Here, the goal is to identify the point where a sharp drop followed by stable decrease occurs in elbow-shaped form. This point is chosen as optimum number of set center for the data set. Clustering diagram for Wss index is depicted in Figure 5.

Figure 6 shows the results of k-Means clustering.

Hierarchical clustering algorithm is of two types: i) AGNES and ii) Divisive Hierarchical clustering algorithm or DIANA (divisive analysis). AGNES works by grouping the data one by one on the basis of the nearest distance measure of all the pairwise distance between the data point. Again distance between the data point is recalculated but which distance to consider when the groups has been formed? For this ward's method -sum of squared euclidean distance is minimized- is used. Figure 7 shows the results of AGNES clustering.

Minpts" and "eps" parameters are to be determined in density-based clustering algorithms. "eps" value can be found out using "KNNdistplot function. The results of KNNdistplot functions are depicted in Figure 8. Being the parameter for number of sets, k determines the termination condition of DBSCAN algorithm. Clustering operation is ended when the desired number of set is obtained. Knndisplot function is utilized in order to find out the eps value corresponding to user provided minpts

Figure 5. Determination of parameter k using wss index

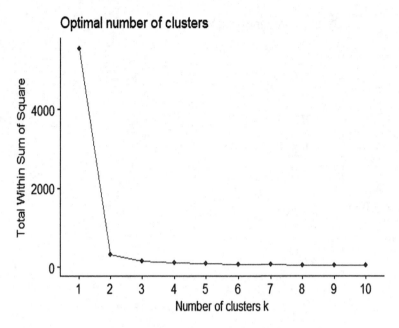

Figure 6. k-Means clustering results for k=2

Figure 7. AGNES clustering results

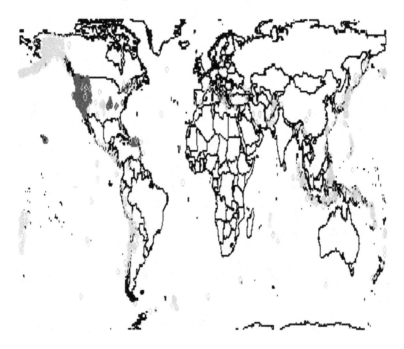

(k value). The points where the diffraction is high in the graph is determined to be eps value.

Figure 9 shows the results of DBSCAN clustering method.

Also, we compare the clustering times under varying size of input. Table 3 shows the performance results.

SUMMARY AND CONCLUSION

This study analyzes three different clustering methods, and reveals their strengths compared to each other. Data obtained from USGS are primarily normalized in the preprocessing phase. One of the important fact revealed according to result is that preprocessing is extremely important. The raw data should be firstly plotted before data mining processes, and then compared with the data resulted from normalization processes. If there are many missing areas in data set after normalization, that definitely means some employed methods should be changed. In this project the data set is firstly plotted, and then compared with the data resulted from normalization processes. It is clearly presented that many important coordinates are lost. During the normalization, it seems that filling NA values with average or correlation is more

Figure 8. Determination of eps value using KNNdistplot function

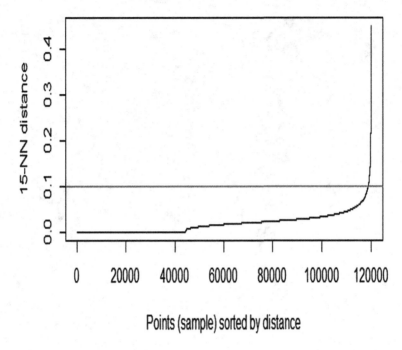

Figure 9. DBSCAN plot representation for Eps values of 1 and 0

Table 3. Comparison of clustering times under varying size of input

Algorithm	Small Dataset (8K Instances)	Big Dataset (20K Instances)
K-means	0.75 sec	1.42 min
DBSCAN	8.32 sec	1.02 min
AGNES	0.61 sec	0.94 sec

suitable than deleting them. As for the quality of clustering, the most important criterion is that inner-set similarity should be maximized while inter-sets similarities are minimized. In this process, the number of sets is one of the most important factors. As a result of executing and testing many different algorithms, the optimum number of sets is determined. So as to determine the similar areas, results are created on non-spatial features and those results are associated with latitudes and longitude values, which makes depicting clustered regions on world map possible. Having done this research in the field of seismology, characteristics of earthquakes can be determined, and necessary measure can be applied in order to decrease death rates if the obtained results are evaluated by earthquake scientists.

REFERENCES

AGNES Algorithm R Packet. (n.d.). Retrieved from https://stat.ethz.ch/R-manual/R-devel/library/cluster/html/agnes.html

Aktas. (2005, June). Implementing geographical information system grid services to support computational geophysics in a service-oriented environment. In *NASA Earth-Sun System Technology Conference*. University of Maryland.

Aktas, M. (2006). iSERVO: Implementing the International Solid Earth Research Virtual Observatory by integrating computational grid and geographical information web services. In Computational Earthquake Physics: Simulations, Analysis and Infrastructure, Part II (pp. 2281-2296). Birkhäuser Basel.

Anderson, J. G., & Nanjo, K. (2013). Distribution of earthquake cluster sizes in the western United States and in Japan. *Bulletin of the Seismological Society of America*, *103*(1), 412–423. doi:10.1785/0120100212

Aydin, G., Sayar, A., Gadgil, H., Aktas, M. S., Fox, G. C., Ko, S., ... Pierce, M. E. (2008). Building and applying geographical information system Grids. *Concurrency and Computation*, *20*(14), 1653–1695. doi:10.1002/cpe.1312

Buscema, P. M., Massini, G., & Maurelli, G. (2015). Artificial Adaptive Systems to predict the magnitude of earthquakes. *Bollettino di Geofisica Teorica ed Applicata*, *56*(2).

DBSCAN Algorithm R Packet. (n.d.). Retrieved from https://cran.r-project.org/web/packages/dbscan/dbscan.pdf

Golghate, A. A., & Shende, S. W. (2014). Parallel K-means clustering based on hadoop and hama. *International Journal of Computers and Technology*, *1*(3), 33–37.

Hashemi, M., & Alesheikh, A. (2011). Spatio-temporal analysis of Tehran's historical earthquakes trends. In *Advancing Geoinformation Science for a Changing World* (pp. 3–20). Berlin: Springer. doi:10.1007/978-3-642-19789-5_1

Hinneburg, A., & Keim, D. A. (1998). An efficient approach to clustering in large multimedia databases with noise. *KDD: Proceedings / International Conference on Knowledge Discovery & Data Mining. International Conference on Knowledge Discovery & Data Mining*, *98*, 58–65.

Lei, L. (2010, July). Identify earthquake hot spots with 3-dimensional density-based clustering analysis. In *Geoscience and Remote Sensing Symposium (IGARSS), 2010 IEEE International* (pp. 530-533). IEEE. 10.1109/IGARSS.2010.5652510

Morales-Esteban, A., Martínez-Álvarez, F., Troncoso, A., Justo, J. L., & Rubio-Escudero, C. (2010). Pattern recognition to forecast seismic time series. *Expert Systems with Applications*, *37*(12), 8333–8342. doi:10.1016/j.eswa.2010.05.050

Pierce, M. E. (2008). The QuakeSim project: Web services for managing geophysical data and applications. In Earthquakes: Simulations, Sources and Tsunamis (pp. 635-651). Birkhäuser Basel.

R Language. (n.d.). Retrieved from https://www.r-project.org/

Sayar, A., Pierce, M., & Fox, G. (2005, November). Developing GIS visualization web services for geophysical applications. In ISPRS 2005 spatial data mining workshop, Ankara, Turkey.

Shekhar, S., Evans, M. R., Kang, J. M., & Mohan, P. (2011). Identifying patterns in spatial information: A survey of methods. *Wiley Interdisciplinary Reviews. Data Mining and Knowledge Discovery*, *1*(3), 193–214. doi:10.1002/widm.25

United States Geological Survey (USGS). (2015). Retrieved from http://earthquake. usgs.gov/earthquakes/search

Zmazek, B., Todorovski, L., Džeroski, S., Vaupotič, J., & Kobal, I. (2003). Application of decision trees to the analysis of soil radon data for earthquake prediction. *Applied Radiation and Isotopes*, *58*(6), 697–706. doi:10.1016/S0969-8043(03)00094-0 PMID:12798380

Chapter 11
Data Imputation Methods for Missing Values in the Context of Clustering

Mehmet S. Aktaş
Yildiz Technical University, Turkey

Oya Kalipsiz
Yildiz Technical University, Turkey

Sinan Kaplan
Lappeenranta University of Technology, Finland

Utku Ketenci
Cybersoft, USA

Umut O. Turgut
Cybersoft, USA

Hasan Abacı
Yildiz Technical University, Turkey

ABSTRACT

Missing data is a common problem for data clustering quality. Most real-life datasets have missing data, which in turn has some effect on clustering tasks. This chapter investigates the appropriate data treatment methods for varying missing data scarcity distributions including gamma, Gaussian, and beta distributions. The analyzed data imputation methods include mean, hot-deck, regression, k-nearest neighbor, expectation maximization, and multiple imputation. To reveal the proper methods to deal with missing data, data mining tasks such as clustering is utilized for evaluation. With the experimental studies, this chapter identifies the correlation between missing data imputation methods and missing data distributions for clustering tasks. The results of the experiments indicated that expectation maximization and k-nearest neighbor methods provide best results for varying missing data scarcity distributions.

DOI: 10.4018/978-1-5225-7519-1.ch011

INTRODUCTION

Information plays a significant role in business to maintain customer satisfaction. Many business successes are based on the availability of information related to marketing strategy. Such information is quite large, and not easy to manage for business purposes. Businesses apply data mining techniques - the process of discovering and processing knowledge from data stored in databases and data warehouses (Han, Micheline, & Jian. 2006) - to overcome information-related problems, such as using analytics to support financial decisions. According to Cios et al (2005), about 20% of the effort is spent on understanding data and problems related to this data, about 60% on data preparation, and about 20% on data mining and knowledge analysis. Specialists spend a great deal of time on data preparation in order to make appropriate decisions because of crucial data quality problems in these datasets in the form of incomplete (missing), redundant or erroneous information. Those problems decrease the quality of data mining tasks such as clustering tasks. Therefore, the treatment of missing data becomes quite important to improve performance of clustering tasks, while missing/incomplete data is the main reason for lack of data quality.

Basically, incomplete/missing data is the missing value of a record in any given dataset/source. Researchers from different areas such as statistics, computer science, etc., have developed many methods and models to analyze large amounts of data to extract valuable information. As has been mentioned above, the quality of information extracted from a dataset is the main concern in knowledge discovery tasks, which is defined as the process of finding and identifying new patterns in the data. These patterns can include relationships, events or trends. In this process, data mining methods are used to extract and verify new patterns. In principle, two types of knowledge discovery tasks can be defined: description and prediction. In a description task, a system finds patterns in order to present these patterns to the user in an understandable way, while a prediction task is defined as finding patterns to anticipate the future behavior of related objects. This study investigates the ways of increasing the quality in description tasks with a particular focus on clustering tasks.

Data quality creates a variety of problems in clustering which is the task of identifying groups of similar objects within a dataset. It is broadly used in many areas such as database marketing, web analysis, bioinformatics, etc. Missing values reduce the power of the clustering process because clustering algorithms usually have no mechanism to handle missing values. A widely used solution for this problem is to fill in the missing values in a preprocessing step. The main goal of this study is to investigate the correlation between missing data imputation methods and missing data distributions for clustering tasks.

Motivations

We observe a number of datasets in various domains where the missing data exists. Such domain include but not limited to banking research datasets, finance research datasets and scientific datasets, As it mentioned before, in datasets, a great deal of damage can be caused by missing data (Luengo, García, & Herrera, 2010).

The mostly commonly encountered problems relating to missing values are as follows:

1. **Loss of Efficiency:** Fewer patterns are extracted from data, and consequently, conclusions are statistically less strong.
2. **Complications in Handling and Analyzing the Data:** This problem lies in the fact that most methods and algorithms are not capable of dealing with missing values. Methods are in general not prepared to handle the missing data.
3. **Bias Resulting From Differences Between Missing and Complete Data:** This problem is related to the possibility that the imputed values are not exactly the same as the observed values in a complete dataset, and this requires finding the most appropriate ways to handle them.

We argue that the quality of information extracted from a dataset is knowledge discovery tasks, which can be defined as the process of finding and identifying new patterns in the data. These patterns could be relationships, events or trends. A commonly used pattern discovery task is clustering the datasets. Data with missing values have fewer properties to conduct clustering and this leads to poor clustering results. Hence, we see an emerging need to identify data imputation techniques that would lead to high quality clustering results.

We argue that there exists various different distributions of missing data in datasets mostly encountered in finance and commercial bank datasets. We see emerging need to investigate whether different distributions of missing data have any effect on the types of missing data handling used.

Data that are missing because a data-collecting mechanism dropped a data-feed notification or data-generating source malfunctioned and skipped some data points are likely to have the missing data mechanism, which is unrelated to the values of any attributes, whether missing or observed. We also see an emerging need to identify the best data imputation techniques for the missing data mechanisms such as missing completely at random.

Statement of the Research Problems

In this book chapter, to remedy the aforementioned motivating problems, we focus on treatment of the missing data in the given datasets. In order to this, we identify the following research questions:

Research Question #1: What are the most effective data handling methods for dealing with the different data scarcity distributions and missing data types?

Research Question #2: What are the least effective data handling methods for dealing with the different data scarcity distributions and missing data types?

Research Question #3: What is the effect of the size of the missing data scarcities on the quality of clustering results?

Research Question #4: What is the effect of the missing data handling methods in terms of achieving high quality in clustering?

Contributions

The main contribution of this research is to investigate missing data handling methods for varying data scarcity distributions in order to achieve a high degree of accuracy in terms of purity in data mining tasks such as clustering. The implications of this research are three-fold. First, this study reviews the research into missing data analysis in recent years. Second, it identifies the appropriate missing data handling methods for a given data density and distribution. Third, it identifies the best missing data handling strategy for the identified data density and distribution to reach high accuracy in clustering tasks.

RELATED WORK

There may be a variety of reasons behind missing data. Therefore, it is important to understand the mechanism behind it. In other words, identifying the nature of the missing data is crucial in order to determine appropriate handling methods. According to Little & Rubin (1987) and Luengo, García, & Herrera (2012), three types of missing data mechanisms have been identified in the literature. These are missing completely at random (MCAR), missing at random (MAR) and missing not at random (MNAR). The amount of missing data impacts differently on the process of Knowledge Discovery Tasks in databases (Fayyad et al., 2016) (Acuna & Caroline, 2004). Based on the conducted studies, there exist different kinds of strategies for working with datasets having missing values. These include imputing or filling in the missing values with other records in the data, involving multiple imputation, complete case analysis, etc. These methods have been broadly grouped into the following three categories by Little and Rubin (1987): (1) Ignoring and Discarding Incomplete Records and Attributes, (2) Parameter Estimation, (3) Imputation Procedures (Rubin, 2004). The treatment of missing data for statistical analysis has been identified in the literature for more than 80 years.

In this book chapter, we choose six commonly used algorithms for data imputation based on the following recently published supporting references that use and explain the application of these algorithms. Masconi et al introduced the applications of six imputation methods in prevalent diabetes prediction research, which are Maximum likelihood, Markov chain Monte Carlo (MCMC), Multiple imputation methods, Hot Decking, Stochastic regression imputation and Conditional Mean imputation (Masconi et al, (2015)). Similar to their work, we also used Multiple Imputation, Hot Decking and Regression imputation in our investigation. García-Laencina & Pedro (2015) studied with some missing data imputation methods on the five-year survival prediction of breast cancer patients with unknown discrete values. These imputation methods are mode imputation, expectation-maximization imputation and k-nearest neighbors' imputation. Similar to their work, we also used KNN, EM and mean imputation methods in our investigation.

Lee et al provides detailed overview of multiple imputation by analyzing two different model, which are multiple imputation with chained equations (MICE) and Multivariate Normal Imputation (MVNI) that applies a Markov Chain Monte Carlo algorithm (Lee et al, 2016). Their study accepts missing data structure as MAR. Different from their study, our work focuses on key issues in missing data distributions and multiple imputation techniques.

Fiero et al conducted a study on the cluster randomized trials, which has hierarchical data structure, to improve imputation accuracy (Fiero, Shuang & Bell, 2015). Inverse Probability Weighting (IPW) is studied by weighting observed cases with the inverse of their probability in the actual data. When there is a monotone pattern of missing values, the IPW can be useful to get better imputation results. The main drawback of this study is that in the presence of quite large weights, it is possible to have instability. In turn, that might cause biased imputation and high variances. Young and David (2015) conducted research to review the key issues and methods for analysis of longitudinal panel data when there is missing data available. Complete case analysis and multiple imputation are used to measure accuracy of the imputation on the data. Root Means Square Error is applied to compare the experimental results and in the presence of the large missing values multiple imputation performed well. They found that if the imputation adds no information to the analysis of the data, then it is not recommended to use imputation methods, since the multiple imputation causes biases on the imputed data. Different from these studies, our work is investigating the most appropriate data imputation methods for varying missing data distributions.

Liu et al analyzed the Bayesian approaches for imputation of the missing values (Liu, Han, Zhao,& Lin, 2015). The method is applied on a schizophrenia clinical trial. The results of the study show that the flexibility of Bayesian approaches increases the accuracy of the imputation methods. Koko & Mohamed (2015) analyzed the effect of imputation on the clustering tasks in. First Little's MCAR test is conducted and missing values in the household health data is imputed by using multiple imputation technique. To reveal implications of the imputation on the clustering tasks Two Step Cluster Analysis is chosen. Results are shown that imputation procedure has positive effect on the clustering tasks when there is a large ratio of missing values. In the existence of outliers, the performance of Pairwise Deletion (PD), Multiple Imputation (MI), random regression imputation (RRI) is studied in Rana, John & Midi (2015). To increase the performance of the imputation in the presence of the outliers Robust Regression Imputation (RRRI) is proposed on 10% missing value. It is shown that when there is no outliers all the methods provide very close results by comparing Mean Square Error (MSE) and residual standard error. When there is outliers, RRRI method superiors the others. None of these studies have investigated the correlation between the missing data distributions and data imputation techniques.

García-Laencina et al conducted a research that revealed the most convenient imputation and prediction method on a real breast cancer dataset from Institute Portuguese of Oncology of Porto with high percentage of missing values (García-Laencina et al (2015). Mode imputation, (Expectation-Maximization imputation and *K*-Nearest Neighbors imputation methods are used for filling the missing values and *K*-Nearest Neighbors, Classification Trees, Logistic Regression and Support Vector Machines are used as a prediction method. The results show *K*-Nearest Neighbors imputation algorithm performs better that with 81% of accuracy. Cleophas found out that the Regression imputation is more sensitive than Mean, Hot-deck imputation and multiple imputation together (Cleopas & Aeilko (2016). It is revealed that in the study multiple imputation provides better results than other methods. Wilks (1932) studied the maximum likelihood of estimation for multivariate normal models involving fragmentary data. After that, important discussions centered on this topic. A general reference to this topic can be found in Little & Rubin (2014). Batista and Monard (2003) analyzed the performance of 10-NNI (Nearest Neighbor Imputation) as an imputation method compared to mean/mode imputation, Hot-Deck, C4.5, and CN2. According to this study, the main advantage of the NNI is that it can predict both qualitative and quantitative attributes. Experimental analysis of this study demonstrates that it provides better results than the other three methods. However, the main disadvantage of this method is that the algorithm looks through all the records in datasets. Wayman (2003) studied Multiple Imputation (MI) as a means of dealing with missing data by comparing it with LD (Listwise Deletion) and MS (Mean Substitution). In this book chapter, MI provides a better result than the other two methods. The main disadvantage of this study is that the authors compared MI with two weak imputation methods as LD and MS. Although, these studies compared different data imputation techniques, it did not look at these techniques with respect to varying missing data scarcities.

Farhangfar et al (2004), experimented with the analysis of several algorithms for the treatment of missing data. They mainly focused on imputation, which included simple statistical algorithms such as Mean and Hot-deck algorithms, and complex imputation algorithms based on Machine Learning such as probabilistic algorithms *(Naive Bayes)*, decision tree algorithms *(C4.5)* and decision rule algorithms *(CLIP4)*. A comprehensive range of databases were used in this book chapter, with MCAR values being introduced randomly. The experimental study contained in this book chapter shows that the *C4.5* has the best overall performance among the other chosen algorithms. However, the study indicated that unsupervised learning methods (Mean and Hot-deck) are more stable with respect to increasing amounts of missing data than supervised methods (*C4.5, CLIP4,* and *Naive Bayes*). The main reason is that the supervised algorithms must have a training dataset to develop a model for imputation. Different from this work, we investigate the performance of different data imputation techniques that do not rely on the existence of a training data.

Kaiser (2014), proposed a comprehensive study of the missing values problem and suggested different approaches for dealing with missing values in datasets. The author suggested that the selection of the data imputation method mostly depends on a given dataset with respect to the structure of attributes and the missing data mechanism in that dataset.

The research in Gómez-Carracedo, (2014), investigated whether major differences occur when five popular imputation methods are applied (four single imputation -*Listwise Deletion, Mean Imputation, PCA (Principal Component Analysis and EM)* methods and a *MI* to datasets with missing data ratios ranging from 24% to 4%, corresponding to three air quality monitoring studies. The results from this study show that all methods performed similarly when the missing ratio was low, but that *MI* performs better when the missing ratio is high. This study also does not investigate the correlation amongst the missing data distributions and data imputation techniques.

Wagstaff (2004) proposed a new method for clustering that divides the dataset into observed data, which are known for all instances, and constraining features that include missing values. A modified clustering algorithm, KSC (k-means for Soft Constraints), combines the set of constraints with the observed features. In the experimental results it was found that KSC can usually perform better than the data imputation methods. More recently, the research in Fatemah & Keivan (2014) studied the effects of different k-means clustering algorithms in terms of missing data and clustering. They combined different versions of the k-means clustering algorithm. To achieve this goal, fuzzy, rough and rough-fuzzy k-means were applied to a normalized dataset with different percentages of missing data. The performance of those algorithms was measured in terms of Root Mean Square Error (RMSE) and accuracy. The results show that the behaviors of the fuzzy k-means and k-means were the same in terms of accuracy, while the fuzzy k-means outperformed the others in terms of RMSE. However, this study only uses the traditional Mean imputation method to deal with the missing data. In our study, we are concerned with both replacing missing data by using different kinds of imputation methods and the effects of these methods on clustering.

Schmitt et al (2015) also studied imputation methods in. They compared six different imputation methods: Mean, K-Nearest Neighbors (KNN), fuzzy K-means (FKM), Singular Value Decomposition (SVD), Bayesian Principal Component Analysis (bPCA) and Multiple Imputations by Chained Equations (MICE). On their study, comparison was performed on four real datasets of various sizes (from 4 to 65 variables), under a missing completely at random (MCAR) assumption, and based on four evaluation criteria: Root Mean Squared Error (RMSE), Unsupervised Classification Error (UCE), Supervised Classification Error (SCE) and execution time. Their results suggest that bPCA and FKM are two imputation methods of interest which deserve further consideration in practice. Different from this study, we investigated EM, Hot-deck, KNN, Mean, Multiple and Regression Imputation methods. Before we performed these techniques, we created missing values with beta, gamma and Gaussian distributions. In our study, we used two evaluation criteria: Root Mean Squared Error (RMSE) and Purity. Furthermore, we investigated the performance of imputation methods on missing data in only one attribute and on missing data in randomly chosen attributes.

He et al. (2015) studied four data filling methods which are Back Propagation Neural Network (BP-NN), Least Squares Support Vector Machine (LSSVM), Gaussian Mixture Model based on Expectation Maximization (GMM-EM) and Multiple Imputation (MI). They resulted that the performance of MI is brilliant and the combination of MI and LS-SVM modelling works well if the deficient rate is low. As the deficient rate rise up to moderate, GMM-EM fills the missing data most effectively and the combination of GMM-EM and LS-SVM modelling is better than others. When the deficient rate becomes severe, GMM-EM is still the best method to fill the missing data whereas the LS-SVM modelling based on LS-SVM fill predicts the values more accurately. However, in our study, we used different imputation methods. We also investigated best of these imputation methods for varying missing data distributions.

Kropho et al (2014), studied Multiple Imputation (MI) - joint Multivariate Normal (MVN) multiple imputation, in which the data are modeled as a sample from a joint MVN distribution; and conditional MI, in which each variable is modeled conditionally on all the others. Their missing values are generated carefully by following the conditions necessary for missingness to be "Missing at Random" (MAR). They found that in these situations conditional MI is more accurate than joint MVN MI whenever the data include categorical variables. They studied only two type of multiple imputation method. However, we studied six different type of imputation methods.

Asian et al (2014) studied with some imputation methods which are Single Arithmetic Average (SAA), Normal Ratio (NR), NR Weighted with Correlations (NRWC), Multilayer Perceptron type Neural Network (MLPNN) and Expectation-Maximization Algorithm based on Monte Carlo Markov Chain (EMMCMC). They used Turkish monthly total precipitation data for comparing the imputation methods. Their results show that both EMMCMC methods perform better than the other imputation methods considered in their study. On the other hand, in this book chapter, we used 3 different datasets. And also, we studied on a different imputation methods. For comparison, we clustered original datasets and datasets which are imputed with imputation methods. After clustering we analyzed RMSE and purity results and we obtained EM and KNN imputations are better than others according to these metrics.

Betrie et al (2014) studied on water-quality data collected from 1971 to 1994 from many locations. They compared three imputation methods to estimate missing water-quality data: Iterative Robust Model-based Imputation (IRMI), multiple imputations of incomplete multivariate data (AMELIA), and sequential imputation for missing values (IMPSEQ). These methods were evaluated based on mean absolute error, relative absolute error, and percent bias techniques. The results showed that IMPSEQ and IRMI are suitable to impute missing values in water-quality databases at mine sites, whereas AMELIA is not. They wanted to find suitable imputation method for their specific data. But this study, we wanted to create general inference from imputation methods for different type of dataset. Also, in this book chapter, we classified the best results according to distribution method and missing ratio. For each distribution and each missing ratio, we obtained best imputation methods. In these distribution results, EM and KNN is shown as best imputation methods mostly.

Thirumahal et al (2014), studied two imputation methods. In their paper KNN and ARL based imputation are introduced to impute missing values and accuracy of both the algorithms are measured by using normalized root mean square error. The result shows that ARL is more accurate and robust method for missing value estimation. They defined k value is in the range of 0-25. But in this book chapter, we also used KNN imputation method and we chose k value is in wide range which is from 2-128. They compared only two methods for a dataset. But our study we used six imputation methods and used three different datasets.

Noor et al (2014), implemented three types of Mean imputation techniques that are mean, mean above and mean above below methods were used to replace the missing values. They used air pollution dataset. Four randomly simulated missing data were evaluated in order to test the efficiency of the methods used. They are 5%, 10%, 15%, 25% and 40%. Three types of performance indicators that are Mean Absolute Error (*MAE*), Root Mean Square Error (*RMSE*) and coefficient of determination (R^2) were calculated to describe the goodness of fit for all the method. From all the method applied, it was found that mean above below method is the best method for estimating data for all percentages of simulated missing values. On their study, they used only one dataset and they created missing values randomly but in this book chapter, we used three dataset and we created missing values according to beta, gamma and Gaussian distribution methods. Also, in this book chapter, we applied K-means clustering, EM clustering and DBSCAN clustering methods, which we evaluated with RMSE and Purity metrics.

Liao et al (2014), developed four variations of K-nearest-neighbor (KNN) methods and compared with two existing methods, Multivariate Imputation by Chained Equations (MICE) and missForest. The four variations are imputation by variables (KNN-V), by subjects (KNN-S), their weighted hybrid (KNN-H) and an adaptively weighted hybrid (KNN-A). They performed simulations and applied different imputation methods and the STS scheme to three lung disease phenomic datasets to evaluate the methods. Simulations and applications to real datasets showed that MICE often did not perform well; KNN-A, KNN-H and random forest were among the top performers although no method universally performed the best. They developed four variations of KNN methods and they used MICE, missForest for comparing. However, we used different imputation methods like EM, Multiple Imputation, Regression, KNN, Hot-deck, Mean imputation methods. They used three datasets but in this book chapter, we studied on a different real dataset and we obtained that EM and KNN are better than others for imputation.

Taylor et al (2016), investigated the effects of seven imputation methods (half minimum substitution, mean substitution, *k*-nearest neighbors, local least squares regression, Bayesian principal components analysis, singular value decomposition and random forest), on the within-subject correlation of compounds between biological matrices and its consequences on MANOVA results. Their results show no one imputation method was universally the best, but the simple substitution methods (Half Minimum and Mean) consistently performed poorly. They studied on three biological real omics datasets and simulation but we studied three different dataset. Two of them are from business area and one of them is from physical area. Like

Taylor et al, we obtained Mean is performed poorly, but we also obtained Hot-deck imputation is performed poorly.

There is a major body of research in data mining on large scale data (Baloglu, Aktas, BlogMiner, 2010) (Chen, Plale, Aktas, 2014) (Chen, Plale, Aktas, 2012). We also observe a number of studies focused on stream data processing Fox et al, 2009) (Aktas & Astekin, 2017) (Aktas, 2018) (Fox et al, 2006). Furthermore, there exists a number of study on distributed data storages (Aktas & Pierce, 2010) (Aktas et al, 2007) (Aktas, Fox & Pierce, 2005). This study differs from such previous work as it mainly focuses on missing data imputation techniques.

METHODS FOR HANDLING MISSING DATA

Based on the literature review, the mostly commonly used algorithms for imputing missing data are chosen for this study. The chosen algorithms are as follows: Mean Method, Hot-Deck Method (Acuna & Caroline, 2004)), Regression Method Little & Rubin (2014), K-Nearest Neighbor (K-NN) (Batista & Monard (2003), Expectation Maximization (EM) (Ghahramani & Michael,1994) and Multiple Imputation (MI) (Wayman, 2003; David, 2000; Bradley, 1979). All methods are implemented in Java separately. We make all the source code available for the readers at the following source code repository at https://github.com/kaplansinan/Imputation-of-Missing-Data.git. Table 1 shows comparison of those methods in detail. We give extensive explanations of the chosen algorithms at a Website that we created for this research. The Website is available at http://www.yildiz.edu.tr/~aktas-/missingdata.

DATA IMPUTATION METHOD EXPLORER

The Data Imputation Method Explorer is an easy to use graphical user interface that harnesses the power of implemented data imputation methods. The Explorer consists of five panels: Preprocess, Data-imputation, Cluster, Data-imputation Explorer. Figure 1 illustrates the Data Imputation Method Explorer.

1. **Preprocess Panel:** The preprocess panel is the starting point for data imputation method exploration. Using this panel, one can load datasets, choose missing-data-scarcity distributions, decide on the percentages of simulated missing data and choose whether the simulation should apply to a constant attribute or to a randomly-selected attribute. This panel allows a user to simulate the missing data distributions on the selected dataset.

Table 1. General comparison of proposed algorithms for imputation of missing data [7, 10, 11, 12, 18, 19, 20]

Imputation Method	Type of missing data	Conceptual idea	Advantages	Disadvantages
Mean	MCAR	•Single imputation. •Missing data are replaced by the mean	•Simple to understand and apply. •Fast	•Weakens covariance and correlation estimates in the data (because ignores relationship between variables) •Reduces variability
Hot-Deck [7]	MCAR	•Single imputation •Replaces missing data with comparable data from the same set	•Most widely used imputation method •Easily be used to impute the missing values	•When several records with missing values occur together on the file, this leads the lack of the precision
Regression [10]	MCAR	•Single imputation. •Replaces missing values with predicted score from a regression equation.	•Uses information from observed data •Fast	•Overestimates model fit and correlation estimates •Weakens variance
K-NNI [11]	MCAR, MAR	•Single Imputation •Use of the k-nearest neighbor algorithm to estimate and substitute missing data •Supervised Learning Algorithm	•k-nearest neighbor can predict both qualitative attributes and quantitative attributes •Do not create a predictive model for each attribute with missing data	•The algorithm searches through all the dataset •The choice of the distance function effects differently (Euclidean, Manhattan, Mahalanobis, Pearson, etc.) •The choice of k, the number of neighbors
EM [18]	MCAR, MAR	•Single imputation. •Medium-high complexity. •The EM algorithm estimates the parameters of a model iteratively. •Starting from initial guess, each iteration consists of an E step (Expectation Step) and a M step (Maximization Step)	•Robust estimations derived from the available data. •Simple and relatively easy to implement.	•Correlation between variables can be affected. •The probability distribution of the imputed variable can be affected. •Single imputation estimates parameters but not variability. •The EM algorithm converges only linearly, with a rate of convergence that depends on the fraction of values, which are missing in the dataset. •Computations can be quite difficult. It requires complex integrations to compute the required expectations and maximization.
MI [12, 19, 20]	MCAR, MAR	•High complexity. •Several imputations are done. •Robust estimators can be obtained.	•Simple to understand, hard to program. •Commercial software available. •Standard errors of the estimates can be calculated.	•Difficult to program (special software required). •The analyst has little control over the imputation model. •The variance is larger than the single-imputation methods. •The choice of m, the number of imputation

2. **Data-imputation Panel:** The data-imputation panel allows a user to choose data-imputation method to be used in the simulation. Once the data-imputation method is selected, the missing values in the selected dataset is filled based on the corresponding data-imputation computation. This stage creates imputed datasets with the selected data imputation technique.

3. **Cluster Panel:** From the cluster panel, once can configure and execute one of the three clustering algorithms (k-means, expected maximization and DBSCAN) on the current dataset. The results of the selected clustering method is shown in the Results Panel.

4. **Data Imputation Explorer Panel:** From the data imputation explorer model, one can configure and execute all three clustering methods on the current dataset. The results will point out the best data imputation technique for both RMSE and Purity values. The results will be shown in the Results Panel.

EXPERIMENTAL EVALUATION

In this section, we investigate the effect of the chosen methods for missing data imputation. To do this, we investigate two strategies. First, we measure RMSE values of each imputed dataset for each algorithm with respect to the missing value ratio based on three different distributions. This way, we explore the quality of imputation. Second, we measure the performance of the clustering tasks applied on

Figure 1. Screenshots of data imputation method explorer

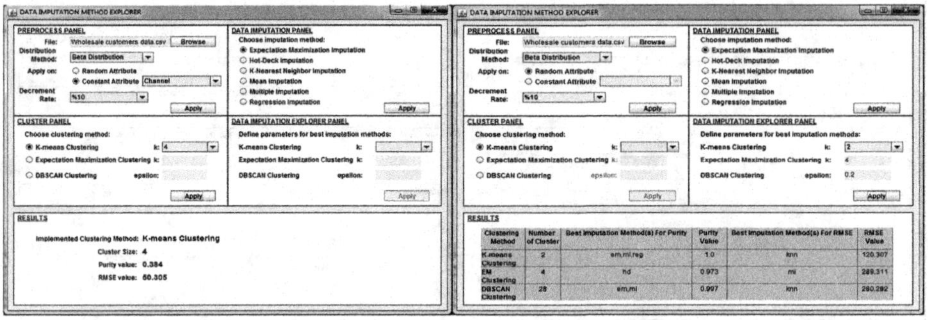

the imputed datasets. To calculate the clustering performance, we use the clustering results obtained from the original datasets (dataset before missing data simulation) and use it as our golden standard in calculation of Purity metric values.

Experimental results are conducted on a different percentage of missing values in each given datasets. Those percentages are 10%, 20%, and 30% respectively. We use four different datasets as described in the following section. Missing values are created by using three different distributions, which are based on the desired percentage of missing values. As for missing data scarcity distributions, Gama, Beta, and Gaussian distributions are used for this purpose (Forbes et al, 2011). Those distributions are applied to create reasonable missing values in the given dataset before the imputation step. We conduct all our experiments by simulating the missing data on a constant attribute and randomly-selected attributes. In this book chapter, we publish our summarized results obtained from both constant attribute and randomly-selected attributes analysis. We give the detailed results for constant attribute analysis, as it is a commonly encountered missing data scenario. Due to lack of space, we publish the detailed results for randomly-selected attribute analysis in the Web site created for this research at http://www.yildiz.edu.tr/~aktas-/missingdata.

We discuss the process of introducing missing values to the datasets in subsection "B. Creating Missing Values".

Dataset Properties

First dataset is a high dimensional dataset, this set contains N=1024 instances and M=64 attributes (http://cs.joensuu.fi/-sipu/datasets). Attributes are named from C1 to C64. Also the dataset has 16 Gaussian clusters without any missing data created. (When using clustering as the evaluation criteria, we use the Purity, which is calculated based on these clusters in this dataset). Table 2 shows the summary of the dataset properties in details.

Table 2. Dataset properties for dim064 dataset

Dataset Characteristics:	Multivariate	Number of Instances:	1024
Attribute Characteristics:	Integer	Number of Attributes:	64
Associated Tasks:	Classification, Clustering	Missing Values?	No

Second dataset is whole sale customer dataset, which is taken from (http://archive.ics.uci.edu/ml/datasets). As a high dimensional dataset, this set contains N=440 instances and M=8 attributes. Table 3 shows the summary of the dataset properties in details.

Another dataset is statlog dataset, which is taken from (http://archive.ics.uci.edu/ml/datasets). As a high dimensional dataset, this set contains N=4435 instances and M=36 attributes. Attributes are named from pixel1 to pixel36. Table 4 shows the summary of the dataset properties in details.

Last dataset is promo dataset, which is taken from (http://clopinet.com/causality/data/promo/). As a high dimensional dataset, this set contains N=1095 instances and M=100 attributes. Table 5 shows the summary of the dataset properties in details.

Creating Missing Values

To simulate the missing values, we repeat the tests for two cases. First, we only use one of the attributes, which has no dependence to others, to simulate the missing values. Second, we randomly select independent attributes and simulate the missing values based on desired scarcity distributions. Figure 2 illustrates the two different

Table 3. Dataset properties for wholesale customer dataset

Dataset Characteristics:	Multivariate	Number of Instances:	440
Attribute Characteristics:	Integer	Number of Attributes:	8
Associated Tasks:	Classification, Clustering	Missing Values?	No

Table 4. Dataset properties for statlog dataset

Dataset Characteristics:	Multivariate	Number of Instances:	4435
Attribute Characteristics:	Integer	Number of Attributes:	36
Associated Tasks:	Classification	Missing Values?	No

Table 5. Dataset properties for promo dataset

Dataset Characteristics:	Multivariate	Number of Instances:	1095
Attribute Characteristics:	Integer	Number of Attributes:	100
Associated Tasks:	Classification	Missing Values?	No

Figure 2. Illustration of simulating missing values on a constant attribute and randomly selected attributes

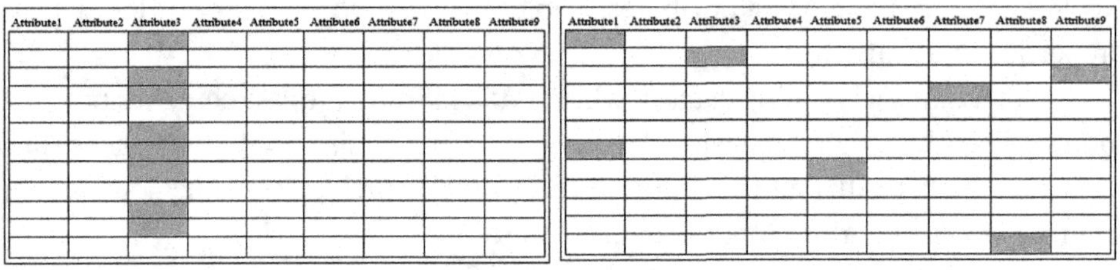

ways of simulating the missing values. Missing values ratio can be 10%, 20% and 30% after applying Gama, Beta and Gaussian distribution. Figure 2 gives an overview of the illustration of how we simulate missing data to the datasets. In the figure, the gray colored cells indicate the missing values.

The original datasets do not have any missing values. Missing values are simulated into the original datasets. By doing this, we aim to measure how close the predicted value and the observed value of the related attribute is. As is aforementioned, the missing values with a ratio of 10%, 20%, and 30% are created by applying Gama, Beta, and Gaussian distributions.

First, to achieve mixed missingness in the dataset we created missing values on randomly-selected attributes in the dataset with ratio of 10%, 20%, and 30% for each distribution. Second, we focused to create missing values with ratio of 10%, 20%, and 30% on specific attributes. For the first dataset (dim064), we choose C6 feature. For both cases, Table 6 shows the number of instances that have missing values, ranging from 10% to 30% respectively.

Table 7 shows the number of instances that have missing values, ranging from 10% to 30% respectively. As for constant attribute missingness analysis, we used "Fresh" feature of wholesale customer dataset.

Table 8 shows the number of instances that have missing values, ranging from 10% to 30% respectively. As for constant attribute missingness analysis, we used "Pixel3" feature of statlog dataset.

Table 6. Number of instances with missing values on dim064 dataset

	Percentage of Missing Values (%)		
	10	20	30
Number of Instances	103	205	307

Note: For missing data simulation on a constant attribute, as for attribute C6 feature is used.

Table 7. Number of instances with missing values on wholesale customers dataset

	Percentage of Missing Values (%)		
	10	20	30
Number of Instances	44	80	122

Note: For missing data simulation on a constant attribute, as for attribute Fresh feature is used.

Table 8. Number of instances with missing values on statlog dataset

	Percentage of Missing Values (%)		
	10	20	30
Number of Instances	430	836	1246

Note: For missing data simulation on a constant attribute, as for attribute Pixel 3 feature is used.

Table 9 shows the number of instances that have missing values, ranging from 10% to 30% respectively. As for constant attribute missingness analysis, we used "Product3" feature of promo dataset.

One of the important issues with missing data is type of the missing data mechanism. In this book chapter, we investigating the best data imputation techniques for different missing data mechanisms such as missing completely at random

Table 9. Number of instances with missing values on promo dataset

	Percentage of Missing Values (%)		
	10	20	30
Number of Instances	106	196	298

Note: For missing data simulation on a constant attribute, as for attribute Product 3 feature is used.

(MCAR) and missing at random (MAR). After creating the missing values on the datasets, Little's MCAR test is performed by using two different software package of a statistics tool "R ". These packages, MissMech package (http://cran.r-project. org/web/packages-/MissMech/index.html) andLitteMCAR package (http://finzi. psych.upenn.edu/library/-BaylorEdPsych/html/LittleMCAR.html) package, are used to specify whether or not the structure of each dataset with missing values is MCAR or MAR. We report the results of these tests in Table 10.

Performance Metrics

To analyze the performance of the proposed algorithms, Root Mean Square Error (RMSE) and Purity are used as performance metrics. RMSE is a commonly used measure of difference between the values predicted by a model and the values actually observed. RMSE is calculated for each attribute. By calculating RMSE, the performance of each data imputation algorithm is measured and compared to determine the most appropriate method based on the distribution and missing ratio of the missing values in each dataset.

To evaluate the performance of these methods in a clustering context, Purity is used. Purity is a simple and transparent evaluation measure. Bad clustering has purity values close to 0, while a perfect clustering has a purity of 1. For lack of space, we leave out the detailed descriptions of these well-known metrics, in this book chapter. However, we give descriptions and formulas for both RMSE and Purity metrics at the Website that we created for this research at http://www.yildiz. edu.tr/~aktas-/missingdata.

Table 10. Types of missing data mechanism for four different datasets for varying missing data distributions and for varying sizes of missingness

		Missingness on a Constant Attribute			Missingness on Randomly Selected Attributes		
		10%	20%	30%	10%	20%	30%
"dim064"	Gaussian	MCAR	MCAR	MCAR	MCAR	MCAR	MCAR
	Gamma	MCAR	MCAR	MAR	MAR	MAR	MCAR
	Beta	MCAR	MCAR	MCAR	MAR	MAR	MCAR
"wholesale customer"	Gaussian	MCAR	MCAR	MCAR	MCAR	MCAR	MCAR
	Gamma	MCAR	MCAR	MCAR	MCAR	MCAR	MCAR
	Beta	MCAR	MCAR	MCAR	MCAR	MCAR	MCAR
"statlog"	Gaussian	MCAR	MCAR	MCAR	MCAR	MCAR	MCAR
	Gamma	MAR	MCAR	MAR	MCAR	MCAR	MCAR
	Beta	MCAR	MCAR	MCAR	MCAR	MCAR	MCAR
"promo"	Gaussian	MCAR	MCAR	MCAR	MCAR	MCAR	MCAR
	Gamma	MCAR	MCAR	MCAR	MCAR	MCAR	MCAR
	Beta	MCAR	MCAR	MCAR	MCAR	MCAR	MCAR

Evaluation of Algorithms for Treatment of Missing Values

After coding all methods separately, the selected algorithms are evaluated by using RMSE values for each distribution of missing values. Figure-3, Figure 4, Figure 5 and Figure 6 indicate the RMSE values of imputed "dimo64", "wholesale customer", "statlog", "promo" datasets, respectively, for each imputed dataset for each algorithm with respect to the missing value ratio based on three different distributions.

Based on the results in Figure 3-to-Figure-6, the EM for 20%, 30% and K-NN for 10% perform better than other methods and Hot- deck and Mean methods give poorer results.

Multiple Imputation (MI) and Regression (REG) give almost the same results because both MI and REG use linear regression lines, which are based on correlation between attributes, to impute missing.

One can easily see that there is not much difference between the results obtained from each method except Mean and Hot-deck methods, which are more primitive methods than others. Also, it can be said that when the ratio of missing values increases, EM algorithm starts to superior other methods.

Figure 3. Evaluation of algorithms for treatment of missing values using RMSE values of missing data with constant variable on dim064 dataset

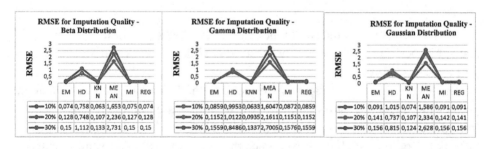

Figure 4. Evaluation of algorithms for treatment of missing values using RMSE values of missing data with constant variable on wholesale customer dataset

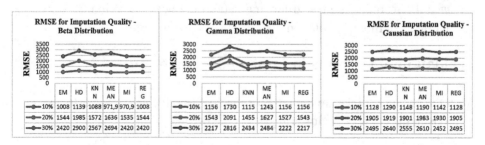

Figure 5. Evaluation of algorithms for treatment of missing values using RMSE values of missing data with constant variable on statlog dataset

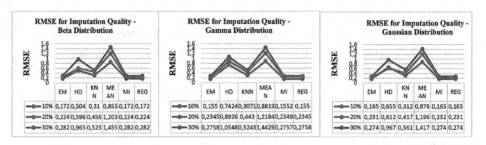

Figure 6. Evaluation of algorithms for treatment of missing values using RMSE values of missing data with constant variable on promo dataset

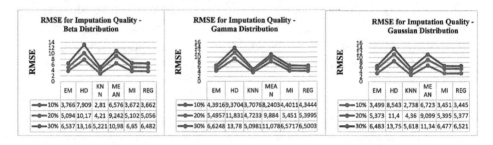

The results also show that, as for the Gamma distribution of the missing data, EM and K-NN performs better than other methods, while Hot-deck and Mean methods give again poorer results.

The RMSE value for Mean and Hot-deck methods increases sharply when the ratio of missing values goes up from 10% to 30%. Based on the results obtained from these experiments, it can be said that EM and K-NN both can be used when the missing ratio is small. However, once the ratio of the missing values increases then it would be wiser to choose EM regardless of structure of missing data.

According to the given results, to get better imputation results in Beta distribution of the missing data, one should apply EM method to impute missing values.

Once the methods are tested for imputation, the next phase in our study is to reveal effects of those imputation methods in clustering tasks.

Evaluation of Methods in Context of Clustering

After the missing values are imputed for each dataset, the next stage is to test those methods in the context of clustering.

On choosing the best unsupervised clustering algorithm for our use, we investigate the performance of three different types of popular clustering algorithms: centroid-based, distribution based and density based, using K-means, DBSCAN and EM algorithms, respectively. The K-Means algorithm is used to cluster the data with respect to different k values, which range from 2 to 128, by taking the power of 2. For k-means clustering, we used 10 seed data points and used 500 as the maximum iteration number. For EM clustering, cluster size is used as 5 for each dataset. DBSCAN clustering gets epsilon parameter instead of k value and cluster size changes according to the epsilon value. For having good cluster size, epsilon parameter should be defined carefully. For this purpose, for datasets cluster size, Weka is used to define epsilon values. As for Epsilon values, we used 0.21, 0.24, 0.615, 1.07 for "dim064", "wholesale customers", "statlog", and "promo" datasets. After injecting these epsilon values, cluster size of each dataset were found to be 20.

To evaluate the results of clustering, we use RMSE as an internal clustering quality measurement. In addition, we use Purity, as an external clustering quality measurement, to analyze the performance of each method in terms of clustering. We list the RMSE clustering results in Figure 7-to-Figure 10. We also list Purity results in Figure 11-to-Figure 14 and Table 11-to-Table 14 for each method conducted on 10%, 20% and 30% missing values for each distribution.

Broadly, for each distribution of missingness EM and K-NN provide the best purity values while Mean gives the worst.

For the Gaussian distribution of missing values, the Mean method for the imputation of missing data provides the worst results for clustering, when the missing data ratio increases, and the EM method gives better clustering results when the amount of missing data increases. One can notice here that when the amount of missing data increases Hot-deck almost provides same results with MI and REG methods.

For the Gamma distribution of missing data, the Mean method for the imputation of missing data provides the worst results for clustering, regardless of the missing data structure and the amount of missing data.

Figure 7. RMSE values of missing data on constant variable for dim064 dataset

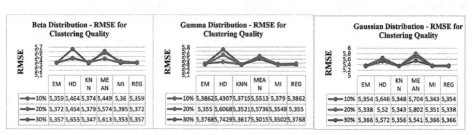

Figure 8. RMSE values of missing data on constant variable for wholesale customer dataset

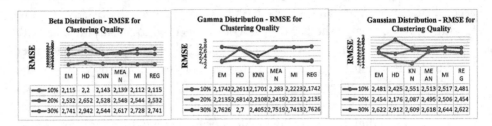

Figure 9. RMSE values of missing data on constant variable for statlog dataset

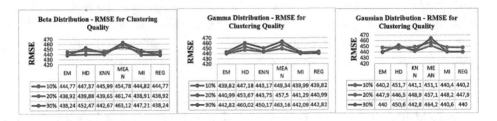

Figure 10. RMSE values of missing data on constant variable for promo dataset

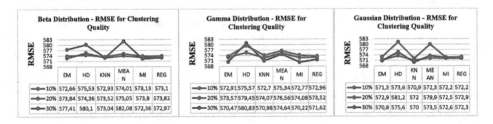

The results show that the Beta distribution of missing data demonstrates that the Mean method for the imputation of missing data provides the worst results for clustering when the missing data ratio increases. The EM method always gives the best results for each amount of missing data, while the KNN, MI, and REG methods provide almost the same Purity results in terms of clustering.

DISCUSSION

In this book chapter, we use clustering techniques to test the data imputation techniques after the missing values are imputed for each dataset. Here, our aim is to detect the best imputation techniques. We use three different types of clustering algorithms: centroid-based, distribution based and density based, using K-means, DBSCAN and EM algorithms, respectively. Here, we cluster the data instances in the imputed datasets. Each cluster is composed of data-instances. For example, let' say, the first imputed dataset that we want to test has 1024 instances, where each instance has 64 attributes. First, we find the number of clusters of the data instances within each imputed dataset. Then, we compare the results against the ground truth data, which has the actual clusters. Based on the results, we compare and contrast the success of different data imputation techniques.

After conducting the experiments for our study, we compare and contrasts the performance of the data imputation methods and produce rankings. Based on the results of our experiments, the answers to each research question are revealed properly. According to the test results these answer are as follows:

Analyzing the results in Table 16, we answer the aforementioned ResearchQuestion#1 as in the following. For each distribution of missing data, the EM algorithm provides better results than other methods. Figure 11-to-Figure 14 and Table 11-to-Table 14 show the Purity results that were conducted on each imputed dataset for each distribution with different clustering algorithms. When analyzing clustering results based on Purity metric, we observe that the datasets imputed with the EM algorithm provide better performance. In general, EM imputations are better because they preserve the relationship with other variables, which is vital if you go on to use factor analysis which is a type of statistical procedure that is conducted to identify clusters or groups of related items. Since, we investigate the best imputation methods that could lead to high quality in clustering tasks, our findings recommends the use EM imputations regardless of the type of missing data scarcity distributions such as Gaussian, Gamma and Beta. In addition to EM, KNN also gives good results. In KNN, the missing values of an attribute are imputed using the given number of attributes that are most similar to the attribute whose values are missing. This method performs better when there exists attributes with multiple missing values. It takes into account correlation structure of the data that is taken into consideration. Similar to EM, KNN also performs well as a data imputation technique regardless of data scarcity distributions. One disadvantage with KNN is that it is time-consuming as it searches through all the dataset looking for similar instances.

Analyzing the results in Table 16, we answer the aforementioned ResearchQuestion#2 as in the following. The Mean and Hot-deck methods lead to poorer imputation results in line with the findings in the aforementioned studies. Apart from other studies, we point out that the performance of these methods remain the same regardless of various missing data scarcity distributions. Mean imputation method is the easiest way for replacing each missing value with the mean of the observed values for that variable. Unfortunately, this strategy severely distorts the distribution for this variable, leading to complications with summary measures and underestimates of the standard deviation. Furthermore, mean imputation distorts relationships between variables by pulling estimates of the correlation toward zero. We argue that the Mean imputation method gives poorer results. Our findings also indicated that Hot-deck imputation gives poorer results. This is mainly because, hot deck imputation method maintains the statistical association of the missing value with assignment variables. However, in turn, this can lead to understatement of its relationship with other variables. Hot-deck procedures replace missing data with the value obtained for a similar row in the same dataset. If similar row data increases root mean square error, replaced missing data increases root mean square error, too.

Analyzing the results in Figure3-to-Figure-10, we answer the aforementioned ResearchQuestion#3 and ResearchQuestion#4 as in the following. The results indicate the EM data imputation method leads to high quality clustering results. The results of this study also reveals that RMSE-for-treatment-of-imputed-values is related to the amount of missing data in the dataset. For instance, when the amount of missing values increases, the RMSE-for-treatment-of-imputed-values value also starts to increase. The EM algorithm gives the lowest RMSE-for-treatment-of-imputed-values when the amount of missing values increases. However, K-NN gives the lowest RMSE-for-treatment-of-imputed-values at Gaussian 10%, Gamma 10%, regardless of the missing data structure. Analyzing the Purity results in Figure 11-to-Figure 14 and Table 11-to-Table 14, another interesting finding of this study is that there is a strong relationship between RMSE-for-treatment-of-imputed-values and Purity. The method that gives lower RMSE-for-treatment-of-imputed-values also gives better Purity. One can conclude that, in order to achieve high accuracy in terms of clustering tasks when the data has missing values, the method that gives lower RMSE-for-treatment-of-imputed-values can be used to achieve better clustering results.

Figure 11 shows the Purity results that were conducted on each "dim064" imputed dataset for k-means clustering. For k-means clustering, we used 10 seed data points and used 500 as the maximum iteration number.

Figure 12 shows the Purity results that were conducted on each "wholesale customer" imputed dataset for k-means clustering. For k-means clustering, we used 10 seed data points and used 500 as the maximum iteration number.

Figure 13 shows the purity results that were conducted on each "statlog" imputed data set for each distribution with different k values.

Figure 14 shows the purity results that were conducted on each "promo" imputed data set for k-means clustering. For k-means clustering, we used 10 seed data points and used 500 as the maximum iteration number.

Table 11, Table 12, Table 13, and Table 14 show the purity results of the datasets "dim064", "wholescale customer", "statlog", and "promo" datasets, respectively for

Figure 11. Purity values with K-means clustering for dim064 dataset; For constant variable missing data simulation and for varying scarcity proportions (10%, 20%, 30%) and scarcity distributions (beta, gamma, gaussian) and K values

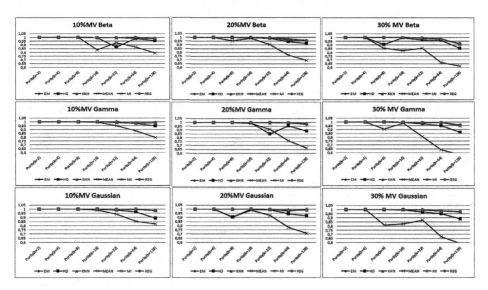

Figure 12. Purity values with K-means clustering for wholesale customer dataset; For constant variable missing data simulation and for varying scarcity proportions (10%, 20%, 30%) and scarcity distributions (beta, gamma, gaussian) and K values

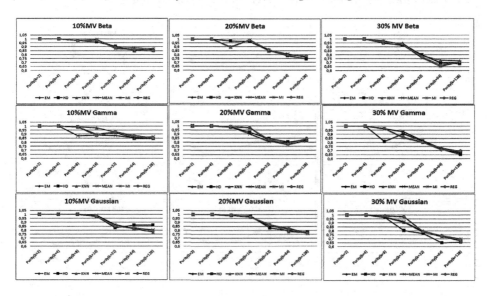

Figure 13. Purity values with K-means clustering for statlog dataset; For constant variable missing data simulation and for varying scarcity proportions (10%, 20%, 30%) and scarcity distributions (beta, gamma, gaussian) and K values

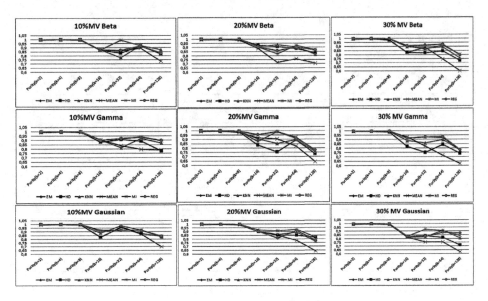

Figure 14. Purity values with K-means clustering for promo dataset; For constant variable missing data simulation and for varying scarcity proportions (10%, 20%, 30%) and scarcity distributions (beta, gamma, gaussian) and K values

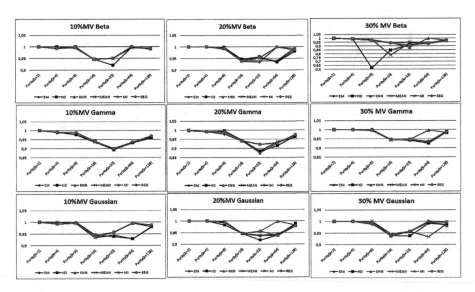

Table 11. Purity values with EM and DBSCAN clustering for dim064 dataset: For constant variable and varying scarcity proportions (10%, 20%, 30%) and varying scarcity distributions (Beta, Gamma, Gaussian)

Beta | | | | **Gamma** | | | | **Gaussian** | | |

DBSCAN	10%	20%	30%	DBSCAN	10%	20%	30%	DBSCAN	10%	20%	30%
EM	1	1	1	EM	1	1	1	EM	1	1	1
HD	0,996	0,996	0,983	HD	0,979	0,987	0,981	HD	0,981	0,987	0,994
KNN	1	1	1	KNN	1	1	1	KNN	1	1	1
MEAN	0,933	0,917	0,876	MEAN	0,934	0,913	0,862	MEAN	0,946	0,908	0,863
MI	1	1	1	MI	1	1	1	MI	1	1	1
REG	1	1	1	REG	1	1	1	REG	1	1	1

EM CLUSTERING	10%	20%	30%	EM CLUSTERING	10%	20%	30%	EM CLUSTERING	10%	20%	30%
EM	1	1	1	EM	1	1	1	EM	1	1	1
HD	1	1	1	HD	1	1	1	HD	1	1	1
KNN	1	1	1	KNN	1	1	1	KNN	1	1	1
MEAN	1	1	1	MEAN	1	1	1	MEAN	1	1	1
MI	1	1	1	MI	1	1	1	MI	1	1	1
REG	1	1	1	REG	1	1	1	REG	1	1	1

Table 12. Purity values with EM and DBSCAN clustering for wholesale customer dataset: For constant variable and varying scarcity proportions (10%, 20%, 30%) and varying scarcity distributions (Beta, Gamma, Gaussian)

Beta | | | | **Gamma** | | | | **Gaussian** | | |

DBSCAN	10%	20%	30%	DBSCAN	10%	20%	30%	DBSCAN	10%	20%	30%
EM	1	0,992	0,983	EM	0,996	0,992	0,975	EM	1	1	0,983
HD	1	0,991	0,983	HD	0,996	0,992	0,98	HD	1	1	0,98
KNN	1	0,992	0,983	KNN	0,996	0,992	0,983	KNN	1	1	0,98
MEAN	1	0,991	0,984	MEAN	0,996	0,992	0,984	MEAN	1	1	0,983
MI	1	0,992	0,983	MI	0,996	0,992	0,975	MI	1	0,997	0,983
REG	1	0,992	0,983	REG	0,996	0,992	0,975	REG	1	1	0,983

EM CLUSTERING	10%	20%	30%	EM CLUSTERING	10%	20%	30%	EM CLUSTERING	10%	20%	30%
EM	0,814	0,819	0,897	EM	0,869	0,816	0,825	EM	0,967	0,995	0,823
HD	0,813	0,815	0,817	HD	0,826	0,818	0,825	HD	0,94	0,933	0,821
KNN	0,81	0,82	0,822	KNN	0,983	0,825	0,821	KNN	0,859	0,984	0,825
MEAN	0,815	0,82	0,82	MEAN	0,981	0,82	0,823	MEAN	0,822	0,825	0,823
MI	0,818	0,819	0,82	MI	1	0,816	0,825	MI	0,967	0,825	0,823
REG	0,814	0,819	0,897	REG	0,869	0,816	0,825	REG	0,967	0,995	0,823

EM and DBScan clustering. Here, EM clustering is configured to have 5 clusters and DBSCAN clustering is configured to have 20 clusters in purity calculation for all datasets. Table 15 shows the list of #1 ranked data imputation methods in different rankings where the agreement ratio for the #1 method is above certain agreement threshold (75%) across all datasets.

Table 13. Purity values with EM and DBSCAN clustering for statlog dataset: For constant variable and varying scarcity proportions (10%, 20%, 30%) and varying scarcity distributions (Beta, Gamma, Gaussian)

	Beta				**Gamma**				**Gaussian**		
DBSCAN	10%	20%	30%	DBSCAN	10%	20%	30%	DBSCAN	10%	20%	30%
EM	1	1	1	EM	1	1	1	EM	1	1	1
HD	1	1	1	HD	1	1	0,999	HD	0,999	1	0,999
KNN	1	1	1	KNN	1	1	1	KNN	1	1	1
MEAN	1	1	1	MEAN	1	0,999	1	MEAN	1	1	1
MI	1	1	1	MI	1	1	1	MI	1	1	1
REG	1	1	1	REG	1	1	1	REG	1	1	1

EM CLUSTERING	10%	20%	30%	EM CLUSTERING	10%	20%	30%	EM CLUSTERING	10%	20%	30%
EM	0,994	0,999	0,998	EM	1	0,995	0,987	EM	1	1	0,999
HD	0,999	0,985	0,99	HD	0,997	0,992	0,993	HD	0,997	0,986	0,995
KNN	0,993	0,996	0,991	KNN	0,997	0,991	0,995	KNN	0,996	0,998	0,99
MEAN	0,996	0,997	0,992	MEAN	0,996	0,993	0,995	MEAN	0,992	0,995	0,993
MI	0,994	0,999	0,998	MI	1	0,995	0,987	MI	1	1	0,999
REG	0,994	0,999	0,998	REG	1	0,995	0,987	REG	1	1	0,999

Table 14. Purity values with EM and DBSCAN clustering for promo dataset: For constant variable and varying scarcity proportions (10%, 20%, 30%) and varying scarcity distributions (Beta, Gamma, Gaussian)

	Beta				**Gamma**				**Gaussian**		
DBSCAN	10%	20%	30%	DBSCAN	10%	20%	30%	DBSCAN	10%	20%	30%
EM	1	1	1	EM	1	1	0,984	EM	1	1	0,984
HD	1	0,983	0,776	HD	0,996	0,76	0,9	HD	0,899	0,982	0,984
KNN	1	1	1	KNN	1	1	1	KNN	1	1	1
MEAN	1	0,884	1	MEAN	1	0,9	0,884	MEAN	0,9	1	0,984
MI	1	1	1	MI	1	1	0,984	MI	1	1	0,984
REG	1	1	1	REG	1	1	0,984	REG	1	1	0,984

EM CLUSTERING	10%	20%	30%	EM CLUSTERING	10%	20%	30%	EM CLUSTERING	10%	20%	30%
EM	0,998	0,974	0,974	EM	0,998	1	1	EM	0,998	0,998	1
HD	0,976	0,976	1	HD	0,998	0,974	0,972	HD	0,974	0,998	0,997
KNN	0,974	0,974	0,998	KNN	0,998	1	1	KNN	0,998	0,998	0,998
MEAN	0,998	1	1	MEAN	0,998	0,972	0,974	MEAN	0,974	0,998	0,998
MI	0,998	0,998	0,974	MI	0,998	1	1	MI	0,998	0,998	1
REG	0,998	0,998	0,974	REG	0,998	1	1	REG	0,998	0,998	1

Table 16 shows the summary results for the list of most appropriate imputation methods for varying missing data scarcities and for different missing data scarcity distributions.

Table 15. The list of #1 ranked data imputation methods in different rankings (coming from clustering evaluation) where the agreement ratio for the #1 method is above certain agreement threshold (75%) across all datasets

Types of Distribution	Missing Data Percentages	Evaluation of Algorithms for Treatment of Missing Values		Evaluation of Methods in Context of Clustering											
		RMSE		External Evaluation Criterion for Cluster Quality (Purity)						Internal Evaluation Criterion for Cluster Quality (RMSE)					
		Ranking RMSE-CONSTANT	Ranking RMSE-RANDOM	Ranking kMEANS-CONSTANT	Ranking kMEANS-RANDOM	Ranking DBSCAN-CONSTANT	Ranking DBSCAN-RANDOM	Ranking DM-CONSTANT	Ranking DM-RANDOM	Ranking kMEANS-CONSTANT	Ranking kMEANS-RANDOM	Ranking DBSCAN-CONSTANT	Ranking DBSCAN-RANDOM	Ranking DM-CONSTANT	Ranking DM-RANDOM
Beta	10%	.	.	K-NN		EM, K-NN, MI, REG	EM, K-NN, MI, REG	MI	HD	EM	.	.	.	HD	.
	20%	.	.	.	.	EM, K-NN, MI, REG	EM, K-NN, MI, REG	MEAN	EM	.	.	.	.	.	.
	30%	.	.	.	.	EM, K-NN, MI, REG	EM, K-NN	EM, REG		.	.	.	.	.	.
Gaussian	10%	.	.	.	.	EM, K-NN, MI, REG, HD	EM, K-NN, MI, REG, HD	EM, MI, REG	.	.	.	.	K-NN	.	.
	20%	K-NN	.	.	K-NN	EM, K-NN, MI, REG	K-NN	EM, MI, REG	EM	.	.	.	.	.	.
	30%	.	K-NN	.	.	EM, MI, REG	EM, MI, REG	EM, MI, REG	EM, MI	K-NN	.	.	.	.	.
Gamma	10%	K-NN	.	EM	.	EM, K-NN, MI, MEAN, REG	EM, K-NN, MI, REG	EM, MI, REG	.	K-NN	.	.	.	HD	.
	20%	K-NN	.	.	.	EM, K-NN, MI, REG	EM, K-NN, MI, REG	EM, K-NN, MI, REG	EM, MI, REG	.	.	HD	.	.	.
	30%	.	K-NN	EM, REG	.	.	EM, K-NN	K-NN, MI	EM, HD	MI	.	.	.	.	.

Table 16. The list of most appropriate imputation methods in descending order (based on # of times each appear as most agreed #1 method): For varying missing data scarcities (10%, 20%, 30%) and per missing data distributions (beta, gamma, gaussian); Results obtained from four datasets (dim064, wholesale customer, statlog, promo)

		10%			20%			30%		
		Overall ranking	method	(#of times selected as #1 ranked method)/(total # of rankings)	Overall ranking	method	(#of times selected as #1 ranked method)/(total # of rankings)	Overall ranking	method	(#of times selected as #1 ranked method)/(total # of rankings)
Beta		1	EM	3/14	1	EM	3/14	1	EM	3/14
		2	KNN	3/14	2	KNN	2/14	2	KNN	2/14
		3	MI	3/14	3	MI	2/14	3	REG	1/14
		4	REG	2/14	4	REG	2/14	4	MI	1/14
		5	HD	1/14	5	HD	1/14	5	HD	0/14
		6	MEAN	0/14	6	MEAN	1/14	6	MEAN	0/14
Gamma		1	EM	4/14	1	EM	4/14	1	EM	3/14
		2	KNN	4/14	2	KNN	4/14	2	KNN	3/14
		3	MI	3/14	3	MI	4/14	3	MI	2/14
		4	REG	3/14	4	REG	4/14	4	HD	1/14
		5	HD	1/14	5	HD	1/14	5	REG	1/14
		6	MEAN	1/14	6	MEAN	0/14	6	MEAN	0/14
Gaussian		1	EM	3/14	1	KNN	4/14	1	EM	3/14
		2	KNN	3/14	2	EM	3/14	2	MI	3/14
		3	MI	3/14	3	MI	1/14	3	KNN	2/14
		4	REG	3/14	4	REG	1/14	4	REG	2/14
		5	HD	1/14	5	HD	0/14	5	HD	0/14
		6	MEAN	0/14	6	MEAN	0/14	6	MEAN	0/14

Scaling missing data imputation techniques can be achieved by using various big data technologies. The book chapter deals with data imputation methods that include Mean, Hot-deck, Regression, K-nearest-neighbor, Expectation Maximization and Multiple Imputation. As the purpose of this chapter is to illustrate the use of data imputation techniques on different datasets with different scarcity distributions, we only show the test results on four different datasets, each stored on a single-node database. However, the data imputation methods utilized in this study can be used to impute missing data, when there is a very large number of records on a dataset and the dataset is kept on distributed databases. Distributed file systems such as HDFS or NoSQL databases, such as HBase and MongoDB, can be used to store very large amounts of data. A scalable data storage system based on such technologies can be utilized to store big data, and the data imputation techniques discussed in this chapter can be extended to read large-scale dataset from these scalable storages. The current data processing technologies such as Spark provides libraries that allows processing of data that may be located in distributed file systems such as HDFS. In other words, such technologies hide the complexities of distributed data processing where the data is distributed and located on multiple nodes. Utilizing the libraries of such data processing technologies, the data imputation algorithms will employ the distributed data processing capabilities of underlying technology. Therefore, once the data are read by using such libraries, then the system would be able to apply imputation algorithms on the dataset. Therefore, scaling data imputation techniques require (a) utilizing data processing libraries such as Spark on the dataset and (b) providing access to the large-scale data stored on distributed data storage systems such as distributed file systems, HDFS, or NoSQL databases.

CONCLUSION AND FUTURE WORK

In this book chapter, we have reviewed and analyzed the missing data imputation methods for handling missing values in datasets and reveal the correlation between missing data imputation ratio and missing data distribution on clustering tasks to determine the most proper method.

To do this, we first implemented various data imputation algorithms (EM, Hot-Deck, Mean, K-NN, MI and Regression) and validated our implementations against their open source implementations from R and Weka tools. To facilitate testing of these methodologies, we formed 4 different datasets having missing values with a ratio of 10%, 20%, 30% by applying Gaussian, Gamma and Beta distributions on the complete data. Then, we analyzed each of the datasets (by using the Little MCAR test) to reveal the mechanism of the missing data. Next, we simulated missing data into the datasets on a constant attribute and on randomly-selected attributes. The missing values for each dataset were imputed by applying the implemented algorithms.

We evaluated the results of imputations by two different strategy. First, we used RMSE metric to investigate the quality of missing data treatments. Second, we investigated the quality of clustering results on the imputed datasets. For quality of clustering, we used RMSE as internal clustering quality, and Purity as external clustering quality metric. Our experimental results show that the EM algorithm provides better results. On the other hand, the Mean and Hot-Deck methods usually give worse results than others in terms of imputation. We argue that EM imputations are better because they preserve the relationship with other variables, which is vital if you go on to use factor analysis which is a type of statistical procedure that is conducted to identify clusters or groups of related items. Mean imputation distorts relationships between variables by pulling estimates of the correlation toward zero. Hot deck imputation method maintains the statistical association of the missing value with assignment variables. In turn, this can lead to understatement of its relationship with other variables.

In this book chapter, we used the K-Means, DBScan and EM clustering algorithms to cluster each imputed dataset, to analyze the effects of the data imputation algorithm in the context of clustering. To evaluate the clustering results we used the RSME and Purity metrics. The datasets imputed with the EM algorithms usually gives much higher Purity values, while the Mean always gives the worst Purity values.

In this chapter, as it is a descriptive property of missing data in our datasets, we investigated the missing data imputations in datasets where the structure of the missing data is MCAR and MAR. Work remains in investigating the data imputation effects when the data mechanism is based on Missing Not At Random (MNAR).

We also argue that the dataset properties also have an impact on the performance of the data imputation methods. In our motivating scenarios, datasets have no interdependent attributes. Work remains in analyzing datasets where there is interdependence. In our future work, we will investigate the relationship between the attributes in the datasets in detail prior to the imputation procedures.

Purity is used to reveal the impact of the missing data handling methods on clustering tasks. To broaden these impacts in addition to Purity, other metrics, such as normalized mutual information, Rand index and F measure, will be used to evaluate the results in the context of clustering in future work.

ACKNOWLEDGMENT

This study conducted within the collaboration activities between Cybersoft Research and Development Division and Yildiz Technical University Software Quality Lab. The authors thank Cybersoft for the working environment and its staff who provided support in order this study to be completed. This study was supported by the YTU BAP Project with ID number: 2013-04-01-KAP03 and by TUBITAK's (3501) National Young Researchers Career Development Program (Project No: 114E781, Project Title: Provenance Use in Social Media Software to Develop Metodologies for Detection of Information Pollution and Violation of Copyrights).

REFERENCES

Acuna, E., & Caroline, R. (2004). The treatment of missing values and its effect on classifier accuracy. Classification, Clustering, and Data Mining Applications. Springer Berlin Heidelberg.

Aktas, M. (2018). Hybrid cloud computing monitoring software architecture. *Concurrency and Computation, 2018*. doi:10.1002/cpe.4694

Aktas, M. S., & Astekin, M. (2017). Provenance aware run-time verification of things for self-healing Internet of Things applications. *Concurrency and Computation, 2017*. doi:10.1002/cpe.4263

Aktas, M. S., Fox, G. C., & Pierce, M. (2005). Information services for dynamically assembled semantic grids. *First International Conference on Semantics, Knowledge and Grid*. 10.1109/SKG.2005.83

Aktas, M. S., Fox, G. C., & Pierce, M. (2007). Fault tolerant high-performance Information Services for dynamic collections of Grid and Web services. *Future Generation Computer Systems, 23*(3), 2007. doi:10.1016/j.future.2006.05.009

Aktas, M. S., & Pierce, M. (2010). High performance hybrid information service architecture. *Concurrency and Computation, 22*(15), 2095–2123.

Asian, S., Yozgatligil, C., Iyigaun, C., Batmaz, İ., Tiirkes, M., & Tatli, H. (2014). *Comparison of missing value imputation methods for Turkish monthly total precipitation data*. Academic Press.

Baloglu, A., & Aktas, M. S. (2010). Web blog mining application for classification of movie reviews. *Fifth International Conference on Internet and Web Applications and Services (ICIW)*, 77-84. 10.1109/ICIW.2010.19

Batista, G. E., & Monard, M. C. (2003). An analysis of four missing data treatment methods for supervised learning. *Applied Artificial Intelligence, 17*(5-6), 519–533. doi:10.1080/713827181

Betrie, G. D., Sadiq, R., Tesfamariam, S., & Morin, K. A. (2014). On the Issue of Incomplete and Missing Water-Quality Data in Mine Site Databases: Comparing Three Imputation Methods. *Mine Water and the Environment*, 1–7.

Bradley, E. (1979). Bootstrap methods: Another look at the jackknife. *Annals of Statistics*, 1–26.

Chen, P., Plale, B., & Aktas, M. S. (2012). Temporal representation for scientific data provenance. *IEEE 8th International Conference on E-Science (e-Science)*, 1-8.

Chen, P., Plale, B., & Aktas, M. S. (2014). Temporal representation for mining scientific data provenance. *Future Generation Computer Systems*, *36*, 363–378. doi:10.1016/j.future.2013.09.032

Cios, K. J., & Lukasz, A. K. (2005). Trends in data mining and knowledge discovery, Advanced techniques in knowledge discovery and data mining. Springer London.

Cleophas, T. J., & Aeilko, H. Z. (2016). *Missing data imputation. In Clinical Data Analysis on a Pocket Calculator* (pp. 93–97). Springer International Publishing. doi:10.1007/978-3-319-27104-0_17

David, B. (2000). The Bootstrap and multiple imputations. *JEP Econometrics Symposium.*

Farhangfar, A., Lukasz, A. K., & Witold, P. (2004). Experimental analysis of methods for imputation of missing values in databases. *Proceedings of the International Society for Optics and Photonics*, *5421*, 172–182.

Fatemah, A. B., & Keivan, M. (2014). Missing Data Analysis: A Survey of Different K-Means Clustering Algortihms. *American Journal of Signal Processing*, *4*(3), 65–70.

Fayyad, U. M., Piatetsky-Shapiro, G., Smyth, P., & Uthurusamy, R. (1996). *Advances in Knowledge Discovery and Data Mining*. MIT Press.

Fiero, M., Shuang, H., & Bell, M. (2015). Statistical analysis and handling of missing data in cluster randomised trials: Protocol for a systematic review. *BMJ Open*, *5*(5), e007378. doi:10.1136/bmjopen-2014-007378 PMID:25971707

Forbes, C., Evans, M., Hastings, N., & Peacock, B. (2011). *Statistical distributions*. John Wiley & Sons.

Fox, G. C., Aktas, M. S., Aydin, G., Bulut, H., Pallickara, S., Pierce, M., ... Zhai, G. (2006). *Real time streaming data grid applications. In Distributed Cooperative Laboratories: Networking, Instrumentation, and Measurements* (pp. 253–267). Boston, MA: Springer. doi:10.1007/0-387-30394-4_17

Fox, G. C., Aktas, M. S., Aydin, G., Gadgil, H., Pallickara, H., Pierce, M., & Sayar, A. (2009). Algorithms and the Grid. *Computing and Visualization in Science*, *12*(3), 115–124. doi:10.100700791-007-0083-8

García-Laencina, P. J., Abreu, P. H., Abreu, M. H., & Afonoso, N. (2015). Missing data imputation on the 5-year survival prediction of breast cancer patients with unknown discrete values. *Computers in Biology and Medicine*, *59*, 125–133. doi:10.1016/j.compbiomed.2015.02.006 PMID:25725446

García-Laencina, P. J., Abreu, P. H., Abreu, M. H., & Afonoso, N. (2015). Missing data imputation on the 5-year survival prediction of breast cancer patients with unknown discrete values. *Computers in Biology and Medicine*, *59*, 125–133. doi:10.1016/j. compbiomed.2015.02.006 PMID:25725446

Ghahramani, Z., & Michael, I. J. (1994). Supervised learning from incomplete data via an EM approach. *Advances in Neural Information Processing Systems*, *6*.

Gómez-Carracedo, M. P., Andrade, J. M., López-Mahía, P., Muniategui, S., & Prada, D. (2014). A practical comparison of single and multiple imputation methods to handle complex missing data in air quality datasets. *Chemometrics and Intelligent Laboratory Systems*, *134*, 23–33. doi:10.1016/j.chemolab.2014.02.007

Han, J., Micheline, K., & Jian, P. (2006). *Data Mining: Concepts and techniques*. Morgan Kaufmann.

He, D. K., Chu, T. S., Lang, Y. B., & Sun, G. X. (2015). *Comparison of Missing Data Imputation Methods for Leaching Process Modelling*. Academic Press.

Kaiser, J. (2014). Dealing with Missing Values in Data. *Journal of Systems Integration*, *5*(1), 42–51. doi:10.20470/jsi.v5i1.178

Koko, E. E. M., & Mohamed, A. I. A. (2015). Missing data treatment method on cluster analysis. International. *Journal of Advanced Statistics and Probability*, *3*(2), 191–209. doi:10.14419/ijasp.v3i2.5318

Kropko, J., Goodrich, B., Gelman, A., & Hill, J. (2014). Multiple imputation for continuous and categorical data: Comparing joint multivariate normal and conditional approaches. *Political Analysis*.

Lee, K. J., Roberts, G., Doyle, L., Anderson, P., & Carlin, J. (2016). Multiple imputation for missing data in a longitudinal cohort study: A tutorial based on a detailed case study involving imputation of missing outcome data. *International Journal of Social Research Methodology*, 1–17.

Liao, S. G., Lin, Y., Kang, D. D., Chandra, D., Bon, J., Kaminski, N., & Tseng, G. C. (2014). Missing value imputation in high-dimensional phenomic data: Imputable or not, and how? *BMC Bioinformatics*, *15*(1), 1. doi:10.118612859-014-0346-6 PMID:25371041

Little, R., & Rubin, D. (1987). *Statistical analysis with missing data* (1st ed.). John Wiley and Sons.

Little, R., & Rubin, D. (2014). *Statistical analysis with missing data*. John Wiley & Sons.

Liu, G. F., Han, B., Zhao, X., & Lin, Q. (2015). A Comparison of Frequentist and Bayesian Model Based Approaches for Missing Data Analysis: Case Study with a Schizophrenia Clinical Trial. *Statistics in Biopharmaceutical Research.* doi:10.1080/19466315.2015.1077725

Luengo, J., García, S., & Herrera, F. (2010). A Study on the Use of Imputation Methods for Experimentation with Radial Basis Function Network Classifiers Handling Missing Attribute Values: The good synergy between RBFs and EventCovering method. *Neural Networks, 23*(3), 406–418. doi:10.1016/j.neunet.2009.11.014 PMID:20015612

Luengo, J., García, S., & Herrera, F. (2012). On the choice of the best imputation methods for missing values considering three groups of classification methods. *Knowledge and Information Systems, 32*(1), 77–108. doi:10.100710115-011-0424-2

Masconi, K., Matsha, T., Echouffo-Tcheugui, J., Erasmus, R., & Kengne, A. (2015). Reporting and handling of missing data in predictive research for prevalent undiagnosed type 2 diabetes mellitus: A systematic review. *The EPMA Journal, 6*(1), 7. doi:10.118613167-015-0028-0 PMID:25829972

Noor, M. N., Yahaya, A. S., Ramli, N. A., & Al Bakri, A. M. M. (2014, March). Mean imputation techniques for filling the missing observations in air pollution dataset. *Key Engineering Materials, 594*, 902–908.

Rana, S., John, A. H., & Midi, H. (2015). Robust Regression Imputation for Missing Data in the Presence of Outliers. Far East Journal of Mathematical Sciences, 97(2).

Rubin, D. B. (2004). *Multiple imputation for nonresponse in surveys.* John Wiley & Sons.

Schmitt, P., Mandel, J., & Guedj, M. (2015). A comparison of six methods for missing data imputation. *Journal of Biometrics & Biostatistics.*

Taylor, S. L., Ruhaak, L. R., Kelly, K., Weiss, R. H., & Kim, K. (2016). Effects of imputation on correlation: Implications for analysis of mass spectrometry data from multiple biological matrices. *Briefings in Bioinformatics.* doi:10.1093/bib/bbw010 PMID:26896791

Thirumahal, R., & Deepali, A. (2014). Patil. (2014). "KNN and ARL Based Imputation to Estimate Missing Values. *Indonesian Journal of Electrical Engineering and Informatics, 2*(3), 119–124.

Wagstaff, K. (2004). *Clustering with missing values: No imputation required.* Springer Berlin Heidelberg.

Wayman, J. C. (2003). *Multiple imputation for missing data: What is it and how can I use it.* Annual Meeting of the American Educational Research Association, Chicago, IL.

Web Site for Project Repository. (n.d.). Retrieved from https://github.com/ kaplansinan/Imputation-of-Missing-Data.git

Web Site for Project Web Site. (n.d.). Retrieved from http://www.yildiz.edu.tr/~aktas-/ missingdata

Wilks, S. S. (1932). Moments and distributions of estimates of population parameters from fragmentary samples. *Annals of Mathematical Statistics, 3*(3), 163–195. doi:10.1214/aoms/1177732885

Young, R., & David, R. J. (2015). Handling missing values in longitudinal panel data with multiple imputation. *Journal of Marriage and the Family, 77*(1), 277–294. doi:10.1111/jomf.12144 PMID:26113748

Compilation of References

Aarts, K. (2007). Parsmony Methodology. *Methodological Inovations Online, 2*(1), 2-10. Retrieved October 1, 2018, from http://journals.sagepub.com/doi/pdf/10.4256/mio.2007.0002

Abeza, G., Pegoraro, A., Naraine, M. L., & Séguin, B., & O'Reilly, N. (2015). Activating a global sport sponsorship with social media: An analysis of TOP sponsors, Twitter, and the 2014 Olympic Games. *International Journal of Sport Management and Marketing, 154*(34), 184–213. doi:10.1504/IJSMM.2014.072010

Abiteboul, S., & Polyzotis, N. (2007). The Data Ring: Community Content Sharing. *Third Biennial Conference on Innovative Data Systems Research (CIDR 2007).*

Abiteboul, S., Benjelloun, & Milo, T. (2002). Web Services and Data Integration. In *Third International Conference on Web Information Systems Engineering (WISE 2002)*. IEEE Computer Society.

Abouelmehdi, K., Beni-Hessane, A., & Khaloufi, H. (2018). Big healthcare data: Preserving security and privacy. *Journal of Big Data, 5*(1).

Abouelmehdi, K., Beni-Hssane, A., Khaloufi, H., & Saadi, M. (2017). Beni., Khaloufi, H., & Saadi, M.(2017). "Big data security and privacy in healthcare: A Review. *Procedia Computer Science, 113*, 73–80. doi:10.1016/j.procs.2017.08.292

Acuna, E., & Caroline, R. (2004). The treatment of missing values and its effect on classifier accuracy. Classification, Clustering, and Data Mining Applications. Springer Berlin Heidelberg.

Adıgüzel, F., & Kennett, C. (2017). *Sport event sponsorship effectiveness: A cross-cultural study*. Working Paper.

AGNES Algorithm R Packet. (n.d.). Retrieved from https://stat.ethz.ch/R-manual/R-devel/library/cluster/html/agnes.html

Agrifoglio, R. (2015). *Knowledge Preservation through Community of Practice*. Springer International Publishing. doi:10.1007/978-3-319-22234-9

Aktas, M. (2006). iSERVO: Implementing the International Solid Earth Research Virtual Observatory by integrating computational grid and geographical information web services. In Computational Earthquake Physics: Simulations, Analysis and Infrastructure, Part II (pp. 2281-2296). Birkhäuser Basel.

Aktas. (2005, June). Implementing geographical information system grid services to support computational geophysics in a service-oriented environment. In *NASA Earth-Sun System Technology Conference*. University of Maryland.

Aktas, M. (2018). Hybrid cloud computing monitoring software architecture. *Concurrency and Computation, 2018*. doi:10.1002/cpe.4694

Aktas, M. S., & Astekin, M. (2017). Provenance aware run-time verification of things for self-healing Internet of Things applications. *Concurrency and Computation, 2017*. doi:10.1002/cpe.4263

Aktas, M. S., Fox, G. C., & Pierce, M. (2005). Information services for dynamically assembled semantic grids. *First International Conference on Semantics, Knowledge and Grid*. 10.1109/SKG.2005.83

Aktas, M. S., Fox, G. C., & Pierce, M. (2007). Fault tolerant high-performance Information Services for dynamic collections of Grid and Web services. *Future Generation Computer Systems, 23*(3), 2007. doi:10.1016/j.future.2006.05.009

Aktas, M. S., & Pierce, M. (2010). High performance hybrid information service architecture. *Concurrency and Computation, 22*(15), 2095–2123.

Aktaş-Polat, S. (2015). Üstgerçeklik ve turizmin sonu. *Celal Bayar Üniversitesi Sosyal Bilimler Dergisi, 13*(1), 120–137.

Akter, S., & Wamba, S. F. (2016). Big data analytics in E-commerce: A systematic review and agenda for future research. *Electronic Markets, 26*(2), 173–194. doi:10.100712525-016-0219-0

Alenezi, H., Tarhini, A., & Sharma, S. K. (2015). Development of quantitative model to investigate the strategic relationship between information quality and e-government benefits. *Transforming Government: People, Process and Policy, 9*(3), 324–351.

Amadeus. (2013). *Amadeus Global Report of 2013*. Retrieved from: https://amadeus.com/

American Society of Travel Agents (ASTA). (2017). *How America travels-sheds light on America's perceptions of travel and better enables ASTA and the travel agent community*. Retrieved from: https://www.asta.org/

Anderson, J. G., & Nanjo, K. (2013). Distribution of earthquake cluster sizes in the western United States and in Japan. *Bulletin of the Seismological Society of America, 103*(1), 412–423. doi:10.1785/0120100212

Andreu, L., Aldas, J., Bigne, J. E., & Mattila, A. S. (2010). An analysis of e-business adoption and its impact on relational quality in travel agency-supplier relationships. *Tourism Management, 31*(6), 777–787. doi:10.1016/j.tourman.2009.08.004

Antoniou, G., & Harmelen, F. V. (2004). *Semantic Web Primer.* MIT Press.

Apache Hadoop. (2018). Retrieved from http://hadoop.apache.org

Archer, B., Cooper, C., & Ruhanen, L. (2004). The positive and negative impacts of tourism. In W. F. Theobald (Ed.), *Global Tourism* (3rd ed.; pp. 79–102). Elsevier.

Asian, S., Yozgatligil, C., Iyigaun, C., Batmaz, İ., Tiirkes, M., & Tatli, H. (2014). *Comparison of missing value imputation methods for Turkish monthly total precipitation data.* Academic Press.

Association, A. L. (2008). *Presidential committee on information literacy.* Retrieved from http:// www. ala. org/ala/acrl/acrlpubs/whitepapers/presidential. cfm

Atenstaedt, R. (2012). Word cloud analysis of the BJGP. *The British Journal of General Practice, 62*(596), 148. doi:10.3399/bjgp12X630142 PMID:22429422

Atos. (2016). *Atos and Quartet FS launch a Big Data appliance that facilitates compliance with the future FRTB banking regulations.* Retrieved from https://atos.net/en/2016/press-release/ general-press-releases_2016_02_22/pr-2016_02_22_01

Aydin, G., Sayar, A., Gadgil, H., Aktas, M. S., Fox, G. C., Ko, S., ... Pierce, M. E. (2008). Building and applying geographical information system Grids. *Concurrency and Computation, 20*(14), 1653–1695. doi:10.1002/cpe.1312

Baer, A., Casas, P., D'Alconzo, A., Fiadino, P., Golab, L., Mellia, M., & Schikuta, E. (2016). DBStream: A holistic approach to large-scale network traffic monitoring and analysis. *Computer Networks, 107*, 5–19. doi:10.1016/j.comnet.2016.04.020

Baker, E. W. (2013). Relational Model Bases: A Technical Approach to Real-Time Business Intelligenec and Decision making. *Communications of the Association for Information Systems, 33*(1).

Baloglu, A., & Aktas, M. S. (2010). Web blog mining application for classification of movie reviews. *Fifth International Conference on Internet and Web Applications and Services (ICIW)*, 77-84. 10.1109/ICIW.2010.19

Baresi, L., & Quinton, C. (2015). Dynamically Evolving the Structural Variability of Dynamic Software Product Lines. *Proceedings of the 10th International Symposium on Software Engineering for Adaptive and Self-Managing Systems*, 57–63. 10.1109/SEAMS.2015.24

Batini, C., Cappiello, C., Francalanci, C., & Maurino, A. (2009). Methodologies for data quality assessment and improvement. *ACM Computing Surveys, 41*(3), 16. doi:10.1145/1541880.1541883

Batini, C., Lenzerini, M., & Navathe, S. B. (1986). A Comparative Analysis of Methodologies for Database Schema Integration. *ACM Computing Surveys, 18*(4), 323–364. doi:10.1145/27633.27634

Batista, G. E., & Monard, M. C. (2003). An analysis of four missing data treatment methods for supervised learning. *Applied Artificial Intelligence, 17*(5-6), 519–533. doi:10.1080/713827181

Batrinca, B., & Treleaven, P. C. (2015). Social Media Analytics: A Survey of Techniques, Tools and Platforms. *AI & Society*, *30*(1), 89–116. doi:10.100700146-014-0549-4

Bauer, H., Baur, C., Mohr, D., Tschiesner, A., Weskamp, T., Alicke, K., & Kelly, R. (2016). *Industry 4.0 after the initial hype–Where manufacturers are finding value and how they can best capture it*. McKinsey Digital.

Bawden, D., & Robinson, L. (2009). The dark side of information: Overload, anxiety and other paradoxes and pathologies. *Journal of Information Science*, *35*(2), 180–191. doi:10.1177/0165551508095781

Bayardo, R. J., Bohrer, B., Brice, R. S., Cichocki, A., Fowler, J., Helal, A., ... Woelk, D. (1997). InfoSleuth: Agent-Based Semantic Integration of Information in Open and Dynamic Environments. *1997 ACM SIGMOD International Conference on Management of Data (SIGMOD 1997)*, 195-206. 10.1145/253260.253294

Beech, J., Kaiser, S., & Kaspar, R. (2014). *The Business of Events Management*. Pearson Education Limited.

Benckendorff, P. J., Sheldon, P. J., & Fesenmaier, D. R. (2014). *Tourism information technology* (2nd ed.). CAB International. doi:10.1079/9781780641850.0000

Beneventtano, D., Bergamaschi, S., Castano, S., Corni, A., Guidetti, R., Malvezzi, G., ... Vincini, M. (2000). Information Integration: the MOMIS Project Demonstration. *Proceeding of the 26th Very Large Database Conference*, 611-614.

Bennett, M. M., & Lai, C. K. (2005). The impact of the internet on travel agencies in Taiwan. *Tourism and Hospitality Research*, *6*(1), 8–23. doi:10.1057/palgrave.thr.6040041

Bergeron, B. (2000). Regional business intelligence: The view from Canada. *Journal of Information Science*, *26*(3), 153–160. doi:10.1177/016555150002600305

Bershadsky, A. M., & Krevsky, I. G. (1996). The Organization of Distance Education in Penza Region of Russian Federation. *Proceedings of the Second International Conference on Distance Education in Russia: Open and Distance Learning as a Development Strategy*, 174-176.

Betrie, G. D., Sadiq, R., Tesfamariam, S., & Morin, K. A. (2014). On the Issue of Incomplete and Missing Water-Quality Data in Mine Site Databases: Comparing Three Imputation Methods. *Mine Water and the Environment*, 1–7.

Bhatia, A. K. (2006). *The business of tourism: Concepts and strategies*. New Delhi: Sterling Publishers.

Big Data in eLearning: The Future of eLearning Industry. (n.d.). Retrieved from https://elearningindustry.com/big-data-in-elearning-future-of-elearning-industry

Big Data Value Association. (2018). *Big data challenges in smart manufacturing*. Retrieved from http://www.bdva.eu/sites/default/files/BDVA_SMI_Discussion_Paper_Web_Version.pdf

Bindner, D., & Ericsson, M. (2011). *A Student's Guide to the Study, Practice and Tools of Modern Mathematics*. CRC Press.

Bjork, E., Ottosson, S., & Thorsteinsdottir, S. (2008). E-Learning for All. In *E-Learning: 21st Century Issues and Challenges* (pp. 49–69). Nova Science Publishers Inc.

Blackman, B. (2008). Uniquely Barbara. *Compass*.

Bologa, A., Bologa, R., & Florea, A. (2010). Big Data and Specific Analysis Methods for Insurance Fraud Detection. Database Systems Journal, 1(1).

Bradley, E. (1979). Bootstrap methods: Another look at the jackknife. *Annals of Statistics*, 1–26.

Browning, B., & Sanderson, J. (2012). The positives and negatives of Twitter: Exploring how student-athletes use Twitter and respond to critical Tweets. *International Journal of Sport Communication*, 5(4), 503–521. doi:10.1123/ijsc.5.4.503

Buhalis, D., & Egger, R. (2008). *Intermediaries*. In R. Egger & D. Buhalis (Eds.), *eTourism case studies: Management and marketing issues* (pp. 83–87). Oxford, UK: Butterworth-Heinemann.

Buhalis, D., & O'Connor, P. (2005). Information communication technology revolutionizing tourism. *Tourism Recreation Research*, 30(3), 7–16. doi:10.1080/02508281.2005.11081482

Buscema, P. M., Massini, G., & Maurelli, G. (2015). Artificial Adaptive Systems to predict the magnitude of earthquakes. *Bollettino di Geofisica Teorica ed Applicata*, 56(2).

Card, J. A., Chen, C. Y., & Cole, S. T. (2003). Online travel products shopping: Differences between shoppers and nonshoppers. *Journal of Travel Research*, 42(2), 133–139. doi:10.1177/0047287503257490

Carey, M., Haas, L., Schwarz, P., Arya, M., Cody, W., Fagin, R., ... Wimmers, E. (1995). Towards Heterogeneous Multimedia Information Systems: The Garlic Approach. *5th International Workshop on Research Issues in Data Engineering-Distributed Object Management (RIDE-DOM 1995)*, 124-131. 10.1109/RIDE.1995.378736

Carnegie Learning. (2018). *Explore Our Products*. Retrieved from https://www.carnegielearning.com/products/our-products/overview/

Castells, M. (2016). A sociology of power: My intellectual journey. *Annual Review of Sociology*, 42(1), 1–19. doi:10.1146/annurev-soc-081715-074158

Cate, F. H., & Cate, B. E. (2012). The Supreme Court and information privacy. *International Data Privacy Law*, 2(4), 255–267. doi:10.1093/idpl/ips024

Cebr. (2012). *Data equity, Unlocking the value of big data*. SAS Reports.

Ceri, S., & Widom, J. (1993). Managing Semantic Heterogeneity with Production Rules and Persistent Queues. *Proceedings of the 19th Very Large Data Base Conference*, 108-119.

Cerrato, P. (2012, July 31). Is Population Health Management the Latest Health IT Fad? *Information Week*. Retrieved from www.informationweek.com/healthcare/clinical-systems/is-population-health-management-ltest-h/240004578

Chaudhuri, S., & Dayal, U. (1997). An Overview of Data Warehousing and OLAP Technology. *SIGMOD Record*, *26*(1), 65–74. doi:10.1145/248603.248616

Chauhan, A., Fontama, V., Hart, M., Hyong, W., & Woody, B. (2014). Introducing Microsoft Azure HDInsight, Technical Overview. Microsoft Press.

Chawathe, S. GarciaMolina, H., Hammer, J., Ireland, K., Papakonstantinou, Y, Ullman, J., & Widom, J. (1994). The TSIMMIS Project: Integration of Heterogeneous Information Sources. *Proceeding of the 1000th Anniversary Meeting of the Information Processing Society of Japan (IPSJ)*, 7-18.

Chen, P., Plale, B., & Aktas, M. S. (2012). Temporal representation for scientific data provenance. *IEEE 8th International Conference on E-Science (e-Science),* 1-8.

Chen, M., Mao, S., & Liu, Y. (2014). Big Data: A Survey. *Mobile Networks and Applications*, *19*(2), 171–209. doi:10.100711036-013-0489-0

Chen, P., Plale, B., & Aktas, M. S. (2014). Temporal representation for mining scientific data provenance. *Future Generation Computer Systems*, *36*, 363–378. doi:10.1016/j.future.2013.09.032

Chen, Y.-C., Shang, R.-A., & Kao, C.-Y. (2009). The effects of information overload on consumers' subjective state towards buying decision in the internet shopping environment. *Electronic Commerce Research and Applications*, *8*(1), 48–58. doi:10.1016/j.elerap.2008.09.001

Chilipirea, C., Petre, A. C., Dobre, C., & Van Steen, M. (2016). Presumably simple: Monitoring crowds using WiFi. In *2016 IEEE 17th international conference on mobile data management (MDM)*. Porto, Portugal: IEEE.

Chumg, H.-F., Seaton, J., Cooke, L., & Ding, W.-Y. (2016). Factors affecting employees' knowledge-sharing behaviour in the virtual organisation from the perspectives of well-being and organisational behaviour. *Computers in Human Behavior*, *64*, 432–448. doi:10.1016/j.chb.2016.07.011

Cios, K. J., & Lukasz, A. K. (2005). Trends in data mining and knowledge discovery, Advanced techniques in knowledge discovery and data mining. Springer London.

Cleophas, T. J., & Aeilko, H. Z. (2016). *Missing data imputation. In Clinical Data Analysis on a Pocket Calculator* (pp. 93–97). Springer International Publishing. doi:10.1007/978-3-319-27104-0_17

Cloudera. (2012). *Explorys Medical: Improving Healthcare Quality & Costs Using a Big Data Platform*. Retrieved from http://blog.cloudera.com/wp-content/uploads/2012/05/Cloudera-Explorys-case-study-final.pdf

Cloudera. (2018). S*mart utilities use smart data*. Retrieved from https://www.cloudera.com/solutions/energy-and-utilities.html

Codd, E. F. (1970). *The Relational Model for Database Management*. Addison Wesley.

Condratov, I. (2013). E-tourism: Concept and evolution. *Ecoforum, 2*(1), 58–61.

Corvello, V., & Migliarese, P. (2007). Virtual forms for the organization of production: A comparative analysis. *International Journal of Production Economics, 110*(1-2), 5–15. doi:10.1016/j.ijpe.2007.02.006

Coult, G. (2008). Managing the 'information pollution'. *Managing Information, 14*(10), 10-12.

Cubeware. (2018). *Business intelligence & performance management solution wholesale trade*. Retrieved from https://www.cubeware.com/en/solutions/industries/wholesale-and-retail-trade/

Cui, Z., Damiani, E., & Leida, M. (2007). Benefits of Ontologies in Real Time Data Access. *Digital Ecosystems and Technologies Conference, DEST '07, 392-397*. 10.1109/DEST.2007.372004

Cure, O., & Blin, G. (2015). *RDF Database Systems Triples Storage and SPARQL Query Processing*. Waltham, MA: Morgan Kaufmann.

Cushard, B. (2018). *Build a Virtual Workforce to Attract Talent and Reduce Costs*. Retrieved from Automatic Data Processing: https://www.adp.com/spark/articles/2018/06/build-a-virtual-workforce-to-attract-talent-and-reduce-costs.aspx

Cyber security Lessons Learned From the Ashley Madison Hack. (2015). Retrieved from https://www.forbes.com/sites/ericbasu/2015/10/26/cybersecurity-lessons-learned-from-the-ashley-madison-hack/#32870cf14c82

Czarnecki, K., & Helsen, S. (2006). Feature-based survey of model transformation approaches. *IBM Systems Journal, 45*(3), 621–646. doi:10.1147j.453.0621

Datawatch. (2018). *Imagine Software Incorporates Panopticon Dashboards into its Real-Time Portfolio, Risk and Compliance Management Solutions*. Retrieved from, http://www.panopticon.com/2018/02/07/imagine-software-incorporates-panopticon-dashboards-real-time-portfolio-risk-compliance-management-solutions/

David, B. (2000). The Bootstrap and multiple imputations. *JEP Econometrics Symposium*.

DBSCAN Algorithm R Packet. (n.d.). Retrieved from https://cran.r-project.org/web/packages/dbscan/dbscan.pdf

De Moragas, M., Kennett, C., & Ginesta, X. (2013). Football and media in Europe. New sport paradigm for the global era. In Sport and the Transformation of Modern Europe. States, Media and Markets 1950-2010. London: Routledge.

de Sousa Jabbour, A. B. L., Jabbour, C. J. C., Godinho Filho, M., & Roubaud, D. (2018). Industry 4.0 and the circular economy: A proposed research agenda and original roadmap for sustainable operations. *Annals of Operations Research*, 1–14.

Dede, C. (2016). Next steps for "Big Data" in education: Utilizing data-intensive research. *Educational Technology, 56*(2), 37–42.

Delia, E. B., & Armstrong, C. G. (2015). #Sponsoring the #FrenchOpen: An examination of social media buzz and sentiment. *Journal of Sport Management, 29*(2), 184–199. doi:10.1123/JSM.2013-0257

Department of Defence (DoD). (2000). *Doctrine for Intelligence Support to Joint Operations, Joint Publications 2-0*. Washington, DC: GPO.

Dietrich, D. (2012). *EMC: Data Science and Big Data Analytics*. EMC Education Services.

Dragland, A. (2013). *Big data–for better or worse*. SINTEF Report. Retrieved from: https://www.sintef.no/en/latest-news/big-data-for-better-or-worse/

DuCharme, B. (2013). *Learning SPARQL: Querying and Updating with SPARQL 1.1*. Sebastopol, CA: O'Reilly Publishing Company.

Dunlop, N. (2015). *Beginning Big Data with Power BI & Excel 2013*. Apress. doi:10.1007/978-1-4842-0529-7

Dupeyras, A., & MacCallum, N. (2013). Indicators for measuring competitiveness in tourism: A guidance gocument. In *OECD Tourism Papers*. OECD Publishing.

Earthquakes, S. J. (2018). *Avaya Stadium - First cloud-enabled stadium in MLS*. Retrieved from https://sanjose-mp7static.mlsdigital.net/elfinderimages/170712_avaya_stadium_infographic_b_print_8-5x11.jpeg

East, D., Osborne, P., Kemp, S., & Woodfine, T. (2017). Combining GPS & survey data improves understanding of visitor behavior. *Tourism Management, 61*, 307–320. doi:10.1016/j.tourman.2017.02.021

Edmunds, A., & Morris, A. (2000). The problem of information overload in business organisations: A review of the literature. *International Journal of Information Management, 20*(1), 17–28. doi:10.1016/S0268-4012(99)00051-1

Elgendy, N., & Elragal, A. (2014). Big Data Analytics: A Literature Review Paper. LNAI, 8557, 214–227.

Epam. (2018). *Transforming the Energy Business with a Digital Services Platform & Data Intelligence*. Retrieved from https://www.epam.com/our-work/customer-stories/transforming-energy-business-with-digital-services-platform-and-data-intelligence

Eppler, M., & Helfert, M. (2004). *A classification and analysis of data quality costs*. Paper presented at the International Conference on Information Quality.

Ericsson, K. A., & Smith, J. (1991). *Toward a General Theory of Expertise: Prospects and Limits*. Cambridge, UK: Cambridge University Press.

Erl, T., Khattak, W., & Buhler, P. (2016). *Big Data Fundamentals: Concepts, Drivers & Techniques*. Prentice Hall.

Esen, M. F., & Turkay, B. (2017). Big data applications in tourism industries. *Journal of Tourism and Gastronomy Studies*, *5*(4), 92–115. doi:10.21325/jotags.2017.140

Evans, J. R. (2013). Business Analytics: Methods, Models & Decisions. Pearson Education, Inc. (Prentice Hall).

Exastax. (2017). *Top 7 big data use cases in insurance industry*. Retrieved from big data https://www.exastax.com/big-data/top-7-big-data-use-cases-in-insurance-industry/

E-Zest. (2018). *Big Data Solutions for Government*. Retrieved from https://www.e-zest.com/big-data-solutions-for-government

Fagin, R., Kolaitis, P. G., Miller, R. J., & Popa, L. (2005a). Data Exchange: Semantics and Query Answering. *Theoretical Computer Science*, *336*(1), 89–124. doi:10.1016/j.tcs.2004.10.033

Fagin, R., Kolaitis, P. G., Popa, L., & Tan, W. (2005b). Composing schema mappings: Second-order dependencies to the rescue. *ACM Transactions on Database Systems*, *30*(4), 994–1055. doi:10.1145/1114244.1114249

Farhangfar, A., Lukasz, A. K., & Witold, P. (2004). Experimental analysis of methods for imputation of missing values in databases. *Proceedings of the International Society for Optics and Photonics*, *5421*, 172–182.

Fatemah, A. B., & Keivan, M. (2014). Missing Data Analysis: A Survey of Different K-Means Clustering Algortihms. *American Journal of Signal Processing*, *4*(3), 65–70.

Fayyad, U. M., Piatetsky-Shapiro, G., Smyth, P., & Uthurusamy, R. (1996). *Advances in Knowledge Discovery and Data Mining*. MIT Press.

Fernández-Miranda, S. S., Marcos, M., Peralta, M., & Aguayo, F. (2017). The challenge of integrating Industry 4.0 in the degree of Mechanical Engineering. *Procedia Manufacturing*, *13*, 1229–1236. doi:10.1016/j.promfg.2017.09.039

Ferreira, P. G. S., de Lima, E. P., & da Costa, S. E. G. (2012). Perception of virtual team's performance: A multinational exercise. *International Journal of Production Economics*, *140*(1), 416–430. doi:10.1016/j.ijpe.2012.06.025

Fiero, M., Shuang, H., & Bell, M. (2015). Statistical analysis and handling of missing data in cluster randomised trials: Protocol for a systematic review. *BMJ Open*, *5*(5), e007378. doi:10.1136/bmjopen-2014-007378 PMID:25971707

Finogeev A. A., Finogeev A. G., Nefedova I. S. (2016). Izvestiya vysshikh uchebnykh zavedeniy. Povolzhskiy region. Tekhnicheskie nauki. *University Proceedings. Volga Region. Engineering Science, 2*(38), 49–60.

Firestone, J. M., & McElroy, M. W. (2003). *Key issues in the new knowledge management*. New York: Routledge.

Firican, G. (2017, February 8). *The 10 V's of Big Data*. Retrieved July 4, 2018, from Transforming Data with Intellignce (TDwI): www.tdwi.org/articles/2017/02/08/10-vs-of-big-data.aspx

Flanagin, A. J., Metzger, M. J., Pure, R., Markov, A., & Hartsell, E. (2014). Mitigating risk in ecommerce transactions: Perceptions of information credibility and the role of user-generated ratings in product quality and purchase intention. *Electronic Commerce Research, 14*(1), 1–23. doi:10.100710660-014-9139-2

Forbes, C., Evans, M., Hastings, N., & Peacock, B. (2011). *Statistical distributions*. John Wiley & Sons.

Fosso Wamba, S., Akter, S., Edwards, A., Chopin, G., & Gnanzou, D. (2015). How 'big data' can make big impact: Findings from a systematic review and a longitudinal case study. *International Journal of Production Economics, 165*, 234–246. doi:10.1016/j.ijpe.2014.12.031

Foster, G., O'Reilly, N., & Davila, A. (2016). *Sports Business Management: Decision Making Around the Globe*. Routledge. doi:10.4324/9781315687827

Fox, G. C., Aktas, M. S., Aydin, G., Bulut, H., Pallickara, S., Pierce, M., ... Zhai, G. (2006). *Real time streaming data grid applications. In Distributed Cooperative Laboratories: Networking, Instrumentation, and Measurements* (pp. 253–267). Boston, MA: Springer. doi:10.1007/0-387-30394-4_17

Fox, G. C., Aktas, M. S., Aydin, G., Gadgil, H., Pallickara, H., Pierce, M., & Sayar, A. (2009). Algorithms and the Grid. *Computing and Visualization in Science, 12*(3), 115–124. doi:10.100700791-007-0083-8

Frampton, M. (2015). *Big Data Made Easy: A Working Guide to the Complete Hadoop Toolset*. Apress. doi:10.1007/978-1-4842-0094-0

Friedman, M., Levy, A., & Millstein, T. (1999). Navigational plans for data integration. In *Proceedings of AAAI* (pp. 67–73). Menlo Park, CA: AAAI Press/MIT Press.

Fujitsu. (2018). *Fujitsu Receives Extended Managed IT Infrastructure and Data Center Services Contract from Orion*. Retrieved from http://www.fujitsu.com/in/

Gantz, J., & Reinsel, D. (2012). *IDC, The digital universe in 2020: big data, bigger digital shadows, and biggest growth in the Far East*. Retrieved from http://www.emc. com/ leadership/ digital-universe/index.htm

García-Laencina, P. J., Abreu, P. H., Abreu, M. H., & Afonoso, N. (2015). Missing data imputation on the 5-year survival prediction of breast cancer patients with unknown discrete values. *Computers in Biology and Medicine, 59*, 125–133. doi:10.1016/j.compbiomed.2015.02.006 PMID:25725446

Garcia-Solaco, M., Saltor, F., & Castellanos, M. (1996). Semantic Heterogeneity in Multidatabase Systems. In O. A. Bukhres & A. K. Elmagarmid (Eds.), Object-Oriented Multidatabase Systems, A Solution for Advanced Applications (pp. 129-202). Prentice-Hall.

Gartner, R., & Gartner, V. (2015). *Gartner Survey Shows More Than 75 Percent of Companies Are Investing or Planning to Invest in Big Data in the Next Two Years, Skills, Governance, Funding and ROI Challenges Set to Increase.* Retrieved from https://www.gartner.com/newsroom/id/3130817

Gasteau, C., & Vilas, V. (2018). *Transportation & Logistics Software And Soft: Technology e-TMS – A web based Transportation Management System.* Retrieved from https://transporttmsandlogisticstms.com/big-data-and-e-tms-software-andsoft/

Gayton, C. M. (2006). Beyond terrorism: Data collection and responsibility for privacy. *Vine*, *36*(4), 377–394. doi:10.1108/03055720610716647

Ge, M., & Helfert, M. (2008). *Data and information quality assessment in information manufacturing systems.* Paper presented at the International Conference on Business Information Systems. 10.1007/978-3-540-79396-0_33

Ghahramani, Z., & Michael, I. J. (1994). Supervised learning from incomplete data via an EM approach. *Advances in Neural Information Processing Systems*, *6*.

Gibbs, C., & Haynes, R. (2013). A phenomenological investigation into how Twitter has changed the nature of sport media relations. *International Journal of Sport Communication*, *6*(4), 394–408. doi:10.1123/ijsc.6.4.394

Gibbs, C., O'Reilly, N., & Brunette, M. (2014). Professional Team Sport and Twitter: Gratifications Sought and Obtained by Followers. *International Journal of Sport Communication*, *7*(2), 188–213. doi:10.1123/IJSC.2014-0005

Goeldner, C. R., & Ritchie, J. R. B. (2009). *Tourism: Principles, practices, philosophies* (11th ed.). Wiley.

Golghate, A. A., & Shende, S. W. (2014). Parallel K-means clustering based on hadoop and hama. *International Journal of Computers and Technology*, *1*(3), 33–37.

Gómez-Carracedo, M. P., Andrade, J. M., López-Mahía, P., Muniategui, S., & Prada, D. (2014). A practical comparison of single and multiple imputation methods to handle complex missing data in air quality datasets. *Chemometrics and Intelligent Laboratory Systems*, *134*, 23–33. doi:10.1016/j.chemolab.2014.02.007

Gratch, J., Lucas, G., Malandrakis, N., Szablowski, E., Fessler, E., & Nichols, J. (2015). GOAALLL!: Using Sentiment in the World Cup to Explore Theories of Emotion. *International Conference on Affective Computing and Intelligent Interaction (ACII)*, 898-903. 10.1109/ACII.2015.7344681

Greenberg. (2016). *Hack Brief: Yahoo Breach Hits Half A Billion Users.* Retrieved from https://www.wired.com/2016/09/hack-brief-yahoo-looks-set-confirm-big-old-data-breach

Gretzel, U., & Fesenmaier, D. R. (2009). Information technology: Shaping the past, present, and future of tourism. In T. Jamal & M. Robinson (Eds.), *The SAGE Handbook of Tourism Studies* (pp. 558–580). London: Sage. doi:10.4135/9780857021076.n31

Gruber, T. R. (1993). A translation approach to portable ontology specifications. *Knowledge Acquisition, 5*(2), 199–220. doi:10.1006/knac.1993.1008

Guo, X., Zheng, X., Ling, L., & Yang, C. (2014). Online coopetition between hotels and online travel agencies: From the perspective of cash back after stay. *Tourism Management Perspectives, 12*, 104–112. doi:10.1016/j.tmp.2014.09.005

Guo, Y., Barnes, S. J., & Jia, Q. (2017). Mining meaning from online ratings and reviews: Tourist satisfaction analysis using latent dirichlet allocation. *Tourism Management, 59*, 467–483. doi:10.1016/j.tourman.2016.09.009

Halevi, G., & Moed, H. F. (2012, September). *The technological impact of library science research*. Paper presented at the 17th International Conference on Science and Technology Indicators (STI), Montreal, Quebec, Canada.

Halevy, A. Y. (2003). Data Integration: A Status Report. *Datenbanksysteme in Business, Technology and Web (BTW 2003), 26*, 24-29.

Halevy, A. Y. (2001). Answering queries using views: A survey. *The VLDB Journal, 10*(4), 270–294. doi:10.1007007780100054

Hammer, J., & Mcleod, D. (1993). An Approach to Resolving Semantic Heterogeneity in a Federation of Autonomous, Heterogeneous Database Systems. *International Journal of Intelligent and Cooperative Information Systems, 2*(1), 51–83. doi:10.1142/S0218215793000046

Han, J., Micheline, K., & Jian, P. (2006). *Data Mining: Concepts and techniques*. Morgan Kaufmann.

Han, J., Pei, J., & Kamber, M. (2011). *Data mining: concepts and techniques*. Elsevier.

Haselton, M. G., Nettle, D., & Andrews, P. W. (2005). The evolution of cognitive bias. In *The Handbook of Evolutionary Psychology*. John Wiley & Sons Inc.

Hashemi, M., & Alesheikh, A. (2011). Spatio-temporal analysis of Tehran's historical earthquakes trends. In *Advancing Geoinformation Science for a Changing World* (pp. 3–20). Berlin: Springer. doi:10.1007/978-3-642-19789-5_1

He, D. K., Chu, T. S., Lang, Y. B., & Sun, G. X. (2015). *Comparison of Missing Data Imputation Methods for Leaching Process Modelling*. Academic Press.

Hellerstein, J., Diao, Y., & Parekh, S. (2004). *Feedback control of computing systems*. Hoboken, NJ: Wiley Interscience. doi:10.1002/047166880X

Hinneburg, A., & Keim, D. A. (1998). An efficient approach to clustering in large multimedia databases with noise. *KDD: Proceedings / International Conference on Knowledge Discovery & Data Mining. International Conference on Knowledge Discovery & Data Mining, 98*, 58–65.

Hoq, K. M. G. (2016). Information Overload: Causes, Consequences and Remedies-A Study. *Philosophy and Progress, 55*(1-2), 49–68. doi:10.3329/pp.v55i1-2.26390

Howson, C. (2006). *Seven Pillars of BI Success, Information Week*. Retrieved from http:// www. informationweek .com/software/ business-intelligence/the-seven-pillars-of-bisuccess/191902420

Huang, G. Q., Zhang, Y., & Jiang, P. (2007). RFID-based wireless manufacturing for walking-worker assembly islands with fixed-position layouts. *Robotics and Computer-integrated Manufacturing*, *23*(4), 469–477. doi:10.1016/j.rcim.2006.05.006

Huhns, M. N., & Singh, M. P. (1997). Agents on the Web: Ontologies for Agents. *IEEE Internet Computing*, *1*(6), 81–83. doi:10.1109/4236.643942

Hull, R. (1997). Managing semantic heterogeneity in databases: A theoretical perspective. *Proceedings of the sixteenth ACM SIGACT-SIGMOD-SIGART symposium on Principles of database systems*, 51-61. 10.1145/263661.263668

Hu, M., & Liu, B. (2004). Mining and summarizing customer reviews. *Proceedings of the ACM SIGKDD International Conference on Knowledge Discovery and Data*.

Hurson, A. R., & Bright, M. W. (1991). Multidatabase Systems: An Advanced Concept in Handling Distributed Data. *Advances in Computers*, *32*, 149–200. doi:10.1016/S0065-2458(08)60247-8

Hwang, H.-G., Ku, C.-Y., Yen, D. V., & Cheng, C.-C. (2004). Critical factors influencing the adoption of data warehouse technology: A study of the banking industry in Taiwan. *Decision Support Systems*, *37*(1), 1–21. doi:10.1016/S0167-9236(02)00191-4

IBM. (2018). *The Four V's of Big Data*. Retrieved from http://www.ibmbigdatahub.com/ infographic/four-vs-big-data

IDC. (2017). *Data age 2025: The evolution of data to life-critical*. IDC White Paper by Seagate. Retrieved from: https://www.seagate.com/tr/tr/www-content/our-story/trends/files/

Iglesia, D. G. (2014). MAPE-K Formal Templates for Self-Adaptive Systems: Specifications and Descriptions. Smaland: Linnaeus University.

Informatica Corporation. (2013). *Big Data for Government*. Retrieved from https://www. informatica.com/content/dam/informatica-com/global/amer/us/collateral/executive-brief/ big_data_government_ebook_2340.pdf

Inmon, W. H. (2005). *Building the Data Warehouse* (4th ed.). Indianapolis, IN: Wiley & Sons.

International Olympic Committee (IOC). (2009). *Games of the XXIX Olympiad, Beijing 2008 Global Television and Online Media Report*. IOC.

Intersec. (2018). Retrieved from https://www.intersec.com/refgb/big-data-analytics-application-in-transportation.html

Iqbal, Q., Hassan, S. H., & Ahmad, N. H. (2018). The assessment of perceived information pollution in banking sector: A scale development and validation study. *Business Information Review*, *35*(2), 68–76. doi:10.1177/0266382118772891

Jackson, T. W., & Farzaneh, P. (2012). Theory-based model of factors affecting information overload. *International Journal of Information Management*, *32*(6), 523–532. doi:10.1016/j.ijinfomgt.2012.04.006

Jang, S., Prasad, A., & Ratchford, B. (2012). How consumers use product reviews in the purchase decision process. *Marketing Letters*, *23*(3), 825–838. doi:10.100711002-012-9191-4

Jarke, M., Lenzerini, M., Vassiliou, Y., & Vassiliadis, P. (2000). *Fundamentals of Data Warehouses*. Springer. doi:10.1007/978-3-662-04138-3

Jayapalan, N. (2001). *An introduction to tourism*. New Delhi, India: Atlantic Publishers and Distributors.

Jin, X., Wah, B. W., Cheng, X., & Wang, Y. (2015). Significance and challenges of big data research. *Big Data Research*, *2*(2), 59–64. doi:10.1016/j.bdr.2015.01.006

Jones, S. (2012, December 27). Why 'Big Data' is the Fourth Factor of Production. *Financial Times*. Retrieved July 5, 2018, from https://www.ft.com/content/5086d700-504a-11e2-9b66-00144feab49a

Joshi, P., Bhandari, A., Jamunkar, K., Warghade, K., & Lokhande, P. (2016). Network Traffic Analysis Measurement and Classification Using Hadoop. *International Journal of Adavanced Research in Computer and Communication Engineering*, *5*(3), 246–249.

Kadiri, J. A., & Adetoro, N. A. (2012). Information Explosion and the Challenges of Information and Communication Technology Utilization in Nigerian Libraries and Information Centres. *Ozean Journal of Social Sciences*, *5*(1), 21–30.

Kagermann, H., Helbig, J., Hellinger, A., & Wahlster, W. (2013). *Recommendations for implementing the strategic initiative INDUSTRIE 4.0: Securing the future of German manufacturing industry; final report of the Industrie 4.0 Working Group*. Forschungsunion.

Kaiser, J. (2014). Dealing with Missing Values in Data. *Journal of Systems Integration*, *5*(1), 42–51. doi:10.20470/jsi.v5i1.178

Kakhani, M. K., Kakhani, S., & Biradar, S. R. (2015). Research issues in big data analytics. *International Journal of Application or Innovation in Engineering & Management*, *2*(8), 228–232.

Kean, T. (2011). *The 9/11 commission report: Final report of the national commission on terrorist attacks upon the United States*. Government Printing Office.

Kelton, K., Fleischmann, K. R., & Wallace, W. A. (2008). Trust in digital information. *Journal of the American Society for Information Science and Technology*, *59*(3), 363–374. doi:10.1002/asi.20722

Keromytis, A. D. (2007). *Characterizing Software Self-healing Systems*. In *Computer Network Security* (pp. 22–33). Berlin: Springer.

Kim, E. H., & Youm, Y. N. (2017). How do social media affect analyst stock recommendations? Evidence from S&P 500 electric power companies' Twitter accounts. *Strategic Management Journal*, *38*(13), 2599–2622. doi:10.1002mj.2678

Kim, W., Choi, I., Gala, S., & Scheevel, M. (1993). On Resolving Schematic Heterogeneity in Multidatabase Systems. *Distributed and Parallel Databases*, *1*(3), 252–279. doi:10.1007/BF01263333

Kim, W., & Seo, J. (1991). Classifying Schematic and Data Heterogeneities in Multidatabase Systems. *IEEE Computer*, *24*(12), 12–18. doi:10.1109/2.116884

Kirsh, D. (2000). A few thoughts on cognitive overload. *Intellectica*, *1*(30), 19–51.

Kntonew. (2016). *Knewton to Accelerate Personalized Learning for Students Worldwide With $52M in Financing*. Retrieved from https://www.knewton.com/resources/press/67525/

Koçel, T. (2015). *İşletme Yöneticiliği*. İstanbul: Beta Basım Yayım Dağıtım.

Kohavi, R., Rothleder, N. J., & Simoudis, E. (2002). Emerging Trends in Business Analytics. *Communications of the ACM*, *45*(8), 45–48.

Koh, S., Gunasekaran, A., & Rajkumar, D. (2008). ERP II: The involvement, benefits and impediments of collaborative information sharing. *International Journal of Production Economics*, *113*(1), 245–268. doi:10.1016/j.ijpe.2007.04.013

Koko, E. E. M., & Mohamed, A. I. A. (2015). Missing data treatment method on cluster analysis. International. *Journal of Advanced Statistics and Probability*, *3*(2), 191–209. doi:10.14419/ijasp.v3i2.5318

Kropko, J., Goodrich, B., Gelman, A., & Hill, J. (2014). Multiple imputation for continuous and categorical data: Comparing joint multivariate normal and conditional approaches. *Political Analysis*.

Kumar, I., & Sebastian, T. M. (2012). Sentiment Analysis on Twitter. *International Journal of Computer Science Issues, 9*(4-3), 372-378.

Kumunzhiev, K. V. (2003). Teoriya sistem i sistemnyy analiz: ucheb. Ulyanovsk: UlGU.

Kuom, M., & Oertel, B. (1999). Virtual travel agencies. *NETNOMICS: Economic Research and Electronic Networking*, *1*(2), 225–235. doi:10.1023/A:1019114208191

Kurbanoglu, S., Grassian, E., Mizrachi, D., Catts, R., & Spiranec, S. (2013). *Worldwide Commonalities and Challenges in Information Literacy Research and Practice: European Conference, ECIL 2013, Istanbul, Turkey, October 22-25, 2013. Revised Selected Papers (Vol. 397)*. Springer. 10.1007/978-3-319-03919-0

Kurniati, A. P., & Surendro, K. (2010). *Designing IQMM as a maturity model for information quality management*. Paper presented at the Informing Science & IT Education Conference (InSITE).

Kuruppuarachchi, P. (2006). Managing virtual project teams: how to maximize performance. Handbook of Business Strategy, 7(1), 71-78.

Kutty, A. D. (2006). *Managing Information Overload for Effective Decision-Making: An Empirical Study on Managers of the South Pacific (Master of Arts)*. The University of the South Pacific.

Lacombe, A. (2018). *Transform Your Fleet with Big Data*. Retrieved from https://www.omnitracs.com/solutions/data-analytics

Landers, T., & Rosenberg, R. L. (1982). An Overview of MULTIBASE. *Second International Symposium on Distributed Data Bases (DDB 1982)*, 153-184.

Laudante, E. (2017). Industry 4.0, Innovation and Design. A new approach for ergonomic analysis in manufacturing system. *The Design Journal, 20*(sup1), S2724-S2734.

Laudon, K. C., & Laudon, J. P. (2002). *Essential of management information systems* (5th ed.). Englewood Cliffs, NJ: Prentice Hall.

Law, R., Leung, K., & Wong, R. J. (2004). The impact of the internet on travel agencies. *International Journal of Contemporary Hospitality Management, 16*(2), 100–107. doi:10.1108/09596110410519982

Law, R., Leung, R., & Buhalis, D. (2009). Information technology applications in hospitality and tourism: A review of publications from 2005 to 2007. *Journal of Travel & Tourism Marketing, 26*(5), 599–623. doi:10.1080/10548400903163160

Leaders, R. (2017). *OTT - The shifting broadcasting landscape*. Retrieved from leadersinsport.com

Leading Core Banking Provider Serving Thousands of Customers Selects NICE Actimize as its Integrated Cloud Financial Crime and Compliance Solution. (2018). Retrieved from https://www.niceactimize.com/press-releases/Leading-Core-Banking-Provider-Serving-Thousands-of-Customers-Selects-NICE-Actimize-as-its-Integrated-Cloud-Financial-Crime-and-Compliance-Solution-209

Lee, J., Kao, H.-A., & Yang, S. (2014). Service innovation and smart analytics for industry 4.0 and big data environment. *Procedia Cirp, 16*, 3–8. doi:10.1016/j.procir.2014.02.001

Lee, J., Park, D.-H., & Han, I. (2008). The effect of negative online consumer reviews on product attitude: An information processing view. *Electronic Commerce Research and Applications, 7*(3), 341–352. doi:10.1016/j.elerap.2007.05.004

Lee, K. J., Roberts, G., Doyle, L., Anderson, P., & Carlin, J. (2016). Multiple imputation for missing data in a longitudinal cohort study: A tutorial based on a detailed case study involving imputation of missing outcome data. *International Journal of Social Research Methodology*, 1–17.

Lei, L. (2010, July). Identify earthquake hot spots with 3-dimensional density-based clustering analysis. In *Geoscience and Remote Sensing Symposium (IGARSS), 2010 IEEE International* (pp. 530-533). IEEE. 10.1109/IGARSS.2010.5652510

Lenzerini, M. (2002). Data integration: A theoretical preceptive. *Proceedings of Twenty-first ACM SIGACT-SIGMOD-SIGART Symposium on Principles of Database System*, 1-14.

LeSueur, D. (2016). *Reasons Healthcare Data Is Unique and Difficult to Measure.* Health Catalyst.

Leuterio, F. C. (2007). Introduction to Tourism. Manila, Philippines: Academic Press.

Levis, M. (2011). *Information quality training requirements analysis guideline demonstrated in a healthcare context.* Dublin City University.

Levy, M., & Powell, P. (1998). SME flexibility and the role of information systems. *Small Business Economics*, *11*(2), 183–196. doi:10.1023/A:1007912714741

Liao, S. G., Lin, Y., Kang, D. D., Chandra, D., Bon, J., Kaminski, N., & Tseng, G. C. (2014). Missing value imputation in high-dimensional phenomic data: Imputable or not, and how? *BMC Bioinformatics*, *15*(1), 1. doi:10.118612859-014-0346-6 PMID:25371041

Li, J., Xu, L., Tang, L., Wang, S., & Li, L. (2018). Big data in tourism research: A literature review. *Tourism Management*, *68*, 301–323. doi:10.1016/j.tourman.2018.03.009

Ling, L., Guo, X., & Yang, C. (2014). Opening the online marketplace: An examination of hotel pricing and travel agency on-line distribution of rooms. *Tourism Management*, *45*, 234–243. doi:10.1016/j.tourman.2014.05.003

Lisi, C. (2016). *Soccer's high-tech future*. Retrieved from https://ussoccerplayers.com/2016/09/soccers-high-tech-future-mls-ifab-video-referee.html

Little, R., & Rubin, D. (1987). *Statistical analysis with missing data* (1st ed.). John Wiley and Sons.

Liu, B., Hu, M., & Cheng, J. (2005). Opinion observer: Analyzing and comparing opinions on the web. *Proceedings of the 14th International World Wide Web conference (WWW 2005)*. 10.1145/1060745.1060797

Liu, G. F., Han, B., Zhao, X., & Lin, Q. (2015). A Comparison of Frequentist and Bayesian Model Based Approaches for Missing Data Analysis: Case Study with a Schizophrenia Clinical Trial. *Statistics in Biopharmaceutical Research*. doi:10.1080/19466315.2015.1077725

Liu, W., & Park, E. K. (2014). *Big Data as an e-Health Service*. IEEE Electronic. doi:10.1109/ICCNC.2014.6785471

Lovett, J. (2011). *Social Media Metrics Secrets*. Wiley Publishing, Inc.

Lubbe, B. (2000). *Tourism distribution: Managing the travel intermediary*. JUTA.

Luengo, J., García, S., & Herrera, F. (2010). A Study on the Use of Imputation Methods for Experimentation with Radial Basis Function Network Classifiers Handling Missing Attribute Values: The good synergy between RBFs and EventCovering method. *Neural Networks*, *23*(3), 406–418. doi:10.1016/j.neunet.2009.11.014 PMID:20015612

Luengo, J., García, S., & Herrera, F. (2012). On the choice of the best imputation methods for missing values considering three groups of classification methods. *Knowledge and Information Systems*, *32*(1), 77–108. doi:10.100710115-011-0424-2

MacDonald, J., Bath, P., & Booth, A. (2011). Information overload and information poverty: Challenges for healthcare services managers? *The Journal of Documentation*, *67*(2), 238–263. doi:10.1108/00220411111109458

Madnick, S. E., Wang, R. Y., Lee, Y. W., & Zhu, H. (2009). Overview and framework for data and information quality research. *Journal of Data and Information Quality*, *1*(1), 2. doi:10.1145/1515693.1516680

Mahler, J. G. (2009). *Organizational learning at NASA: The Challenger and Columbia accidents.* Georgetown University Press.

Masconi, K., Matsha, T., Echouffo-Tcheugui, J., Erasmus, R., & Kengne, A. (2015). Reporting and handling of missing data in predictive research for prevalent undiagnosed type 2 diabetes mellitus: A systematic review. *The EPMA Journal*, *6*(1), 7. doi:10.118613167-015-0028-0 PMID:25829972

Matos, L. M., & Afsarmanesh, H. (2006). Creation of virtual organizations in a breeding environment. *Proceedings of INCOM*, *6*, 595–603.

Mayer, V. V., & Cukier, K. (2013). *Big Data: A Revolution That Will Transform How We Live, Work and Think.* John Murray Press.

McCarter, M. W., & Northcraft, G. B. (2007). Happy together? Insights and implications of viewing managed supply chains as a social dilemma. *Journal of Operations Management*, *25*(2), 498–511. doi:10.1016/j.jom.2006.05.005

McDowell, D. (2009). *A Handbook for Practitioners, Managers and Users: Strategic Intelligence.* The Scarecrow Press, Inc.

McFadzean, E., Ezingeard, J.-N., & Birchall, D. (2007). *Perception of Risk & the Strategic Impact of existing IT on Information Security Strategy at the Board level.* Academic Press.

McKinsey & Co. (2011). *Big Data: The Next Frontier for Innovation, Competition and Productivity.* McKinsey & Co.

McKinsey, D. (2016). Industry 4.0 after the initial hype. Retrieved from McKinsey&Company: https://www.mckinsey.com/~/media/mckinsey/business%20functions/mckinsey%20digital/our%20insights/getting%20the%20most%20out%20of%20industry%204%200/mckinsey_industry_40_2016.ashx

McKinsey. (2011). *Big Data: The next frontier for innovation, competition, and productivity.* Retrieved from: https://www.mckinsey.com/

Medlik, S. (2016). *Managing tourism.* Butterworth-Heinemann.

Mena, E., Kashyap, V., Sheth, A. P., & Illarramendi, A. (1996). OBSERVER: An Approach for Query Processing in Global Information Systems based on Interoperation across Pre-existing Ontologies. *First IFCIS International Conference on Cooperative Information Systems (CoopIS 1996)*, 14-25. 10.1109/COOPIS.1996.554955

Meng, M. D., Stavros, C., & Westberg, K. (2015). Engaging fans through social media: Implications for team identification. *Sport, Business and Management. International Journal (Toronto, Ont.)*, *5*(3), 199–217.

Metzger, M. J., & Flanagin, A. J. (2008). *Digital media, youth, and credibility*. Cambridge, MA: MIT Press.

Miah, S. J., Vu, H. Q., Gammack, J., & McGrath, M. (2017). A big data analytics method for tourist behaviour analysis. *Information & Management*, *54*(6), 771–785. doi:10.1016/j.im.2016.11.011

Mind Fire Solutions. (2018). *The impact of Cloud and Big Data on Healthcare Sector*. Retrieved from,https://medium.com/@mindfiresolutions.usa/the-impact-of-cloud-and-big-data-on-healthcare-sector-e26509a01071

Mkrtchian, V., Bershadsky, A., Bozhday, A., & Fionova, L. (2015). Model in SM of DEE Based on Service-Oriented Interactions at Dynamic Software Product Lines. In Identification, Evaluation, and Perceptions of Distance Education Experts (pp. 231-248). Hershey, PA: IGI Global.

Mkrttchian, V. (2012). Avatar manager and student reflective conversations as the base for describing meta-communication model. In Meta-communication for reflective online conversations: Models for distance education (pp. 340–351). Hershey, PA: IGI Global.

Mkrttchian, V., & Stephanova, G. (2013). Training of Avatar Moderator in Sliding Mode Control. In Enterprise Resource Planning: Concepts, Methodologies, Tools, and Applications (pp. 1376-1405), Hershey PA: IGI Global.

Mkrttchian, V. (2011). Use 'hhh" technology in transformative models of online education. In G. Kurubacak & T. V. Yuzer (Eds.), *Handbook of research on transformative online education and liberation: Models for social equality* (pp. 340–351). Hershey, PA: IGI Global. doi:10.4018/978-1-60960-046-4.ch018

Mkrttchian, V. (2014). Modeling using of Triple H-Avatar Technology in online Multi-Cloud Platform Lab. In M. Khosrow-Pour (Ed.), *Encyclopedia of Information Science and Technology* (3rd ed.; pp. 116–141). Hershey, PA: IGI Global.

Mkrttchian, V., & Aleshina, E. (2017). *Sliding Mode in Intellectual Control and Communication: Emerging Research and Opportunities*. Hershey, PA: IGI Global. doi:10.4018/978-1-5225-2292-8

Mkrttchian, V., Kataev, M., Hwang, W., Bedi, S., & Fedotova, A. (2014). Using Plug-Avatars "hhh" Technology Education as Service-Oriented Virtual Learning Environment in Sliding Mode. In G. Eby & T. V. Yuzer (Eds.), *Emerging Priorities and Trends in Distance Education: Communication, Pedagogy, and Technology* (pp. 43–55). Hershey, PA: IGI Global. doi:10.4018/978-1-4666-5162-3.ch004

Mohapatra, S., Agrawal, A., & Satpathy, A (2016). *Designing Knowledge Management-Enabled Business Strategies A Top-Down Approach*. Springer International Publishing.

Monash, C. (2008). *The 1-petabyte barrier is crumbling*. Retrieved from http://www.networkworld.com/community/node/31439

Morales-Esteban, A., Martínez-Álvarez, F., Troncoso, A., Justo, J. L., & Rubio-Escudero, C. (2010). Pattern recognition to forecast seismic time series. *Expert Systems with Applications*, *37*(12), 8333–8342. doi:10.1016/j.eswa.2010.05.050

Morley, C. K., & Nixon, C. W. (2016). Topological characteristics of simple and complex normal fault networks. *Journal of Structural Geology*, *84*, 68–84. doi:10.1016/j.jsg.2016.01.005

Mowshowitz, A. (2001). Virtual organization: The new feudalism. *Computer*, *34*(4), 100–111. doi:10.1109/MC.2001.917551

Munster W. W. U. OpenUSS. (n.d.). Retrieved from https://www.uni-muenster.de/studium/orga/openuss.html.

Naik, H. C., & Joshi, D. (2016). A Hadoop Framework Require to Process Bigdata very Easily and Efficiently. *IJSRSET*, *2*(2), 1206–1209.

Nami, N. R. (2008). Virtual Organizations: An Overview. In *Intelligent Information Processing IV. IIP 2008. IFIP – The International Federation for Information Processing*. Boston, MA: Springer. doi:10.1007/978-0-387-87685-6_26

Naviance. (2018). *Connecting learning to life*. Retrieved from https://www.naviance.com/

Negash, S. (2004). Business Intelligence. *Communications of the AIS*, *13*, 177–195.

Neilson, L. C., & Chadha, M. (2008). International marketing strategy in the retail banking industry: The case of ICICI Bank in Canada. *Journal of Financial Services Marketing*, *13*(3), 204–220. doi:10.1057/fsm.2008.21

Nelson, R. R., Todd, P. A., & Wixom, B. H. (2005). Antecedents of information and system quality: An empirical examination within the context of data warehousing. *Journal of Management Information Systems*, *21*(4), 199–235. doi:10.1080/07421222.2005.11045823

NewVantage Partners. (2018). *Big data executive survey of 2018*. Retrieved from: http://newvantage.com/

Noor, M. N., Yahaya, A. S., Ramli, N. A., & Al Bakri, A. M. M. (2014, March). Mean imputation techniques for filling the missing observations in air pollution dataset. *Key Engineering Materials*, *594*, 902–908.

Norman, C. D. (2009). Health Promotion as a Systems Science and Practice. *Journal of Evaluation in Clinical Practice*, *15*(5), 868–872. doi:10.1111/j.1365-2753.2009.01273.x PMID:19811602

O'Connell, E. (2016). *Avaya giving San Jose Earthquakes digital boost for in-stadium fan experience*. Retrieved from https://www.sporttechie.com/avaya-giving-san-jose-earthquakes-digital-boost-for-in-stadium-fan-experience/

OctoTelematics. (2015). *The promise of insurance telematics*. Retrieved from https://www.octotelematics.com/news/the-promise-of-insurance-telematics

Oracle Enterprise Architecture White Paper. (2015). *Improving Manufacturing Performance with Big Data Architect's Guide and Reference Architecture Introduction*. Retrieved from http://www.oracle.com/us/technologies/big-data/big-data-manufacturing-2511058.pdf

Ou, C. X., & Davison, R. M. (2011). Interactive or interruptive? Instant messaging at work. *Decision Support Systems*, *52*(1), 61–72. doi:10.1016/j.dss.2011.05.004

Ozcan, A. (2018). *Senior Trader*. Retrieved from https://www.tibco.com/customers/kuveytturk-bank

Ozdemir, Ş. (2016). Individual contributions to infollution (information pollution): Trust and share. *International Journal on New Trends in Education and Their Implications*, *7*(3), 23–33.

Pal, K. (2017). Supply Chain Coordination Based on Web Service. In H. K. Chan, N. Subramanian, & M. D. Abdulrahman (Eds.), *Supply Chain Management in the Big Data Era* (pp. 137–171). Hershey, PA: IGI Global Publishing. doi:10.4018/978-1-5225-0956-1.ch009

Pandita, R. (2014). Information pollution, a mounting threat: Internet a major causality. *Journal of Information Science Theory and Practice*, *2*(2), 49–60. doi:10.1633/JISTaP.2014.2.4.4

Papazoglou, M. P., & Heuvel, W.-J. (2007). Service oriented architectures: Approaches, technologies and research issues. *The VLDB Journal*, *16*(3), 389–415. doi:10.100700778-007-0044-3

Parganas, P., Anagnostopoulos, C., & Chadwick, S. (2015). 'You'll never tweet alone': Managing sports brands through social media. *Journal of Brand Management*, *22*(7), 551–568. doi:10.1057/bm.2015.32

Patil, H. K., & Ravi, S. (2014). Big data security and privacy issues in healthcare. *Big Data (BigData Congress), 2014 IEEE International Congress on. IEEE*. 10.1109/BigData.Congress.2014.112

Pelyushenko, A. V. (2006). Izvestiya Volgogradskogo gosudarstvennogo tekhnicheskogo universiteta, *University proceedings. Volga region. Engineering and Science*, (8): 48–50.

Phillips-Wren, G., Iyer, L. S., Kulkarni, U., & Ariyachandra, T. (2015). Business Analytics in the Context of Big Data: A Roadmap for Research. *Communications of the Association for Information Systems*, *37*, 23.

Piccoli, G. (2013). *Information Systems for Managers: Text & Cases* (2nd ed.). John Wiley & Sons, Inc.

Pierce, M. E. (2008). The QuakeSim project: Web services for managing geophysical data and applications. In Earthquakes: Simulations, Sources and Tsunamis (pp. 635-651). Birkhäuser Basel.

Ponemon, Institute Research Report. (2016). *Sixth Annual Benchmark Study on Privacy & Security of Healthcare Data*. Author.

Pottinger, R., & Halevy, A. (2001). MiniCon: A Scalable Algorithm for Answering Queries Using Views. *The Very Large Dabase Journal*, *10*, 182–198.

Prause, G. (2015). Sustainable business models and structures for Industry 4.0. *Journal of Security & Sustainability Issues*, *5*(2), 159–169. doi:10.9770/jssi.2015.5.2(3)

Preator, B. (2018, June). Delivering Big Data Expectations. *CIO Review*. Retrieved July 24, 2018, from www.bigdata.cioreview.com

Preece, A., Missier, P., Embury, S., Jin, B., & Greenwood, M. (2008). An ontology-based approach to handling information quality in e-Science. *Concurrency and Computation*, *20*(3), 253–264. doi:10.1002/cpe.1195

Press, G. (2016). *Cleaning Big Data: Most Time-Consuming, Least Enjoyable Data Science Task, Survey Says*. Retrieved from https://www.forbes.com/sites/gilpress/2016/03/23/data-preparation-most-time-consuming-least-enjoyable-data-science-task-survey-says/#7955038a6f63

Price, J., Farrington, N., & Hall, L. (2013). Changing the game? The impact of Twitter on relationships between football clubs, supporters and the sports media. *Soccer and Society*, *14*(4), 446–461. doi:10.1080/14660970.2013.810431

Prud'hommeaux, E., & Seaborne, A. (2013). *SPARQL Query Language for RDF*. Retrieved from http://www.w3.org/TR/rdf-sparql-query

Quitzau, A. (2014). *Big Data & Analytics*. Retrieved from https://www.slideshare.net/AndersQuitzauIbm/big-data-analyticsin-energy-utilities

R Language. (n.d.). Retrieved from https://www.r-project.org/

Rana, S., John, A. H., & Midi, H. (2015). Robust Regression Imputation for Missing Data in the Presence of Outliers. *Far East Journal of Mathematical Sciences*, *97*(2).

Raun, J., Ahas, R., & Tiru, M. (2016). Measuring tourism destinations using mobile tracking data. *Tourism Management*, *57*, 202–212. doi:10.1016/j.tourman.2016.06.006

Reddy, T. (2016). *5 ways to turn data into insights and revenue in 2016*. Retrieved from: https://www.ibm.com/blogs/watson/2016/02/5-ways-to-turn-data-into-insights-and-revenue-in-2016/

Reedy, K., Mallett, E., & Soma, N. (2013). iKnow: Information skills in the 21st century workplace. *Library and Information Research*, *37*(114), 105-122.

Research and Markets. (2015). *Global Big Data in Healthcare Study 2015-2020 Featuring Explorys, Humedica, InterSystems, Pervasive, Clinical Query, GNS Healthcare, OmedaRX, and Sogeti Healthcare*. Retrieved from https://www.prnewswire.com/news-releases/global-big-data-in-healthcare-study-2015-2020-featuring-explorys-humedica-intersystems-pervasive-clinical-query-gns-healthcare-omedarx-and-sogeti-healthcare-300104781.html

Rinaldi, M., Himpe, W., & Tampère, M. J. (2016). A sensitivity-based approach for adaptive decomposition of anticipatory network traffic control. *Transportation Research Part C, Emerging Technologies*, *66*, 150–175. doi:10.1016/j.trc.2016.01.005

Robert, P. B., Weng, T. K., & Simon, F. (2016). Big data analytics for transportation: Problems and prospects for its application in China. *2016 IEEE Region 10 Symposium (TENSYMP)*.

Robinson, P. (2009). Travel and management: An introduction. In P. Robinson (Ed.), *Operations management in the travel industry* (pp. 1–13). Cambridge, UK: CAB International. doi:10.1079/9781845935030.0001

Rocha, L. (2015, August 15). *The 5 Steps of the Intelligence Cycle*. Retrieved from Security Monitoring, Threat Intelligence: www.countuponsecurity.com/2015/08/15/the-5-steps-of-the-intelligence-cycle/

Rubin, D. B. (2004). *Multiple imputation for nonresponse in surveys*. John Wiley & Sons.

Russom, P. (2011). Big Data Analytics. TDWI Best Practices Report.

Sager, T. (2014). *An Intelligent Approach to Attack Prevention*. SANS Institute.

Samadi, M., & Yaghoob-Nejadi, A. (2009). A survey of the effect of consumers' perceived risk on purchase intention in e-shopping. *Business Intelligence Journal*, *2*(2), 261–275.

Samra, B., & Wos, A. (2014). Consumer in Sports: Fan typology analysis. *Journal of Intercultural Management*, *6*(4–1), 263–288. doi:10.2478/joim-2014-0050

Santomier, J. P., Hogan, P. I., & Kunz, R. (2016). The 2012 London Olympics: Innovations in ICT and social media marketing. *Innovation: Management*, *Policy & Practice*, *18*(3), 251–269. doi:10.1080/14479338.2016.1237305

Sasaki, Y., Kawai, D., & Kitamura, S. (2015). The anatomy of tweet overload: How number of tweets received, number of friends, and egocentric network density affect perceived information overload. *Telematics and Informatics*, *32*(4), 853–861. doi:10.1016/j.tele.2015.04.008

Sawar, A. (2012). *Virtual organizations*. Retrieved from https://www.slideshare.net/aijazansf/virtual-organisations

Sayar, A., Pierce, M., & Fox, G. (2005, November). Developing GIS visualization web services for geophysical applications. In ISPRS 2005 spatial data mining workshop, Ankara, Turkey.

Schindler, R. M., & Bickart, B. (2012). Perceived helpfulness of online consumer reviews: The role of message content and style. *Journal of Consumer Behaviour*, *11*(3), 234–243. doi:10.1002/cb.1372

Schmitt, P., Mandel, J., & Guedj, M. (2015). A comparison of six methods for missing data imputation. *Journal of Biometrics & Biostatistics*.

Schobbens, P. E., Heymans, P., & Trigaux, J. C. (2011). 14th IEEE International Requirements Engineering Conference (RE'06). *Computers & Society*, *2011*, 139–148.

Schott, W. (2017). *4 ways to protect information in data-driven healthcare system.* HealthCare Business & Technology. Retrieved from http://www.healthcarebusinesstech.com/protect-data-healthcare-system/

Schuler, B. (2010). *Virtual travel: Embrace or expire.* iUniverse.

Scott Morton, M. S. (1991). *The Corporation of the 1990s: Information Technology and Organizational Transformation.* New York: Oxford University Press.

Shafer, T. (2017). *The 42 V's of Big Data and Data Science.* Retrieved from https://www.elderresearch.com/blog/42-v-of-big-data

Shank, M. D., & Beasley, F. M. (1998). Fan or fanatic: Refining a measure of sports involvement. *Journal of Sport Behavior, 21*(4), 435–443.

Shanmugam, C. G. (2002). The Need for Knowledge Management in Special Libraries. In *Proceedings of the National Conference on Information Management in e-Libraries (ImeL).* New Delhi: Allied Publishers.

Shao, Y., Lee, M., & Liao, S. (2000). Virtual organizations: the key dimensions. *Proceedings Academia/Industry Working Conference on Research Challenges '00. Next Generation Enterprises: Virtual Organizations and Mobile/Pervasive Technologies.*

Sharma, R., Yetton, P. W., & Zmud, R. W. (2008). Implementation Costs of IS-Enabled Organizational Change. *Information and Organization, 18*(2), 73–100. doi:10.1016/j.infoandorg.2007.09.001

Shekhar, S., Evans, M. R., Kang, J. M., & Mohan, P. (2011). Identifying patterns in spatial information: A survey of methods. *Wiley Interdisciplinary Reviews. Data Mining and Knowledge Discovery, 1*(3), 193–214. doi:10.1002/widm.25

Sheth, A. P., Gala, S. K., & Navathe, S. B. (1993). On Automatic Reasoning for Shema Integration. *International Journal of Intelligent and Cooperative Information Systems, 2*(1), 23–50. doi:10.1142/S0218215793000034

Sheth, A. P., & Larson, J. A. (1990). Federated Database Systems for Managing Distributed, Heterogenous, and Autonomous Databases. *ACM Computing Surveys, 22*(3), 183–236. doi:10.1145/96602.96604

Silberschatz, A., Korth, H. F., & Sudarshan, S. (1997). *Database System Concepts.* McGraw-Hill.

Singh, A. J., & Kasavana, M. L. (2005). The impact of information technology on future management of lodging operations: A delphi study to predict key technological events in 2007 and 2027. *Tourism and Hospitality Research, 6*(1), 24–37. doi:10.1057/palgrave.thr.6040042

Sivasubramanian, S. (2016). *Process Model for Knowledge Management* (Doctoral thesis). CMU-LTI-16-003 Language Technologies Institute School of Computer Science Carnegie Mellon University. Retrieved from www.lti.cs.cmu.edu

Smartsparrow. (n.d.). Retrieved from https://www.smartsparrow.com/

Smith, L. R., & Smith, K. D. (2012). Identity in Twitter's Hashtag Culture: A Sport-Media Consumption Case Study. *International Journal of Sport Communication*, *5*(4), 539–557. doi:10.1123/ijsc.5.4.539

Song, H., & Liu, H. (2017). Predicting tourist demand using big data. In *Analytics in smart tourism design* (pp. 13–29). Springer.

Soucek, R., & Moser, K. (2010). Coping with information overload in email communication: Evaluation of a training intervention. *Computers in Human Behavior*, *26*(6), 1458–1466. doi:10.1016/j.chb.2010.04.024

Spotfire Blogging Team. (2015). *4 Ways Big Data Is Transforming the Insurance Industry.* Retrieved from https://www.tibco.com/blog/2015/07/20/4-ways-big-data-is-transforming-the-insurance-industry/

Stackowiak, R., Rayman, J., & Greenwald, R. (2007). *Oracle Data Warehousing and Business Intelligence Solutions*. Indianapolis, IN: Wiley Publishing, Inc.

Sterne, J. (2010). *Social Media Metrics: How to Measure and Optimze Your Marketing Investment*. Hoboken, NJ: John Wiley & Sons, Inc.

Stover, A., & Nielsen, J. (2002). *E-mail newsletter usability: 79 design guidelines for subscription, newsletter content and account maintenance based on usability studies*. Fremont, CA: Nielsen Norman Group.

Strong, D. M., Lee, Y. W., & Wang, R. Y. (1997). Data quality in context. *Communications of the ACM*, *40*(5), 103–110. doi:10.1145/253769.253804

Swar, B., Hameed, T., & Reychav, I. (2017). Information overload, psychological ill-being, and behavioral intention to continue online healthcare information search. *Computers in Human Behavior*, *70*, 416–425. doi:10.1016/j.chb.2016.12.068

Syler, R., & Schwager, P. H. (2000). Virtual Organization as a Source of Competitive: A Framework from the Resource-Based. *AMCIS 2000 Proceedings, 390*.

Tableau. (2018). *Retail and Wholesale Analytics*. Retrieved from https://www.tableau.com/solutions/retail-and-wholesale-analytics

Taylor, S. L., Ruhaak, L. R., Kelly, K., Weiss, R. H., & Kim, K. (2016). Effects of imputation on correlation: Implications for analysis of mass spectrometry data from multiple biological matrices. *Briefings in Bioinformatics*. doi:10.1093/bib/bbw010 PMID:26896791

Tchetchik, A., Fleischer, A., & Shoval, N. (2009). Segmentation of visitors to a heritage site using high-resolution time-space data. *Journal of Travel Research*, *48*(2), 216–229. doi:10.1177/0047287509332307

The Next Evolution of ERP. (n.d.). *Adaptive ERP // ERP the Right Way: Changing the game for ERP Cloud implementations*. Retrieved from https://gbeaubouef.wordpress.com/2012/09/05/adaptive-erp/

Thirumahal, R., & Deepali, A. (2014). Patil. (2014). "KNN and ARL Based Imputation to Estimate Missing Values. *Indonesian Journal of Electrical Engineering and Informatics*, *2*(3), 119–124.

Thomas, D., Therlal, G., & Danytel, J. (2015). Worldwide Big Data Technology and Services: 2012-2015 Forecast. *Clinical Pharmacology and Therapeutics*, *92*(1), 77–95.

Thron, C., Tran, K., Smith, D., & Benincasa, D. (2017). Design and simulation of sensor networks for tracking Wifi users in outdoor urban environments. *Proceedings of SPIE*.

Tsai, C. Y., Chang, H. T., & Kuo, R. J. (2017). An ant colony based optimization for RFID reader deployment in theme parks under service level consideration. *Tourism Management*, *58*, 1–14. doi:10.1016/j.tourman.2016.10.003

Tvrdikova, M. (2007), Support of Decision Making by Business Intelligence Tools. *Computer Information Systems and Industrial Management Applications, 2007. CISIM '07. 6th International Conference*, 368.

Ullman, J. D. (1997). Information integration using logical views. *Proceedings of International Conference on Database Theory*, 19-40.

United States Geological Survey (USGS). (2015). Retrieved from http://earthquake.usgs.gov/earthquakes/search

Unver, H., & Sadigh, B. L. (2013). Small and medium enterprises: Concepts, methodologies, tools, and applications. In *An agent-based operational virtual enterprise framework enabled by RFID* (pp. 198–215). IGI Global.

Vale, L., & Fernandes, T. (2018). Social media and sports: Driving fan engagement with football clubs on Facebook. *Journal of Strategic Marketing*, *26*(1), 37–55. doi:10.1080/0965254X.2017.1359655

van Rijmenam, M. (2018). *How Big Data Enabled Spotify To Change The Music Industry*. Retrieved from https://datafloq.com/read/big-data-enabled-spotify-change-music-industry/391

Versichele, M., De Groote, L., Bouuaert, M. C., Neutens, T., Moerman, I., & Van de Weghe, N. (2014). Pattern mining in tourist attraction visits through association rule learning on bluetooth tracking data: A case study of Ghent, Belgium. *Tourism Management*, *44*, 67–81. doi:10.1016/j.tourman.2014.02.009

Villegas, N. M., Muller, H. A., Tamura, G., Duchien, L., & Casallas, R. A. (2011). Framework for evaluating quality- driven self-adaptive software systems. *Proceeding of the 6th International Symposium on Software Engineering for Adaptive and Self-Managing Systems*, 80-89. 10.1145/1988008.1988020

Virkus, S. (2014). *Theoretical Models of Information and Knowledge Management*. Retrieved from http://www.tlu.ee/~sirvir/IKM/Theoretical_models_of_Information_ and_ Knowledge_ Management/the_von_krogh_and_roos_model_of_organizational_epistemology.html

Wache, H., Vogele, T., Visser, U., Struckenschmidt, H., Schuster, G., Neumann, H., & Hubner, S. (2001). Ontology-Based Integration of Information – A Survey of Existing Approaches. *IJCAI-2001 Workshop on Ontologies and Information Sharing*, 108-117.

Wagstaff, K. (2004). *Clustering with missing values: No imputation required*. Springer Berlin Heidelberg.

Wang, R. Y. (1998). A product perspective on total data quality management. *Communications of the ACM*, *41*(2), 58–65. doi:10.1145/269012.269022

Wang, W. Y., & Chan, H. K. (2010). Virtual organization for supply chain integration: Two cases in the textile and fashion retailing industry. *International Journal of Production Economics*, *127*(2), 333–342. doi:10.1016/j.ijpe.2009.08.006

Wardle, C., & Derakhshan, H. (2017). *Information Disorder: Toward an interdisciplinary framework for research and policymaking*. Council of Europe report, DGI(2017), 9.

Watanabe, N. M., Yan, G., & Soebbing, B. P. (2016). Consumer Interest in Major League Baseball: An Analytical Modeling of Twitter. *Journal of Sport Management*, *30*(2), 207–220. doi:10.1123/jsm.2015-0121

Watanabe, N., Yan, G., & Soebbing, B. P. (2015). Major League Baseball and Twitter Usage: The Economics of Social Media Use. *Journal of Sport Management*, *29*(6), 619–632. doi:10.1123/JSM.2014-0229

Wayman, J. C. (2003). *Multiple imputation for missing data: What is it and how can I use it*. Annual Meeting of the American Educational Research Association, Chicago, IL.

Web Site for Project Repository. (n.d.). Retrieved from https://github.com/kaplansinan/Imputation-of-Missing-Data.git

Web Site for Project Web Site. (n.d.). Retrieved from http://www.yildiz.edu.tr/~aktas-/missingdata

WebC. T. (n.d.). Retrieved from http://www.cuhk.edu.hk/eLearning/c_systems/webct6/

Weiss, S. M., Indurkhya, N., Zhang, T., & Damerau, F. J. (2005). *Text Mining-Predictive Methods for Analyzing Unstructured Information*. Springer Verlag.

West, D. M. (2012). *Big Data for Education: Data Mining, Data Analytics, and Web Dashboards*. Gov. Stud. Brook. US Reuters.

White, T. (2008). *HDFS Reliability*. Retrieved from www.cloudera.com/HDFS

Widen, G., Steinerová, J., & Voisey, P. (2014). Conceptual modelling of workplace information practices: a literature review. *Information Research*, *19*(4).

Wiederhold, G. (1992). Mediators in the architecture of future information systems. *IEEE Computer*, 38-49.

Wilks, S. S. (1932). Moments and distributions of estimates of population parameters from fragmentary samples. *Annals of Mathematical Statistics*, *3*(3), 163–195. doi:10.1214/aoms/1177732885

Wills, J. (2016). *7 Ways Amazon Uses Big Data to Stalk You (AMZN)*. Retrieved from, https://www.investopedia.com/articles/insights/090716/7-ways-amazon-uses-big-data-stalk-you-amzn.asp

Witteman, C., & Krol, N. (2005). Knowledge-Based Systems: Acquiring, Modeling, and Representing Human Expertsie for Information Systems. In *Creation, Use, and Deployment of Digital Information* (pp. 177–198). Mahwah, NJ: Lawrence Erlbaum Associates, Inc.

Wixom, B., & Watson, H. J. (2001). An empirical investigation of the factors affecting data warehousing success. *Management Information Systems Quarterly*, *25*(1), 17–41. doi:10.2307/3250957

Wolff, M. (1995*). Ki-Net - New Organizational Structures for Engineering Design*. Retrieved from http://www.ki-net/part1.html

Xiang, Z., & Fesenmaier, D. R. (2016). *Analytics in smart tourism design: Concepts and methods*. Springer.

Xiong, B., Yang, K., Zhao, J., & Li, K. (2017). Robust dynamic network traffic partitioning against malicious attacks. *Journal of Network and Computer Applications*, *87*, 20–31. doi:10.1016/j.jnca.2016.04.013

Yeboah-Boateng, E. O. (2017). Cyber-Security Concerns with Cloud Computing: Business Value Creation & Performance Perspectives. In A. K. Turuk, B. Sahoo, & S. K. Addya (Eds.), Resource Management & Efficiency in Cloud Computing Environment (pp. 106-137). IGI Global Publishers.

Yeboah-Boateng, E. O. (2013). *Cyber-Security Challenges with SMEs in Developing Economies: Issues of Confidentiality, Integrity & Availablity (CIA)*. Aalborg University.

Young, R., & David, R. J. (2015). Handling missing values in longitudinal panel data with multiple imputation. *Journal of Marriage and the Family*, *77*(1), 277–294. doi:10.1111/jomf.12144 PMID:26113748

Younis O., Ghoul S., Alomari M. H. (2013). Systems Variability Modeling: A Textual Model Mixing Class and Feature Concepts. *International Journal of Computer Science & Information Technology*, *2013*(5), 127–139.

Zaher, A. A., & Laith, M. A. (2017). Big data and E-government: A review. *2017 8th International Conference on Information Technology (ICIT)*, 580-587.

Zaveri, A., Rula, A., Maurino, A., Pietrobon, R., Lehmann, J., & Auer, S. (2016). Quality assessment for linked data: A survey. *Semantic Web*, *7*(1), 63–93. doi:10.3233/SW-150175

Zhang, Y., Qu, T., Ho, O. K., & Huang, G. Q. (2011). Agent-based smart gateway for RFID-enabled real-time wireless manufacturing. *International Journal of Production Research*, *49*(5), 1337–1352. doi:10.1080/00207543.2010.518743

Compilation of References

Zhang, Y., Zhang, G., Wang, J., Sun, S., Si, S., & Yang, T. (2015). Real-time information capturing and integration framework of the internet of manufacturing things. *International Journal of Computer Integrated Manufacturing, 28*(8), 811–822. doi:10.1080/0951192X.2014.900874

Ziegler, P., & Dittrich, K. R. (2007). *Data Integration – Problems, Approaches, and Perspectives, Database Technology Research Group.* Department of Informatics, University of Zurich.

Zmazek, B., Todorovski, L., Džeroski, S., Vaupotič, J., & Kobal, I. (2003). Application of decision trees to the analysis of soil radon data for earthquake prediction. *Applied Radiation and Isotopes, 58*(6), 697–706. doi:10.1016/S0969-8043(03)00094-0 PMID:12798380

About the Contributors

Albert Gyamfi has a PhD in Knowledge Management from Aalborg University, Denmark. He is a consultant and an expert who has researched into media richness and web applications for knowledge management process and organisational learning. He is currently attached to Centre for Communication, Media and Information Technologies (CMI), Aalborg University Copenhagen.

Idongesit Williams is a lecturer and Post-Doctoral researcher at Center for Communication, Media and Information Technologies (CMI) located at Aalborg University Copenhagen. He lectures on Internet economics and governance. He holds a Bachelor in Physics, a Master degree in Information and Communications Technologies and a Ph.D. He has since 2010 researched into Knowledge Management, Organizational Learning, socioeconomic, socio-technical related to Information and Communications Technologies. He has authored and co-authored more than 40 research publications, including journal papers, books, book chapters, conference papers and magazine articles. He is the co-editor of the Books, The African Mobile Story, and the Handbook on ICT for developing countries:5G perspectives and Evaluating Media Richness in Organization Learning.

* * *

Ratish Agrawal has a PhD in Mobile Ad-hoc Network from Rajiv Gandhi Proudyogiki Vishwavidyalaya Bhopal, India. Presently he is working as Assistant Professor Department of Information Technology, UIT, RGPV a State Technological University, Bhopal MP, India. His research interest in Mobile Ad-hoc Network and Wireless communication.

Mehmet S. Aktas received his Ph.D. degree from Computer Science Department of School of Informatics and Computing at Indiana University, Bloomington in 2007 and his M.Sc. degree from Electrical Engineering and Computer Science Department at Syracuse University, Syracuse NY, where he gave undergraduate-level lectures as an assistant instructor. Both degrees are in Computer Sciences. Aktas worked at Los Alamos National Laboratory (New Mexico, USA) and Turkish National Science Foundation (Gebze, Turkey) as a Researcher. Since 2013, he is a Professor at Computer Engineering Department, Yildiz Technical University, Turkey. His current research interests include Distributed Systems, Provenance, Data-Intensive Computing, Distributed Machine Learning, Big Data and Cloud Computing.

Emrah Bilgic completed MSc at Statistics Department in 2005 in Turkey. He started his master degree in Skovde/Sweden in 2006 and got a Master of Finance degree there. He worked at retailing companies in Turkey before he started his position as a research assistant in Istanbul at Marmara University, Business Faculty. He was a visiting researcher in University of Louisville during 2014-2015 in Data Mining Lab. with the supervision of Prof. Dr. Mehmed Kantardzic. After returning to Turkey he completed his PhD degree in Quantitative Methods at Business Department in 2016 in Istanbul Marmara University. He is still teaching at Mus Alparslan University in Turkey.

Nirav Bhatt is working at Department of Information Technology in Chandubhai S Patel Institute of Technology, CHARUSAT. He had received degree of Master of Engineering in Computer Engineering from Dharmsinh Desai Institute of Technology and currently pursuing his Ph.D. in the area of Big Data Stream Analytics. His research interests include Database System, Data Mining and Big Data Stream Analytics. He is also a member of Computer Society of India and ACM and member of ACM Chapter at the institute. He is also coordinator of SWAYAM-NPTEL Local Chapter which is the National MOOCs portal being developed by MHRD, Govt. of India.

Süleyman Eken received M.Sc. in Computer Science (2012) from Kocaeli University and now he is pursuing his PhD at the Kocaeli University under the supervision of Dr. Ahmet Sayar. Since 2010, he is a research assistant at Computer Engineering Department, Kocaeli University, Turkey. His main research work focuses on distributed systems, remote sensing, and spatial data analysis. He has co-authored around 30 papers.

M. Fevzi Esen has received his M.A. and Ph.D. in quantitative sciences from Istanbul University. He now works at İstanbul Medeniyet University, Faculty of Tourism, as assistant professor. His main interest fields are: data mining, statistics and big data applications in tourism industries.

Marcela Garza Segovia is a researcher and a PhD student at the Department of Business and Technology in La Salle - Universitat Ramon Llull in Barcelona, Spain, with the support of the National Council for Science and Technology, Mexico (CONACYT). Her research focuses on the analysis of sports events sponsorship activations in the digital environment, the use of online channels and technological trends in sports events.

Sachin Goyal has a PhD from Rajiv Gandhi Proudyogiki Vishwavidyalaya Bhopal, India. Presently he is working as an Assistant Professor Department of Information Technology, UIT, RGPV a State Technological University, Bhopal MP, India. His research interest in Compiler Design and Algorithm Design and Machine Learning.

Burçin Güçlü is assistant professor of Management in BES La Salle, Universitat Ramon Llull. Regarding her research, she is interested in quantitative methods in marketing, working on the applications of behavioural decision theory to managerial issues in marketing. Previously, she earned BA degrees in Business Administration and Economics from Koç University, and a Master of Research in Management (MRM) and PhD in Management from IESE Business School, University of Navarra. She also held teaching positions in EADA Business School, Toulouse Business School and Universitat Internacional de Catalunya.

Nirali Honest is working as an Assistant Professor, at Smt. Chandaben Mo-hanbhai Patel Institute of Computer Applications, since August 2005. She has completed her Master of Computer Applications from Gujarat University in 2005 and Bachelor of Computer Applications in 2002 from Dharamsinh Desai University. During her tenure at academics she has conducted sessions on various courses like Software Quality Assurance, Software Engineering and Quality Assurance, Web Technologies and Applications, Database Management Concepts, System Analysis and designing, Network Technologies, Object Oriented Designing and Modeling, Parallel Processing, Operating Systems, Object Oriented concepts and programming in java, Computer based management systems, Data Structures, Fundamentals of Commerce and Business Processes. She has completed her Ph.D. in Computer Science in November,2016, her area of work is Web Usage Mining. She has published nine research papers in reputed International journals and presented four papers in conference. She has passion to work in the academics take different courses and deliver interesting content to the students and the target audience. With this intense she is writing the chapters on Knowledge Management and Business Analytics as part of the book Big Data and Knowledge Sharing in Virtual Organizations.

Cevat İkibaş received his Master's degree from Syracuse University Computer & Information Science Department in 2001 and then started PhD studies in Indiana University, Bloomington, USA. He worked as a Research Assistant in Pervasive Technologies Labs at Indiana University between 2001 and 2004. He worked on some software development projects in the Pervasive Technology Labs. He continued and completed his PhD in 2012 in Computer Engineering Department of Karadeniz Technical University in Turkey. His PhD thesis is titled as "Detection of optic disc and macula and their evaluation in retinal fundus images". His research area includes Medical Image processing, machine learning and related subjects. As part of his IT experience, he worked in Turk Telekom, the leading Telecom operator of Turkey in terms of mobile, fixed line and data services, as a Project Manager and then as a Department Manager of Resource and Inventory Management, under Information Technology Directorate between 2010 and 2017. He holds Project Management Professional (PMP) and Certified Business Analysis Professional (CBAP) certificates which are related with project management and software development processes. He was appointed as an Assistant professor of Computer Science in American University of Malta as of August 2017. He teaches Computer science related courses such as programming C++, algorithms, data structures in game development program.

Qaisar Iqbal is pursuing his Ph.D. in organizational behavior at School of Management, Universiti Sains Malaysia, Malaysia. He has published many research papers in national and international journals including Global Business Review, Business Information Review, Lahore Journal of Business, World Journal of Science, Technology, and Sustainable Development etc. He is currently providing academic services as associate editor at Probe: Business and Management, and Probe-Accounting, Auditing, and Taxation. He is a member of the editorial board at the Journal of Business Administration Research, and Probe-Insight Information as well. He has also five years of professional experience at a managerial level in the banking sector.

Vardan Mkrttchian received his Doctorate of Sciences (Engineering) in Control Systems from Lomonosov Moscow State University (former USSR). Dr. Vardan Mkrttchian taught for undergraduate and graduate student's courses of control system, information sciences and technology, at the Astrakhan State University (Russian Federation), where he was is the Professor of the Information Systems (www.aspu.ru) six years. Now he is full professor in CAD department of Penza State University (www.pnzgu.ru). He is currently chief executive of HHH University, Australia and team leader of the international academics (www.hhhuniversity. com). He also serves as executive director of the HHH Technology Incorporation. Professor Vardan Mkrttchian has authored over 400 refereed publications. He is the author of over twenty books published of IGI Global, included ten books indexed of SCOPUS in IT, Control System, Digital Economy, and Education Technology. He is also has authored more than 200 articles published in various conference proceedings and journals.

Rashid Nawaz is currently pursuing his degree in Mathematics at the School of Mathematical Sciences, University of Education, Attock, Pakistan. His research area is applied mathematics with a special focus on numerical methods, approximate analytical methods, and mathematical modeling. He intends to get his Ph.D. from a reputable mathematical school.

Kamalendu Pal is with the Department of Computer Science, School of Mathematics, Computer Science and Engineering, City, University London. Kamalendu received his BSc (Hons) degree in Physics from Calcutta University, India, Postgraduate Diploma in Computer Science from Pune, India; MSc degree in Software Systems Technology from Sheffield University, Postgraduate Diploma in Artificial Intelligence from Kingston University, MPhil degree in Computer Science from University College London, and MBA degree from University of Hull, United Kingdom. He has published dozens of research papers in international journals and conferences. His research interests include knowledge-based systems, decision support systems, computer integrated design, software engineering, and service oriented computing. He is a member of the British Computer Society, the Institution of Engineering and Technology, and the IEEE Computer Society.

Svetlana Panasenko is Head of Department of Trade Policy in Plekhanov Russian University of Economics, Moscow, Russia.

Anjana Pandey has a PhD in Data Mining from MANIT, Bhopal, India. Presently she is working as an Assistant Professor Department of Information Technology, UIT, RGPV a State Technological University, Bhopal MP, India. Her research interest in Data Mining, Data Analysis and Machine Learning.

Atul Patel is working as a Professor, Dean and Principal at Smt. Chandaben Mohanbhai Patel Institute of Computer Applications since April 2010. He has completed his Ph.D in Computer Science in August 2012; his area of work is Wireless Communication. He has completed his M.Phil in Computer Science in July 2007 and Master of Computer Applications from D.D.I.T., Nadiad, Gujarat University in 1993. He has served as System Officer at Anand Urban cooperative bank, Anand, and Faculty member at Faculty of Technology, DD University, Nadiad. During his tenure at academics he has conducted sessions on various courses like Mobile Ad hoc Networks, Wireless Communications System Analysis and Design, Database Management Systems, Cloud Computing, Network Technologies, Data Mining, Big Data etc. He has published/presented eight papers in National Conferences/ Journals. He has published forty papers in International Journals having Impact factor that varies from 0.59 to 2.80. He has attended more than 20 Workshops, Conferences and Seminars as Participant, Guest Speaker and Session Chairman. He has conducted various sessions at UGC staff colleges in Gujarat and Rajasthan for Orientation Programmes, Refresher Courses, STTP and FDP Programmes He has a teaching experience of more 16 years and industrial experience of 6 years. With the exposure of knowledge in teaching as well as industry standards he would like to share his thoughts on the importance of data to be handled in the organizations which are getting virtual in the current changing environment. So he is contributing to write the chapters on Knowledge Management and Business Analytics as part of the book Big Data and Knowledge Sharing in Virtual Organizations.

Mahesh Kumar Pawar has a PhD in Component Based Software Engineering from Rajiv Gandhi Proudyogiki Vishwavidyalaya Bhopal, India. He is Professionally qualified Sr. Faculty with more than Fifteen years of experience in academic as well as IT Industry. Presently he is working as Assistant Professor Department of Information Technology, UIT, RGPV a State Technological University, Bhopal MP, India. His research interest in Software Engineering, Big data Analysis and Database Management System.

Serkan Polat is an assistant professor of gastronomy and culinary arts at Istanbul Medeniyet University. He earned his BAs in Tourism Management from Boğaziçi University in Turkey. He gained his MSc in Tourism Management from Istanbul University and his PhD in Tourism Management from Sakarya University in Turkey.

Cihan Savaş was born in 1985 in the central district of Diyarbakır. primary school İstanbul Güngören Primary School and Secondary School completed. He completed his high school education in İstanbul İzzet Ünver High School. Associate Degree Computer Engineering and Programming in Selçuk University in 2006 In 2008 and graduated in 2008. At the same time the second university He graduated from Anadolu University, Department of Business Administration in 2012. Between November 2013 and May 2014 military service as a short-term infantry did his duty. Between 2009 and 2015, he worked as a clerk in the Bakırköy Courthouse. served. he was appointed to Kocaeli, Kocaeli since 2015 He worked in the Administrative and Tax Court. In 2018, he started working as a software engineer at the Department of Information Technology of the Ministry of Justice. He is married and has two children.

Ahmet Sayar received M.Sc. in Computer Science (2001) from Syracuse University and PhD in Computer Science (2009) from Indiana University, USA. He has worked at Los Alamos National Laboratory (New Mexico, USA) and Community Grids Laboratory (Indiana, USA) as a researcher. Since 2010, he is a professor at Computer Engineering Department, Kocaeli University, Turkey. He is currently a Member of Advisory Committee, TUBİTAK (The Scientific And Technological Research Council Of Turkey), Technology and Innovation Support Programs Presidency (TEYDEB). He is also a Member of Board of Directors at Kocaeli University Institute of Science and Technology. He is an associate editor for six journals. These are Kocaeli Journal of Science and Engineering, International Journal of Computer Engineering Research, Journal of Geography, Environment and Earth Science International, Journal of Mechatronics and Robotics, Journal of Aircraft and Spacecraft Technology and American Journal of Engineering and Applied Sciences. His current research interests include Distributed Systems, Big Data, Data-Intensive Computing, Geographic Information Systems (GIS) and Exploratory Data Analysis (EDA). He has (co-)authored 1 book 15 book chapters and around 150 papers.

Amit Thakkar is working as an assistant professor at Department of Information Technology in Chandubhai S Patel Institute of Technology, CHARUSAT. He has 10+ years of teaching experience including worked as I/C head of IT at Chandubhai S Patel Institute of Engineering and teaching As proficiency in C language, C++, .NET, software engineering, Data Mining, Soft computing.

Ezer Yeboah-Boateng is a professional ICT Specialist and Telecoms Engineer with a strong background in cyber-security, digital forensics, business development, change management, knowledge management, strategic IT-enabled business value creation and capabilities to develop market-oriented strategies aimed at promoting growth and market share. An Executive with 25 years of domestic and global experience conceptualizing ideas, seizing opportunities, building operations, leading highly successful new business development initiatives and ventures. A Consultant with emphasis on Cyber-security, digital forensics, telecommunications, Internet, and network integration technologies, with additional experience related to dealing with refurbished and overstock equipment, and manufacturing. His research focuses on cyber-security vulnerabilities, digital forensics, cyber-crime, cloud computing, Big Data, digital transformations and fuzzy systems. Strong presentation, negotiation, and team building skills. Dr. Yeboah-Boateng is also a Governing Board member of the National Information Technology Agency (NITA) in Ghana.

Mehmet Samet Yıldız received BSc. in Computer Engineering (2018) from Kocaeli University, Turkey. His main research work focuses on machine learning and spatial data analysis

Index

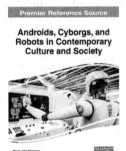

Ensure Quality Research is Introduced to the Academic Community

Become an IGI Global Reviewer for Authored Book Projects

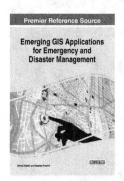

Premier Reference Source

Emerging GIS Applications for Emergency and Disaster Management

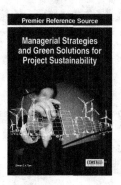

Premier Reference Source

Managerial Strategies and Green Solutions for Project Sustainability

Premier Reference Source

Comparative Approaches to Using R and Python for Statistical Data Analysis

Premier Reference Source

Solutions for High-Touch Communications in a High-Tech World

The overall success of an authored book project is dependent on quality and timely reviews.

In this competitive age of scholarly publishing, constructive and timely feedback significantly expedites the turnaround time of manuscripts from submission to acceptance, allowing the publication and discovery of forward-thinking research at a much more expeditious rate. Several IGI Global authored book projects are currently seeking highly qualified experts in the field to fill vacancies on their respective editorial review boards:

Applications may be sent to:
development@igi-global.com

Applicants must have a doctorate (or an equivalent degree) as well as publishing and reviewing experience. Reviewers are asked to write reviews in a timely, collegial, and constructive manner. All reviewers will begin their role on an ad-hoc basis for a period of one year, and upon successful completion of this term can be considered for full editorial review board status, with the potential for a subsequent promotion to Associate Editor.

If you have a colleague that may be interested in this opportunity, we encourage you to share this information with them.

Printed in the United States
By Bookmasters